Julie

a fellow pu,

with my daughter. Enjoy my

book

Dave True

GANGSTERS, OUTLAWS,
AND MOBSTERS

GANGSTERS, OUTLAWS, AND MOBSTERS

A MISSOURI HISTORY OF TWENTIETH CENTURY CRIMES AND CRIMINALS

BY
DAVID TRUE
ATF (RETIRED)

Acclaim Press
MORLEY, MISSOURI

Acclaim Press
— Your Next Great Book —

P.O. Box 238
Morley, MO 63767
(573) 472-9800
www.acclaimpress.com

Editor: Randy Baumgardner
Book & Cover Design: Rodney Atchley

ISBN: 978-1-948901-87-1 | 1-948901-87-0
Library of Congress Control Number: 2021936042

First Print 2021
Printed in the United States of America
10 9 8 7 6 5 4 3 2 1

This publication was produced using available information.
The publisher regrets it cannot assume responsibility for errors or omissions.

CONTENTS

Dedicated to my loving wife, Kathy.
Without her efforts, this book would not have been written.

ACKNOWLEDGMENTS

I express my thanks, appreciation, and gratitude to my family, friends, and professional associates who helped me with the project.

I wish to extend a special thanks to those who helped type and edit the book: Susan Steen, Jenna Brooks, Reana Sinclair, Kim Carter, my daughter Lauren and her husband Kyle Weeks, and my son Justin.

I thank each true crime research author who came before me for helping with the historical material of the book. Also, thanks to the staff at the numerous archives and libraries in Missouri and beyond, who provided direction and material for this project.

A special thanks to all who supported me during my early life and career in St. Louis, especially my parents, sisters, brothers and in-laws, my adopted son, his mother, her parents, and sister. And my friends, too many to name. You know who you are.

Thank you to the men and women of ATF, law enforcement officials with all the police departments, highway patrol, sheriff's departments, federal agencies, and fire service personnel for keeping our cities safe and playing such an important part in this book. And thanks to you, the reader, for taking the time to read what I have written.

PREFACE

Most authors writing about nonfiction crime and criminals describe their fascination with movies, news articles, and magazine articles about these personalities as the author's reason for getting published. Mine is my fascination combined with my personal association with gangsters, outlaws, and mobsters who committed their crimes in and around Missouri.

I lived and grew up in the Soulard Market neighborhood of the "Bloody" Third Police District of St. Louis, Missouri, in my early childhood, within walking distance to the historic Soulard Market and City Hospital Number One, where many gangsters went to be treated for stabbings and gunshot wounds or simply to be pronounced dead on arrival.

This was the neighborhood where the notorious Cuckoo Gang originated and operated in the early 1900s, a neighborhood that featured the Anheuser-Busch Brewing Company and a tavern on every corner. It provided me with a firsthand account of the rough and tumble ways of South Broadway bookies, street fighters, and common thieves.

I attended McKinley High School on Russell Avenue in South St. Louis, Missouri, and played sports and socialized at Dunn Center in the Darst-Webbe projects, growing up with personalities who would choose occupations as police officers, firemen, gangsters, or mobsters in later years.

In 1962, after graduating from high school, I hitched a ride with a high school classmate, Paul Leisure, and headed to Cape Girardeau, Missouri, to attend SEMO State. Our driver was Leisure's cousin. Within three years, Leisure's cousin was murdered gangland-style; Leisure became the bodyguard and driver for St. Louis mob boss Tony Giordano. I became a St. Louis Teamster dockhand, loading freight and paying into the Teamsters Central States Pension Fund. This same fund provided loans to fund casino construction in Las Vegas, Nevada, because Roy Williams—the Teamster leader in Kansas City, Missouri—took money from our pension fund to do so, under the influence of Kansas City mob boss Nick Civella.

While working on the midnight shift at the freight dock, I became friends with a fellow employee who would later be charged, convicted, and sentenced to federal prison for helping plan the attempted murder of fellow high school classmate, Paul Leisure, in a car bombing, an investigation in St. Louis I was personally involved in as an ATF federal agent.

I then did a stint in the army as an Explosive Ordnance Disposal Specialist, stationed at Granite City, Madison County, Illinois. This county was once controlled by mob boss Buster Wortman, who reported directly to Al Capone in Chicago.

I would later infiltrate the underworld characters living in Madison and St. Clair, Illinois, near St. Louis, Missouri, during my early years as an ATF agent in an undercover capacity.

I moved on after the military service and became a cop and detective on the St. Louis Police Department, then a special agent with the Bureau of Alcohol, Tobacco and Firearms (ATF) of the US Treasury Department. For the next twenty-six years, I was assigned to the St. Louis and Kansas City, Missouri ATF offices, investigating—among other assignments—gangsters, outlaws, mobsters, cult groups, right-wing radicals, kidnappers, rapists, and murderers operating and living in and around Missouri.

Upon retiring in 1997, I started employment with Yellow Roadway Trucking Company as a manager and investigator with the Corporate Security Department, and for the next sixteen years, I investigated company and teamster employees throughout the Midwest, including the terminals located in Kansas City; St. Louis, Missouri; and Madison County, Illinois. This experience gave me tremendous additional insight into the history and current workings of the Teamster International Union.

As I read through more than 100 nonfiction books and numerous magazines, periodicals, and newspaper accounts about gangsters, outlaws, and mobsters in preparation for my own nonfiction narrative on crime and criminals, I made several observations.

Most authors suggested that all big gangsters and mobsters originated in New York, Detroit, Cleveland, or Chicago, some migrating to cities in California, Nevada, or Florida, downplaying the Missouri gangs and mobsters' influence in the United States.

Research authors writing on the Missouri criminal history primarily limited their books to St. Louis or Kansas City area incidents.

An author would have to purchase or read more than 100 books to capture the entire Missouri criminal history to compile it in one book. I know—I have done just that to complete this project, capturing captivating events that have occurred throughout the state of Missouri and surrounding areas, costing me hundreds of dollars.

In my book, you will learn when and where the most tragic law enforcement shootout massacre occurred and who the actual shooters were in the St. Valentine's Day Massacre in Chicago and the Union Station Massacre in Kansas City, two brutal crimes that shocked the nation. You will hear where the fingerprint identification system in the United States was initiated and who was responsible for its inception and what two events inspired the FBI to establish the single fingerprint identification files.

You will find out who had the mansion built that Chicago mob boss Al Capone purchased and lived in, which mobsters were involved in the Nevada casino industry, where the loan money to build and remodel the casinos came from, and where the illegally skimmed money from the casinos went and passed through. You will also learn how the late Senator Estes Kefauver originated his Senate Committee on organized crime and what gangland event caused it to pass the Senate and President Truman's approval. You will learn how the infamous Black Book of Nevada started and who some of the select mobster charter members banned from casinos for life were and where the Thompson submachine gun was most often used and who introduced the weapon in contract murders to Detroit, Michigan, and New York, New York.

The reader will learn where some of the deadliest gangs in the United States originated and how some of the members carried out murderous crimes throughout the United States; the detailed criminal history of some of the most notorious gangsters, outlaws and mobsters; the prison they spent time in; and the crimes they committed, including robberies, bootlegging, kidnappings, bank robberies, fraud schemes, and brutal murders.

Readers will also learn where the first FBI wanted fugitive was captured and where he came from; where the killer who shot and killed the first FBI agent in the United States was captured; where the first daylight bank robbery occurred and who committed the heist; who killed a well-known Chicago newspaper reporter and created a national newspaper scandal and who committed the only successful robbery of a Las Vegas casino, where they hailed from, and what price they paid for robbing a mob-controlled casino; and the inside story of the man who assassinated Dr. Martin Luther King, Jr.

This is just a sampling of what lies ahead as you learn about the fascinating and infamous history of gangsters, outlaws, and mobsters living and operating in Missouri throughout the twentieth century, including the Depression, Prohibition, the Roaring Twenties, and the modern crime era.

This is the first and only comprehensive nonfiction narrative history of the state of Missouri crime and criminals and its nearby areas. A cast of characters whose actions will stretch your imagination.

Much of the material in this book is based on research of crime authors, newspaper articles, and my personal firsthand involvement, as well as the involvement of fellow ATF agents and dedicated law enforcement officials at the city, state, and federal levels during my thirty-two-year career in law enforcement public service, combined with my Yellow Roadway Freight experiences.

In 1770, John Adams wrote, "Facts are stubborn things and whatever may be our wishes, our inclination, or the dictates of our passions, they cannot alter the state of facts and evidence."

I adhered to this premise throughout my career as a public servant and maintained it in the writing of this book. Wherever possible, I corroborated information through independent sources and solid evidence. I learned early in my career as a fact finder that evidence, when handled properly, does not lie.

I spent the past ten years of my life writing the book. I spent the past sixty years of my life living the book.

I hope you enjoy reading the book as much as I enjoyed the many years of researching, traveling, conducting interviews, and preparing the manuscript, using case facts and evidence whenever possible to get accurate, fascinating stories of the gangsters, outlaws, and mobsters who operated in and around the state of Missouri.

INTRODUCTION

As 1900 arrived, Americans and Missourians awakened to one of the most interesting and dynamic centuries in the history of the United States.

The massive influx of immigrants from different countries hoping to get a piece of the American dream streamed into cities across the country, including St. Louis, the "Gateway to the West," and Kansas City, an open city.

New inhabitants consisting primarily of Germans, Dutch, Irish, Jews, African Americans, and Italians squeezed into tenements and shacks in highly populated areas of the two inner cities known as the "Kerry Patch" and "Little Italy." At the same time, smaller Missouri cities and towns also experienced the arrival of these immigrants.

Gone were the days of the Wild West cowboys, the likes of Frank and Jesse James of Kearney, the Younger brothers of Lee's Summit, and their gangs that operated and plagued the citizens of Missouri, Kansas, Oklahoma, and Texas in the mid- to late-1800s.

Gone were the days of the Bald Knobbers of Christian and Taney Counties in the hills of the Missouri Ozarks, law-abiding citizens in the 1880s who turned to vigilante justice, so named when the men met on the treeless "bald top" hills or "knobs," wearing masks to hide their identities while discussing their vigilante plans. Their reign of terror ended in 1889 when three captured Bald Knobbers were hanged on the Christian County Courthouse lawn, putting an end to vigilante justice in Missouri.

"In 1881 in press reports around the country, editorialists talked about Missouri as the sovereign state of crime; Missouri, the law of bushwhackers and bank robbers; and Missouri, the state of banditry."

The state prison, located in Jefferson City, the only maximum security prison operated by the state, was considered one of the largest prisons in the United States. Many of its prisoners were put to work in several shoe and boot factories, producing as many as 10,000 pairs of shoes and boots every two weeks. The prison housed a saddle factory, producing over 60,000 saddle trees each year. The Missouri State Prison became known as the "poster child of the growing popularity of the growth of labor unions, showing why in the free industrial markets convict labor should not be used in competition with union labor."

In 1900 at the turn of the century, Missouri offered accredited state and public colleges in Rolla, St. Louis, Jefferson City, Cape Girardeau, Kirksville,

Warrensburg, and Maryville, as well as the University Missouri in Columbia (the state's major university), plus a University of Springfield, Missouri, and Maryville, Missouri, in 1905.

The state also had sheriff's departments established in 115 counties, and in 1931, the state highway patrol was established, with an initial staff of one superintendent and fifty-five male troopers. Six troops were located throughout the state, including Kansas City, Macon, Kirkwood, Joplin, Sikeston, and headquarters in Jefferson City, the state's capital. The highway patrol had statewide jurisdiction as a state agency.

At the turn of the century, the population of St. Louis was 575,238, placing it as the fourth largest city behind only New York, Chicago, and Philadelphia. St. Louis was recognized as the largest shoe manufacturing center in the world, home of Buster Brown and other famous brands.

The Missouri Botanical Garden was among the top three botanical gardens in the world, and in 1900, the bread slicer was invented in St. Louis. The city offered ninety-five hotels, thirty brick factories, twenty-seven breweries, and thirteen sausage makers. A used buggy (horse not included) cost thirty dollars.

The citizens of St. Louis proudly touted the always busy waterfront of the mighty Mississippi and their well-respected professional baseball team, the St. Louis Cardinals.

The St. Louis World's Fair of 1904 put St. Louis and Missouri on the international map, declaring the state the "Gateway to the West," hoping to downplay the crime that was in process and about to follow. Dr. Pepper was first introduced at the World's Fair, along with the ice cream cone and iced tea. Hot dogs and hamburgers were also popularized to a wide audience at the fair.

In the first of the century 1900, Kansas City hosted the Democratic National Convention, opening the eyes of delegates from all around the United States. An East Coast reporter from the *New York Daily Tribune* wrote in amazement:

> How open the city was with nickel-in-the slot gambling machines everywhere and 147 brothels operated openly within the city limits. The delegates also enjoyed the open flow of alcohol available in more saloons than they could count.

The Jazz Age was fast developing, and nowhere in America was it more prevalent than Kansas City, with the likes of Duke Ellington and the bright lights of Eighteenth and Vine in the Roaring Twenties.

In 1922, Kansas City proudly displayed the Country Club Plaza, the first shopping center in the world designed to accommodate shoppers arriving by automobile. Designed after the city of Seville, Spain, it consisted of quality retail shops, restaurants, and offices surrounded by mansions and upscale apartments.

In the early 1900s, gangs dominated the streets of St. Louis, including the likes of the Cuckoo gang, the Green Ones, the Russo and Hogens, the Sheltons, the Santino/Pillow gang, and the most notorious of them all, the Egan's Rats, which boasted over 400 members specializing in crime and criminal activities. With the gangs came turf wars and brutal battles in the process of their never-ending quest for power and money. Between 1900 and 1932, these wars were responsible for no fewer than 260 murders and untold number of injuries.

At the same time, the Italian mobsters of Kansas City were carrying on their crimes of extortion, known as the Black Hand crimes, victimizing their own people, quite often using hit men out of St. Louis to do the dirty work—one of the earliest connections between criminals from both sides of the state.

Most research authors agree that the golden age of twentieth-century crime occurred between 1920 and 1940, two decades when America experienced the invention of the automobile, the airplane, the telephone, radio, and motion pictures.

It was during this period that a reform effort called Prohibition, known as "The Noble Experiment," designed (or intended) to ensure the survival of traditional American values system, instead created unintended consequences—the rise of organized crime at a time in American history when law enforcement was slow to take steps toward the professionalism that was needed to control the rising crime and organized criminal enterprises.

These early years included the Roaring Twenties, Prohibition, and the Great Depression. With so many out of work and losing all their hard-earned money during the Depression, banks were forced to take away people's houses and farms for failure to make payments on their mortgages. Murders were on the rise. In 1927, Kansas City had more murders per capita than Al Capone's Chicago.

This era gave rise to the popularity of the "yeggs" (criminal parlance for bank robbers) who gained "Robin Hood" status while robbing banks and taking money from the rich bankers who the poor felt were stealing from them.

The repeal of Prohibition in 1933 did not slow down the growth of organized crime in America. The underworld mobsters directed their attention to prostitution, narcotics syndicates, and the control of organized labor and gambling operations.

In concert, the outlaw yeggs took on the art of bank robberies and train robberies, primarily focusing their efforts in the Midwest of America. This was known as the crime corridor, stretching from Texas to as far east as Minnesota, with Missouri in the heart of the corridor.

New gangs were formed in the Midwest, including the likes of the Barker-Karpis Gang, the Shelton and Birger Gangs, the "Pretty Boy" Floyd gangs, the Bailey-Underhill Gang, and the "Bloody" Barrow Gang, all inflicting their pillage and murderous ways in Missouri along their way.

In the decade of the 1940s, the political machines in Missouri were very active in Jefferson City from both sides of the state. In St. Louis you had mobster "Jelly Roll" Hogen, a gang leader and Missouri state senator, and on the Kansas City side, you had the Pendergast machine acting in concert with mob boss Charlie Binaggio in efforts to legalize gambling until it was broken up in a major Kansas City case.

At the same time, the St. Louis and Kansas City mob structures were actively engaged in a major national narcotics syndicate as they moved away from the bootlegging business.

In the decade of the 1950s, the Missouri mob bosses involved themselves in infiltrating the labor unions, especially the Teamsters and their lucrative Central States Pension Fund. In concert with these efforts, the mob bosses and mob attorneys in Missouri focused their efforts on getting a piece of the enormous growth of the Nevada casino and gaming industry and the popularity of the illegal gambling industry in Missouri.

These efforts would continue throughout the 1960s and 1970s until broken up by law enforcement's successful efforts.

The decades of the 1970s and 1980s saw a drastic increase in mob and outlaw violence, using the explosive bomb as the weapon of choice to intimidate and kill unsuspecting victims and mob rivals. Of course, the underworld never was without their firearms used routinely in support of the dynamite bomb.

The pages that follow provide a history of the gangs, outlaws, mobsters, kidnappers, ultra right-wing militant groups, cults, and murderers in and around Missouri that penetrated so deep into the very structure of the state of Missouri throughout the twentieth century. It was a fascinating century, indeed—one when newspaper reporters, true crime authors, detective story writers, and television anchormen found more real-life drama than even Hollywood writers could ever dream up.

OUTLAW MALES AND GANGSTER MOLLS BEHIND MISSOURI PRISON WALLS 1900-2000

The Missouri State Penitentiary, located in Jefferson City, Missouri, initiated its construction in 1834, growing in size from forty cell blocks housing fourteen inmates to a population of around 5,000 in 1932 on a thirty-seven-acre plat, becoming one of the largest prisons in the United States.

In the 1960s, a national publication—overstating its size—described this prison as the bloodiest "47 acres in America."

Among the inmates who did time behind these walls included abolitionists, authors, soldiers, politicians, cop killers, assassins, kidnappers, arsonists, robbers, rapists, molls, boxing champions, mobsters, gangsters, and outlaws, to name a few.

In his books *Shanks to Shakers, Reflections of the Missouri State Penitentiary* and *Somewhere in Time, 170 Years of Missouri Corrections*, Mark S. Schreiber—who served in several positions at the prison, including as deputy warden for forty-two years "working with staff and inmates"— compiled a large collection of artifacts that he documents about the prison's 162-year history, a fascinating read.

If not for the stories of these inmates, who passed through its walls in its 168 years of operation, the Missouri State Prison—known as "The Big House"—would be only that of buildings and walls, leaving little to learn about Missouri criminal history.

Some left after serving their time, some escaped successfully, some were captured and returned, some were received on more than one sentence, and some left in a box after dying in prison or being executed by the state for their crimes. There is one fact that cannot be denied—everyone in this chapter who left continued their sordid life of crime; some of the crimes committed were so heinous they shocked the conscience of Missouri and the nation. Many of the ex-cons met with a violent death either by the hand of fellow criminals or law enforcement.

There are too many stories to document in one book, let alone one chapter. I have selected several criminal ex-cons who passed through the walls over the years, until the old prison officially closed in 2004.

Although the prison population included primarily male inmates, women were housed behind the walls from 1842 to 1926. A comment about female inmates:

Webster's *New Collegiate Dictionary* defines a moll as "a gangster's girl-friend" — a prostitute. Missouri has had its share of gangster girlfriends and gangster prostitutes; however, research proves the definition is too narrow when looking at our bad ladies of Missouri. Here you need to include wives, mothers, and other female relations to make the list complete.

Researchers agree the evidence is pretty vague regarding the level of involvement these gangster molls had in the actual perpetration of the crimes committed, with a few exceptions.

The inmates chosen for this chapter represent at least one or more for each decade of the 1900s and are presented to the reader in chronological order. The criminal personalities include both male and female prison inmates, each one telling a gruesome tale of crime.

LEE SHELTON
a.k.a Stack Lee

Lee Shelton, inmate number 21390, was first received at the Missouri State Penitentiary on October 7, 1897, sentenced to twenty-five years for murder in the second degree. He was paroled on Thanksgiving Day, 1909. Soon, Shelton was in trouble again and returned to prison on May 7, 1911, to serve five years for robbery and assault. He was sick with tuberculosis and died in prison hospital on March 11, 1912.

Was this just another sad story of a black man getting in trouble in St. Louis, Missouri, at the beginning of the 1900s . . . or is there more to this story?

Shelton's first conviction was for the murder of another black man named Lyons in a St. Louis South Side tavern during an argument over a hat.

To put a dramatic spin on this murder, the documented evidence shows the shooter's nickname was "Stagolee" and the victim's first name was Billy. They were allegedly shooting craps, and the argument was over Lee's white Stetson hat.

This incident created the ballad "Stagolee Shot Billy," which would be sung for many years.

The year 1895 was the birth of the blues and the original version of the song was blues. In later years, the words were sang in ragtime, folklore, jazz, pop, and even rap songs released throughout the 1900s.

In his book *Stagolee Shot Billy*, scholar Cecil Brown documents the story behind the song and the many versions of the lyrics. Through the help of and material from archives of Saint Louis University, the St. Louis Public Library, and the Missouri Historical Society, Brown compiled a complete history of the incident and the growth of the legend surrounding the shooting incident.

In 1959, a young black musician, rhythm and blues singer Lloyd Price, recorded a song entitled "Stagger Lee." It became a number one hit and is considered the most popular song of the legend of Stagolee and Billy in the United States.

The lyrics described the shooting of Billy by Stagolee "the classic black bad-man narrative":

The night was clear and the moon was yellow
And the leaves came tumbling down.

I was standin' on the corner when I heard my bulldog bark,
He was barkin' at the two men who were gamblin' in the dark.
It was Stagger Lee and Billy, two men who gambled late.
Stagger Lee threw seven, Billy swore that he threw eight.

Stagger told Billy, 'I can't let you go with that.
You have won all my money and my brand new Stetson hat.'
Stagger Lee started off goin' down that railroad track.
He said, 'I can't get you, Billy, but don't be here when I come back.'

Stagger Lee went home and he got his forty-four
Said, 'I'm goin' to the barroom just to pay that debt I owe.'
Stagger Lee went to the barroom and he stood across the barroom door
He said, 'Nobody move,' and he pulled his forty-four.

Stagger Lee shot Billy; oh he shot that poor boy so bad
Till the bullet came through Billy and it broke the bartender's glass.

Not a fictional account—a scene played out in real life in a tavern known as Bill Curtis's Saloon, located at 1101 Morgan Street at the corner of Thirteenth in the "Bloody Third District" of St Louis.

Court records document that Lee Shelton was tried twice for the murder of Billy Lyons and finally convicted and sentenced to prison in the second trial.

Court transcripts of the trial document that Frank Boyd, the bartender; Leslie Stevenson, a customer; and George G. McFaro, another customer and eyewitness to the murder, all testified at the trial resulting in Lee's conviction.

In the actual real-life incident, the witnesses testified the two men were not shooting craps and that Billy Lyons didn't die instantly. These "discrepancies" fostered many different episodes in ensuing version of the ballad of Stago Lee Shot Billy.

St. Louis records document that Shelton was a waiter, a carriage driver, and a pimp who made connections with well-heeled men looking for prostitutes, according to author Cecil Brown.

At the time of the murder, Shelton, a political figure, owned a "lid" club called the Modern Horseshoe club known "as an underground establishment that kept a 'lid' on such criminal activities as gambling while serving as a front for other activities…" (such a prostitution). Brown went on to explain, "Since Ragtime and Blues music would have flourished in such a place, it is not surprising that Stagolee first emerged as a blues song."

In his well-researched book, Brown documents no fewer than sixty versions of the Legend of Stago Lee and Billy.

According to Brown, the first recording of Stago Lee was sung by "Ma" Rainey, the mother of the blues in 1926.

In the years following her release, Duke Ellington, James Brown, Wilson Pickett, Bob Dylan, and the Isley Brothers sang the song. The versions "were also used as a model of numerous authors for short stories, poems and plays."

Cecil Brown, in the summary of his book, writes:

A black on black crime that barely made headlines . . . this tale of dignity and death, violence and sex has been given countless forms by artists ranging from 'Ma' Rainey to the Clash. Though bits of actual history have been associated with the song, the true story told in its entirety for the first time in his book—is more complex, more deeply rooted, than anything anyone would dare to invent. It tells of the first generation of free black men, crushed by a Genteel America that was both black and white.

It tells of the wild place this country was in the nineteenth century. . . ."

In the early years of the 1900s, it was sang . . . in hollers and prison work songs in the south. . . . But this story, turned into a song, is one that black Americans have never tired of repeating and reliving.

It is very appropriate that Lee Shelton is featured as our selection of inmates for the first decade of the 1900s.

VAUGHN, MORRIS, AND ROSENAUER
TRAIN ROBBERS, MURDERERS

Harry H. Vaughn, inmate number 4410, was received at the Missouri State Prison on January 21, 1897, after being convicted of robbing the train crew in Nevada, Missouri, along with William Bruce Morris, inmate number 4412, who also was found guilty and received on January 21, 1897.

They both served seven years, six months, of a ten-year sentence and were released in 1904. Albert G. Rosenauer, inmate number 2299, was received at the Missouri State Penitentiary in 1899 after being convicted of murder in St. Louis.

He was released on May 23, 1903.

When Vaughn and Morris were released from prison, they swore they would never be taken alive again by law enforcement officers and continued their criminal ways.

Vaughn was suspected of belonging to a gang who robbed in five Southern states and allegedly killed a police officer in Birmingham, Alabama, and the Cincinnati, Ohio police had a complete record on Vaughn. He was known as New York Harry, Harry O'Dowd, and Graham.

The three ex-convicts made their way to St. Louis after robbing an Illinois Central train on August 1, 1904.

The account of what transpired while the outlaws were in St. Louis is provided by the St. Louis Police Department historian, taken from official police files, and published in the book *To Serve and Protect, A Tribute to American Law Enforcement.*

The official account is provided as follows:

In September 1904, Detective James from the St. Louis Police Dept. received information from a former guard at the Jefferson City Penitentiary about the robbery. The guard believed the robbers were three ex-convicts of the penitentiary. Detective James and his partner, Detective Doyle, learned the suspected train robbers were living in a rooming house at 1324 Pine Street, which is today the location of the Soldier's Memorial.

The two detectives asked for the help of Detectives John Shea, Thomas Dwyer, and James McClusky before confronting the robbery suspects. At 4 p.m. on Oct. 20, 1904, the five detectives went to the Pine Street address. As the detectives arrived, they recognized a man coming out of the house as Harry Vaughn, one of the train robbers. After a brief struggle, the officers arrested Vaughn who was then taken to police headquarters by Detectives James and Doyle. Detectives Shea, Dwyer, and McClusky remained at the boarding house to arrest the other two robbers.

As the three remaining detectives entered the darkened room they were met by a barrage of gunshots. The entire gunfight lasted about five minutes, during which time the room was literally shot to pieces. Every man involved in the shooting emptied his revolver. Every man in the room, including the detectives, was shot. Several received more than one wound.

Firing from an ambush position in the darkened room, the robbers had the advantage. Struck by two bullets, one at the side of his nose and over his heart, Detective Shea staggered through the door of the room to the hallway. He died in the hallway.

Detective Doyle returned to the house as Shea, critically wounded, staggered into the hallway. After moving Detective Shea from the line of fire, Detective Doyle entered the room and immediately began firing his weapon. In the room, Doyle found Detectives Dwyer and McClusky making their last stand in the gun battle. Detective Doyle continued firing his revolver until it was empty.

Detective McClusky, also shot through the breast, died at City Hospital the following day. Despite the wounds to the three detectives, their gunfire had been accurate enough to critically injure the two robbers, Albert Rose and William Morris.

Detective Doyle helped Dwyer who, though mortally wounded, insisted upon walking to a drug store at Fourteenth and Pine. Placed on a stretcher, he was rushed to the hospital. Shot through the breast, Detective Dwyer died one hour after being taken to City Hospital.

William Morris, the leader of the robbers, was literally shot to pieces. Ironically, he was last to die. Morris lived for about two weeks in much pain, but always kept cursing the police. An hour before he died, he became delirious. Morris began reenacting the gun battle, screaming, 'If I had my two big guns I would clean the whole bunch and get away.'

The train crew of the Illinois Central train positively identified Harry Vaughn, Albert Rose and William Morris as the train robbers. Harry Vaughn was tried before a jury and sentenced to two-seven years in prison. He later led a revolt in prison, which resulted in the deaths of several guards. Vaughn was hanged for his involvement in the prison riot.

WILBUR "TRI-STATE TERROR" UNDERHILL

Missouri prison inmate number 25456 was first received at the Missouri State Prison in 1916, convicted of burglaries and larceny.

Born on March 16, 1901, as Henry Wilbur Underhill in Newtonia, Missouri, he grew up on the streets of Joplin, Missouri.

After being released from prison on his first sentence in 1921, he returned to Joplin and started robbing couples in "necking" areas in and around Joplin, earning him his first nickname, the "Lover's Lane Bandit." He was eventually apprehended in 1923 and returned to prison on September 14, 1923, convicted of robbery in the first degree in Joplin.

Three of his brothers were also serving time at the Missouri State Prison. His older brother, Charles Ernest Underhill, inmate number 15191, was received on November 17, 1913, and serving a life sentence for killing a hot tamale vender in Joplin. He received a pardon from Governor Park on May 22, 1936, and died in Kansas City, Missouri on May 15, 1937.

Wilbur's other brothers, George Underhill, inmate number 29569, and Earl Underhill, inmate number 29036, were serving time for burglaries and larceny.

Wilbur was released from prison for the second time in the fall of 1926.

Wilbur Underhill, like many of fellow outlaws of their time in the 1920s and 1930s, spent time drinking and gambling in the wide open city of Kansas City. One of his favorite stops was the Boulevard Club at 512 Southwest Boulevard, which was run by mobsters Joe and Sam Capra.

Most of the outlaws who came into have a drink and do a little gambling were peaceful. Not Underhill, who generated concerns for the bartenders and patrons. They were happy when he would leave.

Shortly after his release, he committed his first documented murder on December 15, 1926, when he and a partner shot and killed a person named Fred Smyth in a holdup in Picher, Oklahoma.

Just a few days later on Christmas Day 1926, Underhill and his partner shot and killed a customer named George Fee during an attempted robbery of a drugstore in Okmulgee.

On February 13, 1927, Underhill killed innocent bystander Earl O'Neal in a shootout in Picher, Oklahoma. He was captured on March 20, 1927, in Panama, Oklahoma, and, on June 23, 1927, was convicted of the Earl O'Neal and Fred Smyth murders and sentenced to life.

He escaped from prison on August 1, 1931. Shortly thereafter, Underhill robbed the Midland Theatre in Coffeeville, Kansas.

On August 6, 1933, Underhill was named as a suspect in the murder of Deputy Sheriff Frank Rohrbach in Kansas City, Kansas, and just a few days later, he murdered police officer Merle Colver in Wichita, Kansas. He was captured and returned to the Kansas State Prison in Lansing, convicted of killing Smyth and O'Neal.

On May 3, 1933, after serving just two years of his life sentence, Wilbur Underhill (along with other convicts, including the famous bank robber Harvey Bailey) pulled off a daring successful escape from the prison.

Now a fugitive once again and needing money, he and three others robbed a gas station in Miami, Oklahoma.

Underhill gained another nickname when the press called him the "Southwest Executioner." He joined in with Harvey Bailey, forming the Bailey/Underhill gang.

Underhill was described by law enforcement and the media as a mentally disturbed cop-hater and four-time murderer in three different states and was nicknamed "The Tri-State Terror" after killing Merle Colver in Wichita, Kansas.

Underhill spent most of the summer and fall of 1933 on the run.

On November 2, 1933, Underhill and others in the gang robbed the Citizens National Bank in Okmulgee, Oklahoma, taking $13,000, and on December 13, 1933, Underhill and others attempted to burglarize the First National Bank in Harrah, Oklahoma.

By now Underhill was recognized as a nationally headlined criminal and a federal fugitive. He was also suspected as a possible suspect in the Union Station Massacre in Kansas City, along with Harvey Bailey.

The day after Christmas, Underhill and his current girlfriend, Eva May Nichols, drove to Shawnee, Oklahoma, and rented a house, hoping to avoid detection. However, local police received a tip that they are holed up in the rented house.

Twenty-four police officers, assisted by the FBI, surrounded the house on December 30, 1933. The house was blasted with rifles, pistols, and shotguns, and as Underhill ran out of the house, he was shot four times on the porch of the house. Somehow, he escaped from the police. He ran to the downtown area with three wounds in his shoulders and stomach and one bullet wound in his head. He ran sixteen blocks before he collapsed and was arrested.

Even though he was shot and badly wounded, he told the news media he was hit only five times, but they put eleven holes in him. Apparently showing signs of recovery, he was shipped one hundred miles to the prison.

On January 6, 1934, Wilbur Underhill died of his wounds. Before dying, he uttered the following words from his prison hospital bed: "Tell the boys I'm coming home."

An FBI press release announced Underhill was the first fugitive to be killed by the FBI.

Underhill was buried in the Ozark Memorial Park Cemetery in Joplin, Missouri, on January 10, 1934. In attendance was an estimated crowd of 2,000 people, the largest funeral in Joplin's history. His tombstone simply reads: Wilbur Underhill.

On March 31, 1965, after serving twenty-nine years in prison, bank robber Harvey Bailey took a job as a cabinetmaker in Joplin, and on March 1, 1979, he died and was buried just a half mile from Wilbur Underhill.

MATTIE B. HOWARD
"Gangster Woman"

Mattie B. Howard, Missouri prison inmate number 24265, was received on November 18, 1921, after being convicted of the robbery and murder of a Kansas City jeweler.

Born in 1894 in Idaho, Howard lived her early years in Denver, Colorado; she relocated to Kansas City, Missouri, in her twenties.

She went by several nicknames, including "Kansas City Underworld Darling," "The Gangster Woman," and "The Bandit Queen," all given to her by police authorities and the print media.

Howard was released from Missouri prison on May 17, 1928.

After her conviction, she served a sentence of seven years of imprisonment. Upon her release from prison, she claimed she was running her own beauty salon on Chicago's South Side and also worked in Hammond, Indiana.

Like so many gangster "molls" of her time, she continued to associate with fellow criminals after serving her time and could not stay out of trouble.

On December 14, 1929, Mattie Howard was arrested at a bungalow located on Lake Shore Drive near Stevensville, Michigan, not too far from Chicago, Illinois.

Her gangster lover, Fred "Killer" Burke, had just involved himself in a minor auto accident and rather than be stopped by an area police officer named Charles Skelly, Burke had shot Skelly during a pursuit. Burke was on the run and attempting to get back to their bungalow.

In a search of Burke's abandoned and damaged vehicle, the police located a piece of paper with the name Fred Dane and the address of the bungalow, sending a team of investigators to the house.

When arriving at the house, they were met by Mattie Howard, who identified herself as Viola Dane. She did not know where her "husband" Fred Dane was and had just returned to the bungalow herself, arriving from Chicago. Fred Dane had failed to pick her up at the train station, and she had to take a cab home.

During an extensive search of the house, the investigators found boxes of ammo, two sacks full of pistol and shotgun shells, all stacked in plain view on a shelf. They also located three bulletproof vests in plain view and several loaded revolvers, one behind a pillow, one in a silverware drawer, and others near the windows.

They found men's shirts in their bedroom drawers with the initials FWD and FRB.

When she was shown two machine guns recovered from a closet, she claimed she had never seen them before. When they showed her stolen bond certificates totaling $319,950, with a woman's handwriting on the wrappers similar to her own handwriting, she said, "I don't know nothing of the bonds." She claimed she had never seen them and denied writing on the bonds. Her handwritten examples would surely prove her wrong.

She maintained not knowing about all the guns or stolen bonds in the house because Burke kept the closet door locked.

She claimed she would always go to the bedroom when men came over to talk to Burke. One of the names she remembered was Willie Heeney. He was a powerful member of Capone's Cicero operation of gambling houses and speakeasies, and he often acted as a liaison between the St. Louis hoodlums and those in Chicago.

Officer Skelly died of his wounds at 11:10 p.m.

The investigators were very aware of the St. Valentine's Day Massacre occurring in Chicago in February 1929, and Fred "Killer" Burke was a prime suspect. They felt certain the cache of weapons, including the machine guns, could be part of the weapons used in the hit in February.

During further questioning, Viola said Burke talked about Jack McGurn (one of Al Capone's enforcers) and McGurn's blond gangster moll, Louise Rolfe. McGurn also always talked about Al Capone.

She admitted meeting gangster Gus Winkler and his wife Georgette Winkler through Burke.

Also, during the search, fingerprints were lifted one off a saltshaker in the kitchen that was sent to Chicago over the weekend and positively identified as that of Fred "Killer" Burke, a.k.a. Fred Dane.

She was taken to the sheriff's department for further questioning and processing. After five hours of intense interrogation during this first interview, she never cracked about her criminal associate and lover, Fred "Killer" Burke. He was described by the national media as the "most dangerous man alive" and the "most wanted man alive," with reward money of over $100,000 "wanted dead or alive." She remained defiant and uncooperative.

While she was being processed and charged at the Berrien County Jail, the authorities learned her true identity. They learned that she also went by Mattie Howard and had done prison time in the Missouri State Prison, convicted of murdering a jeweler in Kansas City in 1921.

They learned she was known as "The Bandit Queen," "The Gangster Woman" and "Kansas City Underworld Darling."

After sitting in the jail for a long period of time, she decided she wanted to talk.

On Monday, Viola asked to speak to prosecutor Cunningham, again realizing the trouble she was in. During this interview she was handed an arrest warrant, charging her with receiving stolen property.

Prosecutor Cunningham told her they had confirmed that Fred Dane was actually Fred "Killer" Burke. When told of this fact, she replied, "What difference does it make? It's him you want, not me."

She was informed the investigators were working with police authorities in Chicago, and they intended to develop evidence of her knowledge and possible involvement as an accessory in the Chicago Massacre by covering for Fred Burke. This obviously got her attention, as she was not too eager to return to a long prison term.

She admitted she was not really married to Burke and was ready to tell the truth. She said her real name was Viola Brenneman and that she had married a man on November 7, 1914, in Kankakee, Illinois, and divorced him on March 3, 1917, on the grounds of desertion.

She said her maiden name was Viola Ostrowski and her mother was still living in Kankakee.

She had met Fred "Killer" Burke at a party during the early summer of 1928.

Viola said when she met Fred Burke, a.k.a. "Fred Dane," she was living at 6214 Evans Avenue in Chicago, Illinois. She lived with Fred Dane in the fall of 1928 and early 1929 at the Cordova Apartments in Hammond, Indiana, under the alias of Reed.

She said she also had gone by the name Callahan at Fred Burke's urging.

The two then moved to 14015 Green Bay Avenue in Burnham, Illinois, just outside Hammond, Indiana.

For a two-month period, they lived at the Dalton Apartments on Fifth Avenue, east of Broadway in Gary, Indiana, under the alias of Church.

When asked about Burke's involvement in the St. Valentine's Day Massacre, she showed her true gangster moll attitude and alibied his whereabouts on that day, claiming "Fred wasn't in on that terrible thing. I know he wasn't. Why, he could not have been in Chicago and got back to Hammond."

She said they moved to Michigan near Stevensville on September 27, 1929, buying the bungalow.

Most of Mattie Howard's account of her days living with Burke occurred in 1928 and 1929. She would have been living with him the day he murdered Frankie Yale, mob boss of New York in July 1, 1928, and also on February 14, 1929, the day he and his gang of "American boys" had killed seven members of the "Bugs" Moran gang in the St. Valentine's Massacre—"the crime of the century."

She alibied Burke for that date and said she was living with him the night he shot and killed police officer Charles Skelly on December 14, 1929, not to mention the robberies and bank robberies Burke was suspected of pulling off during their time living together.

These facts and timeline give Mattie Howard another dubious nickname — the "reigning queen" of the Missouri gangster molls — a title that still stands today.

With Burke now a fugitive wanted for the murder of Police Officer Skelly and hiding out in Missouri, Mattie Howard took the heat in Michigan and moved on with her life. She never saw Burke again, moved on to Denver, and became an evangelist.

In 1937, Howard published her journal in which she asserted her innocence of his crimes in Kansas City, Missouri. Her journal can be found in the Spencer Library on the campus of the University of Kansas in Lawrence, Kansas.

JENNINGS YOUNG
Cop Killers

Jennings Young, Missouri prison inmate number 21853, was first received in 1918, convicted of burglary and sentenced to six years. He was released on April 11, 1922. On April 14, 1924, he pled guilty of Dyer Act violations and was sentenced to three years at the federal penitentiary in Leavenworth, Kansas.

HARRY YOUNG

Harry Young, Missouri prison inmate number 31358 and brother of Jennings Young, was received at the Missouri State Prison on March 28, 1927, after pleading guilty to larceny. He was released on September 26, 1928.

He accumulated a number of arrests and convictions during his criminal career in the 1920s, including for burglaries and buying stolen property.

On June 2, 1919, Harry Young's criminal involvement escalated to murder when he shot and killed the city marshal in Republic, Missouri, Mark S. Noe, after Noe had arrested him and an associate for drunkenness. The autopsy report revealed Noe had been shot three times, two of the bullets in the head, and his body was dumped on a road just outside of Republic. Harry disappeared and was not heard of again until January 2, 1932. He was suspected of living in Texas and possibly in Wichita, Kansas, a fugitive from justice, wanted for murder.

In their book *Young Brothers Massacre*, Paul W. Barrett and Mary H. Barrett detail the deadly law enforcement massacre that left six officers dead and three more wounded—a record to this day—in one shooting incident in the history of the United States and what has been called "the greatest manhunt in the history of Texas, ending in the two brothers' death in Houston."

Information also drawn for this story is provided by William J. Helmer and Rick Mattix in their book *The Complete Public Enemy Almanac.*

THE MASSACRE

January 2, 1932, began much like any other day at a hundred-acre farm in Green County, Missouri, owned by James David and Willie Florence Young, who had given birth to eight children, including Jennings and Harry, the youngest of the boys.

They were a dysfunctional family, whose father James was suspicious of authorities and whose mother Florence defended the youngest of the boys, petty outlaws who rose from stealing to burglary, robbery, safecracking, and even murder.

By the latter part of 1931, the Young outlaws, who were wanted in several states, were believed by law enforcement to have returned to the family farm.

Green County Sheriff Marcel Hendrix made plans to raid the farmhouse during the afternoon and assembled a raiding party consisting of seven county officers, two police officers, the sheriff, and one civilian going along for the ride.

Sheriff Hendrix knew the Youngs didn't know they were the danger. The posse gathered in the vicinity of the farm and surrounded the farmhouse. Not hearing any noise on the ground floor, the party believed the occupants were upstairs.

A tear gas shell was launched through a second-floor bedroom window, and a second tear gas shell missed the window and bounced off the house.

Running out of tear gas shells, Hendrix and deputy Wiley Mashburn kicked in a door. As they entered, Mashburn was met with a shotgun blast, striking him around his eyes and removing his facial skin from his skull.

As Sheriff Hendrix yelled out, "They mean business!" a second shotgun blast rang out, hitting him in the upper part of his shoulder. Both men died from their wounds.

The gun battle continued, and four more lawmen were shot and killed, including Springfield Officer Charlie Houser, Police Detective Sid Meadows, Deputy Ollie Crosswhite, and Chief of Detectives Tony Oliver, marking the deadliest law enforcement shooting massacre in Missouri and the United States history.

THE MANHUNT

The two shooters, Jennings and Harry Young, who were deadly marksmen with rifles and shotguns, escaped from the property, most likely through the cornfield after dark as the raiding party lost track of each other during the chaos.

A massive multistate manhunt was mounted. The two brothers left the state and fled to Houston, Texas.

It took three days to locate the two Young brothers when a carpenter, who rented them a room in his house, recognized their photographs in a newspaper and called the police.

The Houston police closed in on the house with numbers, heavy artillery, and gas guns. The brothers were able to get off only three shots as they escaped the gas going to the bathroom.

The police heard one of the brothers shout, "We're dead — come and get us!" as they shot each other to avoid capture.

John R. Woodward, the author of a booklet also titled *The Young Brothers Massacre* that describes the farm massacre and aftermath, wrote, "trapped like rattlesnakes they played the ace to cheat at least society and their god. What they thought cannot be written or told, but what they did in history — Harry and Jennings Young, at bay at last to square accounts, spat their venom into each other and died."

Today a monument stands in the Green County Sheriff's Department in Springfield, Missouri, commemorating the six slain officers.

The Ralph Foster Museum, located on the campus of the College of the Ozarks south of Branson, contains many displays that describe events in Missouri law enforcement history.

One of the displays is the Young Brothers Massacre, which includes a summary of the shootout, a news article, photographs of the victims and murderers, and revolvers belonging to Sheriff Marcel Hendrix and Deputy Ollie Crosswhite.

On the morning of April 8, 2017, at the Forest Park Cemetery in Joplin, Missouri, a headstone was placed on the unmarked grave of Springfield Police Officer Charles Houser through the efforts of the Missouri Police Officers Association (MPOA) at the direction and efforts of Association President Dale Schmidt, a retired Missouri Highway Patrol commander.

EDNA "THE KISSING BANDIT" MURRAY

Edna Murray, Missouri female inmate number 28973, was first admitted to the Missouri State Penitentiary on December 3, 1925, after being convicted of armed robbery of a man in Kansas City, Missouri, a man she had kissed while conducting the robbery with her husband, Jack Murray, Missouri inmate number 28972, giving her the nickname "The Kissing Bandit." She escaped from the Missouri prison on December 13, 1932, her third successful escape, earning a second nickname, "Rabbit."

Edna Murray, much like a fellow outlaw moll Bonnie Parker, started out as a waitress, and much like Bonnie Parker, she enjoyed the wild life and the excitement.

William Helmer and Rick Mattix, in their book *The Complete Public Enemy Almanac*, document that she was married to no fewer than three men.

The first was a man named Paden in 1917. They had a son named Preston. She then married Walter Price, a marriage that was also short-lived. Her third marriage was to a jewel thief "Diamond Joe" Sullivan, who was convicted of murder and executed for his crime in Arkansas.

Edna Murray gained a distinction that few gangster molls have ever earned. She was named as a member of the Barker-Karpis gang. As a member, she involved herself in the conspiracy to kidnap St. Paul businessman Edward George Bremer, president of the State Bank of St. Paul, Minnesota, on January 17, 1934. He was released unharmed only after the gang was paid a ransom of $200,000.

Edna, along with her boyfriend and fellow gang member Volney Davis, were indicted for their part in the kidnapping on January 22, 1935, along with twenty other gang members.

On February 6, Volney Davis was captured in St. Louis by federal agents, only to escape from custody on February 7 on his way to an Illinois prison.

On that same date, gangster moll Edna Murray and Jess Doyle of the gang were captured in Kansas. Eventually Volney Davis was recaptured.

On April 23, 1934, fellow gangster John Hamilton was mortally wounded, after a shootout with deputies near Hastings, Minnesota. Also involved in the shootout was the notorious John Dillinger and Homer Van Meter.

Hamilton was taken to Aurora, Illinois, a hideout of Edna Murray and Volney Davis. Hamilton died of his wounds and was allegedly buried near Aurora, Illinois on April 30.

Acting on the information provided by Davis and Murray, the FBI, on August 28, 1935, dug up the remains of a badly decomposed body believed to be John "Red" Hamilton in Oswego, Illinois.

The body was so decomposed it could not be positively identified as that of John Hamilton. A controversy unfolded when Hamilton's brother claimed John Hamilton was still alive.

Murray beat the kidnapping charges but was returned to the Missouri State Prison to finish her term before she escaped.

She decided to go straight and cooperated with law enforcement authorities against criminal associates.

She always considered herself as a "gangster moll," and with such a colorful personality, she was written up in newspapers and journals and depicted in a film and television adaptation.

Murray was pardoned from prison on December 20, 1940. She lived to the age of seventy-seven and died in San Francisco in 1966 as Martha Edna Patton.

BENNIE DICKSON

Bennie Dickson, prison inmate number 39211, was first received in Missouri State Prison in 1931, convicted of robbery. Dickson, along with his young wife, Stella, were Depression-era bank robbers.

He married Stella when she was a fifteen-year-old, and she started robbing banks at the age of sixteen.

In an eight-month period between August 1938 to April 1939, they stole over $50,000 in two bank robberies in South Dakota. The two bank robbers eluded police on several occasions in 1938, including one incident during which Stella, the young gangster moll, shot the tires out of the pursuing police car, earning her the nickname Stella "Sure Shot" Dickson.

Shortly after the two arrived in St. Louis, Missouri, Bennie Dickson was shot and killed by federal agents on April 6, 1939, at a hamburger stand. Stella was arrested the next day in Kansas City.

Stella "Sure Shot" Dickson avoided going to the Missouri State Prison by escaping from the Clay County Jail in Liberty, Missouri. Eventually captured, she served prison time in South Dakota.

After serving a federal sentence of ten years, she lived in Raytown, Missouri, for a period of time and went straight.

She died in 1995 at the age of seventy-two.

WILLIAM ISAAC RADKAY
The Pride of Alcatraz

William Isaac Radkay, Missouri state prison inmate (number not found), was received at the prison in 1935 after being convicted of a robbery of a jewelry store in Kansas City, Missouri, and sentenced to a ten-year term. He was paroled in October 1940.

In William Helmer's book *The Complete Public Enemy Almanac*, he documented the criminal career of Willie Radkay and portions of his material are included, along with information obtained from the Missouri State Archives in this interesting summary of one 1900s outlaw.

It is interesting to point out that Radkay was shot twelve times by police when he was caught after this robbery but somehow survived.

When his niece asked him years later how he survived, Radkay replied "tough skin, soft bullets, and they didn't hit anything important." He was severely wounded in the arms, back, and upper legs.

In the early days of his criminal career, Radkay was called "one of the most notorious armed robbers in Kansas City history by the police." The Baptist church he attended as a youth called him the "incarnation of the devil."

Surely one of the most colorful criminals to ever spend time in the Missouri prison, he first started as a delivery boy for bootleggers, and by the age of sixteen, he had elevated his talents to armed robbery, declaring he was a "Little Al Capone" as a leader of a youth gang robbing stores.

He progressed to hijacking liquor and robbing speakeasies. In 1932, he was sentenced to ten to twenty-one years in prison in the state Industrial Reformatory at Hutchison, Kansas; however, he was paroled after only serving two years.

After getting out of reformatory prison, he left Kansas City, Missouri, as it was too hot. He went to Covington, Kentucky, robbing casinos, then on to Buffalo, New York, robbing gambling spots before returning to the Midwest to commit bank robberies. In the process during this period of his criminal career, he met "Pretty Boy" Floyd and "Machine Gun" Kelly, to name a few fellow outlaws.

In 1934, Radkay was shot six times by police in Kansas City, Kansas, during an encounter in his hometown. Placed in jail, somehow, he survived his wounds, escaping from a hospital to freedom.

After his parole from the Missouri State Prison, he was sentenced to a federal prison term of twenty years in 1943 for bank robbery convictions.

Radkay's records as an escape artist earned him a trip to Alcatraz, "The Rock," where he was in prison with such notable famous fellow inmates like "Machine Gun" Kelly, Basil Banghart, Jimmy Murray, Harvey Bailey, and his old criminal friend, Alvin Karpis.

Radkay was transferred to federal prison in Leavenworth, Kansas, and paroled in 1954.

Reverting back to a life of crime, he was convicted of a bank robbery in Flint, Michigan, and returned to Leavenworth. He was paroled in 1969, married, and moved to Prescott, Kansas, settling down as a janitor.

In 1994, Willie Radkay attended annual reunions of formal Alcatraz inmates, appearing in a number of television documentaries.

Through these numerous national appearances, he was declared "the most famous 'Rock' star" you'll ever meet.

In his final years, he was in a nursing home in Fort Scott, Kansas, collaborating with his niece, Patty Terry, on his autobiography, *A Devil Incarnate*.

Considered the "last surviving Depression outlaw" by national media, Radkay died on September 24, 2006, at the age of ninety-five.

William Radkay, in this writer's opinion, was the most colorful inmate to ever spend time in the Missouri State Prison in the 1900s, having survived eighteen slugs in his body received while fleeing from the police. He also had a sense of humor regarding his criminal antics, the pride of Alcatraz, and lived to the ripe old age of ninety-five in spite of his lifestyle. He earns the right to be included in the rogue's gallery of twentieth-century Missouri prison inmates.

CHARLES L. "SONNY" LISTON
An American Boxing Icon

Charles L. "Sonny" Liston, inmate number 63723, entered the Missouri State Penitentiary on June 2, 1950, after his conviction for robbing a service station, cab stand, and a café on Market Street in St. Louis. Liston was one of seventeen children born to Helen Liston (Baskin). Liston came to St. Louis as a teenager, living with his mother in an apartment at North Tenth and O'Fallon.

While in the Missouri prison, he was taught how to box and became very good at it, rising to the top of the amateur rankings after his release. His abilities caught the eyes of sports editor Bob Burnes of the *St. Louis Glob Democrat* newspaper, as well as Frank W. Mitchell, who owned the *St. Louis Argus* newspaper.

Burns and Mitchell were successful in getting Liston paroled on Halloween 1952, and Mitchell secured him a job as a laborer.

Liston also started his amateur boxing career, winning the area Golden Gloves Championship. After a short amateur career, he became a professional fighter on September 2, 1953.

Liston signed a contract with Mitchell, giving Mitchell half of all purses Liston won in exchange for all expenses. What Liston did not know was that Mitchell was a front man for St. Louis mob associates John Vitale, Frank "Blinky" Palermo, "Killer" Frank Carbo, and one of labors' leading enforcers, Barney Baker.

Liston won his first nine professional fights before losing an eight-round decision fight.

Liston did not stay out of trouble. His police rap sheet documents fourteen arrests from 1953 until 1958.

His run-ins with the police were often violent. Take the case of Patrolman Thomas Mellow, age forty-one, who, on May 5, 1956, had his revolver taken from him by Liston, who placed it at his head, threatening to shoot him. Liston preceded to hit him in the head. Mellow's leg was also broken at the knee in the struggle. Liston was charged and pled guilty and, on January 1957, was sentenced to nine months in the city workhouse, interrupting his boxing career for almost one year.

John Auble, a crime reporter in St. Louis, wrote in his book *A History of St. Louis Gangsters*,

> Sonny Liston's suspicious connections caught the attention of Senator Estes Kefauver's anti-trust and monopoly committee who subpoenaed Liston to testify before the committee held in the early 1950s.
>
> Liston testified stating he knew his contract was owned by several people but wasn't sure who they were. During his testimony he admitted he knew Frank 'Blinky' Palermo, that everybody knew 'Blinky' and was aware of the hoodlum element in his career.
>
> He was warned by the committee that—
>
> If he did not divest himself from the likes of Vitali, Palermo and Carbo he would never get a chance to win the heavyweight boxing title and may not be able to fight anywhere and his dream of a world title championship would collapse.

Sonny Liston was quoted as saying he had little choice about his associates in the boxing business if he wanted to get ahead. "What was I to do, starve to death?"

There was little doubt Charles "Sonny" Liston was owned by the organized crime bosses of the era.

Rumors has it that St. Louis Police Captain James Reddick Black, commander of the Ruskin Avenue Police District station, used to beat Liston around in the back room of the station house and Major John Doherty, Chief of the Detective Bureau, worked Liston over on more than one occasion. One rumor has it that Doherty took Liston to the edge of the city and told him to get out of town. It is reported he said, "If you don't, they'll find you in an alley."

While this author was a police officer with the St. Louis Police Department, I had the privilege of working for both Jim Reddick as a patrolman and Major John Doherty while in the homicide division, and I was told by more than one fellow detective these stories were more than just rumors.

In the years that followed, Liston himself confirmed these rumors, telling his boxing friends he was persuaded to leave St. Louis.

After his release from his nine-month jail sentence, Liston relocated to Philadelphia, Pennsylvania, where his boxing career took off.

He won twenty-six consecutive fights and set his sights on the heavyweight championship.

Liston was not liked in Philadelphia, and during his boxing career, he moved on to Denver, Colorado, and then to Las Vegas, Nevada, where he was more accepted by fight fans visiting the casinos.

On September 25, 1962, he knocked out Floyd Patterson, winning the professional boxing heavyweight championship.

In his professional career, he earned a career record of fifty wins with four losses. Of his wins, he scored thirty-nine knockouts.

On February 25, 1964, he lost his heavyweight title to a young, determined fighter named Cassius Clay, who would later change his name to Muhammad Ali.

Following two losses to Clay, Liston, in a comeback effort, won eleven consecutive fights by knockouts in 1968 and three more in 1969 before losing a fight.

He entered the ring one more time in the summer of 1970, winning the fight.

On January 5, 1971, Charles "Sonny" Liston was found dead in his Las Vegas home by his wife, Geraldine. Drugs were involved in his accidental death. He was buried in Paradise Memorial Park Cemetery in Las Vegas, Nevada.

On Liston's gravesite, his epitaph reads, "A man."

An extraordinary story of a man who became a national sports figure that all started in the Missouri State Prison.

BONNIE HEADY
Gangster Moll, Kidnapper, Murderer

Bonnie Brown Heady, inmate EX and her boyfriend, Carl Austin Hall, inmate letters EX, were received at the Missouri State Prison on November 20, 1953, charged with the kidnapping and the vicious murder of six-year-old

Bobby Greenlease, which occurred earlier in the year—crimes they both had confessed to after their arrest. The inmates received mug shots bearing the letters EX, which possibly documents they both were to be executed.

Bobby's father, Robert Greenlease, was a wealthy automobile dealer in Kansas City at the time of the kidnapping and murder that received national attention.

Kidnappers Heady and Hall appeared at the private Catholic school in Kansas City that Bobby was attending, introducing themselves as Bobby's aunt and uncle and telling the nuns that Bobby's mother was seriously ill.

The nuns failed to check out their story and released Bobby to the couple.

Heady and Hall first tried to kill Bobby by strangling him, and when that failed, Hall shot the young boy in the head, killing him. They then drove to Heady's residence in St. Joseph, Missouri, and buried his body in her backyard.

The two contacted the parents, convincing them Bobby was still alive, and collected a ransom of $600,000, the largest ever paid in the United States at the time.

Murderers Heady and Hall then traveled to St. Louis, Missouri, with the money, where they first rented a motel room at the infamous Coral Courts Motel. They then rented an apartment on Arsenal Street near Tower Grove Park, freely spending some of the marked money.

The two were eventually arrested by the St. Louis Police, who recovered some of the money; however, half the ransom was missing and has never been recovered.

An investigation revealed the arresting officers, Lt. Louis I. Shoulders and Patrolman Elmer Dolan, had kept half the money in a shakedown when they arrested the pair. The two officers were eventually convicted of perjury in the theft of money and fired from the department.

Heady and Hall were returned to Kansas City, where they confessed to the kidnapping and brutal murder six days after Bobby's body was recovered.

The two were sentenced to death. They waived all appeals and were sent to the Missouri State Penitentiary, where they were executed on December 18, 1953, in the Missouri state gas chamber.

According to reports, Hall appeared remorseful; however, Heady showed no remorse. She was the only woman ever put to death in Missouri.

The mystery of the money whereabouts is still unknown. The FBI's best guess is the money was laundered through the Teamster's rackets in Chicago. The media published the complete list of the serial numbers on the bills, and a few bills showed up in the states of Indiana and Michigan.

Bobby's parents, in recognition of their son, donated a large sum of money to Rockhurst High School and College in Kansas City. The college art gallery and library are named after the Greenleases and the high school, built in 1962, is called Greenlease Memorial Campus in memory of Robert C. Greenlease.

JAMES EARL RAY
American Assasin

James Earl Ray, inmate number 00416, was received in the Missouri State Penitentiary on April 17, 1960. He was convicted in St. Louis, Missouri, of operating a motor vehicle without the permission of the owner and robbery in the first degree by means of a dangerous and deadly weapon. Ray was sentenced to twenty years.

James Earl Ray was born on March 10, 1928, in Alton, Illinois, and was the eldest of nine children. The Ray family left Alton, Illinois, in 1935 and relocated to Ewing, Missouri, after his father, George Ray, was wanted by Alton police for passing a bad check. Ray left high school at the age of fifteen. He later enlisted in the US Army at the close of World War II; however, he failed to adept to military life.

His first conviction was in 1949 in California for a burglary and armed robbery in Illinois. He was then convicted of mail fraud in Hannibal, Missouri.

He served four years in Leavenworth Federal Penitentiary before being sentenced to the Missouri State Penitentiary for his St. Louis conviction.

Now a hardened criminal, Ray escaped from the Missouri State Penitentiary in 1967 by hiding in a truck that was transporting bread from the prison bakery where he was assigned.

As an escaped fugitive, he moved throughout the United States and Canada, finally settling in Puerto Vallarta, Mexico, in October 1967, establishing an alias—Eric Starvo Galt. He left Mexico in November 1967, arriving in Los Angeles, California, where he became interested in the George Wallace presidential campaign.

He was extremely prejudiced toward black people, and on March 24, 1968, he drove to Atlanta, Georgia, setting in place a crime he would soon commit that would shock the world and change the course of history.

On March 30, 1968, Ray drove to Birmingham, Alabama, and purchased a Remington model 760 Gamemaster .30-06 rifle and a box of shells from Aero Marine Supply Company. He also purchased a Redfield 2x-7x scope.

During the purchase, Ray used the name Harvey Lowmeyer.

He drove back to Atlanta to a rooming house that he had rented on March 24. Ray spent time reading newspapers and learned the Reverend Martin Luther King Jr. planned a trip to Memphis, Tennessee, scheduled on April 1, 1968. Ray drove to Memphis and rented a room at a rooming house across the street from the Lorraine Motel, where King was staying during his visit.

On April 4, 1968, James Earl Ray, using the rifle, killed the Reverend Martin Luther King Jr. while King was standing on the second-floor balcony. Witnesses saw Ray running from the rooming house and the rifle Ray used was found, including his fingerprints on the rifle and telescope.

During the investigation, authorities searched the room Ray had rented in Atlanta and recovered a map he had purchased and circled the residence and church of Martin Luther King, Jr.

Ray was a fugitive from justice for two months, first going to Toronto, Canada, acquiring a passport in the name Ramon George Sneyd; he then fled to England, staying in London and Portugal.

On June 8, 1968, Ray was arrested at the airport in London as he was trying to get to Brussels. The name on the passport—Sneyd—was on the Canadian watch list and Ray was detained.

He was extradited to Tennessee, where he was charged with King's murder. Ray confessed to killing Martin Luther King Jr. on March 10, 1969, and was sentenced to ninety-nine years in prison, avoiding the death penalty by pleading guilty.

Three days later, Ray recanted his confession, claiming he was not the person who killed Martin Luther King Jr. but was partially responsible for King's death, suggesting a conspiracy.

Ray told his story to a reporter named William Huie, who found Ray was lying about some of what he told him. On the advice of his attorney, Jack Kershaw, Ray took a polygraph test as part of an interview with *Playboy* magazine. The results showed Ray alone did kill Martin Luther King, Jr.

On June 10, 1977, Ray escaped from the Brush Mountain Tennessee Penitentiary. He was recaptured on June 13, adding one more year to his ninety-nine-year sentence. A second escape attempt also failed.

The King assassination conspiracy theory raised its ugly head, pointing directly back to the Missouri State Penitentiary and Ray's connection with a St. Louis area hoodlum named John Paul Spica, Missouri inmate number 7035, who was serving a term for conspiracy to commit murder. Spica had been received at the prison on July 1, 1963, for the murder conviction.

Ray was serving his prison term and was in the same cell block with Spica in the 1960s.

In the House Assassination Committee Report in 1978, Spica was identified as a possible — but "not substantiated" — link between Dr. Martin Luther King Jr. and James Earl Ray. The committee said it was possible that an offer to kill King had been transmitted through Spica to Ray. Spica was the brother-in-law of Russell G. Byers, a businessman from Rockhill, Missouri, who the committee said was reported to have received an offer of $50,000 for King's assassination.

Spica was subpoenaed in 1978 to appear before the committee; however, nothing further developed on this possible motive.

Spica was killed in a gangland car bombing as he left his residence in Richmond Heights, Missouri, in November 1979, during a labor union power struggle between rival mobster factions. The Martin Luther King Jr. assassination was one of several possible motives considered for Spica's murder until it was proven that two local gangsters named Ray Flynn and Anthony Leisure committed the murder, a series of cases this author investigated while employed with the Bureau of Alcohol and Tobacco (ATF) in the 1970s and early 1980s.

The Missouri Department of Corrections held an escape warrant for James Earl Ray until his death of natural causes on April 23, 1998, at the age of seventy.

GEORGE "TINY" MERCER
Motorcycle Gang Leader, Murderer

George "Tiny" Mercer, Missouri Division of Corrections number CP2, was received at the Missouri State Penitentiary on November 9, 1979, after being convicted of the rape and brutal murder of Karen Keeton, an attractive twenty-two-year-old waitress working in Grandview, Missouri.

On August 31, 1978, Mercer was drinking with some biker associates at the Blue Seven Lounge in Grandview, Missouri, when he told one of his criminal associates, Steve Gardner, he wanted to have sex with waitress Karen Keeton.

Tiny Mercer was the leader of two motorcycle gangs named the "Missing Links" and "the Rancid Riders," both operating out of Belton.

When he barked an order, his fellow bikers jumped.

Gardner brought an unsuspecting Keeton to Mercer's house in Belton, Missouri, where Mercer put a sawed-off shotgun at her head and forced her up to his bedroom.

Also present in the house during this rape was David Gee, who was drinking with Mercer, and John Campbell, who was at the house babysitting Mercer's ten-year-old daughter.

When victim Keeton yelled for help, Gardner told Tiny Mercer "Happy birthday" then said to the others in the room, "Seconds."

Mercer brutally raped her and returned downstairs to his criminal associates.

Mercer took a shower and declared he was going upstairs to have sex with her again. Gee and Campbell also went to the bedroom, and Mercer forced her to perform oral sex on Gee.

Mercer, Gee, Gardner, and Campbell returned downstairs. Mercer asked Gardner what he wanted to do with Keeton, and Gardner said, "Kill the bitch."

Mercer verbally agreed, returned to the bedroom, and strangled Keeton, hitting her at least one time in the head.

With Campbell's help, they put her dead body in Campbell's truck. She was taken to a field, and her body was put over a fence in the field.

At the time of Keeton's murder, he was under charges of raping a seventeen-year-old girl. When they returned to his house, Mercer said he should have killed the seventeen-year-old and he wouldn't have any charges pending.

Mercer had Campbell hide the shotgun and burned her purse.

A few weeks later, Campbell, along with his attorney, looked for and located her badly decomposed body.

Hoping to reduce his exposure, he and his attorney reported this to the police.

Her body was decomposed, and authorities had to identify her with her dental records.

Both Mercer and Campbell were arrested and convicted.

Campbell received a life sentence; however, his conviction was overturned on his appeal. Campbell then pled guilty to a lesser charge.

George "Tiny" Mercer was convicted and sentenced to die. He was executed at the Missouri State Prison by lethal injection on January 6, 1989, becoming the first prisoner executed in Missouri since 1965.

MAURICE OSCAR BYRD

Robber, Rapist, Serial Murderer

Maurice Oscar Byrd, inmate number 99921, was received in the Missouri State Prison on August 18, 1982, convicted of the murder of four victims in Des Peres, Missouri, and sentenced to the death penalty. On August 23, 1991, Byrd was executed by lethal injection.

This entire section is drawn from my discussions with Ronald Martin. Ron served as a St. Louis Firefighter, Jefferson County Deputy Sheriff, Director of Police for the City of Des Peres's Department of Public Safety (DPS) from 1982 to 1996, and an author.

Material is also drawn from Ron Martin's book, *Murder at Pope's Cafeteria*.

Ron Martin and I grew up together in South St. Louis, playing sports together, and were both classmates at McKinley High School from 1958 to 1962. We each went on to careers in the public service sector as law enforcement officials, and we both started our careers in 1968. Mine continued until I retired in 1997, while Ron retired in 2009.

This is his firsthand account of the investigation of the murders of four victims in a restaurant in a quiet suburban St. Louis County community after they were robbed of the restaurant's cash proceeds and all their personal property.

THE POPE'S CAFETERIA MURDERS

The morning of October 23, 1980, started out as just another day for employees arriving at work at the Pope's Cafeteria located in the West County Mall in the city of Des Peres, Missouri. It would turn out to be the last day of their lives.

It would also affect the lives of many more, including relatives, friends, the public, and the law enforcement officials who were tasked with determining who committed the murders and why.

A brutal murder that took over eleven years to bring to final closure to those affected.

Ron Martin, then captain of the Des Peres DPS, was arriving at his office at about 7:44 a.m. when he received the call on his police radio to go to Pope's Cafeteria. Upon his arrival, he was met by DPS officers Frank Florence and Mark Demes, learning there had been "an armed robbery with people shot."

Once the officers determined the robbers were gone and the building was safe, the officers initiated a scene investigation, discovering three dead victims had been shot and one was seriously wounded.

The victims were identified as James Wood, the cafeteria manager, and two kitchen employees — Carolyn Turner and Edna Ince.

The investigation determined the location of the bodies were secluded in an inner office. The evidence at the scene, combined with an eyewitness, indicated the robbery was carried out by three black males seen leaving the building. They also suspected the victims knew one or more of the killers and concluded the victims were killed for that reason.

The fourth victim, Judy Cazaco, died of her wounds ten days after the robbery/murders. Evidence later revealed she had been sexually assaulted then shot in each eye and left to die.

In describing the grizzly scene, Ron Martin wrote in his book:

> When you work in the line of police work, you are forced to encounter the tragedies of death. We had all responded to death and had seen death scenes. . . . But this situation is much more difficult to process.

Ron Martin realized early on his department would need all the help he could get. He requested the Major Case Squad of the Greater St. Louis Metropolitan Area be activated and join in the investigation; this was a group of trained homicide detectives very experienced in this type of crime. He also requested assistance from the St. Louis County Crime Scene Unit to process and preserve the evidence.

Several early motives and suspects for the robbery were developed. According to Captain Martin, one motive was that it was an effort to get drug money for their drug enterprise. The group used a religious cover of MSTA (Moorish Science Temple of America) as a shield for concealing their criminal enterprise. They were actively selling drugs in the St. Louis metropolitan community.

Another suspect was developed named Maurice Oscar Byrd. The investigators learned Byrd had performed a previous service call at the cafeteria for Master Pest Control and had left a set of keys in the office as a "ruse" to gain access that morning.

Captain Martin developed a strong sense this was not the first and possibly not the last robbery/murder committed by one or more of the three suspects. Evidence developed over the next several years by his department and the major case squad proved Ron Martin right.

Captain Martin's suspicions were realized when the investigators learned others were killed by the serial killer before he was arrested and charged with the murders of the Pope's Cafeteria employees.

As the major case squad team of detectives' investigation proceeded from days to weeks to months, their hopes of solving the murders quickly faded. The squad needed a break.

THE BIG BREAK

On May 27, 1981, Detective Colon McCoy, with the St. Louis City Police Department, called Ron Martin, telling him the Savannah, Georgia Police Department had contacted the St. Louis PD, advising them they had a suspect in jail charged with killing Fred Oliver Johnson, an employee of a local liquor store. The suspect had taken the victim to a secluded walk-in cooler and shot him three times in his back and once in the head, killing him—a very similar modus operandi used in the Pope murders.

The Savannah Police learned a liquor delivery driver named Oscelious Green reported he had found the victim in the cooler upon his arrival and ran to a service station next door for help.

A witness at the scene said one of the robbers leaving the scene was wearing a red windbreaker with the word "Germany" on the back of it.

Green got the word he was wanted for questioning and turned himself into the police department.

Investigators determined Green was lying when they learned that a check completed by the victim was filled out and given to Green, documenting the victim was alive when Green made his delivery.

The interviewing detectives informed Green they knew he was inside the liquor store before victim, Johnson, was killed.

Green admitted during his interview his involvement in the robbery but claimed he was not involved in the murder of the store clerk Johnson. He described how his ex-brother-in-law had taken a handgun away from the clerk and taken him to a cooler. Green said he heard four shots. He then told police his brother-in-law was named Maurice Oscar Byrd.

At the same time that Green was being interviewed, Maurice Byrd was committing another armed robbery at a different liquor store in Savannah, Georgia. This time Byrd was not so successful and was arrested after a shootout between him and a Good Samaritan storekeeper working next to the liquor store robbery location. The Good Samaritan was shot twice by Byrd, leaving him wounded while he escaped from the scene.

Byrd was apprehended shortly after the shootout.

Detectives went to Byrd's apartment in Savannah and located a red windbreaker jacket with the word "Germany" on the back, which was given to them by Byrd's ex-wife.

Later that evening the Savannah Detectives served a search warrant at Byrd's house. During the search they recovered one black holster, one black cap, one .38 cartridge R-P, two .38 caliber Federal brand cartridges, one security badge of the Savannah State College Security Police, and—very importantly—one identification holder containing a St. Louis Metropolitan Police Department Identification Card, with Byrd's photograph glued to the ID card and a St. Louis Metro PD Badge.

The detectives also located witnesses placing Byrd with Green shortly before the morning of the murder and robbery. Byrd admitted being with Green while Green went into the liquor store, still denying he was in the liquor store, stating Green killed the employee.

Both Byrd and Green were in custody and eventually indicted for the robbery and murder of Freddie Johnson, the liquor store employee.

The suspect that Ron Martin and his team had been looking for since his disappearance from St. Louis, Missouri, shortly after the murders was now in custody in the jail in Chatham County, Georgia.

Ron Martin called the Chatham County Police, placing a hold on Maurice Byrd.

At 10:40 a.m. the next morning, May 28, 1981, Captain Martin and Special County, St. Louis County Prosecutor Gordon Ankney arrived at the airport in Savannah and were met by Detectives Bobby Wedlock and Steve Hill of the Chatham County Police Department.

Martin and Ankney spent the rest of the day learning how the police were able to arrest Byrd for the robbery/murder at the local liquor store in Savannah.

Captain Martin was hoping to find evidence connecting suspect Byrd with the Pope's Cafeteria murder.

He and Detective Wedlock secured a second search warrant for Byrd's residence and arranged to conduct interviews with Byrd's family members, one at a time after their search efforts.

During the search, a briefcase with the initials MB was located in the apartment. Inside the briefcase, Captain Martin found a 3 x 5 postcard from the St. Louis Fire Department, advising Byrd he was ranked 402 for employment for a probationary position after scoring 70.67 percent on the employment test.

Also located in the briefcase was a piece of adding machine tape with some numbers on it, possibly a safe combination. Byrd had been suspected of obtaining safe combination numbers when he was employed as a security guard at the St. Louis University Security Office and stealing property from the safes.

Ron Martin also found a cash bag with a drawstring. Martin suspected Byrd placed the robbery money from the Pope's murder in a tote bag. His suspicions were confirmed later when an inmate in jail in Chatham County said Byrd had bragged about putting the robbery money in a tote bag. Additional inmates would add details of statements made by Byrd's involvement in the Pope's murders.

On a hunch, Captain Martin asked the police to check with the Savannah State College official with the numbers on the adding machine, where Byrd had also been employed as a security guard. Martin wanted to know if the numbers matched the safe combinations at the college.

Ron Martin then conducted interviews with Byrd's family members. He first interviewed Byrd's "wife," Saundra Yvonne Sanders.

She said Byrd arrived in Savannah on October 26, 1980, with the briefcase containing approximately $4,000 in various denominations.

One time during an argument, Byrd told her he killed three people in St. Louis and the victims had been two women and one man. Byrd did not know the fourth victim died.

Byrd was already married to Evelyn McQueen Dorn Byrd, his legal wife, in St. Louis and was not divorced when he later married Saundra Sanders in Savannah.

This would later prove significant in Byrd's eventual trial for the four victims he murdered in the Pope's Cafeteria. A legally married spouse cannot testify against her husband unless she is also involved in a criminal conspiracy.

On the other hand, since he was not legally married to Saundra Sanders, she would be required to testify, whether she wanted to or not. Ron Martin wisely tape-recorded Sanders' information against Byrd, so if she failed to testify truthfully, her taped statement could be played for the jury. This happened at Byrd's eventual trial and proved very successful for the prosecutors.

Martin then interviewed Saundra's brother, Eric Sanders. He also said Byrd arrived in Savannah with the briefcase full of money. He said the money was assorted in denominations of twenties, tens, and ones wrapped in bundles with rubber bands.

Eric added that the day after Byrd's arrival, two black males arrived from St. Louis, delivering Byrd's motorcycle and his belongings. They left the same day.

Eric told how he went with Byrd the next day to purchase a vehicle. He said Byrd had paid cash for the vehicle with money from the briefcase.

The briefcase and items were taken into custody, and the two witnesses' statements were tape-recorded at the police department.

Now it was time for Captain Martin and Prosecutor Ankney to meet with their suspected killer, Byrd.

Byrd was brought into the interview room, looking very unconcerned.

Ron Martin identified himself, telling Byrd, "I've been looking forward to meeting you since Thursday, October 23, 1980." Then Prosecutor Ankney identified himself and told Byrd, "I'm going to prosecute you and witness your execution."

Byrd all a sudden did not look so confident and started sweating.

He was advised of his Miranda rights, and he refused to make a statement. Captain Martin secured a set of his fingerprints and mug shots of Byrd. Later that night Byrd made a monitored phone call to Sanders, telling her something about a robbery in St. Louis, providing the names of "Bootsy," a friend named Eric, and O. C., the nickname of Oscelious Green, his ex-brother-in-law.

Martin later learned "Bootsy" was a moniker for Robert Selvey Jr., who had prior arrests in St. Louis.

During dinner with the Savannah Police, Sergeant Findley reported Byrd was sweating profusely after they left him and while he was being fingerprinted.

Their day proved very positive, but they were not done yet.

The next morning, they learned the numbers found on the piece of adding machine tape were in fact the combination to the admission office safe at the local college, and the safe would contain a large amount of cash in a couple weeks.

While in Savannah, they collected documents verifying Byrd had purchased the vehicle and confirmed through interviews he had paid cash from a briefcase. The money was wrapped in bundles with rubber bands, just the way the money was wrapped at Pope's Cafeteria.

GATHERING EVIDENCE

The evidence against Byrd continued to mount regarding his involvement in the murders at the Pope's Cafeteria.

Statements were taken from Mrs. Francene Sanders, the mother of Saundra Byrd, providing additional leads for the investigators to follow.

Johnny Sanders, father of Saundra Sanders, said he had looked into the briefcase and seen a large quantity of cash wrapped in bundles with rubber bands and paper clips.

The investigator learned Byrd paid cash to rent the apartment in Savannah with cash wrapped in bundles of 100 one-dollar bills. This was exactly how Pope's bundled their one-dollar bills.

In addition, confidential witnesses were providing information on Byrd's criminal activities.

In June, Oscar Ford, an eyewitness to the Pope's Cafeteria murders, was flown to Savannah and positively identified Byrd as one of the men leaving the cafeteria. Some of the primary leads leading to the successful solving of the robbery and murders at Pope's Cafeteria came from the mouth of the shooter, Maurice Byrd, who had bragged to fellow prisoners while he was in jail at the Chatham County Jail in Savannah, Georgia.

Byrd talked about how he placed all the victims in the secluded office in such a fashion to avoid the bullets from striking him. He boasted he shot them in the head with a .22 caliber weapon and that he disposed of the weapon shortly after the murders. He claimed he disposed of his murder weapons in numerous similar murders before. He exclaimed excitedly he got a "thrill out of killing his victims."

He told inmates he had robbed the M&M Grocery Store in Savannah and immediately returned to St. Louis with Saundra and their baby.

Byrd was obviously a big bragger about his robberies and murders in Savannah and St. Louis according to the inmates in Chatham County Jail.

His bragging would help the prosecutor's case in his eventual murder trial for the Pope's Cafeteria murders.

As interviews with witnesses, relatives, friends, and employees at the shopping mall were conducted, tips and leads followed and evidence collected, all the information was entered into their computer system, providing easy access and correlation from one lead to another.

JUSTICE AND CLOSURE

Captain Martin and his team could now prepare their case for indictment.

Captain Martin prepared his case for the prosecutor's office, and Byrd was indicted in June 1981.

Maurice Oscar Byrd was tried on August 11, 1982, and convicted by a jury on August 16, 1982—found guilty on all four counts of murder.

On the same day, Judge James Ruddy sentenced Byrd to the death penalty.

Maurice Byrd was placed in the Missouri State Prison in Jefferson City. Eventually Byrd was moved to the Mineral Point Facility just outside Potosi, Missouri.

During the investigation of Byrd, Ron Martin and his team of investigators conducted a thorough search of his criminal background, dating back to his military history when he enlisted at the age of eighteen in 1972.

While Byrd was stationed in Korea in 1973, two unsolved murders had occurred near his two bases. While he was stationed in Fort Riley, Kansas, in 1974, a robbery/homicide had occurred in Manhattan, Kansas, and a robbery/homicide in Junction City, Kansas—all still unsolved. In May 1978, Byrd had abducted and assaulted his wife; in June 1978, a robbery/murder had occurred at a Burger King in Savannah, Georgia, while he was living there. In June 1979, a double robbery/homicide had occurred at a restaurant in St. Louis; Byrd had eaten lunch there and had admitted to friends he committed this crime. Victims were taken into a storage area and shot in the head. On April 24, 1980, an armed robbery/homicide at a Dairy Queen in St. Louis County had occurred; the victim was shot in the head with a .45 caliber weapon. Byrd owned one and claimed it was stolen. On October 23, 1980, the Pope's robbery/homicide had happened, and then on November 14, 1980, a double homicide had occurred on Walsh Street in St. Louis City, where both victims were shot in the head. These two victims were attending St. Louis University when Byrd was a security guard there. He was suspected of the killings.

While back in Georgia in 1981, he had set up an attempted armed robbery at a Popeyes chicken fast food restaurant and committed an armed robbery at a Krispy Chicken Restaurant, which he admitted to fellow inmates. On May 27, 1981, he had robbed and murdered Fred Johnson at the liquor store in Savannah, Georgia, and was caught and convicted of the murder also.

Wherever Byrd was, homicides and robberies occurred. He was suspected of some, he admitted to some, and he was convicted and sentenced to five murders.

There is an interesting side story to this case. Ron Martin, the lead investigator, went to McKinley High School in South St. Louis. Detective Colon McCoy of the St. Louis City Police Department, who advised Ron Martin of Byrd's arrest in Savannah, Georgia, was a McKinley High School graduate. Ed Haskins, captain with the Des Pares DPS and Des Pares Police Officer "Big" Joe Sutton (who provided assistance, positive thoughts, and opinions to Ron Martin) were also both McKinley High School graduates.

Your author also attended McKinley High School in South St Louis and was professionally and socially close to all these McKinley High School graduates who selected careers as public servants serving the citizens of St. Louis, Missouri, and beyond.

On August 23, 1991, after eleven years of numerous appeals and stays of execution, Maurice Oscar Byrd was executed by lethal injection, bringing his brutal life of crime to a close.

Ron Martin and prosecutor Gordon Ankney witnessed Byrd's execution.

GLENNON ENGLEMAN
Doctor Death

Glenn Engleman, Missouri prison inmate number 40277, was received at the prison on December 5, 1985, after he was convicted of the murder of Peter Halm in September 1980.

Engleman, a dentist with offices in South St. Louis, lived a dark, secret second life involving a series of vicious murders dating back to 1958.

In all, over his twenty-two years of terror, he was responsible for no fewer than seven murders, all committed for financial gain from the proceeds of the insurance policies of the dead victims.

His first murder occurred when he shot and killed James Bullock on December 17, 1958. The shooting took place at the rear of the St. Louis Art Museum in Forest Park in St. Louis. Two witnesses saw the victim running to the front of the museum and fall dead by the statue in front of the museum. They saw a man with a gun lean over his fallen body and then run away. He was described as a heavy-built man wearing a brown hat and a dark overcoat.

St. Louis police detectives from the Homicide Unit found the victim's car parked in a drive leading to the rear of the museum. It was still running, and they found blood inside the car. He had been shot in his car.

Bullock had been shot once between his eyes, once near the top of his head, and once in his neck.

The detectives learned that Bullock's wife of six months had been married before to a dentist named Glennon Engleman, whom she married in 1953. Her name was Ruth Bullock. She said she had divorced Engleman in 1956.

When Glennon Engleman was questioned by police shortly after the murder, he was wearing a dark topcoat and a hat. The investigation revealed the widow was to collect $64,000 in insurance proceeds and that, prior to her current marriage, she was described by at least a dozen men as a "nymphomaniac" whom they had sex with after picking her up at St. Louis West End bars.

The St. Louis news stories of the murder and follow-up investigation grew wilder as the rumors grew. Why was the victim murdered at a place where homosexuals met? Did the victim's widow really once possess a black book naming men in high places?

The police also learned that Engleman had purchased a 22-caliber weapon from a hardware store in Belleville, Illinois. He claimed he had given the gun to his father-in-law, who had reported it stolen.

As more intriguing motives and evidence were developed, the news stories became more scandalous, describing the hit as the "murder of the decade."

The investigating detectives knew Engleman was good for the murder; however, they could not develop enough evidence to charge him, and the case grew cold. He was never convicted of this murder.

Twenty-two years later, on January 14, 1980, at about 4:45 p.m. as Sophie Marie Barrera started her Pinto vehicle parked behind the dental lab she owned in the Grandview Arcade building on South Grand, just ten minutes from Glennon Engleman's dental office, she was killed when a bomb deto-nated under her vehicle.

She was backing up when she rolled over a pressure device containing a number of sticks of dynamite that had been placed under her front tire.

In a prior incident on March 20, 1979, an attempt was made on Berrera's life when a bomb containing eight sticks of dynamite was placed outside her garage. The bomb got soaked when it rained and had failed to detonate. Dur-ing the investigation of the recovered bomb, it was discovered that Berrera had been owed $15,000 in back lab bills by dentist Engleman for lab work she had performed for him.

Since a bomb was used to kill her, the investigation was conducted by the St. Louis Police Department Bomb and Arson Unit and the Bureau of Alco-hol, Tobacco and Firearms (ATF), who was responsible for the federal bomb-ing laws.

The ATF agent assigned to the case was William J. McGarvey of the St. Louis office. He was assisted by ATF Agent John Bobb and Detective Ron Lin-gle, who was assigned to the case on behalf of the St. Louis Police Department.

When Engleman was interviewed shortly after the murder, he did not show any remorse for Berrera, saying she was cheating him out of money and had it coming. He added, "If I had done it, I would have hired someone else to do it."

Agent Bill McGarvey, a tenacious investigator with a strong desire for the truth, suspected Glennon Engleman from the very beginning.

He gathered files on all the previous murders that Engleman was suspected of committing, back to the 1958 murder of Bullock.

He also approached Ruth Engleman, his ex-wife, and gained her confi-dence, and she started talking. She also agreed to wear a wire while talking to her ex-husband, with whom she was still involved in a sexual relationship.

After three weeks of tape-recorded conversations, combined with the co-operation of the suspects who were also involved with Engleman in previous murders over the past twenty-two years, enough evidence was gained to arrest and convict Engleman of three of the murders, as well as his own confession of three other murders.

In all, he conspired in the murder of James Bullock on December 17, 1958; the murder of Eric Frey on September 26, 1963, in Pacific, Missouri; the mur-der of Peter Halm on September 5, 1976; the murders of Vernita Gusewelle and her husband, Arthur Gusewelle, in Edwardsville, Illinois, in May 1978; the murder of their son Ron Gusewelle on March 31, 1979 (leaving his body in his car in East St. Louis, Illinois); and the murder of Sophie Marie Berrera on January 14, 1980.

During Engleman's confession to the murders of the Gusewelle family, he said, "I killed them. I like to kill. It sets a man apart from his fellow man if he can kill."

In her nonfiction book, *Appointment for Murder*, renowned author Susan Crain Bakos wrote of ATF Agent Bill McGarvey:

The most shocking crime of the decade that stunned a hardworking, blue-collar community and compelled a dedicated investigator [Bill McGarvey] to search for the unbelievable but undeniable truth. . . .

The series of murders was solved by the efforts of ATF Agents Bill McGarvey and John Bobb, along with the detectives of the St. Louis Police Department and a group of state and federal prosecutors who joined in to successfully convict Engleman in federal and Missouri state court trials.

On March 3, 1999 at the age of seventy-three, Glennon Edward Engleman died of natural causes while serving three life sentences for murder in the Missouri State Penitentiary.

ATF Agent Bill McGarvey's work on this case received high praise from his fellow agents, the United States Attorney's Office, and the St. Louis City and St. Louis County Prosecuting Attorney's offices.

A FINAL COMMENT FOR THIS CHAPTER

Several other notorious inmates who also spent time at the Missouri "Big House" in the 1900s have their criminal histories documented in their own chapters in this book due to the detailed nature of their criminal lives. They are:

Thomas Camp, a.k.a. Fred "Killer" Burke—prison inmate 23468 was first received on February 25, 1920, after being convicted of forgery. His entire criminal career is documented in the "AKA Fred "Killer" Burke" chapter.

Charles "Pretty Boy" Floyd—prison inmate 29078 was first received on December 18, 1925, after being convicted of robbery in St. Louis. His criminal career and violent death are documented in the "Charles Arthur Floyd and the Kansas City Massacre" chapter.

Blanche Barrow—female prison inmate 43454 was received on September 4, 1933, after being convicted of assault with intent to kill Sheriff Holt Coffey in Platte City during a shootout with the law enforcement. A member of the notorious Bonnie and Clyde gang, her criminal history is detailed in the "The Story of Bonnie and Clyde" chapter.

Charles Gargotta—Missouri prison inmate number 52546 was received at the Missouri Penitentiary on June 19, 1939, after being convicted of assault with intent to kill and sentenced to three years. This enforcer for the Kansas City Nick Civella Outfit was released on January 28, 1941, after serving nineteen months in prison. Gargotta's criminal history and violent death is documented in the "Mobster Violence, Kansas City Style" chapter.

Carl Spero—prison inmate number 07688 was received on November 27, 1963, convicted of attempted burglary in Kansas City, Missouri, and his brother, *Mike Spero*, prison inmate number 08564, received on May 22, 1965; 1964 convicted of attempted burglary. Their criminal careers and violent deaths are documented in the "Mobster Violence, Kansas City Style" chapter.

John Paul Leisure—Missouri inmate number 166527 arrived in prison on November 9, 1988, after being convicted of murder in St. Louis, Missouri.

Anthony J. Leisure—prison inmate number 1160146 arrived in prison on February 25, 1988, convicted of murder in St. Louis, Missouri.

David R. Leisure—Missouri inmate number 99976 arrived in prison on March 29, 1989, after being convicted of murder in St. Louis. He was executed by the state on September 1, 2000. The Leisures' criminal history is documented in the "Mob Violence and Justice, St. Louis Style" chapter.

Tony Emery—Missouri prison inmate number 40494 arrived at the prison in 1979 after being convicted of possession of burglary tools. Emery was released on August 5, 1981, and entered into the business of trafficking methamphetamine. His criminal history is documented in the "Tony Emery, Narcotics Kingpin and Murderer" chapter.

This book documents at least one inmate spending time in the Missouri State prison every decade of the 1900s, each one committing serious crimes that put them in prison. Each one also continued a life of crime upon their release—a selection of twenty-five inmates from a population of thousands of inmates entering "The Big House" during the 1900s.

I found no good in this group—some were the baddest of the bad and the ugliest of the ugly.

CHAPTER TWO
THE FINGERPRINT IDENTIFICATION SYSTEM
1904-PRESENT

S omewhere in America at this very moment either a law enforcement
forensic technician is lifting a latent fingerprint at a crime scene or a suspect or prisoner is having his or her fingerprints processed on 8 x 8-inch white
print cards at a police jail or prison. Once the process is completed, the latent
print, or one of the print cards, is forwarded to the FBI Fingerprint Identification Division in Washington, DC, and then filed or compared with the mil-
lions of fingerprint cards already on file at the identification division.

In many cases, matches will be made and unsolved crimes will be solved—
fugitives from justice will be identified and returned to serve their sentences
or stand trial for their crimes. "More than any other factor, the fingerprint
today still is bearing the brunt of the fight against law breaking" (Cooper
Book, page 105). No two individuals possess the same fingerprints—not even
identical twins. You might be thinking by now, what does this have to do with
Missouri? The answer is—everything. Allow me to explain.

As early as 1883, America was introduced to the process of the identification of a person through his fingerprints. No, this was not developed
by a famous law enforcement forensic official of the day nor was it from an
anatomy professor staring intently through the newly developed microscope.
Instead, it was presented by a man named Samuel Langhorne Clemens, born
in Florida, Missouri, in 1835, and raised in Hannibal, Missouri, whose career
encompassed occupations as a printer, riverboat pilot, publisher, and writer
under the name Mark Twain.

In his 1883 book *Life on the Mississippi*, he writes about the identification
of a murderer by his thumbprint. In 1894, Twain published *Pudd'nhead Wilson*, set in a small town just south of St. Louis, Missouri (Almanac, page 489).
This book is "The story of a man who was looked upon by the entire village
as a sort of nitwit until he used a fingerprint to establish the proof of a questioned identity. So popular was the book it became a play which ran for years
throughout the United States" (Cooper book, page 99). These two fictional
accounts did much for fingerprinting awareness in America; however, law enforcement was slow in adopting the system for identification purposes.

All law enforcement departments in the United States and all prison systems at the time used the Bertillon Method of criminal identification. This
method was developed in France in the 1870s by a French anthropologist

named Alphonse Bertillon and consisted of a complicated system of tracking anthropometrical measurements and physical marks (such as tattoos and moles), which were documented on a card and accompanied with a photograph of the person. It was a time-consuming process that took up to an hour to complete and was replete with human error.

The idea of the fingerprint system for criminal identification purposes was introduced to the United States at the St. Louis World's Fair in 1904 by Sergeant Ferrier of Scotland Yard while on assignment at the fair, guarding the Queen's Jubilee exhibit. Sergeant Ferrier talked fingerprinting to anyone who would listen, including Edward J. Brennan of the St. Louis Police Department. Edward Brennan became so interested in the fingerprint system that he traveled to Scotland Yard and studied the subject as a means to identify criminals. "Brennon also learned the simple 'Henry' Classification System developed and introduced in 1901 by Sir E.R. Henry, the commissioner of Scotland Yard, which formed the basis of the present classifications employed by identification bureaus even today in the United States" (Cooper Book page 99).

Brennan returned to the United States and implemented the fingerprint identification system in the St. Louis City Police Department, the first US law enforcement agency to establish a fingerprint identification unit. Brennan then took a position with the United States Secret Service and implemented the system there.

In 1908, Edward Brennan was one of eight secret service agents to join the newly created Bureau of Investigation in the Department of Justice, the forerunner of the FBI. He was credited with getting the new agency up and running and introduced the fingerprint system to the newly formed bureau.

Charles Appel, who would later build J. Edgars Hoover's Vaunted Forensics Laboratory and become an icon in his own right, studied at the feet of Edward Brennan before Brennan retired from the FBI in 1925, according to *The Grapevine*, the FBI retirees' newsletter.

In his 1935 book, *Ten Thousand Public Enemies,* Courtney Ryley Cooper, who was J. Edgar Hoover's publicist and an ex-Kansas City newspaper reporter, gives great credit to Hoover for the fingerprint division's success. Unfortunately, Cooper fails to mention Edward J. Brennan.

Cases of Interest

On May 23, 1928, Jacob Henry "Jake" Fleagle, leader of the notorious Fleagle gang who spent time in both Kansas City and St. Louis, pulled off a robbery of the First National Bank at Lamar, Colorado. This resulted in the murder of several men, including a doctor who was killed in Kansas after he treated one of the wounded gang members. Fleagle left a single latent fingerprint behind at the doctor's murder scene, but the print went unidentified as time passed. Then a person using the alias William Hanson Holden was arrested in Stockton, California, and fingerprinted, and a print card forwarded to the identification laboratory in Washington, DC, matched Jake Fleagle's print card on file from a prison in Oklahoma, where he had spent some prison time.

On October 14, 1930, fugitive Jake Fleagle was shot and killed by local officers and federal agents while boarding a train in Branson, Missouri. "The FBI later claimed that Fleagle was the first criminal to be identified by means of a single fingerprint." (Almanac P# 52)

So important was the single fingerprint identification that publicist Courtney Ryley Cooper devoted a complete chapter on this case in his book, *Ten Thousand Public Enemies*. He wrote, ". . . because of the Fleagle's there is now a different procedure when a widely known bandit leaves a latent fingerprint at the scene of a crime." Almost immediately, Mr. Hoover began the building of what now is known as the "single fingerprint file" in the Division of Investigation.

Author Cooper goes on to explain how the system was developed, creating a "'who's who' of vicious crime. Breaking down the regular fingerprint cards of these men in single prints."

Another successful single fingerprint case in the early 1930s involved an extortion attempt that was solved when a set of prints were sent to the identification unit from the Hannibal Police Department after arresting a man using the alias "Joseph Phillips," who was charged with a minor offense. This single print was matched to a set of prints of Theodore Roosevelt Waddel, who was wanted for the extortion attempt in Grange, Tennessee. Waddel went to Tennessee, where he received a fifteen-year sentence for the extortion attempt. It was "an excellent example of a small Missouri town's police department doing its job." (Cooper Book)

In January 1933, the fingerprint system was put to use as a result of an event in Cape Girardeau to identify a dead criminal just as it had done to identify living criminals. Two robbers were killed in a shootout with police. Efforts to identify the two were unsuccessful until the fingerprint identification unit received sets of prints from officials with the St. Louis and San Francisco Railway in St. Louis of the two dead robbers, marked "Unknown #1" and "Unknown #2." A search was conducted and the set of Unknown #2 matched up with another set in the files. He was identified as Thomas Crawford, who had been a fugitive for over four years and wanted for murder of a police officer in Pennsylvania (Cooper Book p110-111).

Then on June 17, 1933 a major incident occurred in Kansas City—a shootout that resulted in the death of two Kansas City police officers, two federal agents, a police chief from McAlester, Oklahoma, and a captured prisoner being returned to the federal prison in Leavenworth, Kansas — a massacre that shook the conscience of an entire nation and became known worldwide as the Kansas City Union Station Massacre. I will detail fully it in another chapter of this book but here will focus on the significance of a single latent fingerprint lifted during the investigation, placing one of the suspected shooters in Kansas City at the time of the massacre.

On June 29, twelve days after the massacre, a house near the shooting was searched by law enforcement and numerous latent prints were lifted, including one single print off a beer bottle found among several in the basement.

The photographs of the prints were eventually sent to the FBI fingerprint unit, including the single print taken from the beer bottle. It was matched to one of the suspects who was now a fugitive. He was arrested in Ohio on October 21, 1934, and eventually tried for one of the murders. On October 7, 1938, he was executed in the gas chamber in the state prison in Jefferson City, hailed by the FBI as one of its most significant fingerprint matches in the bureau's history.

Efforts to Beat the System

The landmark advancements in the fingerprint identification system in the early 1900s and its eventual acceptance by law enforcement institutions created a serious concern for the criminal community and a strong desire to avoid detection. Numerous efforts to alter facial appearances and fingerprint patterns were for the most part "conspicuously unsuccessful." However, there are two successful efforts documented, and coincidentally, both criminals had strong Missouri connections.

In the spring of 1932, St. Louis-born Henry (Gus) Winkeler (a.k.a. "Big Mike," James Ray, Rand) and spelled Winkler by police and the press contacted a plastic surgeon in Chicago, who altered his facial features and successfully altered his fingertips by means of skin transplants that changed the fingerprint patterns.

Winkler was a St. Louis Egan's Rats gang member and partner of Fred "Killer" Burke in numerous bank robberies, the St. Valentine's Day Massacre, and the murder of New York head mobster Frankie Yale. (You will hear much more about Winkler in a later chapter).

In March 1934, bank robber Alvin Karpis (and partner of Missouri-born Fred Barker of the Barker-Karpis Gang) met with family physician, Dr. Joseph Moran, in Chicago. Moran was a one-time skilled physician who unsuccessfully tried to alter their faces through plastic surgery. He did, however, succeed in removing the fingerprints of Alvin Karpis, using a scalpel and skin grafts. Karpis was deported back to his native Canada after he had served thirty-three years in prison, but the operation had been so successful than the Canadians were reluctant to accept him without fingerprints. (page 474, Almanac Book)

The Growth of the System

By 1939, the number of fingerprint cards numbered nearly ten million, and by 1946, the FBI announced the number of fingerprint cards on file had reached 100 million, an achievement that in no small part was accomplished with the assistance of professionals and events that occurred in Missouri during the years of its early development.

CHAPTER THREE

AKA FRED "KILLER" BURKE AND THE ST. VALENTINE'S DAY MASSACRE 1893-1940

T homas Camp [1893–1940] born in Mapleton, Kansas, near Kansas City, Missouri, was arguably the most notorious gangster in Missouri criminal history and destined in the late 1920s to become "America's most wanted man" under the name Fred "Killer" Burke.

Camp's life of crime began in 1910 at age seventeen when he was charged in a swindling scheme for selling phony land deeds to unsuspecting investors.

Camp spent his early years in Kansas City, committing petty crimes, and somewhere along the way, he took the name Fred Burke.

In his book *Egan's Rats*, Daniel Waugh, provides a detailed account of Burke's arrival in St. Louis at the end of 1915, joining the Egan's Rats gang, and documenting the numerous crimes he committed along with his fellow Rats gang members between 1915 and 1923. Details of Waugh's research are included in this chapter.

Near the end of 1915, at the age of twenty-two, Burke left Kansas City to avoid his land deed charges and moved on to St Louis, joining in with the Egan's Rats gang and becoming a regular at Egan's saloons. Burke formed a strong criminal relationship with fellow Rats gangsters—Missouri-born Robert "Gimpy" Carey, August "Gus" Winkler, Johnny Reid, and Army mate Raymond "Crane Neck" Nugent, who arrived in St. Louis from Cincinnati to join the Egan gang.

While the Rats were involved in a heated war with rival gangs, Burke and fellow gangsters continued to rob and steal at an alarming rate.

It's estimated by researchers that Burke and his gangsters were responsible for as many as fifty bank robberies throughout the United States, numerous kidnappings for ransom money, and too many burglaries and thefts to count.

Fred Burke was personally responsible for no fewer than fifteen documented murders, and it's unknown how many more he got away with—giving him the moniker from newspaper reporters Fred "Killer" Burke.

On June 15, 1917, America went to war, and Burke enlisted under his real name, not for patriotic reasons but rather to avoid pending arrest warrants and indictment under aliases he used. It was during his enlistment that he developed a fascination with automatic weapons, becoming a proficient marksman with the machine gun. While in the Army, Burke was in the same unit with a soldier named Raymond "Crane Neck" Nugent from Cincinnati. They became friends, and Burke would later invite Nugent to join him with the Egan's Rats gang in St. Louis.

He returned from the war, discharged in May 1919, and headed to the Detroit area for the first time and was soon charged with another land fraud scheme, this time receiving a five-year sentence.

Burke returned to St. Louis in 1922 after serving a one-year sentence in Michigan, followed by a one-year term in the Missouri State Prison in Jefferson City for a 1917 forgery conviction. (Daniel Waugh)

Burke's cleverness as a gangster at times paralleled his ruthlessness, as he created disguises and elaborate schemes, garnering admiration among fellow criminals.

On April 25, 1923, Burke demonstrated his intelligence while robbing a secured federal warehouse at 4116 North Union Boulevard in St. Louis, where whiskey was stored for medical purposes.

Shortly after midnight, Burke knocked on the door of the warehouse, wearing a police uniform, and asked the security guard for help in identifying a burglary suspect. As the unsuspecting guard opened the door, he was greeted with pistols and four or five additional gangsters. The crew made off with about fifty barrels of whiskey valued at some $80,000, which provided a nice nest egg for the Egan gang and surely a round of laughter, high fives, and praise from his fellow hoods.

Just two months later, Burke's brashness and indifference reared its ugly head when, on July 3, Burke led six fellow Rats on a payroll robbery of the United Railway office located at Park and Thirty Ninth Street, a provider of street cars for the city of St. Louis. The six rushed in the building, all displaying weapons and wearing hoods except Burke, who strolled in wearing a shirt and hat. The heist netted $38,306 cash, and upon making their getaway, a shootout occurred. Fortunately, no one was hit. Burke was identified by witnesses as the leader of the gang and charged with the robbery.

In December 1923, Burke left St. Louis, heading east back to Detroit, joining his friend and ex-Egan's Rat—Johnny Reid—who had preceded Burke to Detroit, opening a saloon and becoming a liquor distributor for the Detroit Purple Gang.

Throughout the 1920s, Burke offered his professional services to gangs and hoodlums, including Detroit's Purple Gang and, eventually, to Chicago's mob boss Al Capone.

On March 10, 1924, Burke—along with ex-Rat Izzy Londe, Bob Carey, and a criminal associate named James Callahan—pulled a robbery at Kay's Jewelry Store in Downtown Detroit, making off with only $7,000 in jewels after failing to convince the owner to open his safe.

Two nights after what appeared to be a successful robbery, a very drunk Burke was stopped and arrested by police after leaving a restaurant and operating his vehicle. During a search of his vehicle, police found most of the stolen jewelry. He was sent back to prison and charged with a parole violation.

Burke was released on October 22, only to be arrested by St. Louis Police detectives, who returned him to St. Louis to stand trial for his part in the United Railway robbery of July 1923.

Burke made bail and returned to Michigan, continuing his crime wave throughout Midwest cities, including Toledo, St. Louis, St. Paul, Kansas City, Cincinnati, and Chicago.

On January 10, 1925, "Killer" Burke, several other ex-Egan's Rats, and Purple Gang members joined forces for possibly the first time in a robbery attempt of a gambling joint at 2439 Milwaukee Avenue in Detroit. At about 3:00 a.m., three gunmen snuck into the building and waited for the owner, Raymond Bishop, to come to his office to count the day's take. As Bishop arrived and realized he was being robbed, he opened fire with his .45 caliber, and a shootout ensued, leaving Bishop and one robber, Arthur Wilson, dead.

Soon after the robbery attempt, Burke was picked up and charged with jumping his bail in the United Railway case in St. Louis.

After posting bail again on April 2, 1925, Burke, Pasqual Lolordo, Paul Morina, and Larry Dougherty robbed the Farmers Bank in Louisville, Kentucky, netting $30,000 and shooting a teller in the process.

The four were eventually identified and former Egan's Rats Pascal, Morina, and Dougherty were convicted and sent to Leavenworth, joining a number of other Egan's Rats already serving time for other crimes.

On April 30, 1925, the Portland Bank in Louisville, Kentucky, was robbed. Burke and Winkler were suspected of the robbery.

On June 5, 1925 Burke, Gus Winkler, and Milford Jones were back in St. Louis and once again in trouble, chased by police in Downtown St. Louis, firing numerous shots into their car, which caused them to crash into a pole and ended their getaway attempt.

Police found a gun case in the car containing a 7.63 mm Mauser machine pistol, one of Burke's collection of dangerous weapons. The three were charged with possessing concealed weapons.

Burke went to trial on November 12 for the United Railway robbery. In the trial, much to the disgust of the presiding judge, Burke was found innocent, even though the evidence against him was strong. The judge admonished the jury panel, declaring their verdict was an insult to intelligence and calling them incompetent to let a "rat" like Burke go free. It was never determined if members of the jury were threatened or paid off.

On the morning of May 18, 1926, Burke, Winkler, Casey, Nugent, Jones, and former Egan's Rats gangster Louis Mulcovey reportedly robbed the North St. Louis Trust Company at 3500 North Grand, armed with a sawed-off shotgun, and netted about $30,000 in cash in the process. The crew escaped without firing a shot.

It was during this period of time in his criminal career that Burke was credited with inventing a clever scheme called "the snatch"—possibly along with the Purple Gang—wherein, hoodlums would kidnap other hoodlums and gamblers and hold them until a ransom was paid for their safe release, a scheme that lacked notoriety or police involvement since it was a hoodlum-against-hoodlum process. This scheme was adopted by many hoods throughout the United States, giving Burke notoriety for his cleverness and blame for many crimes he did not commit.

In early August 1926, Burke was summoned back to Detroit by friend Johnny Reid, who was having issues with a Sicilian mobster named Mike Dipisa. He was a confessed killer and hijacker who was trying to extort Reid's profits, sending two of his hoods, Clarence "Bud" Gilboe and Paul Clark, into Reid's saloon to demand money using Mike Dipisa's name. Reid, having none of this nonsense, pulled his gun and started shooting at the startled extortionist. A friend of Reid's named "Tennessee Slim" Hurley, who was having a drink in the saloon, also started shooting at the hoods as they ran from the bar.

Several shootouts occurred the following weeks between Dipisa's gang and Reid and his host of Egan's Rats, including "Killer" Burke, which resulted in several of Dipisa's goons being killed or wounded.

Dipisa, realizing he was doomed, called a meeting with Reid, claiming the two extortionists, Gilboe and Clark, were not sent by him , that they had used his name without his knowledge. The two were turned over to Reid and promptly killed.

The truce prevailed until Dipisa's brother was killed in November. Dipisa blamed Reid and planned his retaliation. On December 25, 1926, Burke's good friend Reid was shot and killed as he returned to his apartment.

In early 1927, "Killer" Burke learned Reid's killer was a jewel thief named Frankie Wright, who had come to Detroit from Chicago and was hired by Dipisa to kill Reid. The Purple Gang was also looking to get Wright and sought Burke out.

THE MILAFLORES APARTMENT MASSACRE IN DETROIT, MICHIGAN

On March 16, 1927, Fred "Killer" Burke, on contract with the Purple Gang and armed with one of his machine guns, ambushed and machine-gunned to death Frank Wright, along with the two East Coast hoods Joseph Bloom and Ruben Cohen, introducing the machine gun to Detroit in the process. Burke was backed up by Purple Gang triggermen Abe Axler and Eddie Fletcher, who were armed with a revolver and two .45 caliber pistols.

The trio of shooters left the apartment by the rear door to an awaiting Gus Winkler then sped away from the scene.

Cohen and Bloom died instantly, riddled with too many bullets for the coroner to count. Wright lived for a few hours (even though he had been hit fourteen times)—long enough to tell police why he went to the apartment—and said they were lured to the apartment by Burke's snatch racket scheme to free a close friend, gambler Meyer "Fish" Bloomfield, who could be found in Apartment 308. When they arrived, they were filled with lead by the shooters.

Fred Burke and Abe Axler were arrested shortly after the massacre on suspicion and released. The Milaflores Massacre gained national media attention and coverage.

"Killer" Burke branched out from Detroit and—with fellow Missouri mobsters Harvey Bailey, Gus Winkler, "Shotgun" George Ziegler, Eddie Bentz, "Big" Homer Wilson, and others—committed bank robberies and kidnappings and other crimes throughout the Midwest, being among the first mobsters to employ the machine gun in their work. Burke eventually moved into the Chicago area.

In early 1928 Al Capone's gang, consisting of Italian and Sicilian nationalities, entered into a professional criminal relationship with a group of criminals primarily from the battlegrounds of St. Louis. They were members of gangs who routinely engaged in robberies, thefts, shootings, murders, and kidnappings. It's the snatch that brought the unholy alliance to the attention of Al Capone. Capone learned one of his men had been kidnapped and held for ransom, and the perpetrators were ex-Egan's Rats from St. Louis, Roy Nugent and Bob Casey.

Al Capone got the word out to Gus Winkler that he wanted his friend released, unharmed, and he wanted the kidnappers to meet with him to discuss the matter. Since Capone knew their names, both Nugent and Casey felt their number was up. Gus cleaned the two up the best he could and brought them to Capone to accept the music. To their surprise, Capone didn't get rough and told them they were in the wrong racket. He requested that they release their victim, offered them some money, and told Gus he could use these guys. The victim was released and the two promised no more snatches.

Shortly after this affair, Fred "Killer" Burke—feeling the heat for the Milaflores Massacre—headed for Chicago and joined with his ex-Rats associates.

Capone was introduced to "Killer" Burke, most likely by Gus Winkler, and joined the team. Much to Capone's approval, he now had a crew of outsiders unknown to Chicago police that formed a special crew he called his "American Boys."

Criminal history was not too far in the future for the members of the "American Boys" from Missouri. On April 16, 1938, Fred Burke, Gus Winkler, Fred Goetz, Byron Batton, Roy Nugent, and Charles Fitzgerald pulled off a safecracking job at the American Express Company in Toledo, Ohio, netting $200,000 and killing a police officer in the process. Capone got wind of this, told them to knock off this type of activity, and put them on his payroll.

The group hung out at the Hawthorne, a gang watering hole where the St. Louis crew got to know Louis "Little New York" Campagna, "Machine Gun" Jack McGurn, Tony Capezio (part-owner with Winkler in the Circus Cafe), Rocco de Grazia, and many other top hoods working for Capone.

THE FRANKIE YALE MURDER

Al Capone learned New York mob boss Yale, his one-time mentor, was stealing Capone's booze shipments from the East Coast. Yale was also trying to move in on Capone's profitable dog tracks and supporting a Capone rival for leadership of Chicago's Union. Al decided enough was enough.

The Missouri hoodlum influence stretched to the East Coast when, on July 1, 1928, Al Capone hired his "American Boys" from St. Louis—Fred "Killer" Burke, Gus Winkler, and Bob Casey,—along with Louis "Little New York" Campagna, and dispatched them to New York.

The team, led by Burke with his machine gun, drilled Brooklyn's mobster boss Yale to his death in broad daylight, in the process introducing New York to its first machine gun murder.

The murder of Frankie Yale persuaded New York gangsters they were behind on the firearms race, causing East Coast mobsters to adopt the Thompson as their weapon of choice, all through the influence of Fred "Killer" Burke's actions.

THE ST. VALENTINE'S DAY MASSACRE, CHICAGO, ILLINOIS

In their book, *The St. Valentine's Day Massacre*, William J. Helmer and Arthur J. Bilek provided a well-documented account of the massacre in Chicago, Illinois, and the eventual downfall of Fred "Killer" Burke. America's most famous hoodlum massacre occurred on February 14, 1929, on an icy, snowy morning with the temperature in the teens at SMC Cartage Company Garage, 2120 Clark Street, North Chicago, Illinois, committed by the "American Boys." Passing as police officers and detectives, the killers used machine guns and shotguns to murder seven men. The newspapers described it as the "crime of the century." It was a gruesome scene, a bloodbath of carnage replayed over the years in books, movies, biographies, and radio and television specials.

Most early accounts, mainly through speculation rather than case facts and evidence, incorrectly fingered the shooters to the Chicago Police as Al Capone's Italian gang members assisted by the Detroit Purple Gang hoods committing the St. Valentine's Day Massacre. The crime was considered so despicable that law enforcement created the largest reward offering in the United States up until that time. It marked the end of Al Capone's empire and the beginning of the repeal of Prohibition.

The victims were six members of the "Bugs" Moran gang and one "wannabe" hanger-on, an optometrist in the wrong place at the wrong time.

The intended target, gang boss "Bugs" Moran, a rival gang leader to Al Capone's gang, was spared the execution after arriving late to the garage and, seeing what he believed were two uniformed policemen vehicles, retreated into a restaurant to avoid an arrest or a police shakedown.

The most popular motive for the massacre, which has withstood the scrutiny of time, involved the ongoing war between Al Capone gang with the "Bugs" Moran gang and the Joey Aiello gang of Sicilians, who were aligned with the "Bugs" Moran gang.

As a lead-up to the massacre, on September 7, 1928, Union President Tony Lombardo, who was supported by Capone, was gunned down at noon on a busy downtown Chicago street. Then on January 8, 1929, just one month before the massacre, Pasquale "Patsy" Lolordo—Lombardo's successor—was murdered by three gunmen, who fired eighteen slugs at Lolordo, many into his body. His grieving wife identified Joey Aiello as one of the shooters, placing Aiello and Moran on Capone's "hit list."

The St. Valentine's Day Massacre was never officially solved. However, over a period of time, the facts and evidence developed—combined with eyewitness accounts, a confession by one of the Massacre participants, and the memo prepared by the wife of one of the participants—clearly documents the crew was made up of Al Capone's "American Boys." They were led by Fred "Killer" Burke and other Egan's Rats from St. Louis.

At the time of the massacre, mob boss Al Capone was safely resting at his estate at Palm Island, Miami, Florida. Capone had purchased this luxurious estate for $140,000 in March 1928. The fourteen-room, Spanish-style oceanfront mansion had been built by St. Louis brewer Clarence M. Busch, and Capone spent another $100,000 in additions and upgrades.

Capone had established his documented whereabouts, meeting with well-known personalities while visiting at his estate in a very public manner.

In 1935, six years after the Massacre, Byron Bolton, who was arrested for kidnapping, confessed to the *Chicago American Newspaper*, giving his version and admitting his part in the massacre.

Bolton admitted he was one of the lookouts and that the original planning had taken place at a resort in Wisconsin, operated by Fred Goetz. Bolton admitted he had purchased one of the two cars used by the gunmen, whom he named as Fred "Killer" Burke, Ray Nugent, Bob Casey, and Gus Winkler — all Missouri gangsters assisted by Fred Goetz. Bolton said he used the name "James Martin" when he purchased the car used in the massacre off a car lot located near the Lexington and Metropol Hotels. This was corroborated by the police investigation, which followed the name "James Martin" as the purchaser of the vehicle.

What Bolton did not know was that Gus Winkler's widow, Georgette, had provided a book-length manuscript to FBI Agent Melvin Purvis a month before Bolton's arrest. In it, she detailed her deceased husband's exploits, including his part in the massacre, independently confirming Bolton's account. She stated that Fred Goetz had brought the two police uniforms used in the massacre to her and Gus Winkler's residence, where they amused themselves wearing the uniforms, to the displeasure of the visiting gangsters.

She named Rocco de Grazia, one of Capone's drivers, as the person harboring the shooters at his apartment until they were notified by the lookouts to go to the garage.

She described how Bolton, as a lookout, mistook someone else as "Bugs" Moran, setting the massacre in motion too soon.

Eyewitness accounts of the massacre lend support to both Bolton and Winkler's accounts, and the investigation after the massacre produced additional physical evidence. For instance, Bolton left a prescription bottle and letter in the room where he was stationed as a lookout that were recovered by police.

Then on February 21, one of the two vehicles used in the massacre exploded in an alley garage rented by the ex-Egan's Rat Claude Maddox under a phony name. Firemen found a loaded Luger, a police siren, and a police gong in the 1927 wrecked Cadillac, and a witness saw a burnt man running from the garage toward a nearby hospital for treatment. He left the hospital before police arrived and could not be interviewed.

Forty years later, Alvin Karpis of the Karpis/Barber Gang identified the burn victim as "Tough Tony" Capezio, an ally to Capone, in his biography. According to Karpis, Capezio had been dismantling the vehicle a few days after the massacre with a cutting torch, when gasoline fumes in the vehicle exploded. Capezio was burned in the explosion. However, he survived, earning the nickname "Tough Tony."

The second murder vehicle, a 1926 Peerless, was found by police on February 27 in the Chicago suburb of Maywood, blasted by explosives and partially destroyed. Items found at the wreckage were another police gong, a gun rack, and a notebook belonging to Albert Weinshank, one of the massacre victims. One of the killers, Claude Maddox, lived in Maywood, a Capone stronghold, lending credence to Maddox's association with the vehicle used in the getaway after the massacre.

This vehicle was identical to the two Peerless vehicles still in use by the Chicago Police Department detectives at the time.

Piecing the information from Bolton and Georgette together provided an account of how the massacre was carried out. Fred "Killer" Burke and Fred Goetz, wearing the police uniforms, entered the garage and lined up the victims, with Bob Casey and Ray Nugent waiting at the rear door, wearing suits and posing as detectives.

After the massacre, Burke and Goetz led Casey and Nugent out with their hands up, as if they were under arrest, to the awaiting getaway cars driven by Winkler and Claude Maddox. According to Bolton, the second lookout was a thug named Jimmy Morand.

The most compelling evidence associating "Killer" Burke with the massacre came on December 14, 1929, when a search of a cottage Burke was living in under an alias produced, among other incriminating evidence, two Thompson submachine guns connecting Burke through ballistic tests to the St. Valentine's Day Massacre.

THE FALL OF FRED "KILLER" BURKE

After the massacre, the main players realized the murders had caused a national outrage and left Chicago to lay low for a while in different states. "Killer" Burke and his girlfriend at the time, Viola, traveled to Burke's resort outside Grand Rapids, Minnesota. In autumn, Burke and Viola took refuge in a cottage on Lake Michigan near St. Joseph, Michigan, under the alias Frederick and Viola Dane.

In October, Burke and Gus Winkler were suspected of robbing a bank in Indiana of $93,000. Then in early December, Winkler drove to Burke's lakeside cottage at the request of fellow bank robber friend Harvey Bailey, stashing about $300,000 in bonds stolen from a bank in Wisconsin by Bailey.

On December 14, a drunk "Killer" Burke had a minor auto accident near St. Joseph, Michigan. When he tried to flee the scene, a Michigan patrol man named Charles Skelly took chase, and Burke, in his effort to get away, shot Skelly three times, killing the patrolman.

In an ensuing investigation, Burke's lakeside cottage was searched, uncovering Viola, Burke's paramour, the stolen bonds, and an enormous arsenal. The investigators sat back in disbelief as they materialized the seized evidence. The contents included:

- Two Thompson submachine guns
- One Winchester .350 automatic high-powered rifle
- One Savage .303 high-powered rifle
- One 20-gauge sawed-off shotgun with pistol grip
- Seven automatic pistols
- Five 100-round drums loaded with .45-caliber ammunition
- Many fifty-round drums
- Three twenty-round stick magazines
- Nine hundred rounds of .45-caliber ammunition
- Two bags estimated at 5,000 shells of miscellaneous ammunition
- Half a dozen fruit jars and tin cans filled with miscellaneous ammunition, including smokeless shotgun shells, shells loaded with iron slugs, and small shot
- Eleven tear gas bombs
- Several bottles of nitroglycerin
- Three Dunrite bulletproof vests
- Detectographs (audio recording device used in wiretaps)
- Acetylene torches

Burke was nowhere to be found.

A nationwide alert was issued, and the two submachine guns were rushed to Chicago. Ballistic tests were conducted by forensic expert Calvin Goddard on the weapons, using comparison microscopes, matching the weapons with slugs recovered at the St. Valentine's Day Massacre and the Frankie Yale murder in New York, connecting Burke with both the Yale murder and the massacre.

Goddard also looked at the ammunition recovered from the cottage and documented the .45 caliber shells were manufactured by the US Cartridge Company and, in a limited run, were stamped with an "S." Some of the slugs removed from the victims bore the "S" marking, further connecting Burke with the evidence recovered at the scene.

One of the two machine guns recovered in Burke's cottage, bearing serial number 2347, was traced by Pat Roche, chief investigator with the Illinois State Attorney's Office. He learned the weapon was purchased by Deputy

Sheriff Les Farmer of Marion, Illinois, on November 12, 1924. At the time of his purchase, Deputy Farmer had aligned himself with the Egan's Rats, who were feuding with the Birger gang and Shelton gang in Illinois over bootlegging territory. After the St. Valentine's Day Massacre, slugs removed from the bodies of Kachellek and Schwimmer were to the machine gun. Also found in Burke's cottage were shirts embroidered with the initials "FRB." Police fingerprint experts lifted prints from the cottage matching those with Fred Burke's fingerprints on file.

After the patrolman Skelly murder, Burke returned to Missouri, hiding out in a farm located near Green City, Missouri, owned by relatives of bank robber Harvey Bailey. Burke assumed the alias Richard F. White, taking on the role of a rich real estate tycoon from Kansas City.

In June 1930, Burke married a twenty-year-old girl named Bonnie Porter. Shortly after the wedding, he was suspected of killing a Chicago hoodlum named Thomas Bonner in Michigan for trying to give Burke up to the Chicago police.

On September 13, Burke and Gus Winkler were identified as two of the three gangsters who had robbed a bank in South Paterson, New Jersey, of $18,000.

Six months later, Burke's luck ran out when Joe Hunsaker Jr., a gas station attendant in Green City, Missouri, saw a picture of Burke in a detective magazine, recognizing the businessman "Richard White" as Burke.

Hunsaker, a professed crime buff, reported his suspicions to area law enforcement and a railway detective. Based on this information, on March 26, 1931, Burke was arrested at the farm and quickly taken to the jail in St. Joseph for processing and questioning. Michigan authorities took custody of Burke, who was charged with the murder of patrolman Skelly.

Burke pled guilty to the murder and was sentenced to life in prison. Burke was never tried for the Milaflores Massacre, the St. Valentine's Day Massacre, the gangland murder of New York Boss Frankie Yale, or numerous other crimes. He died of a heart attack in prison on July 10, 1940, ending the criminal career of Missouri's most notorious gangster and America's "Most Dangerous Man."

CHAPTER FOUR
THE GUN OF THE ROARING TWENTIES
1917–1942

The Thompson fully automatic submachine gun—named after its creator, retired Brigadier General John T. Thompson—was invented shortly after 1916, weighing about ten pounds and firing a .45 caliber pistol cartridge at the rate of 800 rounds per minute.

Believing the military needed more firepower in World War I in Europe, Thompson intended to have it sold to the United States Army. Little did he realize eventual evil intentions by the criminal element, and how they would use his invention.

In 1920, Thompson produced a working prototype, and the production of 15,000 weapons was initiated by Auto-Ordnance Corporation of New York, to their misfortune just as World War I ended.

The company, hoping to market the weapon, commercially released an ad in 1920 to the general public, describing the weapon as "the most effective portable firearm in existence providing increasingly wider use by banks, industrial plants, railroads, mines, ranches, plantations, etc., it has been adopted by leading police and constabulary forces throughout the world and is unsurpassed for military purposes." There was no mention of mob interest. These efforts met with limited success, and the weapons set on shelves until around 1925/1926, when mobsters throughout the country developed a fascination with the machine gun, gaining it a reputation as a gangster weapon of choice.

The weapon was initially popularized in a series of gangland murders, occurring primarily in Chicago, Southern Illinois, and St. Louis, in battles between various gangs that erupted in 1925. They were dubbed the "Beer Wars" during the Prohibition era, gaining media attention.

Interestingly, a series of brutal machine-gun massacres and murders in the late 1920s that occurred in Detroit, New York, and Chicago brought the most national attention and public outcry and was the work of a Missouri gangster nicknamed Fred "Killer" Burke. He was a graduate of the St. Louis Egan's Rats gang who had headed east, putting his talents out for hire as a professional hit man. In each of these incidents, Burke drew on support from fellow St. Louis gangsters, also from the Cuckoo and Egan's Rats Gangs, to participate in the murders.

Not knowing the identity of the actual shooters, the national media focused its news coverage primarily on East Coast cities and Chicago, attributing the use of the weapon to Chicago and East Coast mobsters. Dubbing the machine gun as the "Chicago typewriter" and proclaiming the first machine-gun murder victim a Chicago mobster named Charles Kelly in 1926, the media downplayed multiple machine gun murders in Downstate Illinois and St. Louis occurring at the same time.

In his *Brothers Notorious*, retired *St. Louis Post-Dispatch* reporter Taylor Pensoneau describes the gang wars of the Roaring Twenties as follows: "The whole world was painfully aware of Chicago, but the bloodshed in Chicago, or in New York for that matter, hardly was more sensational than the gang violence that erupted with astonishing ferocity in Southern Illinois and St. Louis during the decade."

"In fact," Pensoneau noted, "the Senator Kefauver committee established in 1950 to investigate crime in America minced no words in concluding that the gang battles in Southern Illinois and St. Louis during the 1920s 'reached a peak in bloodiness unparalleled in United States crime history.'" Both Pensoneau and Senator Kefauver's committee were, of course, talking about the gang wars in St. Louis and the gang war between the Sheltons and the Birger gangs in Southern Illinois, not far from Missouri.

Both the Sheltons, Carl and Earl, wound up in St. Louis, in the years before World War I, working as cab drivers and holding other jobs, committing crimes, and making connections with St. Louis tough guys. In 1921, they focused their criminal attentions in nearby East St. Louis, Illinois, staying well into the 1930s, when the Shelton gang originated. As for the Birger gang, Charlie Birger lived as a youngster in St. Louis, working as a newsboy, then lived in nearby Glen Carbon in Madison County, Illinois, and, in later years, emerged as the underworld chief of Saline County in southeastern Illinois.

According to Birger, he met the Sheltons in 1923 in Southern Illinois and teamed up with them in mutual criminal bootlegging operations; however, a vicious gang war erupted in 1926 between the Birger gang members and the Sheltons after a fallout between the two gangs.

In 1925, St. Louis Cuckoo gang boss, Herman Tipton, formed an alliance with the bootleg boss, Carl Shelton, and provided support to the Sheltons in their battle with the Birger gang.

To support this position, the following chronology has been prepared utilizing material from true crime books published by authors who have researched the weapons used by gangsters, outlaws, and mobsters.

William Helmer and Rick Mattix document no fewer than twenty-two criminal incidents occurring between 1926 and 1951 in *The Complete Public Enemy Almanac*:

September 12, 1926—Shelton Gang member "Wild Bill" Holland is tommy-gunned to death while leaving a roadhouse near Herrin, Illinois, by rival Birger Gang members.

September 17, 1926—Lyle "Shag" Warsham is machine-gunned to death by members of the Birger Gang and cremated in a barn near Pulley'sMill, Illinois.

September 23, 1926—Ex-Cuckoo Gang members Milford Jones and Gus Winkler—along with ex-Egan's Rats Fred "Killer" Burke, Bob Carey, and Roy

Nugent—are called back to St. Louis by Cuckoo Gang boss, Herman Tipton, and commence a machine-gun attack on the Russo gang in the Submarine Bar in Downtown St. Louis, killing three and wounding several others.

October 16, 1926—The Charlie Birger Gang is suspected of stealing tommy guns at a business in Rosiclare, Illinois.

October 26, 1926—Birger Gang members "High Packets" McQuay and Ward "Casey" Jones are machine-gunned near Herrin and Equality, Illinois. The Shelton Gang is blamed.

November 6, 1926— The mayor of Colp, Illinois, and mobster John "Apie" Melroy are shot to death in the Birger-Shelton gang war, reportedly by a tripod-mounted machine gun.

March 16, 1927—St. Louis gangster Fred "Killer" Burke (on contract with the Purple Gang of Detroit, Michigan) machine-gunned to death three gamblers at an apartment complex in Detroit, gaining national attention as the Milaflores Apartment Massacre.

August 10, 1927—St. Louis gangsters Anthony K. Russo and Vincent Spicuzza, while in Chicago considering an attempt on mob boss Al Capone's life, are machine-gunned to death near the intersection of North and Mannheim. St. Louis gangster Alphonso Palazzolo is suspected of arranging the murders and is murdered a month later in St. Louis in retaliation.

December 19, 1927—During a robbery attempt, a bank messenger, John Hopson, is the first victim slain by machine-gun fire in St. Louis.

December 28, 1927—St. Louis gangster Vito Giannola, a leader of the Green Dagos Gang, is machine-gunned to death by a rival gang at his girlfriend's house in St. Louis. Jack Griffin of St. Louis, suspected of this murder, is killed in Kirkwood, Missouri, just six hours later.

July 1, 1928—Brooklyn's top mob boss, Frankie Yale, is machine-gunned to death by St. Louis gangster Fred "Killer" Burke on contract to Al Capone of Chicago. The media declares Chicago the machine gun capital of the world.

February 14, 1929—St. Louis gangster Fred "Killer" Burke, along with other St. Louis gangsters, use machine guns in the St. Valentine Massacre in Chicago, Illinois, killing six rival gang bootleggers and one gang groupie, making national attention in every newspaper in the United States.

June 1, 1930—Three Capone-affiliated gangsters are machine-gunned to death at a resort in Fox Lake, Illinois. The murder is attributed to St. Louis killer Verne Miller in revenge for the murder of his friend "Red" McLaughlin. Miller, using a machine gun, gains national attention after arranging and participating in the Kansas City Union Station massacre.

October 2, 1930—Peter McTigue and William Boody, members of the St. Louis Cuckoo Gang, are killed in a machine-gun attack on a cabin distillery near Valmeyer, Illinois, by a dissident gang faction led by "Mad Dog" Tommy Hayes.

November 22, 1930—Dewey "The $500 Kid" Goebbels and Lester Barth, members of the rebellious Tommy Hayes faction of the St. Louis Cuckoo Gang, are machine-gunned to death in a parked car in St. Louis. Other Cuckoo Gang members are suspected.

February 2, 1931—Shelton Gang member Joseph Caroll, a pawnbroker and former police officer, Theodore Kamenski, and jewelry salesman David Hoffman are found near Granite City, Illinois, after being machine-gunned to death the night before at a gambling house in East St. Louis, Illinois. St. Louis Cuckoo Gang member Tommy "Mad Dog" Hayes and Carl Shelton are named as suspects.

June 17, 1933—Kansas City killer Verne Miller, assisted by Arthur "Pretty Boy" Floyd and Missouri-born gangster Adam Richetti, armed with machine guns and .45 caliber pistols, bungle an attempt to rescue bank robber Frank Nash at the Union Station in Kansas City, Missouri. Three officers, one federal agent, and Nash are killed in an ensuing shootout. The blood bath did much to launch J. Edger Hoover's FBI and the arming of federal agents and set the stage for the federal government's "war on crime."

July 10, 1934—John Lazia, boss of the Kansas City Italian Mob and connected to the Tom Prendergast Democrat machine, is killed outside the Park Central Hotel in Kansas City with a machine gun that ballistics tests indicates had been used in the Union Station Massacre, which was probably provided to the massacre shooters by Lazia. The shooters are Jack Griffin, a St. Louis gangster, and James "Jimmy Needles" La Capra, a Kansas City thug.

October 22, 1934—Charles Arthur "Pretty Boy" Floyd is executed by an FBI agent with a machine gun during his capture in East Liverpool, Ohio, after Floyd refused to answer questions about his involvement in the Kansas City Union Station Massacre, according to Police Officer Chester Smith, who assisted in the capture.

February 14, 1936—"Machine Gun" Jack McGurn of the Chicago Capone Gang is machine-gunned to death in a bowling alley in Chicago on the seventh anniversary of the St. Valentine's Day Massacre. According to an undercover FBI taped recording, one of the shooters was ex-St. Louis gangster Claude Maddox, acting on orders from mob boss Frank Nitti.

February 17, 1943—William Dinty Colbeck, ex-leader of the St. Louis Cuckoo Gang, is machine-gunned to death in St. Louis after returning from East St. Louis, Illinois. East St. Louis mobster Buster Wortman is suspected of being behind the killing.

June 25, 1951—Lula Shelton Pennington and her husband, Guy, are wounded in a machine-gun ambush in Fairfield, Illinois. She was a sister of the notorious Shelton Brothers.

Retired FBI agent and true crime researcher William Ousley adds the following murder to the list in his book *Open City*:

February 12, 1931—Bootlegger Jimmy Howard is murdered with machine-gun fire at the ABC Auto Livery Company, located at 1111 Broadway in Kansas City. He is killed for failure to share in his profits, and his death is officially considered the first victim killed by a machine gun in Kansas City, Missouri.

Retired *St. Louis Post-Dispatch* crime reporter William Lhotka provides a detailed account of another vicious murder in his book *St. Louis Crime Chronicles*:

August 10, 1932—Oliver Alden Moore, president of the East St. Louis Central Trades Council and Business Manager of the boilermakers local, is gunned down by machine-gun fire outside his union office shortly after he told a *St. Louis Post-Dispatch* reporter he cannot be intimidated. He was struck with thirty-four slugs during the ambush.

According to St. Louis native and true crime author Daniel Waugh in his book, *Gangs of St. Louis,* by the summer of 1927, the St. Louis Police Department was outfitted with a number of Thompson submachine guns, making St. Louis one of the only Prohibition-era American cities where the cops got their hands on the infamous tommy gun before the gangsters. He added, "Ironically in 1927, John Q. Public did not need a permit to own the Thompson sub machine gun though it was illegal for him to carry a pistol without authorization."

Police Detective Lieutenant Jon Carroll and his squad of men were provided the weapons to arm themselves when going up against gangs and gangsters.

Author Waugh provided the following machine gun-related incidents in his book:

April 27, 1928—Well-respected Cuckoo Gang member Piggy Weller, who ran a roadhouse on Collinsville Road called Villa Iris (a favorite hangout for members of the Cuckoo Gang), was machine-gunned to death at about 9:45 p.m. by two masked killers when he entered the roadhouse. His business partner, Louis Mandel, was the likely suspect, having him killed over an argument they had a few days before the murder. Mandel was murdered a few days later during a one-way ride in South St. Louis County. Cuckoo Gang members were suspected in the hit as revenge to Wellers death.

January 19, 1928—Charlie Fresina, a boss of the St. Louis Santino/Pillow Gang, is shot and wounded by machine-gun fire, and fellow gang members Tony DiTrapani and Dominick Cataldo are killed during a failed extortion attempt at the home of Charlie Spicuzza at 6129 Clayton Street in St. Louis. Members of the Russo Gang are suspected.

April 1928—During a roadside ambush near Edwardsville, Illinois, a failed machine-gun murder attempt is made on St. Louis "Pillow" Gang members Joe Lupo, Joseph Cincomavo, and Frank Coslontino after they conducted an extortion attempt on Italian businessmen in Benld, Illinois. Members of the rival Russo Gang are suspected.

July 16, 1931—Gus Buselaki is machine-gunned to death as he is leaving his gas station located at Twentieth and Washington in St. Louis. Two women, who were also in the station, were injured and claimed "that redhead is responsible for this." Cuckoo Gang member and strongman Timothy "Red" Cronin was brought in for questioning but never charged with the murder.

January 15, 1932—Milton Rost, a twenty-four year-old ex-con doing jobs for Cuckoo gangster Tommy Hayes, is shot nine times on Wabada in St. Louis in a drive-by shooting after bragging he had been offered $10,000 to kill "Mad Dog" Tommy Hayes. Witnesses said a machine gun was used. One of the shooters, Peter Stevens, later claimed they only used pistols.

March 24, 1932—-The machine gun-riddled bodies of Joseph Colone, a former Madison County Deputy Sheriff, and Charles Bowers, a Collinsville bootlegger, are found on the side of Caseyville Road in St. Clair County, Illinois. Colone was hit thirty-five times and Bowers a half dozen times. The double murder was attributed to St. Louis Tommy Hayes and his crew by the Sheriff's Department.

April 14, 1932—"Mad Dog" Tommy Hayes, former St. Louis Cuckoo Gang member, is murdered by machine-gun fire from a bodyguard during an inside hit in the village of Madison, in Madison County, Illinois. Hit by a dozen slugs, he died instantly. Also killed were Willie G. Wilbert and "Pretty Boy" Legler. Hayes obviously knew and trusted his killer, who was probably on contract for the Shelton Gang members who wanted Hayes killed.

December 7, 1943—Two of Shelton Strongarm gang members, Norman Farr and Harley Grizzell, are machine-gunned to death while driving north of Caseville, Illinois. Former Cuckoo Gang member, Wincel "Jackie" Urban, known as one of the best safecrackers in St. Louis history and doing freelance work for Eastside mob boss Buster Wertman, is named as a prime suspect in the murders.

Given the documented research conducted by numerous respected true crime historians, coupled with undisputed forensic ballistics evidence, first-hand memoirs, confessions, documented eyewitness accounts, and printed newspaper articles, one can make the case that gangsters, outlaws, and mobsters associated with Missouri criminal lore were in the forefront of national history in the United States in the criminal use of the Thompson submachine gun.

This author would have little problem debating the issue with anyone interested in taking on the question.

CHAPTER FIVE

"PRETTY BOY" FLOYD
AND THE UNION STATION MASSACRE
1925-1934

C harles Arthur Floyd ranks high among outlaws born outside Missouri, yet he spent so much time in Missouri, involving himself in serious criminal activities, and was also a part-time resident, which warrants him a chapter in this book.

His name means little to most readers until one adds his given nickname—"Pretty Boy" Floyd.

Born in 1904 in Adairsville, Georgia, and moving as a child to a farm near the Cookson Hills of Oklahoma—a safe haven area for bandits, robbers, and outlaws during the early 1900s—Floyd chose legendary Missouri-born outlaw Jesse James as his idol and role model, using the stories of Jesse James in later years as his blueprint for his own criminal actions.

As a teenager and young adult, he spent time in Joplin, frequenting the bars and houses of prostitution (Bandit King, P 212-236).

Floyd would later in life become the first of the Depression-era outlaws to attract national attention, as "Pretty Boy" Floyd. He was described by the *Literary Digest* as "Oklahoma's Bandit King" for his audacity, cockiness, use of a machine gun, and lack of fear of notoriety (Almanac, p 423).

Early in his career, he was admired by common folks in Oklahoma for his alleged destruction of mortgage loan records while robbing banks, making it more difficult for the banks to carry out foreclosures, which turned Floyd into a sort of Robin Hood figure to many poor Depression-era farmers (Almanac, P 423).

Floyd's first notable entry into this life of crime occurred on September 11, 1925, at the age of twenty-one, when he, along with criminal associate Fred Hilderbrand and a third outlaw, robbed a Kroger store headquarters in St. Louis of $11,934. Floyd and Hilderbrand fled to Oklahoma, where they had purchased new clothes and fancy Studebaker vehicles and flashed large sums of money, drawing the attention of a local sheriff's deputy who arrested the two on suspicion (Lhotka Book, p 154).

When the deputy searched Hilderbrand, he had $1,750 in his possession, still in the wrappers of the Tower Grove Bank of St. Louis, the bank used by the Kroger Headquarters in St. Louis (Lhotka Book, P 154).

Two days later, Floyd and Hilderbrand were returned to St. Louis and charged with the Kroger robbery. Hilderbrand confessed, implicating Floyd and another outlaw, Joe Hlavaty as taking part in the robbery.

According to historian and St. Louis area police chief Michael Webb, it was during this investigation where the moniker "Pretty Boy" was first attached to Charles Arthur Floyd when St. Louis police investigating the Kroger robbery confused Floyd with another criminal named "Pretty Boy" Smith, and the moniker stuck (Almanac, P419, see Footnote).

However, Floyd repeatedly claimed his paramour Beulah Baird, a Kansas City native, gave him the nickname during his time with her in Kansas City.

On December 8, 1925, Floyd pled guilty to the Kroger robbery, was sentenced to a term of five years, and took up residency at the Missouri State Prison in Jefferson City.

During his prison time, Floyd met numerous veteran Missouri outlaws and became a student of their outlaw ways.

After serving almost three years and six months, Floyd was paroled on March 7, 1929, and made his way to the Kansas City area to continue his criminal activities—now better equipped with his prison training.

Floyd was arrested no fewer than three times on suspicion of robbery and vagrancy during his stay in the Kansas City area, and on December 2, 1929, "Pretty Boy" was identified by Kansas City Police Detective Burt Haycock as the person shooting at him near South Sixty-First Street.

It was about this same period of time that Floyd's father was shot to death in Oklahoma during an argument with a neighbor, Jim Mills. The neighbor, after being acquitted of the shooting, disappeared, never to be seen again. It was rumored that Floyd killed the man to revenge his father's death; however, he was never charged.

On March 8, 1930, Floyd was arrested, with others, suspected of killing Patrolman Harland Manes in Akron, Ohio.

On September 3, Floyd's outlaw associate Willis "The Killer" Miller and an unidentified man robbed the National Bank and Trust Company in North Kansas City of $14,544. "Pretty Boy" Floyd was suspected as being the unidentified man in the robbery.

On November 24, "Pretty Boy" Floyd was convicted of bank robbery in Sylvania, Ohio. He was sentenced to twelve to fifteen years at the state prison in Columbus, Ohio; however, Floyd escaped from a train en route to the state prison on December 10, 1930.

In 1931, "fugitive" Floyd continued his criminal activities, robbing banks in Kentucky, Ohio, and Oklahoma, including one bank in Oklahoma he robbed twice.

On March 25, "Pretty Boy" and outlaw partner Willis "the Killer" Miller murdered fellow outlaws William Ash and Wallace Ash in Kansas City, Kansas, allegedly during a dispute about whether the Ashes were informing to law enforcement.

On April 16, Floyd, along with "Killer" Miller, murdered Patrolman Ralph Costner in a shootout with police in Bowling Green, Ohio. Miller was killed and criminal molls Rose Ash and Beulah Baird were captured.

On July 22, as reported in the Prohibition agency's official report:

Prohibition Special Agents Curtis Burks, George Small, Glen Palmer, Mark Weiser, Kenneth Thompson, George Craig, Clifford McMaster, Allen Aldridge, Ray Gaston, and A.C. Anderson, along with six local officers, were conducting liquor investigations along the north side of Kansas City, MO. While executing a search warrant at the Lusco-Note Flower Shop, the agents discovered a well dressed young man, later identified by the agents as Charles Arthur 'Pretty Boy' Floyd, in a back bedroom. Observed on the bed were a number of .45 caliber bullets. Agent Burks searched the man and removed a .45 caliber pistol from his waistband. However, before he could continue the search, the suspect drew another .45 caliber pistol from the opposite side of his body and shot Agent Burks twice. Agent Burks died two days later.

'Pretty Boy' Floyd then ran into a hallway where he encountered Agent Anderson, who he also shot. As Floyd ran from the building, he shot and wounded Kansas City Police Officer Clarence Reedy and a civilian, M. Wilson, all while making a clean escape.

Agents later searched the room where Floyd was first encountered and uncovered laundry bills and a man's suit bearing cleaner's marks and a label from a Chicago tailor. A trace of the suit revealed that it had been handmade for Charles Arthur Floyd. Special agents at the scene later positively identified Floyd's picture as being the same person that had killed Agent Burks (ATF History Book).

During the remainder of 1931, Floyd and another outlaw partner, George Birdwell, robbed no fewer than six banks in Oklahoma.

In January 1932, Floyd and his outlaw associates robbed a bank in Castle, Oklahoma, and one in Dover, Oklahoma.

On February 7, Floyd and Birdwell engaged in a gun battle with police in Tulsa, Oklahoma. They both escaped after wounding officer W. E. Wilson (Almanac, P 332).

The next day, February 8, in a robbery attempt of the Mercantile Bank in Kansas City, Police officer O. P. Carpenter was killed. Floyd, Birdwell, and Kansas City outlaw Victor Maddi were named as suspects (Almanac, P 332). Victor Maddi was captured in Houston, Texas, and charged with the Mercantile Trust robbery and murder in Kansas City (Almanac, P 332).

On February 10, Floyd and Birdwell again were spotted by Tulsa police and again escaped after a running gun battle.

The next day, Floyd and Birdwell battled Tulsa police in a house located at 513 Young Street. Once again, they both escaped; however, Floyd's wife and young son were taken into custody (Almanac, P 332).

On March 9, Floyd's outlaw partner Adam Richetti, along with L. C. "Blackie" Smalley and Fred Hammer, engaged in a robbery attempt of the First National Bank in Mill Creek, Oklahoma. Hammer was killed, Smalley wounded and captured, and later in the day, Richetti was captured and taken to the state prison at McAlester, Oklahoma (Almanac, P 333).

On March 23, Floyd and Birdwell robbed a bank in Meeker, Oklahoma, taking $500.00.

On April 6, "Pretty Boy" Floyd murdered a state investigator near Bixby, Oklahoma.

On April 20, Floyd and Birdwell captured deputies at a funeral parlor in Earlsboro, Oklahoma, so Birdwell could pay his last respects to his recently deceased father (Almanac, P 333-334).

The next day after paying their respects, Floyd and Birdwell robbed the First State Bank in Stonewell, Oklahoma of $600.00.

On June 7, Floyd and Birdwell escaped a police trap in Ada, Oklahoma. Police claimed the two were wearing bulletproof vests (Almanac, P334).

On August 25, Adam Richetti, Floyd's outlaw partner, was released from Oklahoma State Prison on $15,000 bond while awaiting trial for bank robbery. He skipped on the bond and was now a fugitive (Almanac, P 336).

On September 30, "Pretty Boy" escaped a police ambush in Sallisaw, Oklahoma (Almanac, P 337).

On November 1, "Pretty Boy" Floyd, George Birdwell, and Aulcie "Aussie" Elliot robbed the State Bank of Sallisaw, Oklahoma, taking $2,530 in the process (Almanac, P 337). This would be the last job Floyd and Birdwell pulled together. A few days later, Birdwell was killed in a bank robbery attempt at Boley, Oklahoma (Almanac, P 346).

Floyd wasted little time in 1933. Five days into the year, he was suspected of robbing a bank in Cleveland, Texas, and on January 11, he was suspected of robbing a bank in Ash Grove, Missouri. The Barrow gang was also suspected of this robbery.

THE KANSAS CITY UNION STATION MASSACRE

On June 16, 1933, "Pretty Boy" Floyd and outlaw associate Adam Richetti were back in Missouri, this time in Richetti's hometown of Bolivar, where they kidnapped the local sheriff, Jack Killingsworth, and drove out of town, heading towards Kansas City. Fearing they would be stopped once the kidnapping was broadcast, they abandoned his vehicle south of Deepwater, Missouri, and commandeered another vehicle, driven by an unsuspecting citizen, Walter Griffith, whom they also took hostage (Almanac, P 351).

According to statements later provided by Killingsworth and Griffith, they document Floyd possessing two .45 caliber firearms and one machine gun, and Richetti carrying one .45 caliber firearm. They also observed a large quantity of .45 caliber ammunition.

For the next several hours, with Floyd driving and Richetti drinking, they traveled the "cat roads" through Missouri, crossing into Kansas and back toward Kansas City. During the trip, an observant Killingsworth noticed the serial number on the machine gun had been removed (L.L. Edge Book).

During the late evening, Floyd brought the vehicle to a halt in the West Bottoms area of Kansas City at the corner of Ninth and Hickory. Floyd left the vehicle for a short while, entering into a nearby building. Within several minutes, a vehicle arrived, picking up Floyd and Richetti, leaving Killingsworth and Griffith unharmed with a warning not to leave the area for a while.

Fearing they were being watched, the two men decided not to report their kidnapping and release immediately. They drove out of town to Lee's Summit, Missouri, where they stopped for a meal and called their families before heading back home. They were relieved they were still alive, not realizing a tragic massacre was to occur about eight hours later.

Reports filed later by Killingworth and Griffith proved critical in documenting their observations, developing a timeline, and placing Floyd and Richetti being picked up by others late in the evening in Kansas City on June 16, 1933.

Also, on June 16 as the two hostages took the ride of their lives, a notorious bank robber and federal prison escapee, Frank "Jelly" Nash," was arrested in Hot Springs, Arkansas. Plans were being made by the arresting lawmen to return Nash to the federal prison in Leavenworth, Kansas. They were to travel by train from Fort Smith, Arkansas, to Union Station in Kansas City then on to the prison by vehicle; Nash would be guarded by a host of FBI agents and police (Almanac, P 351).

This seemingly unrelated event put into motion the most notorious law enforcement massacre in Kansas City's history, forever to be known as the Kansas City Union Station Massacre.

It will involve a host of outlaws, Midwest mobsters, and assorted criminal characters, including "Pretty Boy" Floyd, Adam Richetti, and outlaw bank robber and contract killer Verne C. Miller, who was living in Kansas City at the time at 6612 Edgevale Road with his mistress Vivian "Vi" Mathis (spelled by some researchers as Mathias), who were renting the house under the alias Vincent C. Moore (Unger, P 64).

Verne Miller was a close criminal associate of the captured Frank Nash, having robbed banks with Nash in the past, and was eager to help Nash if the opportunity ever presented itself.

At about 10:45 p.m., according to an FBI source, the following events took place as the released hostage Killingsworth and Griffith left Kansas City.

"Pretty Boy" Floyd met with a Kansas City contact Steve Oliver and his brother-in-law Dominick Binaggio, a local gambler, nightclub owner, and associate of the Kansas City Mob. Boss Johnny Lazia offered to provide the two with temporary shelter in the West Bottoms, after learning that Floyd and an associate were in town. This was a required obligation of Boss Lazia, who wanted to be informed of anything that was going on in a city he controlled.

At the same time, Verne Miller was meeting with Johnny Lazia at his favorite restaurant located in the Union Station, asking to borrow a couple of Lazia's boys to help free Frank Nash away from the lawmen when they arrive at the Union Station in the morning.

Lazia, knowing Floyd was in town, offered up Floyd and his partner, Adam Richetti, and provided Miller with a machine gun—Miller accepted the offer (Unger, P 40).

Shortly thereafter, Miller met with Floyd and Richetti at a mob drugstore located at Grand and Missouri and laid out his plan to free bank robber Frank Nash by scaring the feds with surprise and firepower, hopefully without a shot being fired. (Unger, P 40-41)

Miller, after the meeting, took his two gunmen to his Edgevale house and informed his mistress, Vi, that two men would be spending the rest of the night.

On June 17, 1933, at 7:15 a.m., the Missouri Pacific slowly rolled into the Union Station in Kansas City fifteen minutes late, carrying its usual load of passengers, as well as three lawmen with Frank Nash in their custody.

The lawmen—FBI Agents Frank Smith and Joe Lackey and McAlester [Oklahoma] Police Chief Otto Reed—were met inside Union Station by local FBI Agents Reed Vetterli and Roy Caffrey, along with Kansas City Police Detectives Bill Grooms and Frank Hermanson. Grooms and Hermanson were assigned to the Kansas City Police Department armored car known as "Hot Shot," which normally contained a machine gun that was, for some unknown reason, missing this day.

The lawmen, along with their prisoner Nash, who was handcuffed in front and held by the back of his belt by an FBI agent, walked to the east door of the station in a wedge-shaped formation to the waiting vehicles parked just outside the station doors.

The plan was to place Nash in Agent Caffrey's vehicle and drive him to the federal prison in Leavenworth, Kansas, some thirty miles to the north.

Passengers and employees in and outside the Union Station watched the procession in awe, taking in their every movement, not realizing in a few minutes most in the group would be dead or wounded. Several traveling passengers and station employees were about to become eyewitnesses to an event that would lay the groundwork for the Federal Bureau of Investigation we know today and the passage of numerous federal laws, giving the power to enforce them to the FBI and propel the criminal status of Vernon Miller, Adam Richetti, and, of course, "Pretty Boy" Floyd to the most hunted and wanted men in America.

The official FBI summary version of what happened next was contained in a report in the FBI's eighty-nine volume file of the Kansas City Union Station Massacre and reads as follows:

> Frank Nash was escorted by the Head of the FBI's Kansas City Office, together with Special Agent Raymond J. Caffrey, two other representatives of the FBI, and Otto Reed, chief of police of the McAlester, Oklahoma, Police Department. Police Officers W.J. Grooms and Frank Hermanson of the Kansas City, Missouri, Police Department, were also given important posts of assignment for this transfer. Frank Nash, upon being removed from the train, was immediately taken to the waiting automobile of Special Agent Caffrey, where he was placed in the left front seat in order that the officers might occupy the rear seat. At this instant

two Special Agents took positions in the rear seat with Chief of Police Otto Reed. Police Officers Grooms and Hermanson, together with the Head of FBI's Kansas City Office, were standing on the right side of Agent Caffrey's automobile during the time Special Agent Caffrey was walking around the car preparatory to entering the driver's seat. It was when Agent Caffrey approached the left door of this automobile that the three assassins surprised the officers from a point in front of and about fifteen to twenty feet to the west of the automobile. These men were observed carrying machine guns and other weapons and in approaching the automobile shouted, 'Up, up.' An instant later the voice of one of the gunmen was heard to say, 'Let 'em have it.' Immediately a fusillade of gunfire came from the weapons of the attackers. Shots were fired from the front and from all sides of Agent Caffrey's car. Police officers Grooms and Hermanson were instantly killed in the positions where they stood. Chief of Police Otto Reed was also instantly killed. One agent was severely wounded by bullets which entered his back, and he was confined to bed for several months. Special Agent Caffrey was instantly killed by a bullet which passed directly through his head as he stood beside the car. The prisoner, Frank Nash, was also killed by a misdirected gunshot that entered his skull, thereby defeating the very purpose of the conspiracy to gain his freedom. The other Special Agent escaped injury, while the Head of the FBI office received a wound in the arm. Apparently, the assassins started at the front right-hand side of the car and at least two of them proceeded around the automobile, making a complete circle and firing recklessly as they went.

The facts surrounding the ambush and law enforcement massacre in Kansas City would be reviewed, researched, wrote about, and debated for years, leaving as many questions for some as answers about who actually assisted Vernon Miller in the tragic shootout.

The investigation process began with the uncovering of a series of long-distance phone calls made the day proceeding the massacre between outlaws in Hot Springs, Arkansas; Joplin, Missouri; Chicago, Illinois; and Kansas City, Missouri—all wanting to help free Frank Nash from his captivity when he arrived in Kansas City the next morning (Unger, P 86).

Indisputable evidence resulted in a string of federal indictments, charging eleven individuals with conspiracy to obstruct justice, was filed on September 13, 1933.

Meanwhile Floyd and Richetti, feeling the heat, skipped out of town, and one day later, Verne Miller and Vi left town, also headed in different directions then meeting up again in Chicago.

In September, Floyd and Richetti headed east first stopping in Toledo, Ohio, meeting up with Beulah Baird and her sister, Rose Ash, moving them out of their apartment, and the foursome continued to Buffalo, New York, hiding out and only leaving the apartment intermittently to pull a robbery when money was running low, until October of 1934, when they decided to return to the Midwest.

It was quite likely this move east was caused by the announcement of the federal indictments and arrest of those involved in the Frank Nash escape attempt. This information was confirmed by both Baird and Ash when they were interviewed by FBI agents later in 1934.

After their indictment and arrest, coconspirators Frances Nash, Frank Nash's wife, as well as Herb Farmer and his wife, Esther, all confirmed they had received a call from Verne Miller from a pay phone at Union Station just after midnight a few hours before the massacre, telling Frances they would get her husband back. Phone records confirmed a call was made from a pay phone from Union Station to the Farmer's Joplin farm phone, supporting their statement as truthful.

On July 24, one of Floyd's outlaw associates, bank robber John Scheck—during an arraignment hearing at the Chicago courts building—attempted an escape, fatally shooting policeman John Sevick. Scheck was wounded and re-captured, and the murder weapon, a revolver, was recovered. Scheck claimed that, while he was in jail prior to the court appearance, the revolver was smuggled to him by "Pretty Boy" Floyd.

On August 28, Floyd and Richetti were suspected of robbing a bank in Galena, Missouri, of $1,000.

On November 1, while Floyd and Richetti were hiding out in Buffalo, New York, Verne Miller—the prime suspect of the Union Station Massacre—escaped a trap to capture him while he was visiting his mistress, Vi Mathis, at a Chicago apartment, bringing focus back to the tragic event.

Later in November, Albert Silvers, a New Jersey mobster who had helped Verne Miller flee Chicago, was found murdered in Connecticut, then several days later, Verne Miller was murdered in Detroit, Michigan, taking his information about the Kansas City Massacre to his grave.

It was not until March 1934 that one of the fingerprints lifted at the Verne Miller house was reexamined, revealing a print taken from one of the beer bottles found in the basement of the house belonged to Adam Richetti, "Pretty Boy" Floyd's partner.

This revelation put an intense focus on Richetti and Floyd, and the manhunt intensified. On June 24, 1934, a large number of state and federal Agents raided a ranch near Branson, Missouri, after receiving information Floyd and John Dillinger were hiding at the farm. The search proved negative. (Almanac, P 384)

On June 30, 1934, a bank was robbed by John Dillinger, criminal associates Homer Van Meter, "Baby Face" Nelson, and two unidentified men in South Bank, Indiana, killing a patrolman in the process. Several outlaw sources claimed one of the unidentified participants was "Pretty Boy" Floyd (Almanac, P 386, 424).

If true, this marked the only occasion Floyd and Dillinger worked together as John Dillinger was killed by FBI agents on July 22, nearly a month after the bank robbery.

On August 31, a middle-aged Kansas City mob associate, Jimmy "Needles" LaCapra, decided he needed police protection and started talking to the FBI after two mob murder attempts on his life, as a result of his alleged involvement in the machine-gun murder of Kansas City mob boss Johnny Lazia one month earlier on July 10 in Kansas City.

LaCapra provided very damaging and intimate firsthand and secondhand knowledge he had about the Union Station Massacre, placing both "Pretty Boy" Floyd and Adam Richetti in Kansas City to meet with Kansas City mobsters Steve Oliver and Dominick Binaggio just after they released their two hostages, Killingsworth and Griffith.

According to LaCapra, Floyd and Richetti were connected to Verne Miller through mob boss Johnny Lazia at a drugstore located at Missouri and Grand. Mob associate Sam Scola was also at the drugstore meeting.

LaCapra then provided details of what took place the next day, naming names along the way. LaCapra claimed he knew Floyd was injured and named the person, a young intern, who had treated Floyd before he left town. LaCapra admitted he provided the getaway car for Floyd and Richetti, a big Buick he had stolen a year earlier in St. Louis and brought to Kansas City, storing it in a garage. This vehicle information was confirmed by several witnesses who working at the parking garage.

Other independent evidence and witnesses supported LaCapra's revelations, making his story believable.

When LaCapra's criminal associate, Edward "Speedy" Wilhite, was shown LaCapra's statement, he agreed that LaCapra knew a lot about the massacre, adding that Johnny Lazia and Sam Scola had told him the same things they told LaCapra. (Unger, P142)

Wilhite was reluctant to snitch on "Pretty Boy" Floyd; however, he told the agents "if you know what LaCapra and I know you have the Union Station Massacre solved," adding "when Floyd and Richetti are dead to come back and he would provide a lot more information."

Shortly after these interviews, the FBI learned the stolen Buick LaCapra talked about was located in Akron, Ohio, burned up with a body found in the car. They found out the car had been discovered a few days after the massacre with the body of Nathan Gerstein, a New York gangster, in the car.

The miles on the vehicle's odometer were consistent with the miles from St. Louis to Kansas City then to Akron, Ohio, further supporting LaCapra's story. Sam Scola had been murdered, so neither Scola nor the now deceased Lazia were available to dispute or verify the stunning information from LaCapra and Wilhite.

Also, in September 1934, Richard Galatas, mobster from Hot Springs, Arkansas, during an interview with the FBI after his arrest in New Orleans, provided information on how the conspiracy to free Frank Nash started with phone calls by him from Hot Springs (Almanac, P 405).

A few days later, Fritz Mulloy, the Kansas City mob insider, during an interview with the FBI in Chicago, filled in additional events he had personal knowledge concerning the day before, the day of, and the days after the massacre.

Then on September 30, 1934, Vivian "Vi" Mathis, Verne Miller's live-in, provided a written statement to the FBI with information that supported the information previously provided by Jimmy "Needles" LaCapra on August 31, 1934. What proved very important was the fact neither storyteller knew the other was talking in different cities to different FBI agents.

LaCapra wanted protection, and Vi Mathis wanted a promise her statement would be kept a secret.

Mathis detailed events that occurred on the day before the massacre, the day of the massacre, and the days and months after the massacre.

She confirmed that Fritz Mulloy, a Kansas City mob insider, had called the house at about 5:00 p.m. on the sixteenth, looking for Verne. She had told Mulloy he could find Verne at the golf course. One hour later, Verne returned to the house, informing her Frank Nash had been arrested by the feds in Hot Springs, Arkansas.

Vi documented the strong criminal relationship between Verne Miller and bank robber Frank Nash and verified answering a phone call at the house from Esther Farmer from Joplin, who left a message for Verne that she wrote down. The party (Nash) left Fort Worth, Arkansas, (by train) en route to Kansas City. She gave the note to Verne as he left the house.

Later that night, Verne returned home, telling her he had brought two men with him who needed a place to sleep.

The next morning, Verne left with the two men while she was sleeping. When he returned to the house about 9:00 a.m. with the two men, he told her that one of the men was "Pretty Boy" Floyd and the three of them had been at the Union Station to free Nash—some shooting had started and Nash was killed.

She added that, after Verne had read the newspaper account of the shooting, which reported there were as many as five or six shooters, he told her there was only three of us shooters.

Vi identified photographs of "Pretty Boy" Floyd and Adam Richetti as the two men she met in her house shortly after the massacre, adding that Floyd was wounded in his left shoulder and Richetti was drinking beer out of bottles while in the house.

She and Verne stayed in the house throughout the day on Sunday, and Floyd and Richetti left during the day. Verne left in his vehicle, and Vi was taken to Des Moines by Martin Schartzberg, a friend of Verne's. She caught a train out of Des Moines to Chicago and met up with Verne Miller.

THE FALL OF CHARLES ARTHUR "PRETTY BOY" FLOYD

On October 19, while traveling from Buffalo, New York, en route to the Midwest, "Pretty Boy" Floyd and Adam Richetti were suspected in a $500 bank robbery at Tiltonsville, Ohio, and two days later, Richetti was wounded and taken into custody during a shootout with police near Wellsville, Ohio. Floyd escaped. His freedom was short-lived (Almanac, P 405).

The next day, October 22, 1934, Charles Arthur "Pretty Boy" Floyd met his Waterloo at a farm near East Liverpool, Ohio, when he was killed by police and federal agents while trying to escape.

Beulah Baird—Floyd's girlfriend—and her sister, Rose Ash, were interviewed by the FBI shortly after Floyd was killed. They confirmed Floyd and Richetti had moved them out of their apartment in Toledo, Ohio, in September 1933, possibly as a result of the heat brought on by the recent federal indictments. They had all traveled to an apartment in Buffalo, New York, and hid out most of the time until October 1934, when they all decided to return to Oklahoma, possibly robbing a bank in Ohio on the way.

The official FBI accounting of the shooting incident claimed a local policeman had spotted a man in a suit running behind a corncrib then running across a field. When Floyd had failed to obey an order to stop, he was mortally wounded, only living long enough to give his name—Charles Arthur Floyd, so ending the criminal career of one of the most wanted, notorious criminals during America's Depression era.

In a most sensational development not too long after Floyd's death, a Kansas City ballistics expert, Merle Gill, who had conducted all the ballistics tests of the evidence recovered at the massacre scene for state law enforcement authorities and the FBI, was provided shell casings from Floyd's two recovered .45 caliber firearms through the Missouri Highway Patrol.

After conducting his ballistics tests, Gill announced he had made a positive match with the casings recovered at the Union Station Massacre scene with the casings recovered from Floyd's weapons when he was killed; finally, there was a link between one of Floyd's guns and the Union Station Massacre.

Simple logic more than suggested that, if Floyd's .45 caliber weapon was at the massacre scene, then Floyd was also at the massacre scene.

It is important to point out that, with Verne Miller and "Pretty Boy" Floyd both dead, the only person left to face the consequences was Adam Richetti, and this would happen at his state murder trial in a courthouse in Jackson County, Missouri, which opened on June 13, 1935. Expert testimony from Merle Gill, who presented convincingly to the jury his ballistics tests and positive findings, placed one of "Pretty Boy" Floyd's weapons at the scene.

Gill's findings have withstood the test of time to this day, with only limited dispute of his results, placing "Pretty Boy" Floyd as a shooter in the Kansas City Union Station Massacre.

At the end of closing arguments, the jury panel found Adam Richetti, "Pretty Boy" Floyd's outlaw partner, guilty of first-degree murder (Unger, P 190-192).

On August 21, 1935, just one month after testifying at the Richetti murder trial, Michael James "Jimmy the Needle" LaCapra was murdered in New Paltz, New York (Almanac, P 421).

On November 26, 1934, Kansas City Police Officer Myron "Mike" Fanning, despondent over witnessing the Union Station Massacre, went on a drunken rampage and fatally shot fellow officer Grand V. Schroder. Fanning would be convicted of murder and sent to the Missouri State Prison, the same prison Floyd had served his time in just a few years earlier (Almanac, P 406).

On January 4, 1935, Richard Galatas, Herbert "Deafy" Farmer, Frank "Fritz" Mulloy, and Louis "Doc" Stacci were convicted of conspiracy to obstruct justice for their part in the Kansas City Union Station Massacre. All were sentenced to two years in prison and fined $10,000 (Almanac, P 408).

Richetti's murder conviction was upheld by the Missouri Supreme Court, and on October 7, 1938, Richetti was executed in the newly constructed gas chamber in the state prison in Jefferson City, the same prison where "Pretty Boy" Floyd had served his time for his first felony conviction and been paroled on March 7, 1929, just nine years earlier (Almanac, P 435).

In 1939, Oklahoma Balladeer Woody Guthrie, a well-known writer of folk music of his time, wrote a song about the outlaw "Pretty Boy" Floyd that elevated his legend to hero status. The first stanza goes like this:

Come and gather 'round me children

A story I will tell

About Pretty Boy Floyd the outlaw

Oklahoma knew him well.

Throughout the years, the song has been sung and recorded by no fewer than eleven artists, including Bob Dylan, Joan Baez, and James Taylor, and three bands named themselves "Pretty Boy" Floyd. His character has been portrayed in at least eight film and TV movies between 1959 and 2009, depicting his life, association with fellow outlaws, and death. Floyd's life and death has been detailed in more publications than one can count.

The character "Flattop Jones" in the Dick Tracey comic strip was modeled after Floyd, and professional boxer Floyd Mayweather Jr. used the alias "Pretty Boy" Floyd for a period of his undefeated professional career. (Wikipedia)

The official FBI version of how Floyd died held up for forty years, until the only surviving police officer at the farm that day, Chester Smith, provided an interview to crime researcher Neal Trickel. Smith was confronting failing health and felt a sense of obligation to clear up long-standing rumors before his own death. He described to Trickel his version of what actually happened.

Smith said he was the local officer that saw Floyd behind the corncrib and take off running across an open field with a .45 caliber weapon in both hands. As Floyd continued running, Smith and another officer fired shots at Floyd, wounding him twice. Smith approached Floyd, still alive, picked up both .45 caliber pistols and started talking to Floyd when FBI Agent Melvin Purvis ordered him to stand back.

When Floyd refused to answer questions, Purvis ordered another FBI agent to "fire into him." The agent complied, firing two single shots into Floyd, killing him execution-style.

Purvis left the group of lawmen for a short while and later returned, telling the officers he had called J. Edgar Hoover to report they had killed Floyd.

A female neighbor, when interviewed at the time of the shooting, supported Smith's version, reporting she heard the shooting and the shots happened twice several minutes apart.

According to researcher Trickel, during the interview, Smith handed him an envelope containing a .45 caliber Cupro-Nickel slug recovered from Floyd's body by the coroner. The rifling marking indicated it came from a Thompson machine gun similar to one the FBI agents possessed at the scene. The slug tested positive for blood dried in the grooves of the metal-jacketed round.

The FBI has steadfastly denied Smith's account of what happened the day Floyd was killed (Almanac, P 405, 406, 425, 426).

As a direct result of the tragic Kansas City Union Station Massacre, the stage was set for the federal government's "war on crime." Franklin D. Roosevelt signed a number of crime bills into law making it a federal crime

- to assault or kill a federal agent
- to rob a national bank
- to flee across a state line to avoid prosecution
- to transport stolen property of more than $5,000 across a state line
- to use interstate communications in extortion attempts
- to take hostages or kidnap victims across state lines

In addition, the president—

- provided federal agents the authority to carry guns
- authorized federal agents full arrest powers throughout the United States

The only thing that is certain: the debates will continue regarding who the third shooter was at the Union Station Massacre, whether Richetti was falsely executed, and how "Pretty Boy" Floyd died on the Ohio farm at the hands of law enforcement officers. The legacy will continue to grow.

CHAPTER SIX

THE STORY OF BONNIE AND CLYDE
1910-1934

C lyde Champion Barrow and Bonnie Elizabeth Parker, two Depression-era outlaws born in Texas, involved themselves in petty crimes throughout the Midwest at a young age, graduating to serious crimes—including burglaries, robberies, kidnappings, and murders—and, in the process, left their mark on Missouri history, becoming known as "Bonnie and Clyde."

A young nineteen-year-old Bonnie Parker was introduced to and fell in love with Clyde Barrow in 1930 while her husband, Roy Thornton (whom she had married at the age of sixteen) was serving a lengthy prison sentence in an Oklahoma prison for bank robbery.

In the late 1920s, Clyde also went to prison. He convinced Bonnie Parker to help him escape, and on March 9, 1930, Barrow escaped from the Texas prison after she smuggled a handgun to him. They drove to Illinois, stealing a number of vehicles on the way, including one in Joplin and one in St. Louis. Clyde was later recaptured and returned to prison to serve out his sentence.

In 1932 Clyde Barrow, upon completion of his prison sentence, once again teamed up with his girlfriend and accomplice Bonnie Parker, forming a gang called by some "The Bloody Barrows," robbing gas stations, grocery stores, and small banks throughout the Southwest and Midwest, including stops in Missouri.

Bonnie and Clyde, both small in physical stature, preferred Browning automatic rifles (BARs), the popular automatic rifle, and an assortment of handguns to commit their criminal acts. They stole many of their weapons from National Guard armories. They killed a dozen or more victims, including two in Missouri, during a well-publicized crime spree between 1932 and 1934 alone.

On Halloween night of 1932, after a brief visit with Bonnie's family in Dallas, Texas, Bonnie and Clyde drove to Carthage, Missouri, meeting with fellow gang members Hollis Hale and Frank Hardy, where the three men committed a number of robberies throughout November. On November 30, 1932, gang members Clyde Barrow, Hollis Hale, and Frank Hardy robbed the Farmers Bank of Oronogo, Missouri, of $115.00. A few days later, on December 5, fellow gang member Raymond Hamilton was captured in Michigan, extradited to Texas, and convicted of murder and robberies. He was sentenced to 263 years.

On January 11, 1933, three men robbed the Ash Grove Bank in Ash Grove, Missouri. The Barrow gang was suspected, as well as the "Pretty Boy" Floyd gang.

A few days later, on January 26, Clyde Barrow, Bonnie Parker, and young gang member W. D. Jones were stopped for speeding in Springfield, Missouri, by a police motorcycle patrolman named Thomas Persell. The trio got the jump on Persell, placed him in their vehicle, and took him for a ride. Fortunately, in a rare display of compassion, he was released unharmed near Poundstone Corner, Missouri, after being relieved of his service revolver.

Marvin Ivan "Buck" Barrow, Clyde's older brother, was released from a prison in Oklahoma on March 22, 1933. Buck spent some time in Fort Smith, Arkansas—with his wife Blanche—before joining up with his brother Clyde near the Oklahoma state line.

In April 1933, members of the Barrow gang robbed a filling station in Springfield then traveled to Joplin, renting a garage apartment located at 3347 1/2 Thirty-Fourth Street. On April 13, Bonnie, Clyde, Buck Barrow, his wife Blanche, and gang member W. D. Jones engaged in a raging daylight gun battle at the rental house with law enforcement officers. During the shootout, Constable J. Wesley Harryman and Joplin detective Harry McGinnis were shot and killed by members of the Barrow gang, while the gang was escaping the rental house.

Also engaged in the tragic shootout was George B. Kahler, a Missouri Highway Patrol trooper who had been investigating the gang. He provided this detailed, firsthand account that was published in a booklet written by Patrol Sergeant Charles E. Walker in 1981 to commemorate the patrol's fiftieth anniversary:

It was April 13, 1933, that I experienced my baptism of fire, so to speak. Somebody had been pulling a lot of robberies in the area; suspicion pointed to the people living in a house on 34th Street in Joplin. Neighbors said the residents of the house had several cars, all with license plates from different states. They rarely left in the daytime, but were seen coming and going at odd hours in the night. Apparently, none of them worked.

The house was built of Carthage stone and had two stories, the upper one consisting of living quarters and the lower a garage large enough to park four cars inside. It sat right on the sidewalk, facing south on 34th Street and was the second house from the corner of 34th and Oak Ridge Drive. The corner house faced Oak Ridge Drive to the west. Neighbors said the occupants always backed two cars into the garage and another between the houses.

I had gone out to the house when the reports were first received and checked the registration plate on the car parked outside. It checked to a person in Kansas on that car, so we didn't think too much more about it, as we had no direct evidence that they were involved in any criminal activity.

Then on April 12 the Neosho Milling Company was robbed. The proprietor, Harry Bacon and his wife were held captive while the robbers rifled the safe. The description of the robbers seemed to fit the folks in the house.

The next step was to secure a search warrant and investigate these people. Most of Joplin is in Jasper County, but the southern one-fourth, where the house was located, is in Newton County, so Trooper Walt Grammer and I went to Neosho, the county seat, where the prosecutor issued the warrant. Wes Harryman, the constable of the township accompanied us back to Joplin. He would serve the warrant, as the law didn't permit us to do it.

We stopped at the Joplin Police Station to make plans. We decided that Grammer and I would go in one car—it was Captain Eslick's Model A sedan—and Harryman and two Joplin detectives, Harry McGinnis and Tom Degraff would follow in the other. While the others served the warrant, Grammer and I were to check identification numbers on the car parked between the houses.

We didn't realize who we were dealing with. If we had, we'd have lined up a lot more help. The people in that house were Bonnie Parker and Clyde Barrow (better known as simply 'Bonnie and Clyde'), Clyde's brother, Buck, and wife, Blanche, and W.D. Jones, all known to Texas law enforcement authorities as dangerous characters.

As I approached the house from the east on 34th Street, I noticed the Barrow brothers standing in front of the house. The garage doors were open. They had evidently just arrived and were talking prior to entering their apartment.

'Step on it,' said Grammer. 'We'll get up there before they get inside.'

So, I stepped on it, but of course those Model As didn't have much scat.

They looked up, saw us coming, and casually moved inside the garage, pulling the doors shut behind them. I drove right up to the garage entrance, and Grammer said, 'Hey, fellows, wait up, we want to talk to you.'

That's when the shooting started. They opened up on us with rifles and shotguns. Luckily, Grammer and I weren't hit.

'Cover the back!' I shouted to Grammer. He ran around to the rear of the Barrow house and after firing a few rounds, I scrambled over behind the adjoining house out of the line of fire.

The police car was a short distance behind us. DeGraff was driving, with Harryman beside him, and McGinnis in the back seat. They should have been alerted to trouble by our quick exit, but instead of stopping down the street, they pulled right in beside the patrol car. Harryman climbed out and walked to the partially open garage doors. As he took his search warrant from his pocket, one of the Barrows shot him point blank in the chest with a sawed-off shotgun, killing him instantly.

DeGraff leaped out and ran around to the back with Grammer, as Harry McGinnis rolled from the passenger side and ran to the right-hand garage door. He smashed out the window and shoved his pistol inside. Before he could fire, one of the criminals shot him through the crack in the doors. The shotgun blast severed his right arm at the elbow. Slugs hit him in the face and body as well.

As I started to reload, I glanced up to see the muzzle of a machine gun protruding from behind the right-hand garage door. It was Clyde Barrow and he was firing at one of the fallen policemen. I aimed about where I judged his body to be and put two or three bullets through the door. He dropped the weapon and ran inside. At the time I thought I'd hit him, but found out later I'd only shot off his necktie!

There was a side window in the apartment. Just as I looked up to check it, W.D. Jones swung a Browning machine rifle out of the garage door and opened up. With the initial burst, I felt sharp pains in my face and neck. I thought, my God, half my head is gone. But the shells had hit the house, and I'd been struck by stone fragments blown free by the slugs.

I knew I had no chance against that kind of firepower with my little .38 pistol, so I ran around the house. He continued to fire, and how he missed, I'll never know. As I rounded the corner, I tripped over a poultry wire that bordered a flowerbed and fell. As I rolled around the corner of the house, I saw Jones turn around.

'Where did the other son of a bitch go?' he said, meaning Grammer. Jones thought he'd killed me.

From about 25 feet away, I took careful aim and fired. The slug hit him just beneath the right shoulder blade. He fell back inside the garage.

This was the last cartridge in my revolver, so I ducked back down and began reloading. Suddenly, I heard someone coming around the opposite side of the house. Again, I thought I'd had it, but it was only Walt Grammer.

'Get in that house and call for help!' I told him, and managed to load two shells in my gun. Meanwhile, the Barrows had pitched the wounded W.D. Jones into one of the cars inside of the garage and, joined by Bonnie Parker and Blanche, started to drive out. The police car blocked the way, so Buck jumped out and released the brake. The car rolled down the street and struck a tree. Degraff and I fired several rounds at their fleeing car, but to no avail.

This whole incident lasted only about one minute from the first shot to the final one. Constable Wes Harryman had been killed instantly and the Joplin police detective, Harry McGinnis, died that night.

In the apartment, we found an old Eastman Kodak camera with a roll of film inside. One of the shots was the now famous one of Bonnie Parker leaning on the headlight of a Model T Ford with her foot hiked up on the bumper, cigar in her mouth, and stag-handle pistol in her right hand. That pistol was stolen from Tom Persell, a Springfield policeman, whom the gang had kidnapped in January of 1933. He had been released unharmed.

On a table lay several sheets of black paper on which Bonnie Parker had been composing a poem, 'Suicide Sal,' in white ink. The poem only lacked a couple of lines before completion. She had evidently been writing when the shooting started, because the ink was still wet.

The gang had also left two of their cars, several pistols, and the Browning machine rifle that is now displayed at the Patrol Museum in Jefferson City.

W.D. Jones left the gang in August of 1933, and was captured on his way back to Dallas. I later interviewed him in the penitentiary at Huntsville. By that time, Buck Barrow was dead from wounds suffered in another gun battle near Platte City, Missouri, and his wife, Blanche, had been caught in Iowa.

Jones showed me the scar left from my bullet. The place it exited his chest left a hole large enough to put your thumb into. The slug had passed completely through him but missed his vital organs. He said they'd stopped at a country store after fleeing Joplin and bought a little bottle of rubbing alcohol. Bonnie Parker pried open the wound with knitting needles and filled it with the alcohol. That was the only treatment he'd had!

Jones had been shot numerous times on other occasions. The backs of his hands felt like beanbags from the buckshot embedded there. He had five buckshot in his lip, and one side of his face was full too. You could put your hand on it and feel the shot rolling around.

I saw an article in the newspaper a year or so ago saying that he'd finally been released from prison, but a short time afterwards somebody shot and killed him in a fight in a beer joint.

After making their escape, the gang members returned to Texas first and, for the next several months, rambled through a good number of states, including Oklahoma, Kansas, Indiana, and Louisiana, continuing their crime wave.

In May, Bonnie and Clyde were declared federal fugitives after being charged with transportation of a stolen vehicle across a state line.

The next month Bonnie was seriously burned in a vehicle accident in Wellington, Texas. In the process of recovering, she participated in crimes in Oklahoma, Arkansas, and Iowa.

In July 1933, members of the Barrow gang returned to Missouri, and on July 20, 1933, Bonnie, Clyde, Buck and Blanche Barrow, and W.D. Jones were surrounded by police at the Red Crown Cabin Camp at Ferrelview near Platte City, Missouri, just north of Kansas City, and once again engaged in a shootout with area law enforcement officers. Missouri State Trooper Thomas E. "Tom" Whitecotton provided this firsthand account, which was also published in a booklet written by State Trooper Sergeant Charles E. Walker in 1981:

You hear a lot of wild talks about the gunfight between law officers and Bonnie and Clyde near Platte City on July 20, 1933. Well, I participated, so I'll add my version.

We had no two-way radios in our patrol cars then, so when the troop headquarters had a message for us, they'd phone restaurants where we made regular stops.

The Red Crown Tavern near Platte City was one of these stopping places. They served good food and a lot of the boys ate there. The owner also had several tourist cabins next to the restaurant.

Word came to our office that three men and two women had rented two of the cabins and were acting suspicious. They never set foot in the Red Crown, but would instead send one man to the restaurant across the highway for carryout meals. When a license check on their car revealed that it had been stolen in Oklahoma from a doctor and his girlfriend, we knew we had some hot customers.

Captain Baxter, the commanding officer of Troop A, Trooper Leonard Ellis and I drove to the scene, arriving about 11 o'clock on the night of July 19. I'd been working in the office all day and was wearing a seersucker suit and a Panama hat instead of my uniform. We met the Platte County Sheriff, Holt Coffey, and several deputies. Holt had asked Sheriff Tom Bash of Jackson County to bring his armored car and a few of his deputies, too.

The cabins were connected by a double car garage. Bonnie Parker and Clyde Barrow were in one cabin, and Blanch (sic) and Buck Barrow and W.D. Jones were in the other. We stationed two Platte County deputies on top of the Red Crown Tavern. The armored car, with two Jackson County men inside, was parked in the driveway, blocking the only escape route. A deputy and I were set up at the end of the driveway as backup and the rest of the officers were arranged strategically around the cabins.

At 1 a.m. Baxter and Coffey, carrying machine guns and protected by armored shields, walked to the door of Bonnie and Clyde's cabin and knocked.

'Who's there?' asked Clyde.

'The sheriff. Open up!' said Coffey.

'Just a minute,' said Clyde, reaching for his 30.06 machine rifle. He blasted several rounds right through the closed door.

Baxter staggered backward, unhurt and still holding his gun and shield, but Holt Coffey ran for cover. You really couldn't blame him with those slugs flying around. In the uncertain light, I mistook him for one of the gang members. I ran after him and yelled at Leonard Ellis, who was closer to the cabins, 'There's one of 'em! Get him!'

And, he did, too! Fortunately, Holt only received a superficial buckshot wound to the neck. He believed 'til his dying day that Clyde Barrow shot him, but it was actually a state trooper.

Bonnie and Clyde could reach the gang's car by an interior door, but Buck, Blanche, and Jones had to come out the front. When they did, Captain Baxter opened up with his machine gun, hitting Buck in the head. He stumbled to the car with Blanche's help, and with Clyde at the wheel, they roared out of the garage. The hail of bullets from both sides was terrific. I hit the dirt, seersucker suit and all. Bullets whizzed overhead for a few seconds, then stopped. I guess they thought they'd hit me. Jones and Clyde concentrated their fire on the armored car, which blocked the exit, and one slug actually penetrated the armor, slightly wounding one of the deputies.

If the lawmen had left that armored car where it was, the gang would never have escaped, but the deputies panicked and moved it out of the way. Clyde zipped the car through the opening. At the end of the road where I had been standing before I mistakenly chased Sheriff Coffey, the deputy fired and shattered a pane, blinding Blanche, but the way was clear now and the Barrow gang escaped. Several of the lawmen were wounded, but none seriously.

After another miraculous escape, the gang headed north to Iowa.

On July 24, Buck and Blanche were captured at a park in Dexter, Iowa, and on July 29, Buck Barrow died of his head wound. A month later, Blanche Barrow was returned to Platte City.

On September 3, 1933, Blanche Barrow was sentenced to ten years in prison for her part in the assault on law enforcement officers in Platte City, to serve her time at the Missouri State Prison for Women in Jefferson City.

While serving her time in prison, Blanche Barrow took pen to hand, writing a manuscript detailing her inside account of the Barrow Gang. Unfortunately, the manuscript was lost, not to be found until ten years after her death by her friend and estate executor, Lorraine Weiser. Her information was authenticated by Barrow historians John Neal Phillips and Ken Holmes in their book, *My Life with Bonnie and Clyde*, which contained much new information.

Bonnie and Clyde continued their crime wave, robbing and kidnapping in Texas throughout 1933.

On November 18, 1933, youthful gang member W. D. Jones provided a lengthy written confession to Winter R. King, assistant district attorney, after being arrested in Houston, Texas, two days earlier. Jones detailed his relationship with Bonnie Parker and Clyde Barrow and Barrow Gang members. He'd been with the gang starting in December 1932, a few days before Christmas, until shortly after the shootouts in Missouri in 1933, escape to Iowa, and capture of Buck and Blanche Barrow. Although self-serving and downplaying his role in the serious criminal actions carried on by the gang members, his firsthand account shed light on the violent personalities of Clyde Barrow and his criminal associates.

On January 16, 1934, Bonnie and Clyde, with the help of gang member James Mullen, raided the Eastham prison farm in Texas, freeing gang member and convicted murderer Raymond Hamilton and four other convicts. During the escape, one guard was killed and another guard was wounded.

On February 10, 1934, law enforcement, completely frustrated with the murderous couple "Bonnie and Clyde," hired famous retired Texas Ranger Frank Hamer to track down the couple and "kill on sight" if necessary.

A few days later, on February 12, the couple once again escaped law enforcement after a running gun battle in Reed Springs, Missouri, fleeing to Oklahoma then into Texas.

On March 7, 1934, Bonnie Parker's husband, Roy Thornton, who was serving fifty-five years in prison for his part in what became known as the "Santa Claus" robbery, attempted to escape the Oklahoma state prison, along with four other prisoners. Captured attempting to scale the prison wall, his motive for the escape attempt was attributed to his continuing love for his estranged wife, Bonnie Parker.

In the month of April 1934 alone, the "Bloody Barrows Gang" murdered Texas highway patrolmen Edward Bryan Wheeler and Holloway David Murphy near Grapevine, Texas, and Clyde Barrow was declared "Public Enemy No. 1" by the authorities.

A few days later, Clyde Barrow was accused of killing a criminal associate, Wade McNabb, over a dispute, and two days later, he murdered Constable Cal Campbell near Commerce, Oklahoma. In the same shootout, he wounded and kidnapped Police Chief Percy Boyd and later released him near Fort Scott, Kansas.

On May 6, 1934, Bonnie and Clyde were again in Dallas, Texas, visiting their relatives. This would prove to be the last time Bonnie Parker's mother would see her alive. In an emotional and tearful meeting, Bonnie handed her mother a poem she had recently written about her and Clyde's escapades entitled "The Story of Bonnie and Clyde," consisting of sixteen verses. This is the first and last verse of the poem:

You have heard the story of Jesse James, of how he lived and died.
If you still are in need of something to read, here is the story of Bonnie
    and Clyde.
Some day they will go down together; and they will bury them side by
    side.
To a few it means grief, to the law it's relief, but it's death to Bonnie and
    Clyde.

On May 18, 1934, Clyde Barrow and fellow gang members Joe Palmer, Raymond Hamilton, and Henry Methvin were indicted by a federal grand jury in Dallas, Texas, charged with the theft of US Army automatic pistols and BARS.

Henry Methvin, in January 1934, helped Clyde Barrow rob a bank in Rembrandt, Iowa. Henry's father and mother, Ivy and Ava, wanted to help their son with his charges and knew where Bonnie and Clyde were hiding out in Louisiana. They provided the information to retired Texas Ranger Frank Hamer and also helped set up an ambush.

On May 23, 1934, Bonnie Parker and Clyde Barrow ran out of luck when they were tracked down by retired Texas Ranger Frank Hamer in Louisiana and were gunned down and killed in a hail of fire, ambushed on a lonely road between Gibsland and Sailes. The spot on Sailes Road where Bonnie and Clyde were killed has been memorialized with a white granite rectangle sitting on a stone slab that reads:

> At this site May 23, 1934
> Clyde Barrow
> and
> Bonnie Parker
> were killed by
> law enforcement officials
> Erected by
> Bienville Parish Police Jury

Clyde Barrow was buried with his brother Buck in Dallas, Texas, with a simple dual headstone. Bonnie Parker was also laid to rest in Dallas, Texas, where her poetry followed her to her grave. On her headstone her short poem reads: "As the flowers are all made sweeter by the sunshine and the dew, so this old world is made brighter by the lives of folks like you."

Texas Trooper Frank Hamer was quoted not too long after the fateful ambush as saying, "I hate to bust a cap on a woman, especially when she's sitting down."

Memorabilia of Bonnie and Clyde's escapades—including weapons, the death car, Clyde's death shirt, site markers, books, movies, photographs, memoirs, and written confessions—can be found in numerous states, including a prominent display at the highway patrol headquarters in Jefferson City for all Missourians and others to visit.

As recently as September 22, 2019, it was reported by Joe Hadsall, digital editor of the *Joplin Globe* newspaper, a sawed-off shotgun used by Bonnie and Clyde in the Joplin shootout with law enforcement was sold at auction by RR Auction, based in Boston, to an anonymous bidder, along with a draft of a police wanted poster for the two outlaws and a wristwatch recovered from Clyde's body after his death. A book of poetry written by Bonnie Parker was withdrawn from the bidding before it could be sold. The winning bidder, who was passionate about the history of Joplin, said, "he was determined to make sure the shotgun remains a part of Joplin history," adding the Western Field Browning Model 30 shotgun would remain in Joplin, Missouri.

Joplin Globe Editor Hadsall reported:

> The Western Field Browning Model 30 shotgun was recovered after a 1933 gunfight at a southern Joplin apartment, which resulted in the

death's [sic] of Detective Harry McGinnis and Newton County Constable John Wesley Harryman. The gang was able to escape, but left behind supplies, including a camera with a roll of film that was developed by the Globe—those pictures were transmitted across the country and gave the public their first look at the criminals.

Detective Tom Degraff, a detective with the Joplin Police Department during that 1933 raid, kept the gun in his office; it was later gifted to him upon his retirement. The shotgun was kept by his children and grandchildren as a family heirloom until current owner Jerry Watson and his siblings decided it was time to sell it.

The gun's authenticity was verified by photo-matching it to one of the photos of Clyde Barrow posing alongside several firearms arranged in front of a car, and through De Graff registering it in 1946 with the Treasury Department. Before the auction, it was valued at $75,000.

Bonnie and Clyde are long gone, dead and buried. However, their gruesome legend lives on, and their story continues to be told.

CHAPTER SEVEN

"MACHINE GUN" KELLY
1916-1954

The Missouri Highway Patrol Public Information and Education Division located in Jefferson City at Patrol Headquarters has on display a number of historical artifacts collected or donated for their history museum. Included are a number of glass-enclosed visual wall displays of various firearms and photographs through the years and the stories of the criminals associated with each item.

One of the displays contains a large collection of handguns and long guns confiscated over the years by highway patrol seizures. Also included in this display is featured a person named George F. Barnes, a.k.a. "Machine Gun Kelly," who like many outlaws of his time committed criminal acts throughout the Midwest, including Missouri, using these type of weapons.

Born around 1900, Kelly started his criminal career as a bootlegger shortly after he dropped out of high school around 1916. He began reselling illegal whiskey he had purchased in Missouri and Kentucky.

Kelly met and married Geneva Ramsey, who was the daughter of a Memphis millionaire family who gave Kelly a parking lot and a dairy farm to operate. Despite this windfall, Kelly preferred bootlegging over a legitimate career. At twenty-four years old, he was caught committing a crime and sentenced to six months in jail. His wife Geneva divorced him, and he went to Kansas City, working for a short while at a supermarket, where he embezzled enough money to purchase a truck. He used the truck to transport illegal whiskey. He was caught selling bootlegged whiskey and went to the federal prison in Leavenworth for five years, meeting a number of bank robbers, including the notorious Frank Nash and some of Nash's associates in crime. He was paroled in 1930 and started associating with bank robbers and crooks in Minnesota, assisting in bank robberies as a tagalong.

Later in 1930, Kelly married Kathryn Thorne, an alcoholic who FBI Director J. Edgar Hoover characterized as a "cold blooded killer."

Hoover wrote in his 1936 book *Persons in Hiding*, "Kathryn Thorne Kelly was one of the most coldly deliberate criminals of my experience." He continued, "If ever there was a henpecked husband, it was George [Machine Gun] Kelly."

Historians document that Kelly was not a very proficient bank robber and very nervous, causing him to be shunned by fellow yeggs in the bank-robbing business. For a period of time, unable to find bank-robbing partners, Kelly lived in a house owned by his wife Kathryn in Fort Worth, Texas.

In January 1932, Kelly made his first attempt at kidnapping, taking an Indiana businessman named Howard Wolverton, whose name Kathryn had picked out of a phone book. Kelly had to release the man after his family was unable to pay the ransom demand.

Kelly proved to be as inept in kidnapping as he was in bank robbing; however, he would try again. Kelly eventually hooked up with bank robbers Eddie Bentz and Albert Bates, robbing banks together in several states in 1932.

Kelly and Kathryn gained the attention of an enterprising police officer named Ed Weatherford to whom Kathryn—thinking he was a corrupt individual—bragged about Kelly's criminal associates and exploits in robbing banks. He would make several undercover contacts with Kathryn over the next month or two.

On July 22, 1933, Kelly and his wife, along with Albert Bates, participated in the kidnapping of an Oklahoma oil well millionaire named Charles Urschel. After he was kidnapped at his Oklahoma residence, he was driven blindfolded from his house to a ranch outside Paradise, Texas, just north of Fort Worth, where Kathryn's mother lived with Robert "Boss" Shannon.

The FBI had developed an interest in the ranch while investigating information from the Fort Worth Police about Kelly's alleged association with bank robbers. Law enforcement arranged with a postmaster for a cover on incoming mail to the ranch.

On July 26, a Western Union messenger delivered a telegram to Joe Catlett, an oilman from Tulsa, Oklahoma, and close friend of Charles Urschel. In it were three of Urschel's business cards and a note from Urschel asking Catlett to take care of his wife. Also included was a note demanding $200,000 ransom money in return for Urshcel's safe release. A third note instructed the Urschels to place an ad in the Oklahoma newspaper and run the ad daily for a week.

E.G. Kirkpatrick—a friend of the Urschels—placed the ad. The next day, the newspaper received a letter from the kidnappers, instructing Kirkpatrick to take the evening train to Kansas City on Saturday night with the money placed in a Gladstone bag.

It further instructed Kirkpatrick to toss the bag from the train after he saw two "signal fires." If something went wrong, he was to continue to Kansas City to the Muehlebach Hotel to receive further instructions. There was also a threat that, if the ransom was not paid, Urschel would be killed, and someone very dear to the family was being watched and would also be harmed.

As instructed, Kirkpatrick headed for Kansas City, failing to drop the bag from the train after not seeing any signals on the way. He arrived in Kansas City and checked into the Muehlebach Hotel, awaiting further instructions.

Soon after, Kirkpatrick received a telegram delivered to him by a bellboy, informing him they had missed the drop.

In the early evening of Saturday, he received a phone call from a man identifying himself as "Mr. Moore," telling him to go to the LaSalle Hotel on Linwood Boulevard, where he would be met. As Kirkpatrick arrived, he walked to the hotel and was met on the sidewalk at the hotel by a man wearing a suit. It was Kelly telling Kirkpatrick he would take the bag.

He questioned the man, asking how he could be sure he had the right contact. After being told Urschel would be released in twelve hours safely at home, Kirkpatrick handed the bag to Kelly and returned to Oklahoma.

In Oklahoma, Kirkpatrick reviewed numerous mug shots at the FBI office with negative results. Had the FBI had a picture of Kelly, the identification would have been a major step in solving the kidnapping.

The FBI doubted Urschel was alive, but to their surprise, he arrived at his house at about 11:00 p.m., unharmed and happy to be alive.

On one occasion while Kelly was out of town working on the ransom notes, Kathryn had invited Weatherford to her house. While sitting on her front porch, she started naming persons her husband Kelly was associated with, including Verne Miller of Kansas City. Weatherford was aware that Miller was a suspect in the Union Station police massacre that had just occurred one month earlier on June 17, 1933.

He also noticed an Oklahoma newspaper on the front seat of a vehicle about the Urschel kidnapping and took note of red dirt caked on the wheels — Oklahoma was known as red dirt country. He was sure they were involved in the Urschel kidnapping and passed his information onto the FBI. For some reason the information was not immediately pursued by the FBI agent who received the tip.

This was the last time that Kelly would come to the attention of the FBI, who learned from Fort Worth local law enforcement authorities that Kelly was proficient in the use of a submachine gun. This was possibly where his nickname came about and later promoted by J. Edgar Hoover and the FBI.

Although tired, Urschel answered questions posed by the agent. He said he was blindfolded and couldn't identify anyone. The FBI agents concentrated on Urschel's memory of his ride to the place he was held. He proved to have an excellent recall of sounds and weather, including rain patterns he had encountered during his frightful trip. He felt he was taken to a farm. He had heard roosters crow. The combination of Urshcel's recall and the corroboration of the FBI's scientific approach proved significant in locating the farm in Texas.

Meanwhile, the Fort Worth and Dallas police pursued leads, as they felt certain the Kellys and the Shannons were somehow involved in the Urschel kidnapping. Eventually acting on the local police tips, the FBI devised a scheme to get into the Shannon ranch with the help of a local barber who knew the Shannons as customers.

On August 12, 1933, the FBI and Texas police were invited into the house by Boss Shannon's son and observed that Urschel's recall of the interior of the house fit the house to a tee, as well as the sounds Urschel at reported coming from the ranch.

The FBI and local officers descended on the ranch, and Charles Urschel joined them. As they entered, they encountered "Boss" Shannon, who asked in a loud voice, "What do you think you're doing here?" Urschel, hearing this, said that "this was the man who was guarding me. I recognize the voice!"

As an added bonus, they searched the rear yard and found notorious bank robber Harvey Bailey sleeping in a cot in the backyard. He was arrested. They also arrested the Shannon's son Armon, who broke down under questioning and told them everything, naming Kelly and Albert Bates as the kidnappers. Boss Shannon also confessed to his part in the scheme. Unfortunately, the Kellys and Albert Bates had left town.

The hunt was on for the kidnappers. Albert Bates was arrested first. He was observed on a train bound for Denver by an alert American Express investigator who had been on the trail of Bates since 1932 for passing bad traveler's checks. The investigator notified Denver Police, who arrested Bates as he arrived.

The hunt for the Kellys got off to a fast start as a nationwide alert was put out. The Kellys first drove to St. Paul after releasing Urschel and laundered some of the ransom money then drove to Cleveland, Ohio, where they learned the outlaws who were laundering the money were arrested. They headed to Chicago, Illinois, then to Des Moines, learning that Kathryn's mother had been arrested at the Shannon Ranch.

They then drove to West Texas in search of a lawyer for Kathryn's mother, and they buried the money at the ranch of Kathryn's uncle Cas Coleman. Kathryn went to Dallas in search of a lawyer, and Kelly took off to Mississippi, leaving a note with Coleman that instructed Kathryn to meet him. She followed in search of Kelly, who went to Biloxi, Mississippi, and checked into a motel where he cashed a number of American Express cashier checks. The clerk recognized him and called the FBI. Kelly learned they were on to him and purchased a bus ticket to Memphis, leaving his luggage and a loaded .45 caliber pistol behind. Kelly then spent time in Texas, meeting up with Kathryn.

Feeling the heat, they packed up and headed to Chicago, taking Kathryn's daughter Geraldine with them. While in Chicago, Kelly was able to purchase a different vehicle, and they left Chicago just ahead of the FBI.

They arrived in Memphis, where, on September 26, 1933, Kelly and Kathryn were arrested by FBI agents and officers from the Memphis Police Department. On October 12, 1933, they both were tried in Oklahoma, convicted, and sentenced to life in prison for the Urschel kidnapping. Kelly went first to Leavenworth then to Alcatraz when it opened.

Kelly was the first national known fugitive the FBI had ever captured, and J. Edgar Hoover talked and wrote about the "Machine Gun Kelly" episode for years to come. Hoover glorified Kelly as making the statement "Don't shoot, G-Men"—the first time the term was heard. It was later learned that Kathryn, not Kelly, had made the statement to an FBI agent who was assisting in their arrest. She uttered, "Honey, I guess it's all up for us. The G-Men won't ever give us a break. I've been living in dread of this."

The nickname "Machine Gun" was given to him by newspaper reporters after they learned a machine gun was taken into custody at the ranch where

Urschel was held. It was traced to a pawnshop, where the records documented the weapon was purchased by Kathryn Kelly for her husband George Kelly.

On July 18, 1954, George F. Barnes, a.k.a. George "Machine Gun" Kelly, died in Leavenworth Prison. Kathryn Kelly died in Oklahoma in 1984.

CHAPTER EIGHT

MISSOURI MOBSTER INFLUENCE IN THE NEVADA CASINO INDUSTRY 1947-1985

A book about the history of Missouri mobsters would not be complete without a chapter detailing their infiltration and influence of the Nevada casino industry, especially the casinos in Las Vegas. It takes very little imagination to understand the association between Las Vegas and mobsters throughout the United States.

Benjamin "Bugsy" Siegel is considered by most researchers to be the visionary of the Las Vegas Strip. He was a New York mobster who used East Coast mob money to finance the construction of the Flamingo, the first luxury hotel-casino on what is now known as the Strip.

"Bugsy" Siegel, seeing the cash profit potential, "skimmed" money from the mob loan proceeds, leading to his untimely murder on June 20, 1947. This ended his hopes to profit during his lifetime from the eventual Flamingo and Las Vegas success story. However, fellow mobsters throughout the country saw a potential gold mine, and many wanted in on the action. It didn't take long for the mobsters and mobster attorneys from Kansas City and St. Louis to move in on the take.

EFFORTS TO CONTROL MOB INFLUENCE

In 1950, Senator Estes Kefauver of Tennessee, a freshman politician with presidential ambitions, "organized a national investigation of organized criminal activity including gambling." Sally Denton and Roger Morris, in their book *The Money and the Power,* commented on the hearings:

> It was a full-blown investigation of what was termed organized crime in interstate commerce in the United States. It was to be the first—and last—of its kind. Both Congress and the White House worked feverishly behind the scenes to emasculate the investigation. Not until a sensational gangland double murder in Kansas City, Missouri . . . could Kefauver break the impasse in authorizing the committee. (Denton 81)

The two victims of the homicide were Kansas City mob bosses Charlie Binaggio and Charlie Gargotta, found shot to death inside the Democratic Club located at 720 Truman Road. Through a review of the crime scene, it was evident the two victims knew their killers, and it was considered a hit ordered by the Mob.

The double homicide in his hometown was an embarrassment to Missouri-born President Harry Truman. He proclaimed he had no association with the mob boss Binaggio, hoping the coverage would just die down. It did not. The *Kansas City Star* and the *Times* newspapers provided extensive reporting on the double homicide.

Retired FBI agent Bill Ousley, in his well-researched book *Open City,* wrote about the murders:

> President Truman's reaction to the furor in his hometown was to side step the murders. His spokesman proclaimed Truman had no association of any kind with Binaggio, and thus had no concern about the case. On the other hand, his political advisors had other thoughts. They feared the killings could become a red-hot political issue causing grave harm to Democrats unless the administration employed every means available to solve the case. . . . Missouri interests in Washington D.C. were aware of Truman's contempt for Binaggio, and his support of Jim Pendergast in resisting Binaggio's political aspirations. . . .
>
> Truman and Democrats, prior to the double murders in Kansas City, were opposed to the idea of such a committee, and their opposition was even stronger after the murders. . . . The administration favored a rival initiative by the Senate Interstate Commerce Committee, anticipated to be far less intrusive, as its inquiry was limited to two interstate gambling bills sent to Congress by the Justice Department.
>
> When news stories focused on the Truman administration's impeding the Kefauver initiative the tide turned. In what the *Kansas City Times* newspaper described as a 'surprise move,' Democrat leadership called for an all-out investigation of interstate crime and gambling syndicates. . . . The *Times* also described the decision as a move seen as recognition of the implications of the Binaggio slaying.' Out of political turmoil and gangland murder the Kefauver Committee was born. (Ousley 293, 294)

The Kefauver Hearings, which started in Kansas City in the summer of 1950, were televised and in "its novel, compelling infancy captured the imagination of a transfixed nation." (Denton 82) More than 30 million people watched. "Over the next ten months his committee would hold sessions in fourteen cities, travel 52,000 miles, hear 800 witnesses and file four reports." (Denton 82) As the committee continued its investigation through the summer and fall of 1950, the primary revelations seemed to converge on the influence of organized crime in the Nevada casino industry, and "in November of 1950 Las Vegas nervously awaited the visit of the famous senator from Tennessee." (Denton 85)

During these hearings in Vegas, the topic of the infamous "skimming" of money from the casino profits and the loss of federal taxes became a hot topic.

"You had to be deaf, dumb and blind not to know about the skim," a Strip operator said of the era throughout the 1950s. (Denton 109)

As the committee continued its inquiries, Max Jaben, who had his hand in the Nevada gaming industry, became part of Nick Civella's trusted inner circle and acted on Civella's behalf on casino matters.

The hearings brought about much conversation regarding the Mob's influence in the Nevada gaming industry and the extent of illegal gambling throughout the United States. Mob bosses and mob associates were subpoenaed to testify in each of the cities the committee visited. Kansas City and St. Louis were no exception. This caused concerns for the mob bosses.

In the end, the hearings came and went, the Nevada casino industry continued its amazing growth, and the mob bosses increased their interests in being a part of the growth and the desire for the profits.

THE KANSAS CITY MOB INFLUENCE

In 1959, the Gaming Control Act was enacted in Nevada, due to concerns of mob involvement in the Nevada casino industry. In 1960 the Nevada Gaming Commission Control Board of Directors, recognizing syndicate crime organizations' efforts to control the casino industry, created the List of Excluded Persons, which soon became known as the Black Book. Entry into the Black Book banned a person for life from all licensed gambling establishments in the state of Nevada. The emergence of the Black Book centered around the conflicts of organized crime interests in Las Vegas and the state's regulatory bodies' desires to address the problem. It's interesting to note the original List of Excluded Persons released on June 13, 1960, identified only eleven mobsters in the United States associated with organized crime. Of those eleven, two were from Kansas City: mob boss Nicholas Civella and his brother Carl James "Corky" Civella.

In the first formal hearing involving the purpose of placing these individuals in the book, the Nevada State Deputy Attorney General wrote in part: "Considering the awesome sanctions that befall an individual who is included in the list and the numerical paucity of individuals who have actually undergone inclusion, I think it is more than fair to conclude that it takes a very special type of person to be considered for candidacy." He continued: "We might even consider the individuals whose names are currently on the list to be members of a very exclusive, if infamous club."

It's not surprising the Civellas were included in the charter member list, considering that Nick Civella, in February 1960, a few months before the list was announced, traveled to Las Vegas with several other Kansas City mobsters and tried to buy into the Las Vegas Riviera Hotel and Casino, only to be refused by the officials of the casino. Furious over this refusal, Civella threatened one of the owners, suggesting someone could get hurt if his offer wasn't considered. (Ousley 224) Instead of getting a piece of the action, Nick Civella was visited by the Las Vegas Police, who told him to leave the city and to never return.

This major setback did not stop Nick Civella's efforts to get a piece of a Las Vegas casino. Civella owned Roy Lee Williams, a major player in the Teamsters and their lucrative Central States Pension Fund, and Civella fully intended to use the fund's money as loans to buy in through hidden ownerships.

In 1962, Frank Caracciolo, the owner of the Flight Deck Hotel and a Kansas City native, was having financial problems and sought a loan from the Teamsters' Central States Pension Fund through Nick Civella and Roy Williams. Several meetings took place. Others involved in the deal were mobster figures Gaetano Lococo, Max Jaben, and Morris "Snag" Klein.

The arrangements didn't go too well at first. However, after several years had passed, the pension fund approved a loan of $5.5 million. In the process, payouts of illegal kickbacks and finder's fees amounting to over $500,000 were parsed out to the players involved. Just when everything seemed to be in place finally in the 1960s, the Nevada Gaming Commission denied Frank Caracciolo license, forcing him to sell to investor Howard Hughes, taking the control away from Nick Civella.

Not surprisingly, federal agents learned through intercepted conversations that Nick Civella and the Kansas City Mob had other hidden interests in the Monte Carlo Hotel and Casino in Lake Tahoe, Nevada, and reportedly were receiving skimmed proceeds in monthly payments. The feds also learned that mob boss Nick Civella for several years was a member of the Desert Inn Country Club in Las Vegas, where he frequently stayed, a guest of hotel management even though he was listed in the Black Book.

Throughout the 1960s and early 1970s, the Kansas City Mob, led by Civella influence and Teamster Union funds, developed interests in the Frontier, Plainsman, and Riviera hotels and casinos. Federal authorities were frustrated for years trying to prove these hidden interests existed until electronic surveillances were legalized and utilized very effectively in the mid-1970s by the Kansas City Organized Crime Strike Force, the FBI, other federal law enforcement agencies, and the Kansas City Police Intelligence Unit. A federal investigation conducted by this multiagency law enforcement group over several years developed very strong federal cases against numerous mobsters in Missouri and several other states.

During these investigations, it was learned that, from 1973 to 1979, Nick Civella had teamed up with mob bosses from Chicago, Milwaukee, and Cleveland to gain hidden interests in several hotels and casinos, securing loans using the Teamsters Central States Pension Fund. These establishments included the Tropicana, the Stardust, the Marina Hotel, and the Fremont, all placed under the Argent Corporation, under the control of an unsuspecting businessman named Allen Glick from San Diego, California. Little did Glick know his corporation was actually being run by the mob boss from Kansas City. At least $1,310,000 was skimmed from the Argent Corporation casinos between 1976 and 1979. In 1978, Allen Glick was forced to get out and mob boss Civella took control of the skimming of large sums of money from the Tropicana Hotel slot machine profits.

THE FALL OF THE KANSAS CITY "OUTFIT"

The following detailed account of how the mob Outfit in Kansas City, as well as the mob Outfits in Chicago, Milwaukee, Cleveland, and Las Vegas, were dismantled is provided from information contained in *Mobsters in our Midst,* written by retired FBI agent and noted crime author Bill Ousley. His book details the investigations and convictions that resulted from the efforts of all the dedicated law enforcement officials assigned to the Organized Crime Task Force in Kansas City and the dedicated United States Attorney Offices located throughout the United States involved in these investigations.

After years of intense investigations, the Organized Crime Strike Force decided in December 1978 that it was time to take the Kansas City mob's gambling operation down.

Plans were made in January 1979 to execute a number of search warrants in conjunction with a delivery of skimmed money being delivered to Kansas City by the courier Carl Caruso on February 14, St. Valentine's Day, 1979.

Upon Caruso's arrival at the KCI airport, he was stopped by federal agents, served with a search warrant, and searched. Seized from his blazer was $80,000 tied in two bundles called "sandwiches"—gambling markers of money rightfully owed to a Las Vegas casino.

Simultaneously, the task force teams searched the personal vehicles and homes of mobsters Nick Civella, Corky Civella, Carl DeLuna, Pete Tamburello, Joe Ragusa, Vince Abbott, Charles Moretina, and William Cammisano Jr.

Recovered from Nick Civella and Cork Civella was $135,000 in cash, $45,000 in certificates of deposit, forty loose diamonds, financial records, and papers with coded names, including percentages associated with the sharing of skimmed proceeds.

The largest seizure was recovered from the residence of Carl "Tuffy" DeLuna. Taken into custody were $60,000 in cash and numerous detailed proceeds of skimmed money, identities of mob figures, and evidence of high-level meetings held in various locations. Also seized were four loaded handguns.

In the search at Pete Tamburello's house, the investigator found a safe deposit box key, records, a notebook, and five handguns. Four of them were loaded. The safe deposit box contained another $10,000.

In all, the searches resulted in the recovery of almost $300,000 cash, various weapons, ski masks, a police scanner, walkie-talkies, binoculars, blackjacks, handcuffs, a tracking device, a roster of employees of DEA, and bulletproof vests that had been stolen from DEA and ATF government vehicles in 1978.

It would take two more years of effort by the Kansas City task force members to compile the evidence for the indictments and eventual convictions of all coconspirators involved.

Nick Civella had his parole revoked and was sent to federal prison on June 11, 1979.

On November 5, 1981, the first indictments were returned regarding the skimming from the Tropicana Casino. Those indicted were Nick and "Corky" Civella, DeLuna, Moretina, Tamburello, Caruso, and Joe Agosto. The indictments also charged Billy Caldwell and Don Shepard, officials of the Tropicana, and Anthony Chiavola, a Chicago policeman who was also a courier of skimmed money from Kansas City to Chicago.

The US attorneys in Kansas City prosecuting the case hoped to have Allen Dorfman and Joe Agosto as witnesses for the government. Dorfman was shot several times and killed in January 1983 by the Mob, who had feared he would testify against other mob figures.

Joe Agosto was also in prison on unrelated convictions and, fearing he would be killed when he got out, agreed to testify and become the star witness in the Tropicana trial.

In all, eight mob defendants were convicted, with sentences ranging from thirty years in prison down to probation. Agosto died before he could be sentenced, and Tamburello was acquitted.

In the next phase, indictments were returned on October 11, 1983, charging conspiracy to control and skim from the four casinos in the Argent Corporation. Those named as defendants were Corky Civella, DeLuna, and Pete Tamburello from Kansas City; Joe Aiuppa, Jack Cerone, Angelo LaPietra, and Joe Lombardo from Chicago; Anthony Chiavola Sr. and Jr.; Milton Rockman from Cleveland; Frank Balistrieri, Milwaukee mob boss, and his two sons, Joe and John—both attorneys—Tony Spilotro living in Las Vegas, and Carl Thomas from Cleveland.

Several of those indicted pled guilty. Spilotro was severed to be tried separately, and the remaining seven went to trial. On January 21, 1986, five were found guilty. Joe and John Balistrieri were found not guilty.

The five who were convicted received sentences ranging from fourteen to twenty-eight-and-a-half years.

Those who pled guilty received sentences of five to sixteen years. Spilotro was murdered gangland-style before he could be tried.

In 1984, five members of the Nick Civella-led mob criminal enterprise were indicted and charged with the federal Racketeering Influence and Corrupt Organization (RICO) Act. They were Nick Civella, Corky Civella, Tony Civella, Carl DeLuna, and Charles Morentina. All pled guilty to the charges.

Fortunately, the intense federal and state investigations conducted in Kansas City, Chicago, Cleveland, and Los Angeles (code-named Strawman and supported with court-ordered legal wiretaps) resulted in the eventual conviction of Kansas City mobsters Nick Civella, Carl "Corky" Civella, Carl DeLuna, Pete Tamburello, Joe Ragusa, Vince Abbott, Charles Moretina, William Cammisano Jr., and Tony Civella. In addition, numerous mobsters from Chicago, Cleveland, and Milwaukee were convicted, along with Teamsters official Roy

Williams and others, finally ending the Kansas City mob influence in the Las Vegas casino industry.

THE ST. LOUIS MOB INFLUENCE

Now, we will take a look at the history of St. Louis mobsters and mobster attorneys' influence in the Nevada casino industry, which is just as intriguing. In doing so, we will also document the long-standing and ongoing connections between the St. Louis Kansas City mobsters, as well as their connections with mob bosses located in other large cities throughout the United States. We will also look at their intimate attachment to the Teamsters Union's Central States Pension Fund monies, which were available to them for large loans to fund investments in the Nevada casino industry.

The primary players involved in the moves to gain control in the Las Vegas hotel and casino industry from St. Louis in the early years of development in the 1950s included mob attorneys Morris Shenker, Sorkis Webbe Sr., and Webbe's brother, St. Louis politician Pete Webbe.

When the Dunes opened in 1955, the licensed owners were Sid Wyman, Kewpie Rich, Butch Goldstein, Major Riddle, Bob Rice, and Howie Engel, according to Ed Reid and Ovid Demaris in *The Green Felt Jungle*.

Morris Shenker, a noted attorney for the Mob and the Teamsters Union, was also an owner of the Dunes with Ray Patriarca, the capo of the New England Cosa Nostra.

Shenker came to Las Vegas the year the Dunes opened but initially was an investor in the Royal Nevada. After Wyman died, Shenker took over at the Dunes, according to Sally Denton and Roger Morris in *The Money and the Power*.

Steven Brill documents in *The Teamsters* the Mob's involvement in the purchase of hotels and casinos in Las Vegas during the years 1959 to 1961, using the Central States, Southeast, and Southwest Areas Pension Funds. He wrote:

> Also, during the years 1959–1961 the Fund took the plunge into Las Vegas. The major loan recipient was a group headed by Morris 'Moe' Dalitz, a well-known former bootlegger who had led a mostly Jewish organized-crime group in Cleveland before moving to Las Vegas in the middle '50s. Eventually, Dalitz and three partners swung another large series of Fund loans, through Dorfman, to build La Costa. But in 1959 their first loan was to build the Sunrise Hospital in Las Vegas. Then beginning in 1960 Dalitz borrowed money to finance the Stardust Hotel and Country Club, the Fremont Hotel, and the Desert Inn, all in Las Vegas. (Brill 210)

These properties were under the control of Shenker, who, in the 1960s, gained national attention for the defense of Teamster boss Jimmy Hoffa, and was dubbed by *Life* magazine in 1967 as the "foremost lawyer of the mob in the U.S."

In 1970, *Life* magazine published an investigative report accusing Morris Shenker and St. Louis mayor Alfonso Cervantes of having "personal ties to the underworld," even while Shenker was head of the St. Louis Commission on Crime and Law Enforcement.

Ronald Farrell and Carole Cas wrote about Chicago mobster Anthony Spilotro in *The Black Book and the Mob*. He gained national interest when Joe Pesci played a fictionalized version of Spilotro in the 1995 movie *Casino*. Spilotro arrived in Las Vegas in the early 1970s to run the Chicago Mob's interests. He began holding court at the poker area of Morris Shenker's Dunes Casino, which was heavily indebted at the time to the Teamsters Central States Pension Fund. Spilotro spent most of 1975 there before regulatory pressure was put on Morris Shenker to get him out. (Farrell 73)

John McGuire once wrote in the *St. Louis Post-Dispatch*:

> Shenker represented organized—and disorganized—crime figures.
>
> Shenker also represented Teamster Leader Jimmy Hoffa. All this attracted the attention of the Kefauver Committee, the IRS and the FBI. There was also his involvement with the Teamsters and his Las Vegas connections. There were union slush funds to probe and casino activities. . . .
>
> Missouri Senator Ed Dowd called Shenker 'the most investigated man in the country.' . . .
>
> It would be difficult to estimate how much we spent trying to get Morris. The Government came the closest during this brilliant attorney's final days on earth. He was indicted by a Federal Grand Jury in Vegas, suspected of concealing funds from the IRS. . . .
>
> 'Shenker's life was like something out of a Mario Puzo novel; or a classic from his native Russia. Such were the twists and turns. The richness of characters.'

In 1974, Nick Civella of Kansas City visited Las Vegas and stayed in Shenker's Dunes Hotel, in violation of his Black Book suspension. He received VIP treatment, causing the Nevada regulators to take action and fine Shenker and the Dunes $10,000.

It was about this period of time that Allen Glick, the wonder boy of investment in Vegas casinos, entered the picture. As reported by Steven Brill in *The Teamsters*:

> The big Glick loan of $62,700,000 was made in May 1974. The money would be used to buy out the Recrion Corporation—owner of the Stardust and the Fremont—from Delbert Coleman and the other stockholders through a tender offer. Originally, former Hoffa lawyer and frequent loan recipient Morris Shenker, who already owned the Dunes

Hotel in Las Vegas, was going to make the deal with Coleman, also using a Dorfman-sponsored pension fund loan. But Shenker backed out at the last minute and Glick was allowed to come in.

The filing Glick made with the Securities Exchange Commission at the time of this loan and his purchase of Recrion showed that he was paying a $421,000 finder's fee for the fund loan to someone named Todd Derlachter. It turned out that Derlachter was a Southern Californian whose name had come up in various organized-crime investigations. Why Shenker suddenly dropped out of the deal, and why Glick needed to pay anyone a finder's fee for the loan, when he had already borrowed from the Fund and from Dorfman in the past and therefore didn't need anyone to 'find' the Fund for him, were two of the more perplexing questions associated with the deal.

Three years later a lawyer involved directly in the deal tied the two mysteries together and provided a plausible solution to both, based, he said, on firsthand knowledge. 'Shenker had to get out,' he explained 'because Dorfman and the others at the Fund wanted him out. They were afraid of all the bad publicity because of all the other loans he had [more than $100,0000,000] at the time for the Dunes and other properties] and because of his past reputation. Also, he had been Hoffa's lawyer, and with Hoffa trying to come back [this was 1974] they were worried about Shenker's loyalty. I heard Dorfman say this. . . . So Bill Presser remembered Glick and said how clean he was and everything. "Let's give it to that nice kid, what's-his-name," he probably said.' The records show that Derlachter was made a $10,000 a month 'consultant' to Glick in addition to getting the finder's fee. The same inside source explained that, 'We told Shenker we wouldn't give it to him, but that he could deliver it to Glick and take something out for himself and his people. So Shenker had Derlachter contact Glick. . . . I think Derlachter's payment [the finder's fee] went to Shenker and to the mob guys Shenker was involved with. That way Shenker didn't feel so bad.' This last part of the explanation is made more plausible by the fact that Derlachter was known to be an associate of Shenker's. (Brill, 236–237)

I will now turn our attention to Sorkis Webbe Sr., with information drawn from the *Las Vegas Sun* newspaper, the Nevada Gaming Commission, the county licensing board, and *Life* magazine.

The property on which the Aladdin long operated consistently failed for decades. The English Tudor-style Tallyho Motel—a resort without gaming—opened on that South Las Vegas Boulevard site in 1962 and closed in October 1963. In 1964 it became the King's Crown Tallyho Inn and failed less than six months after it was denied a gaming license.

In 1966, Milton Prell purchased the resort. Its Arabian Nights theme befitted its name, the Aladdin. By 1969 Parvin Dohrman [Parvin-Dorhmann] Corp. took over the Aladdin. In 1972, using the name Recrion Corp., the Aladdin was sold to veteran casino executive Sam Diamond, St. Louis politician Peter Webbe, attorney Sorkis Webbe and Richard Daly for $5 million, the Las Vegas Sun reported in 1979.

Under the Webbes, the hotel got a $60 million face-lift, including the addition of a 19-story tower and a new 7,500-seat performing arts center.

Sorkis Webbe was a longtime mob attorney and it did not take long for the Aladdin to get tainted as a mob joint.

In August 1979, James Abraham, Charles Goldfarb, James Tamer, and Edward Monazym were convicted by a federal grand jury in Detroit of conspiring to allow hidden owners to exert control over the Aladdin.

The Nevada Gaming Commission then closed the hotel but U.S. District Judge Harry Claiborne opened it three hours later, saying he had 'special powers' as a federal judge. (lasvegassun.com/history/mob-ties, accessed January 28, 2020)

The Webbes had their share of run-ins with the law. On December 31, 1970, I was a detective with the St. Louis Police Department Bomb and Arson Unit. On that New Year's Eve, I received an assignment to investigate an intentionally set fire at the Congress Hotel, located at 6543 Chippewa in St. Louis. We learned Sorkis Webbe Jr., a high school student, was hosting a New Year's Eve party at the hotel, and we suspected his party was involved in setting the fire.

During the investigation, Sorkis Webbe Sr. made arrangements for me to interview his son at his home on Rhodes Street in St. Louis. I conducted the interview with Junior in the presence of Webbe Sr.. Early into the interview, I could tell I wasn't going to get any information or admissions of involvement in the fire. Junior denied any knowledge or involvement in the fire, and the interview was discontinued. I left with a firsthand understanding of how the Mob worked in St. Louis.

More information from the *Las Vegas Sun* about Sorkis Webbe Sr.:

In 1976, he was acquitted of tax evasion charges stemming from losses he claimed in a now defunct Hollywood film company.

Webbe's attorney argued that the Justice Department's organized crime strike force in St. Louis was "out to get" Webbe, although it had little or no evidence against him.

On March 4, 1975, St. Louis mob boss Tony "G" Giordano was added to the Nevada Black Book after he was convicted of federal racketeering charges arising out of his hidden interests in the Frontier Casino in Las Vegas, Nevada, along with Detroit mobsters Antony Joseph Zerilli and Michael Santo Polizzi.

The Frontier Hotel and Casinos was owned at the time by an ailing Howard Hughes, and the mobsters were able to penetrate his organization.

On Sept. 5, 1979, the Aladdin Hotel Corporation., Sorkis Webbe, and Del Webb Corporation were indicted along with five individuals on charges of conspiracy to defraud the Teamsters Union during the 1975–76 Aladdin re-modeling, according to the *Sun*.

The indictment alleged that subcontractors were forced to pay kickbacks during the Aladdin construction project, including to Webbe, who allegedly got $1 million.

A month later, five Clark County commissioners, sitting as the County Licensing Board, agreed to revoke the Aladdin's slot and unrestricted gaming license.

By Oct. 25, 1979, entertainer Johnny Carson and former Del Webb executive Ed Nigro offered to buy the Aladdin but were rejected, opening the door for entertainer Wayne Newton to buy the resort. That ended mob influence over the property. (lasvegassun.com/history/mob-ties, accessed January 28, 2020)

On November 23, 1983, Sorkis Webbe Jr., was indicted by a federal grand jury the same day he was sworn in as Seventh Ward Alderman in St. Louis. He was charged with harboring a federal fugitive, David Leisure. Leisure had been indicted earlier in April 1983.

In January 1984, Sorkis Webbe Jr. was sentenced to twenty-six years in prison on charges of corruption, vote fraud, obstruction of justice, and harboring a fugitive. In 1985, Sorkis Webbe Sr. died of natural causes.

According to government documents filed in 1985 to oppose defense efforts to throw out the electronically recorded conversations monitored by FBI Agents, Sorkis Webb Sr. had an interest in a casino in the Bahamas and was skimming $100,000 from casinos profits.

In one conversation, Sorkis Webbe Jr. said his father was the "goose that laid the golden egg for the St. Louis La Cosa Nostra."

The conversations also revealed Webbe Sr. was involved in the casino with the Detroit La Cosa Nostra in the Bahamas and that the money used to purchase the casino came from the profits of the sale of the Aladdin Hotel in Las Vegas by Webbe and the Detroit Mob.

At a federal court jury trial in St. Louis in 1985, it was revealed through the testimony of John Ramo that St. Louis mob boss Tony Giordano, Sorkis Webbe Sr., Jimmy Michaels Sr., and mob enforcer Paul Leisure had hidden interests in the Aladdin. Leisure told Ramo they were to share in the illegal interests after Michaels was killed. That was one of the reasons Michaels was killed in a car bombing in 1980.

St. Louis Post-Dispatch reporter Ron Lawrence followed that trial and reported about it in an article titled "Casino Was Motive in Killing," published on February 28, 1985. He reported that United States prosecuting attorney Tom Dittmeier, in his opening statement, told about the Mob's hidden interest in the Aladdin Hotel and Casino. Lawrence's reporting follows:

> . . . that hidden, illegal interests in a casino had been held by Paul Leisure; Michaels; the late Anthony Giordano, a mob boss; Sorkis J. Webbe, Sr., a hotel owner, lawyer and political figure; and Arthur Berne, a rackets boss in Metro East. But he did not elaborate.

Paul Leisure's interest in the Aladdin demonstrates his stature in the underworld here, authorities on organized crime have said. In numerous other instances of mob infiltration of casinos in Nevada, they said, only the upper echelon of the underworld has been permitted to participate in hidden ownership.

Ownership of the Aladdin was divided among interests in St. Louis and Detroit. The Aladdin's principal owner of record and officer was Peter J. Webbe, a former deputy license collector in St. Louis and a brother of Sorkis Webbe. Sorkis Webbe was the Aladdin's general counsel.

JUSTICE IS SERVED

In similar fashion to those in Kansas City, the successful law enforcement investigations and court actions, along with the deaths of Morris Shenker and Sorkis Webbe, Sr., ended the St. Louis Mob's influence in the Nevada casino industry in the 1980s. I hope readers are left with a better understanding of how the Mob operated when they controlled the casino industry.

The next two chapters, "Mobster Violence East Missouri Style" and "Mobster Violence West Missouri Style," will complete the trilogy of the underworld, gangland, and mobster history of Missouri in the 1900s, while providing readers with an even more thorough understanding of this subculture of American society.

CHAPTER NINE

MOBSTER CRIME, VIOLENCE, AND JUSTICE, EAST MISSOURI STYLE 1920-2002

There are several common denominators associated with all mobster hits and bombings occurring in Missouri over the years. They all involved individual organized crime figures; they all involved the use of firearms or explosives; the motives behind the violence were almost always related to wars between mobster factions, revenge, desires to infiltrate local labor unions and politicians, and occasionally the need to silence a fellow mobster. The criminal violations on the federal level are all under the jurisdiction of the Bureau of ATF, requiring their investigative involvement. So was the case of the mob violence occurring in the St. Louis area in the 1960s, 1970s, and 1980s as outlined in this chapter.

Information for this chapter was obtained from true crime researchers, the ATF agents who investigated these cases (including, in some instances, your author during his years in law enforcement at the state and federal levels), and from the files of the ATF offices in St. Louis, Springfield, and Kansas City, Missouri. Information was also drawn from the state and local police and sheriff's department officers' files and reports and from the various newspapers that covered and reported on the investigations.

EARLY HISTORY

Gangster and mob violence in the St. Louis area in the early 1900s was caused by several gangs, their gang members, and gang associates. The gangs of most notoriety were the Egan's Rats, the Cuckoo Gang, the Hogan Gang, the Russo Gang, the Santino/Pillow Gang, the Green Dagoes Gang, the Shelton Gang, and the Birger Gang. Collectively, they spanned a reign of crime and corruption between 1900 and the 1940s.

St. Louis native David Waugh, in his two books *Egan's Rats* and *The Gangs of St. Louis: Men of Respect*, and authors William Helmer and Rick Mattix, in their book *The Complete Public Enemy Almanac* separately documented the activities of gang members and mobsters who were from St. Louis and moved to and operated in other cities in the United States.

The demise of these criminal characters and their group was the result of prison sentences, natural deaths, and victims of death caused by underworld homicide. As pointed out in the introduction chapter, between 1900 and 1932 alone, these gangs were responsible for no fewer than 200 murders and untold numbers of injuries. The national media of the era seemed to focus on under-world activities of East Coast mobsters, giving little or no attention to the influ-ence the St. Louis mobsters inflicted on numerous East Coast mob-controlled cities from Chicago to New York.

This is a false impression and far from the actual facts. To support this posi-tion, I present to the reader the following case facts and evidence documented by these crime researchers. Their research confirms that no fewer than twenty St. Louis mobsters and gangsters relocated to mob cities from Illinois all the way to the East Coast, mostly in the 1920s. They were motivated by greed, revenge, bootlegging opportunities, and the desire to join existing underworld organiza-tions or to establish their own organization and capitalize on enormous illegal profits. Examples are as follows:

John Reid—Born in Kansas City and a member of the Egan's Rats Gang of St. Louis in the early 1900s. He went east to Detroit, Michigan in the early '20s and joined up with the notorious Purple Gang. He was a major distributor of illegal liquor and established himself as a major player in Detroit. He was mur-dered by a rival gang member on December 25, 1926.

Max "Big Maxey" Greenberg—He joined in with the Egan's Rats and was convicted of robbing freight train cars in Danville, Illinois. He went to the fed-eral prison in Leavenworth, Kansas, to serve his time. With the help of Willie Egan and Senator Mike Kinney, he was released early and returned to St. Louis. He double-crossed Willie Egan after his release and had to get out of town.

He moved to New York in the 1920s and became involved in rum-running operations with East Coast mobsters "Waxey" Gordon and Arnold Rothstein, rising to a position of lieutenant in the mob organization. He was murdered in Elizabeth, New Jersey, in 1933.

Anthony Spicuzza And Anthony "Shorty" Russo—Members of the Green Dagoes in St. Louis, both traveled to Chicago and joined up with the Aiello Gang, who were a rival gang fighting Al Capone. They were machine-gunned to death on a Chicago street on August 10, 1927, when Capone got word they were there to kill him.

Fred "Killer" Burke—A member of the Egan's Rats. He relocated to Detroit in the summer of 1917 and joined in with the Purple Gang, involved in snatch racket kidnappings, bank robberies, and professional killings, murdering several rivals in Detroit. He moved to Chicago and joined in with Al Capone, becoming the main shooter in the St. Valentine's Day Massacre in Chicago. He also com-mitted the machine-gun murder of Frankie Yale, mob boss in New York, all at the direction of Al Capone and Frank Nitti.

Claude Maddox [Aka John Moore]—An Egan's Rat who went to Chicago in the early '20s and became a main player in the Al Capone syndicate. He ran Capone's Circus Gang and brought the St. Louis Burke Winkler group into the Capone Organization. He organized the St. Valentine's Day Massacre with Fred Burke. He died of natural causes in his Riverside home.

Willie Haney—An Egan's Rats gang member who moved to Chicago and became a prominent member of the Capone Criminal syndicate along with Claude Maddox.

Charles Joseph "Big Fitz" Fitzgerald—Born in St. Louis in 1877, a bank robber who took his mob activities to St. Paul, Minnesota, and Toledo, Ohio. He was involved in the kidnapping of brewing magnet William Hamm and was convicted of the kidnapping and sent to Alcatraz then to Leavenworth, where he died in prison in 1945.

Giovanni "John" Mirabella—A member of the Green Dagoes in St. Louis, he relocated to Toledo, Ohio, where he murdered bootlegger Jackie Kennedy, with the help of Joe "The Wop" English and Russel Syracuse. They were charged with the murders; however, they vanished. The three were also accused of the murder of newscaster Gerald Buckley at the LaSalle Hotel in Toledo Ohio. Mirabella settled in Youngstown, Ohio, under the alias Paul Mangine and was protected from arrest by the local underworld until his death of natural causes in 1955.

Peter Joseph Licavoli And Thomas "Yonnie" Licavoli—Members of the Green Dagoes in St. Louis and introduced to the Egan's Rats by Joseph "Green Onions" Cupola, who joined in with the Rats in the early 1900s. He was murdered by the Rats after a botched robbery in Dupo, Illinois. The Licavoli brothers relocated to Detroit in the mid-1920s, along with several cousins, and established a gang known as the River Gang. The gang was a major rum-running operation in concert with other Italian factions. They were rivals to the Purple Gang. The Licavolis left Detroit for the Cleveland Underworld syndicate. Peter returned to Detroit and joined in with the Zerilli-Tocco Gang that he ruled until the 1960s. "Yonnie" stayed in Toledo, Ohio, and was convicted of the murder of the bootlegger Jackie Kennedy in 1933. He was sentenced to life in prison. He was paroled in 1972 and died in 1973.

James "Blackie" Licavoli—A cousin of the Licavoli's who in later years became boss of the Cleveland, Ohio syndicate. Peter "Horse Shoe" Licavoli also moved north and went to prison for the murder of a rival Detroit bootlegger. He served thirty-three years and died in prison in 1953.

Leo Vincent Brothers—A member of the Egan's Rats Gang who lived his life of crime by the bullet until his death by a bullet. In his early years, he hung out at the Rats' Max Welton Clubhouse, working for boss Dinty Colbeck, stealing cars and providing beatings to those failing to pay their debts to the gang boss.

He was the victim of beating as a young person inflicted by a bully named Kane. On August 5, 1923, he took his revenge by beating Kane and then murdering him in St. Louis.

Brothers, who was known to be proficient with a pistol, shot his way to infamy in August 1929 when he was accused of the contract killing of St. Louis labor official John DeBlase while Brothers was an enforcer in the city's labor rackets, working for union organizer Edwards "Toots" Clark. He then moved to Chicago and joined in with the Capone Mob.

On June 9, 1930, he gunned down a *Chicago Tribune* reporter named Jake Lingle in an underground pedestrian tunnel in downtown Chicago. It's believed that mob boss Al Capone let the public know it was Brothers that killed Lingle. He was tried and convicted of the killing and received a fourteen-year sentence. He only served six years and was released, most likely the handiwork of Brother attorney Louis Piquett.

Ironically, at his death, Lingle was found wearing an expensive belt given to him by Al Capone for "special" friends. An exposé series of stories were written by a *St. Louis Post-Dispatch* reporter, who had discovered that Lingle himself was very involved in the rackets.

In 1940, Brother returned to St. Louis to face his charges of killing John DeBlase. Fortunately for Brother, he was acquitted, and it was never proven that he killed the bully Kane.

On September 18, 1950, Brothers was shot by a gunman three times while drinking a beer at his home in St. Louis. He initially survived his wounds, claiming he was going to quit the rackets. He didn't have time to fulfill his boast, succumbing to an infection of his wounds and dying on December 23, 1950.

August "Gus" Winkeler—An Egan's Rat who migrated to Chicago and was one of Al Capone's "American Boys." He was involved in the St. Valentine's Day Massacre and was murdered gangland-style on October 9, 1933, most likely on orders from Chicago mob boss Frank Nitti.

Solly "Cutcherheadoff" Weissman—He was a St. Louis native and member of the Egan's Rats Gang. The 300-pound Weissman arrived in Kansas City during the beginning of Prohibition and involved himself in numerous crimes. He teamed up with Kansas City mob boss John Lazia and took control of a dog track. He moved to Minneapolis in 1929 and began hijacking liquor. In 1930, three of his criminal partners were murdered either by "Bugs" Moran or Verne Miller. He returned to Kansas City on October 28 to fight several charges involving Prohibition violations, but the charges were dismissed. A few hours later he was shot to death by a wire service manager of a bookie operation named Charlie Haughton during an argument. The service manager Haughton claimed self-defense and was never charged.

William "Two Gun" Weissman—A St. Louis gangster (not related to Sally Weissman) who left St. Louis and joined up with Zwillman Mob and "Waxey" Gordon on the East Coast. He was murdered in Irving, New Jersey, in 1941.

William J. "Willie" Harrison—He was an Egan's Rat and criminal associate of Gus Winkler, Jack Klutas, Fred Goetz, "Big Homer" Wilson, and Fred "Killer" Burke. He was a bootlegger who moved to Cleveland, Ohio, and operated speakeasies in Cleveland and Toledo in Ohio and in Calumet, Illinois. He joined in with the Barker-Karpis Gang and was involved in the Bremer kidnapping. He was considered unreliable by the gang and was murdered in January 1935 by "Doc" Barker and thrown into a burning barn in Illinois.

Bob Carey [Aka Conroy, Newberry Sandon, Etc.] — A member of the Egan's Rats and a criminal associate of Fred "Killer" Burke, Gus Winkler, Fred Goetz, Ray Nugent, and Charles Fitzgerald. He went to Detroit, along with a number of Capone's "American Boys" from St. Louis to assist another ex-Egan's Rat, Johnny Reid. While there, the group committed a number of murders during the battle with Reid's rival gang. He also organized a successful kidnapping ring. He moved to Chicago and joined in with the Capone syndicate. Carey was one of the shooters in the St. Valentine's Day murders in Chicago on February 14, 1926, and one of the shooters in the murder of Frankie Yale in New York.

On April 16, 1928, Carey (along with Burke, Winkler, Goetz, Nugent, and Charles Fitzgerald) murdered a policeman in Toledo, Ohio, after robbing an American Express truck of $200,000. On November 25, 1928, Carey, (along with Gus Winkler, Fred Goetz, Carl Conley, Ray Nugent, and Herman Tipton) were charged with robbing the Farmers and Merchants Bank in Jefferson, Wisconsin, of $252,000 in cash and bonds. Carey moved to New York and was involved in counterfeiting and blackmailing wealthy victims with his girlfriend.

In 1932, he, along with his girlfriend, were found dead in an apartment in New York, and it was called a murder-suicide. It appeared it was actually a murder caused by "Bugs" Moran as a revenge for Carey's involvement in the St. Valentine's Day Massacre in Chicago in 1929. "Bugs" Moran would take credit for the hit, telling this to a longtime associate in confidence, who then revealed this to law enforcement.

Joseph "Red" O'riordan—An Egan's Rat Gang member and cousin to Bob Carey. He moved to Detroit before Prohibition and involved himself in snatch racket kidnapping, with Fred "Killer" Burke, and murder, eventually becoming the leader of the gang. Wanted by law enforcement, he fled to California, and on September 15, 1933, he was captured in Los Angeles.

Ezra Milford Jonas (Aka "Jones")—A twenty-six-year-old St. Louis Cuckoo Gang member who was introduced to the Egan's Rats by Fred "Killer" Burke and also became an Egan's Rat. Jones was involved in a shootout in St. Louis with members of the Green Ones Italian Gang, leaving two of Jones' companions, Ben Milner and Ben "Cotton" Fanke, dead. Danny O'Neil was also shot but survived. Jones already had a hatred for Italians, and this incident heightened his hatred even more.

He went on to a criminal life as a hit man for hire and murdered a number of Italians in the wake. Between 1923 and 1927, he was arrested by the St. Louis Police a reported 130 times for crimes ranging from bank robberies to rape. Jones joined up with Fred Burke and a number of Egan's Rats Gang members in Detroit to help their St. Louis criminal associate and ex-Egan's Rat Johnny Reid in a battle with gang rivals. He, along with the other Rats, committed a number of murders during the gang rival battles.

In 1927, Jones joined up with ex-Rat Claude Maddox's faction of the Capone gang in Chicago. Milford Ezra Jones was murdered, shot to death on June 15, 1927, by four Italian gunmen at the Posh Stark Club in Detroit, Michigan, in revenge for his hatred of Italians and career of killing them. Some crime researchers have claimed he may have killed more men than Fred "Killer" Burke.

Tommy "Maddog" Hayes—He was a Cuckoo Gang member who served as its leader from 1930 to 1932. He joined in with the Shelton Gang in Illinois and fought against the Birger Gang of Illinois. He later turned against the Shelton Gang and murdered three of the Shelton Gang members in a road-house near Valmeyer, Illinois, machine-gunning them to death. Hayes was arrested on May 8, 1931, by state and federal authorities in a gangster flat in East St. Louis, Illinois, along with several other gang members. They were suspected of committing more than sixty bank robberies throughout the Midwest. They were also suspected of involvement in kidnappings and murder.

On April 15, 1932, Hayes was found shot to death near Granite City, Illinois, along with "Pretty Boy" Legler and Conrad "Willie" G. Wilbert. The Sheltons were suspected of these murders.

—m—

These well-documented findings establish beyond a reasonable doubt the amount of influence and violence Missouri gangsters inflicted on a national level that is equal to, if not greater than, most East Coast mobsters and gangsters. We will now focus on the St. Louis mobsters, mob violence, and legal law enforcement justice.

THE 1960s

The violent criminal episodes began in the early 1960s during my early teenage and high school years, long before I began my career as a public servant, when I actually knew and associated with some of the criminal characters who are featured in this chapter. They continued through the 1980s, when the underworld influence was diminished due to the successful results of an intensive multiagency investigation. Some episodes are so revealing that the reader will learn how, at times, fact is more sensational than fiction.

Bombing at Cahokia Downs—June 29, 1962

On June 29, 1962, an East St. Louis hoodlum named Charles J. Hollis was critically injured when a bomb detonated in his vehicle in the parking lot of the Cahokia Downs horse racetrack in Cahokia, Illinois, just across the river from St. Louis. Two men with him were also injured.

Gangland Robbery And Murder—July 25, 1963

On July 25, 1963, St. Louis area gangster Paul Leisure, who had strong aspirations of becoming a mob enforcer for St. Louis mobsters, robbed and murdered a person near the intersection of Eighth Street and Chouteau in the Downtown St. Louis area. Another criminal associate of Leisure's named Jerry Box participated in the robbery and the murder of this victim. After the robbery, Leisure and Box went to East St. Louis, Illinois, across the Mississippi

River to drink and ended up shooting a black man, for which they were arrested by the East St. Louis Police Department and charged with aggravated battery, police mug shot number 36380.

The Jerry Box Gangland Murder—1963

Also in 1963, St. Louis gangsters Paul J. Leisure and his cousin Rich Leisure took criminal associate Jerry Box out drinking. Soon after, Box beat up Rich over a girl. While driving in the area of Twelfth and Calhoun Streets in St. Louis, they pulled the car over to relieve themselves. When Box got out of the car, Paul shot him in the head, killing him. Years later, Paul Leisure confided in a mob associate named Fred Prater, who revealed the details to federal ATF agents. In 1964, Paul Leisure became the driver and bodyguard for St. Louis mob boss Tony Giordano.

The Lou and Cecil's Tavern Murders

On July 26, 1964, Richard P. Leisure and a criminal associate of the Leisures named Larry Chaffin were murdered gangland-style while drinking at the Lou and Cecil's Tavern in East St. Louis. The shooters were actually looking for Paul Leisure.

I had met Chaffin and became acquainted with him while playing sports and socializing at the Dunn Center, located in the Dorst Webbe projects in the inner city of St. Louis in the late 1950s and early '60s.

Several years before his murder, in August 1962, Rich drove me and Paul Leisure to Cape Girardeau to attend college at Southeast Missouri State University after we both had graduated from McKinley High School in St. Louis.

Norm Peters, a St. Louis bookmaker, and his associate, Jack Issa, were charged with the murders of Leisure and Chaffin. Witnesses in the tavern on the night of the shootings identified the two as the shooters. News accounts reported that Jimmy Michaels Sr., a high-ranking mob associate, influenced the witnesses to change their stories, and the charges were dropped. Norm Peters then left St. Louis. Years later a friend of mine who was a close associate of Peters confided that he was the person who had driven Peters out of town after the hit. Peters has since passed away.

Mob enforcer Paul Leisure, learning of the developments in the death of his cousin and criminal associate, held a grudge against Peters and Jimmy Michaels Sr. for years. This was just one of a series of hits and bombings that were about to unfold throughout the 1970s and 1980s around St. Louis, all related to mobsters and underworld figures.

Hoodlum Hits

On November 12, 1965, Michael J. Buckley, a construction worker with underworld connections, was killed in a car bombing on an Uplands Park Street, just outside St. Louis, and on May 10, 1967 Richard L. Bodecker, a burglar and small-time hoodlum in St. Louis, was killed in another car bombing in a Normandy Shopping Center parking lot just north of St. Louis. Investigators believed five sticks of dynamite were wired to the car's taillight.

On May 16, 1967, Paul Leisure and James Anthony Michaels Jr., son of Michaels Sr., a high-ranking mob leader, shot and killed Richard Timothy Otis and Grady Lloyd Carter at Carter's Corner Tavern in Wellston, just outside St. Louis. Richard Otis was under indictment for killing Joseph F. Michaels, son of Francis Michaels, and nephew of James Michaels Sr. The incident occurred on December 17, 1966, at a clubhouse along the Meramec River in St. Louis County as a result of a fight. Otis was killed at the request of James Michaels Sr. in retaliation for the murder of Joseph Michaels. Leisure, in admitting to the murders, claimed Carter was killed because he was a witness to the killing of Otis.

Your author remembers the clubhouse shooting all too well. I had just been drafted into the Army in November 1966, and when I was on furlough during Christmas, my younger brother Rodney told me he was at the clubhouse and was nearly shot when the bullets started flying.

Two other young men at the party were not so lucky; one was Gary Radcliff, a friend of my brother's, who drove him to the party. He was killed, hit by a stray bullet as my brother stood next to him.

Michael Tinsley, the younger brother of Ron Tinsley, a high school classmate of mine, was also killed when hit with a stray bullet. Ron would discuss with me the death of his brother on numerous occasions over the years. Neither Leisure nor Michaels were ever charged with the hit.

These were two more notches on the killing belt of my high school choir partner. After graduating, I remained a tenor, but Paul Leisure was becoming a real-life Soprano.

Sometime after the shooting of Richard Otis and Grady Carter, James A. Michaels Sr., using his influence within the St. Louis Pipefitters Union, arranged for Paul Leisure and James A. Michaels Jr. to work as pipefitters on a jobsite in Outstate Missouri. The shooting incident generated a considerable amount of publicity, and according to Paul, Michaels Sr. moved him and Michaels Jr. out of the St. Louis area to alleviate some of the pressure caused by the publicity. During this period when Paul and Michaels Jr. were working out of town, they were to receive a certain amount of money over and above their salaries for being part of Michaels Sr.'s "operation." However, Paul claims that, while Michaels Jr. was receiving his payments, he (Paul) was not. Paul also claimed that the Michaels family was planning to kill him because they were "putting the word out" that Paul Leisure was no longer part of their "operation."

THE 1970s

On March 16, 1970 Jesse Wilcox, an ex-convict, was killed on a South St. Louis street in another car bombing. This gangland hit was the first of no fewer than fourteen gangland bombings occurring in and around St. Louis throughout the remainder of the 1970s—the decade of the bomb in the St. Louis area.

The Telephone Executive Bombing Homicide

The carnage continued on July 24, 1970. Phillip J. Lucier, a telephone executive who owned the Continental Telephone Company—the nation's third-largest independent system—was murdered when a bomb detonated as he started his 1966 Fleetwood Cadillac. The bombing occurred in the parking lot of the Pierre Laclede Center at 7701 Forsyth Boulevard in Clayton, Missouri, after Lucier was having lunch with two fellow associates who were not injured in the blast. Lucier, a model citizen, had no known enemies, and the major case squad, which investigated the bombing along with ATF agents from the St. Louis office, speculated the murder was a mistaken bombing meant for a local mobster.

I was a detective with the St. Louis Missouri Police Department assigned to the Bomb and Arson Unit of the Homicide Department and assisted in the investigation. The case went unsolved for five years.

Then in 1975, five years after Lucier's murder, ATF Agents John Liedtke and Dale Wiggins initiated a cold case review of all the files and newspaper articles written on the mysterious killing. They needed a motive, a witness, a suspect, and a storyteller—not an easy task. No one had a reason to kill Lucier, but Lucier was dead, leaving behind a widow and eight children.

The witness was the easy part of the puzzle. A man looking for a parking spot had seen a man in the front seat of a vehicle who seemed to be doing something with his hands near the windshield of the car. The witness got a good look, and he said he could identify the man if he saw him again. He was hypnotized, and an artist sketched the suspect's face. The media published the sketch; however, the person of interest was not identified.

One of the ATF agents located a small mention in an article that "Attorney Swartz escapes injury." He reported to police a few days after the 1970 murder that his black Lincoln looked much like Lucier's vehicle, sported a four-digit license plate similar to Lucier's, and had a telephone antenna similar to Lucier's. Could this attorney have been the bomber's actual target and the bomb was placed in Lucier's vehicle by mistake?

Swartz was reinterviewed by Agents Lietke and Wiggins. He said he had told the FBI this information, adding he had two clients who had swindled a mobster from New Orleans out of $150,000. He said he or his clients who visited him at the Laclede Tower Building were very possibly the actual targets. The suspect's name was Santo Difatta.

When the ATF agents confronted the FBI agent, he said Santo Difatta was the FBI's confidential source in a bank swindling case at the time, and for that reason, they did not disseminate the information to ATF in 1970. The ATF agents subpoenaed Difatta, bringing him before the federal grand jury, and placed him in a room with several other persons called to the grand jury session.

The eyewitness was also subpoenaed and sent into the grand jury room to see if he could identify anyone in the room. In a very short period of time, he came out and said he positively identified Difatta as the man he had seen in the front seat of Lucier's vehicle. This was shortly before Lucier got into his parked vehicle and started the engine and the vehicle exploded, killing him.

When the ATF agents interviewed Difatta, he neither admitted nor denied he was in Lucier's vehicle on July 24, 1970. Difatta simply asked questions and talked only in hypothetical terms. In his book entitled *Very Special Agents*, retired ATF agent and supervisor James Moore documented the interview as provided to author Moore by the agents. Difatta asked:

What if I was the bomber, or what if I was the bomber with my attorney, or what if my attorney was the bomber? Could he go and lie to the Grand Jury and make me stand alone? And, just where would I be if... let's just suppose that I was the bomber . . . that I was in the car or my attorney was involved with me in this . . . or even if my attorney acted alone—could they frame me for this? [The agents shrugged] Could they put my fingerprints in the car that was bombed?"

The federal statute of limitation had expired, so the information was presented to the St. Louis County attorney's office. Their office found several problems with charging Difatta: the case was five years old, the bomber suspect did not provide a confession, and the eyewitness had been hypnotized while having his recall diagrammed in a sketch. His testimony would be challenged since hypnotized witnesses would not be allowed to testify.

Although solved, the case would never be prosecuted.

I began my career as a federal agent with ATF in May 1971. I was assigned to the East Group, responsible for enforcing the federal firearms and explosives laws, in Madison and St. Clair Counties in Illinois located near St. Louis. I had learned while I was assigned to the St. Louis Police Department Homicide Unit that many of the firearms used in homicides in St. Louis were sold by illegal firearms dealers in those counties.

A group of ATF agents under the supervision of John Durako initiated undercover operations to apprehend some of these criminals. In the following thirty-seven months from December 1971 to Summer 1975, the group purchased or seized over 160 firearms, including revolvers, pistols, rifles, and shotguns, some of them sawed-off and intended for armed robberies.

We purchased or seized 36,000 rounds of stolen ammunition and approximately 600 cases of stolen whiskey, all taken from freight train cars and transit trucks, all money in interstate commerce. We also purchased two manufactured explosive pipe bombs and numerous chemicals to make bombs. The project netted fifty-five criminals convicted of federal felonies in violation of firearms, explosives, and gambling violations. Twenty-three of the fifty-five convicted had previously been convicted of felonies ranging from burglary, armed robberies, assaults, or murders. The convictions resulted in prison sentences of two years to twenty-two years.

Most of the purchases were made from vehicles, houses, or East Side taverns and one cabstand. In each and every purchase, the sellers knew the weapons, ammo, and whiskey were going to be sold in St. Louis. They didn't know these items were actually placed into evidence and used to convict them of federal crimes.

The success of the project didn't go unnoticed by the media. Newspaper reporters Joe Melosi and Bill Lhotka of the *Alton Telegraph* wrote in part in an article heading "2 Agencies Fight Organized Crime in County."

With few exceptions little has changed since the days in 1950 when the Kefauver Crime Committee excoriated law enforcement in Madison County.

The article went on to say:

Some experts say organized crime activities can be stopped here. It is not always a question of manpower but one of willingness and initiative. Take the case of David True, or the FBI's activities in dealing with a Wood River bookie operation. True, an investigator for the Treasury Department's Alcohol, Tobacco and Firearms Division, gained the confidence of area hoodlums last winter while working here as an undercover agent. His individual efforts cracked a stolen gun ring, led to seven indictments, and closed off one highly profitable interstate criminal operation. The FBI, in one of its most diligent local efforts, monitored phone calls at a taxi stand and two Wood River taverns around the clock for 30 days. The surveillance paid off in the arrest and indictments of seven men charged with operating a $2,000-per-day interstate handbook.

What the reporters didn't know was that ATF Agent True was placing bets over the phone to the gamblers and, on occasion, even taking the phone calls from bettors for one of the men convicted of running the gambling operation, making it easier for the FBI to perfect their case. The gambling operator was also one of those convicted of federal firearms violation in the ATF undercover operation.

The Union Labor Business Manager Hit

On February 24, 1972, Edward J. Steska, the business manager for Pipefitters Local Union 562, was shot five times. He was killed while he sat at his desk at the union hall located at 1242 Pierce Avenue in St. Louis. The murder weapon, a .45 caliber pistol, was left at the scene. Steska was on the phone at the time of the murder, talking to James Michaels Jr., who was a business agent for Local 562 and a grandson of Jimmy Michaels Sr. Steska, who was hand-picked by Larry Callanan to be his successor, had promised to rid the union of hoodlums. Apparently, some of the hoodlums didn't agree with Steska's promises.

The Union Member Bombing Homicide

On August 25, 1972, Louis P. Shoulders Jr., the son of a crooked St. Louis cop named Lou Shoulders Sr., was killed when a bomb wired to his vehicle detonated. His bodyguard, T.J. Harvell, was seriously injured in the blast. The two had been fishing at the Long Creek boat dock in Taney County, Missouri.

Shoulders and Harvell were employed at the Pipefitters Local Union 562 in St. Louis at the time of his murder. Shoulders was also working for mob boss "Buster" Wortman of Madison County, Illinois, at the time. The homicide was investigated by the Taney County Sheriff's Office, the ATF agents assigned to the Springfield office, the St. Louis ATF office, and the St. Louis Police Department.

Shoulders was a convicted felon who had been recently convicted of "possessing a firearm by a convicted felon," a case perfected by ATF agents from the St. Louis office. Shoulders's associates included mobsters from both St. Louis and East Side, Illinois, including Anthony Giordano, Norman "Bosco" Owens, Terry Tweat, Landon Fischer, Art Berne, Jon Vitale, Ray Flynn, and Malcom Flynn, to name a few.

Shortly after the bombing, Glenn Sweet of Springfield was interviewed at the scene by ATF agents. He said he was "Employed as a guide at Andersen's Boat Deck. Was the guide who Lou used most of the time. Said Lou told him not to go with him this trip because it was too dangerous but would not explain further. Liked Lou very much and had asked Lou to take him to St. Louis, but Lou refused saying he would get killed there. Saw nothing unusual to report."

Shoulders obviously knew something was up, expressing danger. ATF agents also interviewed Sharon Stuckenschneider, Shoulders's girlfriend, when she was brought to the scene by sheriff's deputies. She would not provide any information about the bombing; however, enough information was gained to obtain a search warrant for Shoulders's St. Louis apartment.

On August 26, 1972, Rick and Jan Andersen, owners of the Long Creek Dock and Café, were interviewed by ATF agents. They stated that Louis Donald Shoulders had been storing his boat at their dock and fishing from it during the last four years. Both said that, during the bass season from April through October, Shoulders came to Table Rock Lake on almost every new moon and fished each night from about 10:00 p.m. to 2:00 a.m., each trip being about six days in length.

Each night, Shoulders had been using the telephone on the boat dock to make telephone calls; the exact recipient of these calls unknown. Shoulders always made this telephone call between 10:00 p.m. and 10:30 p.m., requested time and charges on these calls, and paid the Andersens in cash. The telephone number of the telephone at the boat dock was 417-334-4860. Each evening Shoulders also asked for two dollars in change prior to going out so that he could make a telephone call from the pay phone outside the Long Creek Cafe on returning from fishing.

On August 24, 1972, Shoulders parked his car on the parking lot of the boat dock at about 6:00 p.m., and it was not observed to have been moved prior to the explosion. At about 6:00 p.m. on August 24, Shoulders, Harvell, and Harvell's son went out in Shoulders's boat. They returned at about 10:00 p.m. and dropped off Harvell's son, and then Shoulders and Harvell went out in the boat alone.

Both witnesses viewed mug shots of known St. Louis hoodlums and picked out photographs of Anthony Giordano, St. Louis Mafia boss, as having been down fishing three to four times that year. They also identified Roy John Conrad, an organized crime figure, as having only been down once that year. They also identified a photograph of John Paul Leisure, organized crime associate, as having been down once that year. They would not state that these persons associated with Shoulders while at the lake.

An intense investigation produced several suspects. ATF learned that St. Louis mob boss Tony Giordano, his bodyguard and driver Paul Leisure, and a mob associate named Roy Conrad, also had stayed at the lake resort over the past several years. Later in the day, a confidential informant telephoned the ATF office and advised that Dave Michaels of Belleville, Illinois, was involved in the Shoulders's bombing, along with a man called "Red" from Granite City, Illinois, and another person, name unknown.

Information was developed that T. J. Harvell, who was seriously injured when the bomb blast killed Louis Shoulders, said to James Robertson (a boat dock employee) that "those sons of bitches got Lou." Harvell was interviewed several times but refused comment about the bombing, referring agents to his St. Louis attorney Norman London. Several motives for the bombing, included the Pipefitters Union power struggle and revenge over Shoulders assaulting a union member and the killing of another union member's brother.

It was suspected Shoulders's death and the gangland murder of Edward Steska in February 1972 were both related to a union struggle and power play in Local Union 562. Sorkis Webbe Sr., a St. Louis mobster defense attorney, became involved in the Steska murder by representing hoodlums of the Pipefitters Union. Webbe was an ally of the Jimmy Michaels mob faction in St. Louis and a counselor to many St. Louis mobsters and thugs. Webbe and Michaels would both become subjects of future homicide investigations—one as a victim and one as a coconspirator in cases that were investigated by ATF and the St. Louis Police Department.

On September 12, 1972, Sheriff Kenneth Buckley of St. Francois County, Missouri, told ATF agents that, a year-and-a-half earlier, St. Louis mob boss Tony Giordano and Lou Shoulders were in Farmington, visiting a local thug named James Pollito, and just a few days before the Shoulders' bombing, Jimmy Michaels Jr. had met with James Pollito and a man named Bill Prescott. A confidential source told him that Bill Prescott, a hoodlum from St. Louis, bombed Shoulders with a bomb made and supplied by Delmar Keith, a powderman for a construction company located about forty miles east of Farmington; it was also reported that Keith drove a tan Plymouth.

Sheriff Buckley said he, along with the highway patrol, were surveilling Keith on the nights of August 24 and 25. He also stated that he had checked a cistern in Keith's yard and observed dynamite. He returned an hour later, and the dynamite was gone. Keith did not return during the surveillance, and Buckley learned that Keith had put his tan Plymouth in his brother's garage in Ironton. Sheriff Buckley turned over two Dupont and one Hercules electric blasting caps that he had received from a confidential source, who said the caps came out of Keith's car within the past few days. This was a strong lead requiring further investigation, so Sheriff Buckley said he would keep in touch if any further information was received.

During interviews with witnesses at the bombing site, ATF agents identified three different witnesses who reported seeing a tan car on the parking lot, parked about three stalls away from Shoulders's vehicle between 1:00 and 1:30 a.m., and another witness remembered hearing someone yell the name "Keith" in the parking lot.

Another suspect developed was James Walter Boyd, a consummate St. Louis gangster and tough guy according to police officials, who grew up in the St. Louis suburb of Normandy. Boyd was unliked by law enforcement and once had threatened to kill Colonel Robert Lowry, the Florissant Police Chief who cofounded the St. Louis area major case squad. Boyd was an associate of Lou Shoulders. He was also a suspect in the gangland killing of gangster Bosco Owens, also an associate of Lou Shoulders, whose body was found in the trunk of a car at Lambert airport in St. Louis.

The multiagency law enforcement team investigating these two bombing homicides reviewed Boyd's admissions with suspicion for several reasons. Why would a person confess to two murders to get out of a federal auto theft indictment? He claimed he had placed the bomb on Lou Shoulders's vehicle after Shoulders beat him up in St. Louis, knocking some of his teeth out. He claimed he had been paid a $3,000 contract to take Shoulders out. He also claimed he had placed the bomb on Lucier's vehicle because Lucier, the telephone executive, refused to issue him and his criminal associates a telephone line after Lucier suspected it would be used to run a gambling operation.

The Shoulders bombing went unsolved for several years.

The St. Louis Cop Bombing Homicide

On October 23, 1972, just two months after the Shoulders hit, Lyman Davis, an ex-St. Louis police officer, was killed when a bomb—estimated to be ten sticks of dynamite placed under his Cadillac—detonated, killing him. The bombing occurred in a parking lot by a tavern he operated in Overland, just outside St. Louis. Davis, who was a heavy gambler, had just returned from Vegas earlier in the day after reportedly losing $10,000 at the St. Louis-owned Aladdin Casino. Davis was a close associate of Shoulders and T. J. Harvell and had expressed fear for his life over the previous several months. Davis and Harvell were running a bookmaking operation out of Davis's apartment, where numerous phones were found during a later search. Harvell was inside the apartment and had reportedly removed their bookmaking documents before the police arrived. Also found in his apartment were thirty-five sticks of dynamite fused with safety fuse and blasting caps.

Police learned that Davis was reportedly planning to bomb a St. Louis restaurant, Cocktail Lounge, a week before his murder. Law enforcement investigators believed Davis was killed over continuing gangland warfare dating back to the shooting death of Edward Steska, the business manager for Pipefitters Union Local 562 on February 24.

Davis had turned down an invitation to go on the fishing trip with Lou Shoulders and T. J. Harvell two months earlier because of his heart condition, missing the bombing of Shoulders. The two bombings were never solved.

Another Union-Related Bombing

On June 15, 1973 Tommy Callanan, brother of Laurence L. Callanan, leader of Pipefitters Local Union 562, lost his legs when a bomb ripped apart a vehicle he was operating in Spanish Lake, just outside St. Louis. Callanan told his rescuer, "They promised they wouldn't do this to me." So much for kept promises in the battlefields of St. Louis. The rescuer, "Tad" Heitzler, testified to this quote at a federal grand jury shortly after the attempt on Callanan's life and went on to become an ATF Agent in the St. Louis office, where I had the privilege of working with him for many years.

Callanan was a business agent for the Pipefitters Union. Investigators believed the remote-controlled bomb consisting of five sticks of dynamite had been placed under the driver's seat of the car. He was blown through the roof of his car, landing about 225 feet from the wreckage.

In 1974, while we were involved in our undercover operation, St. Louis Police detectives in the Intelligence Unit and Narcotics Unit were busy conducting their own investigation involving robberies and firearms violations. In September 1975, William Poe, a reporter with the *St. Louis Globe-Democrat*, wrote an entire front-page article with the headline "Contract For Crime: The Rent-A-Gun Business."

Poe wrote:

> As the rock group Lynyrd Skynyrd sings it, the Saturday night special is an accepted component of American Life. However, police now say that illegal gun traffic in the St. Louis area has become so sophisticated that some dealers, who normally just sell guns for illicit purposes, have entered into a new kind of contract with criminals—the rent-a-gun business.
>
> Under this scheme, police say, a criminal can rent a weapon for a set price from a dealer who, in turn, will demand part of the 'take' from the impending 'job.' Or the dealer may simply demand more cash upon receipt of the gun. The same gun may be rented for another six or seven various 'jobs' until it becomes traceable.
>
> 'It's scary to think that some of the guns used in today's killings and holdups are passed back and forth over the counter like candy,' one city

homicide detective said. While gun experts in St. Louis emphasize that guns are still more commonly sold than rented illegally, they say 'community' guns, especially sawed-off shotguns, are becoming increasingly responsible for area slayings and holdups.

Sgt. Thomas Rowane of the homicide division said illegal dealers in the city 'pawn guns out to young dudes in street gangs.' The gang members will pass the same weapon among themselves for use in many crimes, he said.

David R. True, a special agent with the federal Bureau of Alcohol, Tobacco and Firearms, told a tale of a huge rent-a-gun organization in a recent interview with The Globe-Democrat. True, who is considered the top expert on St. Louis area gun traffic, recalled a series of pharmacy holdups and shootings that plagued the area last year. The robberies were conducted by an illegal gun and holdup ring consisting of about 12 men responsible for 50 or 60 pharmacy holdups in the Midwest area, True said.

The holdup ring members were concentrated in Missouri, Illinois and Tennessee and were supplied with 20 or 30 'available' weapons from another group concentrated 'somewhere on the East Side,' True said. This syndicate of 'traveling criminals' was spurred on by the promise of drugs obtained from the pharmacy robberies, True said.

The gun financiers would rent the weapons and in return, would have 'first crack' at the stolen narcotics, True said. After the holdup, the robbers would return to the financier and turn over the guns and some of the drugs at a reduced price, True said. After another pharmacy was 'cased,' another deal would be set, True said. The ring operated for 12 months before it was broken up [by the detectives]. St. Louis is especially suited to large-scale gun-running operations, he said.

The city's geographic location at the hub of interstate highways, railroads and trucking lines leads to a large number of guns stolen from legitimate shipments, he said. However, most guns rented or sold illegally are stolen from area residences, True said.

The gun network is now so well organized that the criminal population is no longer so dependent upon a large quantity of guns, True said, because only one gun is needed for many jobs. (Poe, 1975)

ATF assisted the detectives by conducting interviews and obtaining police files on some of the pharmacy robberies in Nashville and Memphis, Tennessee. These two successful projects clearly emphasized the extent of illegal firearm trafficking between St. Louis and nearby Illinois.

The Mob Associate Business Bombing
On September 24, 1974, the Pillow Manufacturing Company, located at 2223 Cole Street in St. Louis, was bombed. The bombing was investigated by agents of the St. Louis ATF and detectives from the St. Louis Police Depart-

ment Bomb and Arson Unit, who all speculated the blast may have been an underworld warning as reported in the *St. Louis Post-Dispatch*. Arthur A. Safron, the owner of the pillow company and a gambler, may have been having trouble with the underworld over gambling debts.

Safron was a known associate of a number of gangland figures, including Anthony Giordano, head of the St. Louis Mafia Mob. Giordano was a frequent guest of Safron on gambling trips to Las Vegas. Safron claimed he had not received any threats and he was not having any labor troubles at the plant that was heavily damaged in the one-story portion of the building.

The bomb had detonated late Tuesday evening and was triggered by a timing device, a professional type of bomb. Evidence of pieces of wire and a blasting cap were located at the scene.

Police reported that, in 1967, Safron had accompanied Giordano to San Diego, California, where Giordano met with Frank "Bomp" Bompensiero, the head of the Mafia there and a longtime friend of Giordano's. In 1968, Safron had attended the funeral of Frank "Buster" Wortman, the Eastside rackets boss and also went to the 1972 funeral for Lou Shoulders Jr., the St. Louis labor racketeer, after he was killed in a car bombing.

Bomb Maker Death

On May 19, 1975 Walter W. Eberhardt, an ironworker and former convict, was killed in a car bombing on a street in Hillsdale, Missouri. Associate Doyle Laurence was injured but survived. Investigators believed the two were transporting the bomb made of military plastic explosive C-4 when it accidentally detonated. When the police searched Eberhardt's home, they found a timer, wires, and diagrams of a bomb device. Eberhardt had served time in 1966 for a forcible rape.

The Teamster Organizers Beating

In 1975, two organizers of the Teamsters Union, Peter Cavata and a man named Herman, were beaten with baseball bats and tire irons when they mistakenly tried to organize drivers at the Paul Leisure-run LN & P Towing Company, located at 2128 Chouteau Avenue in St. Louis. Both were hospitalized for long periods after incurring numerous injuries, including broken legs, with one Teamster requiring 300 stitches and the other 50. Both were associated with Teamster Local 618. They were beaten in the office of LN & P by Paul Leisure, David Leisure, and Fred Prater. Anthony Leisure held a pistol on the victims while the others beat them.

The Parking Lot Bombings

On October 7, 1977, Ronald T. Sterghos was lucky and escaped injury from a bomb wired to his vehicle in a South County apartment complex. Then, on October 18, 1977, Ronald L. Jackson, a parcel service supervisor, was killed in a South St. Louis County apartment complex parking lot bombing.

On November 3, 1977, Shirley Marie Flynn, a girlfriend of a local hoodlum named William Ohlhausen, was killed when her vehicle blew up as she started her car in the parking lot of a South St. Louis apartment complex parking lot. Authorities believed the bomb was actually meant for Ohlhausen. Five months later, on March 7, 1978, William Ohlhausen was seriously injured when a bomb detonated in his truck in a motel parking lot in Paducah, Kentucky.

Businessman Bombing

On April 10, 1979, a St. Louis businessman, Louis H. Ritter, was injured by a bomb as he drove near his suburban Clarkson Valley home. Ritter was president of the American Water Treatment Company. He received burns over 27 percent of his body when a black powder pipe bomb went off in his car as he was returning to his West County office. There was no known motive for the bombing.

The Political Figure House Bombing

On April 27, 1978, a house located at 6736 Eichelberger in South St. Louis, the home of Alex Aboussie, a well-known political figure, received minor damage when a bomb blast ignited outside the bedroom of Aboussie's daughter. Investigators learned the bombing was a warning for Alex Aboussie, not meant to harm anyone.

The Convicted Hit Man Bombing Murder

On November 8, 1979, John Paul Spica, a St. Louis hoodlum and previously convicted murderer, was killed when a bomb placed under his 1977 Cadillac Coupe detonated. The bombing occurred as Spica drove away from his apartment in a residential street in Richmond Heights, Missouri, a suburb of St. Louis. Spica, who operated a produce stand in St. Louis, also was active in the mob-linked vending and amusement machines operation near Fairmont, Illinois.

The crime scene and follow-up investigation was conducted by the St. Louis area major case squad, the Richmond Heights Police, and St. Louis ATF. Numerous motives were developed as to who might have killed Spica.

The *Post-Dispatch* reported in an article published on November 8, 1979:

Spica, who was 42, had been mentioned in the House Assassinations Committee report last year as a possible—but unsubstantiated—link between Dr. Martin Luther King Jr. and James Earl Ray, King's convicted assassin. Spica served a term for conspiracy to murder in the Missouri Penitentiary at the same time that Ray was there in the 1960's, and the House Assassinations Committee said it was possible that an offer to kill King had been transmitted through Spica to Ray. Spica was the brother-in-law of Russell G. Byers, a Rock Hill businessman who the committee said was reported to have received an offer of $50,000 for King's assassination.

Spica was convicted in the 1962 fatal shooting of John J. Myszak, a Normandy real estate dealer, who was shot down outside a friend's house. Spica was accused of arranging the killing after he was approached by Myszak's wife, Marie, who wanted her husband murdered. Spica was sentenced to a life term, but was paroled in 1973.

On June 22, 1980 the *Post-Dispatch* reported in an article headlined "Kansas City Mob Figure Carrying Bomb Is Killed":

A Kansas City underworld figure who authorities believe had ties with murdered St. Louis hoodlum John Paul Spica was killed Friday when a bomb he was carrying exploded.

Authorities said Saturday they believed that Joseph Spero, 48, was killed when the bomb was accidentally detonated, possibly by remote control. The bomb exploded as Spero apparently was carrying it into a rental storage facility in suburban Library, in Clay County. Spica had become close to Carl Spero while they both were in the Missouri State Penitentiary in Jefferson City. Spero had been convicted in a murder conspiracy. Authorities investigating Spica's murder believe that he might have honored his friendship with Carl Spero and had sided with the rump gang in the warfare. Spica was an associate of St. Louis underworld leader Anthony Giordano. Spica's aid to the Speros, sources said, apparently incurred the wrath of the Civella crime family, which has close ties to the Giordano mob. The Post-Dispatch reported last month that in the days immediately preceding Spica's death, Giordano sent two lieutenants to Kansas City. But they broke off their visit and returned to St. Louis because of what Giordano told a friend was a 'lot of problems there.'

Another motive theory, according to a source, indicated Spica had made trips to Las Vegas in the 1970s and may have accumulated gambling debts. Some authorities also speculated he may have tried to take over an operation that smuggled drugs into the Missouri Penitentiary, and that effort caused his death.

In a *Globe Democratic* article published on November 12, 1979 entitled "Top Priority in Bombing Case—Find Someone to Talk," the reporter wrote:

Unless some unexpected break occurs the car-bomb killing of John could end in another dusty unsolved murder file along with those of Lyman Davis, Louis D. Shoulders and Richard L. Bodecker. This is another of those gangland killings that is very difficult to investigate, one police officer said. 'It may never be solved.' One break that could solve the murder of Spica, and perhaps those of Shoulders, Bodecker and others, would be for someone inside the St. Louis gangland establishment to talk. But the underworld code of silence backed by the threat of death, makes that unlikely.

Little did the reporter know what intense investigative efforts were unfolding in the St. Louis office of the Bureau of ATF, headed by case agent Gordon Holdiman; the St. Louis Police Department Bomb and Arson Unit; and the

United States Attorney's Office, headed by Assistant United States Attorney Tom Dittmeier.

The Union Officer Second Bombing Attempt

On December 1, 1979, a van belonging to Thomas J. Callanan, a Pipefitters Union officer, was bombed in the parking lot of a North St. Louis toy store in Black Jack. The bombs, meant for Thomas Callanan, injured his wife Harriet, who suffered minor injuries when the bomb detonated as she opened the door to start the vehicle and prepared its hydraulic lift for her husband. Callanan, a business agent for the union, was in a wheelchair because he had been critically injured in a previous car bombing murder attempt seven years earlier, which blew off both of his legs and part of his hands. Two weeks after this bombing, a man arrested in Syracuse, New York, for not paying a motel bill was carrying newspaper clippings of the St. Louis bombing. He was brought to St. Louis by the county police for questioning.

As reported in several *Post-Dispatch* news articles, the man said he was on the fringes of the underworld and claimed he was brought to St. Louis by an underworld figure involved in the December 1 bombing. The man, who was not identified, said he also had information on the fatal John Paul Spica bombing that had occurred on November 8 in Richmond Heights. The unidentified man claimed he took the man who had planned the bombing of Callanan's van to the explosion site and then returned to his hotel. Later, the man planning the bombing came to his hotel and told him the device had not worked properly.

Investigators said the unidentified man told several versions of the bombing and was not considered believable. Neither of the two Callanan bombings were solved.

The Last Of The Old Cuckoo Gang Member Bombing Homicide

On September 17, 1980, James A. "Horseshoe" Michaels Sr., area mob associate, was killed gangland-style when the car he was driving, a 1977 Chrysler Cordoba, blew up, killing Michaels instantly. He was the only remaining Cuckoo Gang member of the early 1900s.

The bombing took place on Highway 55 near the Reavis Barracks road exit, propelling Michaels from his vehicle and spreading debris and body parts all over Highway 55. The crime scene and follow-up investigation was conducted by the St. Louis Police Department's Bomb and Arson Unit and agents from the ATF, St. Louis office. ATF agents assigned to the ATF National Response Team were also called in to assist in the investigation. ATF Agent Gordon Holdiman of the St. Louis office was assigned as the case agent.

A St. Louis mob enforcer, Paul J. Leisure, was developed as an early suspect. Leisure was the former bodyguard for area mob boss Tony Giordano, a close associate with Jimmy Michaels who had just died of cancer only nineteen days earlier. It was suspected the Leisure Mob felt, with Giordano's death, it would be safe to kill Michaels and make a move to take control of a local labor union. With the two mobsters out of the way, the Leisure Mob would not receive any resistance from the Italian Mob faction. Paul Leisure now felt he was untouchable.

The death of Jimmy Michaels would unleash a war over the next several years between the Michaels faction and the Leisure faction, resulting in more bombings and hoodlum hits, and set the stage for St. Louis's last big-time gang war.

The bombing also ignited the investigative instincts of Federal Agent Gordon Holdiman, a modern-day ATF Untouchable similar to the forerunner of the ATF, Prohibition Agent Elliot Ness of the 1920s and 1930s. Agent Holdiman would mount his own group of Untouchables, including fellow ATF agents, the St. Louis Bomb and Arson Detectives and the assistance of local FBI agents.

Over the next two years, a number of bombings and murder attempts using firearms occurred in and around St. Louis.

THE 1980s
The Mob Boss Bombing

On August 11, 1981, mob enforcer Paul Leisure was critically injured when a remote-controlled bomb placed under his Cadillac detonated as he started his car in front of his house. On the morning of this bombing, your author was in St. Louis visiting a relative near the Leisure bombing on Nottingham. After hearing the explosion, I drove to the scene, where I met with the St. Louis police officers and fellow ATF agents from our St. Louis office, who were also just arriving at the scene.

Leisure had been removed from the vehicle and taken to the hospital in critical condition yet still alive. I discussed the bombing with the ATF agents, reminding them of my association with the victim, his brother Anthony, and their associates. Special Agent in Charge Jim Elder said he would involve me in their follow-up investigation. I then left the scene, returning to Kansas City.

Shortly thereafter, I received a phone call from the St. Louis ATF office, advising me that an anonymous caller had contacted their office requesting to speak to me regarding the Leisure bombing. He related to the secretary that he had seen me at the scene of the bombing and wanted to talk about the incident—that he knew me.

I was personally acquainted with Paul Leisure and his brother Anthony. We were classmates at McKinley High School in St. Louis in 1962. I was involved with Paul Leisure in sports and socialized with Anthony Leisure for a period during the early 1960s. Paul Leisure and I drove to Cape Girardeau to attend college together in September of 1962. Rich Leisure drove us to Cape Girardeau; however, Paul Leisure left college after a week or two and returned to St. Louis. Rich Leisure was shot and killed, along with two other individuals, the following summer in a gangland-style ambush at Lew & Cecil's Tavern in East St. Louis, Illinois.

I left telephone numbers where I could be reached with the ATF secretary, and a short while later, the caller contacted me at the St. Louis number and stated he wanted to talk to me about the Leisure bombing. He would not give me his name, and I could not recognize the individual by his voice. He said we had mutual friends and indicated that we knew each other during high school.

I attempted to arrange a meeting with him immediately, but he put me off, stating that he had to go to work. I told him I had to return to Kansas City but would be willing to meet with him anywhere he wanted to meet. He told me that he would be in Osage Beach at the Osage House Lodge in the near future and would meet me there. I gave him several telephone numbers where I could be reached, and he said he would call and let me know when he would meet with me. He would not give me his name. I told him to use the name "Don" when he called, so I would know who he was. He then hung up.

On August 14, 1981, I returned to St. Louis to assist in the investigation. I learned the ATF answering service had taken a message from an individual earlier in the week using the name "Don" who had said, "Tell True 'Don' will be in Osage Beach the week of August 24; this message may not mean anything to you, but True will know what I mean."

I responded to the Firmin Desloge Hospital in an attempt to speak with the victim Paul Leisure; however, he was in no condition to talk. I did talk with Anthony Leisure, his brother, at Firmin Desloge Hospital, Grand Avenue, St. Louis. He stated he didn't know who was responsible for his brother's bombing and attempted murder, but if he could get his hands on them, he would choke them to death. I requested an opportunity to talk to Paul when he was able to talk, and Anthony agreed to arrange a meeting. Anthony stated he may be willing to talk to me after his brother was able to take care of himself, provided he survived.

On August 15, I assisted Special Agents Young, Cook, Holdiman, Bobb, Cooper, and Beattie, and police officers from Arnold, Missouri at 2706 Arnold Tenbrook in Arnold, securing an apartment and the search of the apartment's trash dumpster. I prepared and distributed lead cards to agents and supervised their activities and coordinated communications between agents in Arnold and agents at the US Attorney's Office in St. Louis in an effort to obtain a federal search warrant for the Arnold Police Department.

While at the apartments, we received license information and physical identification from several residents at the Arnold department. Agent Young took notes and license information. It is to be noted that one license plate turned over to ATF was "SCHEPP." This plate was shown issued to Russ Schepp. At the time, Schepp was a police chief near St. Louis who had previously worked for the St. Louis County Police Department as a detective.

Schepp and I had worked together from 1964 to 1966 at Yellow Transit Freight System in St. Louis. On several occasions Schepp had indicated that a relative of his named Norm Peters may have been responsible for the ambush murder of Rich Leisure and others at Lew & Cecil's Tavern in East St. Louis,

Illinois in 1964. He also indicated that Norm Peters had left town shortly after the killings and had never been seen since that day. The FBI contacted Schepp each year and asked him if he had heard from or seen Norm Peters. He said he always told them he didn't know where Peters was.

It was common knowledge to me, as well as to other South St. Louis associates, that Norm Peters had been a bookie in South St. Louis during the early sixties and that Peters had a run-in with Paul Leisure just prior to the killing of Rich Leisure. It was also known in these circles that Paul Leisure was actually the target but escaped death by not going to the tavern that night. It was rumored that Jimmy Michaels Sr. was the man responsible for getting Norm Peters out of St. Louis or even out of the United States.

On August 16, 1981, I assisted in the examination of evidence recovered from the dumpster at the Arnold Missouri apartment building and returned to Kansas City. The evidence was quite damaging to Russ Schepp and members of the Jimmy Michaels family. It included bomb making evidence, explosive residue, and a police magazine containing fingerprints.

On August 23, I traveled to Osage Beach and registered at the Osage House Hotel. I remained at Osage House Hotel and awaited the arrival of the anonymous caller "Don," who claimed to have information about the Paul Leisure bombing. During the day, I reviewed the records of individuals and groups who had reserved rooms during the week of August 24 to August 27, 1981.

During the early afternoon, an individual known to me as Ken Griffey arrived at the hotel with his family. We had attended high school together in St. Louis, and he was associated with the individuals involved in this investigation. He was very surprised to see me, and it was obvious he was uneasy while we talked by the pool. He told me that a number of individuals from St. Louis would be arriving at the hotel throughout the week from South St. Louis. Several of these individuals arriving were associated with the criminal element in St. Louis. I remained very visible throughout the day and evening, but I did not receive any contact regarding this matter from any other individuals from St. Louis.

On September 14, 1981, I received a call from Arthur Thomason, a reporter from the *St. Louis Globe-Democrat*. Thomason was inquiring about any connection between the Leisure bombing and the arrest of organized crime figures James "Cork" Civella and Arthur Shepherd by ATF in Kansas City on September 10, 1981, on a bombing charge. I advised him there was no apparent connection but that we were in contact with the St. Louis office on all organized crime-related bombings.

The Shotgun Murder Attempt

On September 11, 1981, Charles J. Michaels, the grandson of Jimmy "Horseshoe" Michaels, was shot while in the parking lot of The Edge restaurant in St. Louis, along with an associate, Dennis Day. They were hit in the back with a pump-action shotgun, and both of them survived the shooting. It was strongly suspected the shooting was linked to the car bombing of Paul

Leisure on August 11, just one month earlier. The shots were fired from a vacant building at the rear of the parking lot. The shotgun and some spent shells were recovered by investigators.

The Revenge Bombing Homicide

On October 18, 1981, George M. Faheen, a nephew of Jimmy "Horseshoe" Michaels, became the latest victim of the Leisure–Michaels mob war when he was murdered as he started his Volkswagen vehicle in the parking lot of the Mansion House Center, a high-rise office and apartment in Downtown St. Louis. The bomb that was placed on his car blew the front half of his car away. The body was found in his car, badly burned.

Law enforcement authorities with the St. Louis Police Department and the ATF task force strongly suspected the murder was another revenge hit for the Paul Leisure bombing a few months earlier. They had taken quick action, arresting Michael A. Kornhardt, a Leisure faction mob member, and charging him with the murder of Faheen. The intensive investigation would continue over the ensuing several months, focusing on the Leisure mob members' movements and putting the pressure on Kornhardt to talk.

Numerous discussions among the Leisure Mob occurred regarding the need to silence Kornhardt. In March 1982, just six months after the Faheen homicide and the arrest of Michael Kornhardt, Frank J. Termine Jr. of Ballwin, Missouri, agreed to cooperate with the federal and state investigators after he was arrested and charged with house invasion and aggravated assault in Alton, Illinois. Realizing he was facing up to sixty years in prison on these charges, he worked out a deal to receive a sentence of sixteen years, to be served in federal prison rather than a very lengthy prison term in Illinois state prison.

On July 22, 1982, the Paul Leisure Mob learned Termine had agreed to testify against Michael Kornhardt, responsible for the Faheen bombing. Termine had assisted on several surveillances of Faheen in the St. Louis Hill area of St. Louis, where Faheen's mother lived, and also at the St. Louis Circuit Court building in Downtown St. Louis, where he was employed. These surveillances had occurred just nine days before Faheen's murder. He also named David Leisure as being involved with these surveillances, along with Charles "Obie" Loewe. Termine agreed to testify to this in any court proceeding, and this information greatly concerned the Leisure faction.

On March 24, 1982, James A. Michaels III and Milton Russell Schepp were charged for the vehicle bombing and murder attempt of Paul Leisure. Michaels surrendered and was released on bond. Russ Schepp dropped out of sight.

The Mob Associate Shooting Homicide

On July 31, 1982, Michael Kornhardt, while out on bond, was shot and killed gangland-style. His body was found in a field in St. Charles, shot in the back of the head, an obvious mob hit. This incident would prove to be the undoing of the Paul Leisure gang and their murderous ways.

Shortly after Kornhardt's body was found, Fred Prater, a Leisure mob member and coconspirator, turned himself into Assistant United States Attorney Tom Dittmeier, seeking federal protection for him and his family. He agreed to provide substantial information. Attorney Dittmeier turned Prater over to ATF agents.

In a series of lengthy interviews with ATF Agents Gordon Holdiman and Bill McGarvey in August and September 1982, Prater admitted his direct knowledge and his own involvement in a series of criminal acts committed by members of the Leisure mob faction. Prater cleared up the George Faheen murder, providing his firsthand knowledge to name who had killed Faheen and why.

Prater said someone told the Leisures that George Faheen was seen at the scene of the bombing that had hurt Paul. They were also informed that Faheen kept going to Anthony's aunt, Mary Pazur, who worked in St. Louis City Hall, and telling her how sorry he was to hear about Paul being hurt. Faheen would ask the aunt to tell Anthony that he would like to meet with him. This drew suspicion on Faheen because it was something highly unusual for him to do. To add to it, Anthony was told by someone that Faheen had been to federal court with a subpoena. Prater remembered an instance in the hospital when he went to visit Paul. Anthony happened to be there, and they told him they were going to "hit" Faheen. Prater said he told them he couldn't believe they would do such a thing, to which they just laughed at him.

David Leisure ran the surveillance on George Faheen. They found out Faheen was living at the Mansion House. He knew, through conversations, that David was using a van to keep an eye on Faheen and was using Charles Loewe, Mike Kornhardt, possibly John Ramo and Malcom Flynn for surveillance.

Prater was asked about Michael Kornhardt and how he came on the scene. He replied Kornhardt worked for LN & P several years ago before quitting and going to work at Mid-Town Motors, Lemay Ferry Road, selling cars. Prater said he hadn't seen Kornhardt for a year or two before he just showed up again at LN & P. His feelings were from conversations he had heard that, while Kornhardt was at Mid-Town Motors, he was involved in the sale of two cars to members of the Michaels group using the name Sims or Simmons. When Kornhardt found out about it, he apparently felt an obligation to the Leisures to tell them about it. The next time he saw Michael Kornhardt, after he had left to go with Mid-Town, was one time when Kornhardt walked in the hospital, with David, to visit Paul.

Prater said David was going to use Kornhardt on the day of the bombing. Prater learned David and Kornhardt went in David's car to the Mansion House garage, where they had met Charles Loewe. They met Loewe on another floor of the garage, different from the one where Faheen's car was parked. It was here Loewe supposedly gave David either the dynamite or the entire explosive device. David drove near Faheen's car and parked, with Kornhardt remaining in the car the entire time. David got out of the car, approached Faheen's car, and was able to enter it by putting a wire through the vent window to pull up the level button. After the device was placed on the car, they left the area.

Prater was at the hospital visiting Paul one time after Faheen was killed. Paul commented to the effect, "you have to say something about the 'Little Man,'" a nickname of David Leisure's; "he gets things done."

When Prater commented on the Leisures' reaction to Kornhardt being arrested for Faheen's murder, he said they were definitely shocked. They were shocked because Kornhardt didn't participate in planting the bomb but stayed in the car. There was a lot of pressure on Michael Kornhardt after his arrest for the capital murder charge.

Prater was asked about the role played by Frank Termine. Prater said, on one occasion, John Ramo commented to him that Termine had been with them on some of the surveillances of Faheen. Paul made comments to Prater that he was going to take Kornhardt across the river into Illinois and dump him. Prater said he knew Paul was referring to killing Kornhardt. He said he objected to what Paul had suggested and later told Paul that wasn't such a good idea. Paul told him it was okay because he was going to dump Kornhardt in St. Charles.

On Friday, the day before Kornhardt was murdered, there was a lot of discussion about killing him while Prater was at the LN & P lot. Prater said he had called Mrs. Kornhardt, Mike's mother, and she told him Mike had been killed. He said later, while in the lot, he had asked Charles Loewe who killed Kornhardt. Loewe said all he knew was David was trying to get Robert Carbaugh, so Carbaugh couldn't snitch on David.

On the Sunday after the death, Prater said he was out in front of his house when Philomena Leisure came by. They both expressed how sorry they were Kornhardt had been killed. Prater said he knew Philomena had been seeing Kornhardt just before his death, so he asked her if she had seen Mike that Friday. She said, "yes, he had come by in the evening when she was taking a shower." Then Philomena told Prater she couldn't say this to the police, but Kornhardt had left her place with David Leisure and never came back.

Fred Prater also provided his knowledge and involvement in the Alex Aboussie house bombing. Sometime in the past, LN & P Towing Company had put a bid in with the City of St. Louis to obtain the towing contract. Their bid was low enough that they would have gotten the contract. However, Prater says Paul was telling him Alex Aboussie went to Walter Able, head of the City Street Department, and had the contract taken away from them.

About a week or so prior to the bombing of Alex Aboussie's residence, Paul said he would "scare the bastard," referring to Aboussie. Prater purchased a battery and some colored wire, which Paul later paid him for getting. Prater said on the evening of the Aboussie bombing, Anthony, Paul, and David came to his house and put part of the bomb together in the basement. He said Paul brought some dynamite sticks, which were about a foot long, and an electric blasting cap with two yellow wires coming out the top. The first Prater heard of the explosion was the following morning over the radio.

Solving the Spica Murder

Fred Prater told ATF Agents Holdiman and Bill McGarvey how John Paul Spica was murdered, the reason for the bombing, and who was responsible.

Prater said it was during the time Paul Leisure was aligned with Tony Giordano that Paul was introduced, by Giordano, to John Paul Spica. Spica, at the time, was operating a fruit stand on the corner of Vandeventer and Shaw Streets in St. Louis but was becoming a key man in Giordano's operation. Spica had some connections with the Spero gang, a known family of organized crime subjects in Kansas City, as he had done prison time with one of them.

Spica supposedly went to the Italian faction of organized crime in St. Louis, namely Tony Giordano, and said they were going to take over Laborers Local 42. Giordano gave the okay for this process, which had the eventual goal of killing Ray Flynn for a total takeover.

Since Anthony Giordano had Paul Leisure aligned with him, he mentioned to Leisure one time the Spica takeover and the fact Flynn would be killed. Paul Leisure realized at that point that, if the Italians took over Local 42, they would not stop there. He saw an eventual takeover of Laborers Local 110, a Syrian union, in which his brother Anthony was a part of. He could see trouble for himself and Anthony if this were to happen. This is about the time the Leisures aligned closer with the Flynns to begin the plan to kill John Paul Spica. Paul Leisure told Prater that Ray Flynn was the person who had killed Lou Shoulders, Jr. by hooking a bomb to his vehicle.

During this time Paul Leisure was buddying up to Spica in order to figure out his routine and his activities. Paul would talk to Spica a lot and would go out to dinner with Spica and his girlfriend.

Prater knew that Anthony Leisure was in on the bombing with Ray Flynn. Prater thought they may have hooked it to the taillights, similar to the Lou Shoulders Jr. bombing.

After Spica's death, the Leisures were afraid of retaliation by the Italians. They were also concerned the Italians would reach beyond St. Louis to take care of it. However, Tony Giordano was pretty sick during this time, and it seemed the Italians just accepted the turn of events.

Prater then cleared up the Michaels and Day murder attempt.

John Vitale had met with Anthony and said "you will read in the newspapers as it's a family thing". When the information came from Vitale, Anthony said he was going to find and kill all the Michaels.

Dave Leisure was told to begin looking down at the brewery (Anheuser-Busch) to keep an eye on a Michaels, who worked down there. At the time, Prater thought they meant James Michaels III. David Leisure did run surveillance in that area, and he did find out that one of the Michaels ate at The Edge Restaurant on LaSalle Street regularly.

Paul then spoke up and said there was an old house back there. Prater knew, before Paul was hurt, that Paul used to go over by that area and bum around and drink. Anthony told Prater they would go down in that area to check it out. Prater went with Anthony in Anthony's car and parked on the street near the old building behind The Edge Restaurant. The two of them went inside, and Anthony told him the place would be all right to shoot Michaels. This particular building overlooked the parking lot of the restaurant.

The next day, Prater said he drove David over there. They went inside, and David started knocking old boards off the windows. Later, David told him to go back to the place and cut the metal fence, so they wouldn't have to climb over it. He got with Charles "Obie" Loewe, who took him over to the building. Loewe returned to LN & P and got a pair of wire cutters from one of the toolboxes for the two trucks, which were kept in the lot office. Prater said he used the cutters to take care of the fence. A day or so after this, John Michaels and Dennis Day were shot at The Edge.

A few days after the shooting, Anthony described how, when he shot John Michaels, he fell down in the parking lot and Anthony thought he was dead. When he shot Dennis Day, he got him in the shoulder, which spun him around. Anthony explained he shot Day because he was afraid Day was going to run. Prater didn't know if Anthony knew who Dennis Day was at that time. Prater also said they had a driver who picked them up in a stolen van. He learned through conversation the driver was Charles "Obie" Loewe.

This was very damaging information, and just like Prater, other mob members fell in line and cooperated with the federal and state investigators and attorneys assigned to the cases. Such was the case of mob member John F. Ramo, who pled guilty to a federal racketeering charge involving a series of these underworld bombings and shootings.

Ramo also pled guilty to second-degree murder in the death of Jimmy Michaels Sr. in St. Louis Circuit Court and received a fifteen-year sentence that ran concurrent with the federal sentence in return for his cooperation with authorities. Ramo was the first of the mob to be sentenced.

As reported in the *St. Louis Globe-Democrat* on August 20, 1982:

James A. Michaels III was convicted in the Leisure bombing by a federal jury in Little Rock, Arkansas, where the trial was moved on a change of venue. U.S. Attorney Thomas E. Dittmeier predicted then that more car bombings would be resolved as a result of the conviction. Michaels is free on bond awaiting appeal of his five-year sentence.

And on October 19, 1982 the *Globe* reported:

Fred Prater was summoned to appear before a federal grand jury investigating the car bombings. Prater is considered a key government witness against the Leisure family. At the time of the scheduled grand jury appearance Prater was employed by Leisure's towing firm. Prater was then given federal protection and went into hiding, where he remains. Prater was named in indictments as one of those accused of conspiracy in the bombing of the elder Michaels.

On November 4, 1982, ATF agents conducted a lengthy interview with Innes James Anderson, who was an installation and repairman for Southwestern Bell Telephone Company in St. Louis. He was married to Brenda Jo, who was the sister of Steven Thomas Wougamon, a Leisure associate.

His first contacts with the Leisures were in February 1981, when he received a phone call from David Leisure regarding Wougamon's arrest for a murder in North St. Louis. Between February and March, he had a number of contacts with David Leisure. Through David, he had met Paul and Anthony Leisure. David asked him for telephone equipment and advice on how to bypass burglar alarms and related systems.

In August, David Leisure introduced him to Michael Kornhardt. David also discussed how Paul Leisure was a victim of a bombing and he suspected Michaels and a person named Norm Peters. He asked him to get some long-distance phone numbers for Norm Peters's brother, Robert, because the Leisures thought Robert was calling Norm Peters, who, in 1964, killed Rich Leisure. He also wanted Anderson to put a tap on Peters's phone. He told Leisure he couldn't do this. At the request of David Leisure, he found the long-distance phone calls of Robert Peters in a telephone record room.

On one occasion during the following six months, David Leisure accused James Michael III (nicknamed "Beans,") of bombing his uncle Paul Leisure. During these numerous conversations, David Leisure made numerous incriminating statements. Anderson said that when he learned about John Michael's shooting on September 11, 1981, he knew David Leisure was involved. About two weeks after the shooting, David Leisure said he and his cousin were responsible for shooting Michaels.

In October right after the George Faheen bombing, he had heard on the news that Michael Kornhardt had been arrested for the bombing murder. During conversations with David Leisure, Leisure admitted he and Kornhardt had killed George Faheen. On one occasion before Christmas 1981, Anderson had met with David Leisure and Robert Carbaugh at a restaurant located at South Broadway and Lafayette.

Shortly after Michael Kornhardt was murdered, Steven T. Wougamon told Anderson he and Carbaugh had killed Kornhardt. He told Anderson in detail how the murder was committed. Anderson's information would prove very damaging against numerous members of the Leisure mob faction.

Clearing the Kornhardt Murder Hit

In April 1983, Robert M. Carbaugh and Steven T. Wougamon, members of the Paul Leisure mob organization, were indicted with federal racketeering violations, including the murder of Michael Kornhardt on July 30, 1982. Evidence had been submitted in federal court through a federal agent that Carbaugh had killed Kornhardt on a country road in St. Charles County and dumped his body in a cornfield while Wougamon watched. The agent testified that Kornhardt was killed because members of the Leisure faction feared he might turn against his associates and cooperate with the government. John

Ramo, who was already cooperating with the government, testified that David Leisure had told him Robert Carbaugh murdered Kornhardt for the Leisures. Then on March 14, 1983 the news media reported:

Schepp surrendered to federal authorities 19 months after dropping out of sight. Two days later Schepp pleaded innocent in the Leisure bombing and was released on $50,000 bond. His trial is scheduled for May 23.

On April 14, 1983, the extensive investigation by ATF, other federal agencies, and the detectives of the St. Louis Bomb and Arson squad resulted in the indictment of eight men on charges of capital murder, racketeering, assault, armed criminal action, obstruction of justice, and conspiracy. As reported in a *Globe-Democrat* news article:

The indictments charge that six of the eight men were associated with the towing business owned by Anthony and John Paul Leisure, LN and P Inc. Those names in the indictment are: Paul John Leisure (also known as John Paul Leisure), business agent for Laborers' Local 42 and a part owner of the firm; Anthony J. Leisure, business agent for Laborers' Local 110 and part owner of the firm; David R. Leisure, part owner of the firm; John F. Ramo, an employee of the firm; Ronald Joseph Broderick, a business agent for Laborers' Local 110, Charles M. Loewe, and employee of the towing firm; and two men—Robert M. Carbaugh and Steven T. Wougamon—named as 'other individuals.'

The firm's purpose, according to the indictment, included:

To enrich its members financially, to obtain and maintain control over various labor unions; to murder leaders and members of rival groups, organizations and families; to retaliate against leaders and members of rival groups, organizations and families for acts committed against associates of the enterprise; avoid, discover and obstruct investigations and prosecutions of associates and activities of the enterprise by law enforcement officials. . . .

On September 9, 1983 Milton Russ Schepp was sentenced to a ten-year term for his role in the Paul Leisure bombing after Schepp was convicted on August 19, 1983 in federal court in Kansas City after a week-long trial.

On November 11, 1983, recently elected city alderman Sorkis Webbe Jr. was indicted by a federal grand jury, charging him with harboring federal fugitive David Leisure, who had been indicted in April 1983.

On January 17, 1984, Ronald J. Broderick pleaded guilty to six state charges in St. Louis Circuit Court. He had pleaded guilty to a federal racketeering charge previously in federal court in St. Louis. On November 16, 1989, Broderick was sentenced to a term of fifteen years for his part in the federal racketeering conspiracy.

On June 17, 1985, Robert M. Carbaugh entered a guilty plea to conspiracy in the federal racketeering case and shortly thereafter entered a guilty plea in state court for conspiracy to murder Michael Kornhardt on July 30, 1982.

On September 23, 1985, Steven T. Wougamon, who pled guilty to a state charge of second-degree murder in the Kornhardt hit, was sentenced to twenty years in prison to run concurrent with his previous sentence of forty-six years in federal court.

On January 21, 1986, Sorkis Webbe Jr. was sentenced to a term of twenty-six years in prison. On April 7, 1987, David Leisure was convicted in St. Louis Circuit Court for the murder of Jimmie Michaels Sr. on September 17, 1980. He was sentenced to death on May 22, 1987.

On May 2, 1987, Charles M. Loewe was found guilty in circuit court in the shooting murder attempt of Charles John Michaels and Dennis Day on September 11, 1981. Loewe had set up the shooting and driven the getaway van. He was sentenced to fifty years. Loewe had previously been convicted in federal court for racketeering and received a thirty-six-year sentence.

On September 25, 1987, Anthony J. Leisure was sentenced to life in prison in the circuit court in St. Louis for the murder of Jimmy Michaels Sr. after he had been sentenced to forty years in federal court in 1985 for racketeering charges.

On February 16, 1988, Anthony Leisure was found guilty in state courts of manslaughter in the George Faheen bombing, receiving a maximum sentence of ten years.

On March 2, 1989, Paul Leisure was sent to the Missouri State Penitentiary, sentenced to fifty-five years.

On July 19, 2000, Paul Leisure died while serving a fifty-five-year sentence at the Federal Medical Center in Springfield for federal prisoners.

On September 1, 2000, David Leisure was put to death by lethal injection for the vehicle bombing death of Jimmy Michaels Sr.

On May 22, 2002 Raymond H. Flynn, convicted of killing George Faheen and John Paul Spica, died in the federal medical prison in Springfield. He was seventy-three.

This marked the end of a thirty-nine-year saga of Paul Leisure and his gang of mobsters.

All those law enforcement officials from the ATF, state, and local police agencies and the state and federal attorneys involved in the successful outcome can look back with pride and a sense of accomplishment for a job well done.

I know Case Agent Gordon Holdiman of the ATF, St. Louis office feels a sense of pride in the outcome. I know because we still talk to each other about the stories behind the investigations.

CHAPTER TEN

MOBSTER CRIME, VIOLENCE, AND JUSTICE, WEST MISSOURI STYLE 1900-1990

I n the 1980s article "Death is a Way of Life for the Mob—55 Murders in 38 Years," *Kansas City Star* reporter Patrick Dunn described Kansas City's crime history:

> As one story after another unfolds the same words and phrases are repeated over the years: found dead in the trunk of a car, bullet wounds in the head, gunned down in a bar, shot down in a hail of bullets on the street, blown up by a car bomb.

Just like St. Louis mobsters, Kansas City mobsters created havoc in the city and surrounding areas, dating back to the turn of the century as summarized in the introductory chapter in the book.

Terence Michael O'Malley, an author and film documentary producer, documents the early history of Kansas City crime in his book *Black Hand/Strawman: The History of Organized Crime in Kansas City*. His work has provided material for this chapter.

At the turn of the century, a large population of immigrants settled in the Kansas City area of Missouri. Many of them were Sicilian immigrants. Most were hardworking individuals trying to make an honest living during very difficult times. A small segment of them were criminals who specialized in extorting money from their fellow honest, hardworking Sicilians. Their method was known as the Black Hand, a very intimidating crime in which the victim was forced to remain silent or his family member would face physical punishment or death. This form of crime was carried out from the late 1890s to about 1920, a period of time when at least forty murders were attributed to Black Hand extortion and homicide crimes.

In 1911 Joseph Raimo, a thirty-four-year-old Kansas City police officer of Italian descent, was murdered shortly after he overheard men talking about a Black Hand murder of an aging female Black Hand victim who had spoken to police. Raimo was murdered by members of the criminal group as he exited the saloon where the conversation took place. This gangland killing of a police officer, killed by two shotgun blasts, shocked the city. It was a ruthless crime that placed utter fear into the Italian community.

Throughout the 1930s, Kansas City mob boss Johnny Lazia operated closely with Kansas City political machine boss Tom Pendergast, providing money to Pendergast and the machine in return for allowing the mobsters to operate uncontrolled. At one time Lazia had over eighty police officers on his payroll after he found them jobs as police officers. They paid Lazia proceeds from their every paycheck.

This ruthless marriage between the two organizations broke up in 1939 when machine boss Pendergast was convicted and sentenced to prison for tax evasion. As for Lazia, his reign ended when he was murdered on July 11, 1934, by two men carrying and using a shotgun and machine gun. He was murdered by two area criminals named Michael James LaCapra (a.k.a. "Jimmy Needles") of Kansas City and Jack Griffin (a.k.a. "Jack Gregory") out of St. Louis. On July 30, 1934, Gregory was shot three times in a gangland hit yet survived his wounds. Then on September 18, 1934, he disappeared and was never seen again.

On August 30, 1934, the first attempted murder of LaCapra occurred in rural Kansas when three hired mobsters out of St. Louis shot him with a shotgun blast; however, he also survived the wounds. He left town and headed to the East Coast, where, on August 26, 1935, his body was found on the side of a road in Plattekill, New York. He was shot in the base of his skull. Another mob hit.

Research author Terence O'Malley documents in his book that mob boss Charlie Binaggio was in with the Kansas City political machine in the late 1940s and had initiated an effort to organize legal gambling in Missouri. His efforts failed, and in 1950, he paid for his failed attempts with his life. This mob murder will be detailed more in the chronology of this chapter.

This chapter will now focus on the mob violence from the 1940s to the late 1980s, involving the same recurring motivations for the carnage, the desire for power, money, greed, and revenge—moving into labor unions, gambling, and vice. In his 1980s article, Dunn went on to describe in dramatic detail the various mob hits detailed in this chapter.

The date is Jan. 30, 1946. The time is 1:15 a.m. Two men, both about the same height and build, walk from a small market on the city's East Side. The men, old friends, talk as they get into a car parked outside the market. One man enters the driver's side and leans the back of his head against the window. The second man slides into the passenger's seat, even though the car is his.

A second car appears up the block and drives slowly by. A Thompson sub-machine gun and a 12-gauge shotgun appear at its windows and the car with the two talking men is sprayed with bullets. The man on the driver's side slumps over the wheel fatally wounded with four bullets in the head. His companion dives for the floor of the car, opens the door and rolls onto the ground. He escapes without a scratch.

Dead is 43-year-old Louis Cuccia, a Jackson County deputy sheriff, a man known well in the city and popular with all who knew him. His friend who escaped without a mark, and who police believe was the actual target, is Nick Civella, later to become regarded as the underworld boss of Kansas City.

That 'hit' more than 30 years ago may stand apart because a man other than the intended victim was killed. But for the Kansas City Crime Commission it is just another statistic, one of 55 killings in Kansas City since 1940 that the commission attributes to organized crime.

In April 1980, the well-known, nationally syndicated reporter Jack Anderson wrote "Mob Not Far Removed from 30's Stereotype" for the *Kansas City Star*. In it, he described a tape-recorded conversation in 1978 between Kansas City mob boss Nick Civella and his brother "Cork" Civella. They were talking about "rubbing" out a mobster rival named Carl Spero. During the conversation, Civella described his murder squad with pride, saying, "We got the best blood hounds in the United States and always have."

Reporter Anderson ended his article with this paragraph:

> The thing to remember about this grisly business is that the transactions involve the violent death of someone who has—innocently or not—gotten in the way of a leader's pursuit of power. The Mafia men may dress like Wall Street brokers, but they're no more respectable than they ever were.

The chronology of murder and mobster mayhem continued through the ensuing years.

In 1920, Kansas City mobsters began to be more organized with the passage of Prohibition, forming what became known as the Sugarhouse Syndicate, which would organize the distribution of illegal alcohol throughout the Midwest.

Also, from the 1920s to the 1940s, the Kansas City Mob controlled the drug distribution network, distributing primarily heroin. The Mob in Kansas City ran these illegal drug operations with crime families from other cities until 1943, when the federal DEA conducted a major investigation resulting in numerous prosecutions, basically dissolving the distribution network.

In their 1961 book, *The Murderers, The Shocking Story of the Narcotic Gangs*, Harry J. Anslinger and Will Oursler wrote about their experience with the crime syndicate's national and international dealing in commercialized drug addiction.

Anslinger was the long-standing director of the National Drug Enforcement Administration, and he detailed a major investigation conducted by his federal agents who engaged in the war against murders for more than thirty years. In the book, he found it important to include a major mob drug syndicate operating primarily in the Midwest United States in St. Louis and Kansas City.

The syndicate mob bosses were distributing heroin brought in from Tampa, Florida, to the Missouri mobsters. Their DEA investigation involved more than fifty top echelon Mafia gangsters. Before the investigation was brought to a successful conclusion, one of the informants was "found dead in San Francisco gangland style." Another witness who was supplying information "who disclosed many inside details of the syndicate organization was murdered in Chicago with a shotgun blast that tore off his head."

Anslinger's investigation revealed that crooked cops in Chicago were involved with the Mob and even one of his DEA agents admitted he was carrying out "hits" for the Mob. When the agent was confronted with this information, he left the DEA office and committed suicide.

On April 5, 1950, in the late evening or early morning, mob political front man Charlie Binaggio and mob associate hit man Charlie Gargotta were murdered gangland-style while meeting with a known mob associate in the First District Democratic Club at 716-18 Truman Road in Kansas City. Their bodies were found the next morning. Both men were shot—both with four bullets to the head. This was clearly a mob inside hit. The execution was planned and carried out by the Kansas City Mob, known by law enforcement as the "Outfit." It was strongly suspected in organized mob circles that Nick Civella was the person who orchestrated and carried out the murder of Gargotta and Binaggio, which put Civella in a position to soon become the mob boss of the Kansas City Mafia family.

The brutal double murders drew the attention of the Senator Estes Kefauver's committee hearings. Their first committee hearings were held in Kansas City in 1950. The committee called numerous local mobsters to the hearings and also drew national attention to Kansas City mobsters, causing the Mob to go into temporary hiding and slow down their mob activities.

At the same time throughout the 1950s, the St. Louis City Police Department created what was referred to as the Hoodlum Squad led by Major John Doherty. The activities in the unit put intense pressure on the St. Louis mobsters, causing them to switch regional mobster meetings to Kansas City and Chicago. Then during the mid-afternoon of November 14, 1957, Officer Edgar Croswell of the New York State Police, his partner Vincent Vasisko, and two ATF Treasury agents were conducting surveillance at the estate owned by Joseph Barbara Sr., owner of a legitimate local bottling company, when they observed numerous vehicles with out-of-state plates. Officer Croswell had come across Barbara's name in connection with gambling and other underworld activities.

As late as the 1950s, the FBI led by J. Edgar Hoover did not recognize that the Mafia ever existed, so the troopers requested the federal assistance with the ATF agents, who had the jurisdiction of firearms at the time. Croswell, however, suspected the secret underworld organization did exist.

They were diligently writing down numerous license plates when they were spotted and one of the visitors yelled out a warning, causing a major exodus of the suspected mobsters. Officer Croswell called for assistance, roadblocks were set up, and sixty-three of Barbara's guests were arrested. According to law enforcement reports, those who attended included mob bosses Joe

Bonanno, Carlo Gambino, Vito Genovese, and Joe Profaci, of prominent New York crime families. Other bosses from around the country were identified as John Scalish (Cleveland), Joe Civello (Dallas), James Colletti (Boulder, Colorado), Frank DiSimone (Los Angeles), Joseph Ida (Philadelphia), and Frank Zito (Springfield, Illinois). Guests from Cuba and Italy were in attendance as well.

Also arrested were two men who gave their names as Joe Filard and Nick Civello, who were actually Nick Civella and Joe Filardo, both of Kansas City.

Sergeant Croswell, Trooper Vasisko and the two ATF agents had disrupted a meeting of Cosa Nostra's national leadership, a meeting officially identified as the Apalachin Gangland Convention. It was now an undisputed fact that the Mafia did exist and Kansas City was in it at the highest level.

In February 1960 Nick Civella, his brother Carl "Cork" Civella, and several of his mob associates went to Las Vegas and attempted to muscle in at the Riviera Hotel and Casino, only to be arrested and chased out of town. On June 13, 1960, the Nevada Gaming Commission Board of Directors enacted the List of Excluded Persons or the Black Book, naming eleven mobsters as excluded for life from Nevada casinos. It should be no surprise that included on this list were Nick Civella and his brother Carl "Cork" Civella. The reader will find more details of mob influence in the Nevada gambling industry in this book's "Missouri Mob Influence on the Nevada Hotel and Casino Industry" chapter.

On June 20, 1960 Kenneth Bruce Sheets, a government witness in a federal narcotics case, was shot four times at the front door of his house in Omaha, Nebraska. Sheets survived the attempted murder and later identified Tiger Cardarella and Felix Ferina, two men who were soldiers in the organized crime faction in Kansas City, as the shooters. Both coconspirators were convicted of the attempted gangland murder and sentenced to ten years in prison.

On February 9, 1961 Stanton Gladden, Kansas City Firefighters Local 42 Union president, was seriously injured at his Kansas City home when a bomb detonated as he started a family vehicle in an obvious gangland murder attempt. Gladden had refused to sign an affidavit regarding union business that mob boss Nick Civella had ordered him to sign.

When then United States Attorney General Robert F. Kennedy learned of the attempted murder hit, he prompted an intensive federal investigation into the Teamsters union activities and connections with the Kansas City underworld. This action broadened the scope of the Organized Criminal Federal Task Force on the inside workings of the Teamsters and the Mob. Kennedy's primary targets were Teamster International President Jimmy Hoffa and Teamster official Roy Williams of Kansas City.

Williams was under indictment for the embezzlement of $200,000 in Teamster Union funds. A person named Floyd Hayes, who was a high-ranking official in Kansas City Local 41 about to testify against Roy Williams, was shotgunned to death in Chicago, and the federal case fell apart. Many crimes in Kansas City went unsolved when turncoat witnesses who had agreed to cooperate or testify against members of the underworld were found dead.

In 1963, police learned a high-level meeting would take place at Uncle Tom's Barbeque at 3809 Broadway. This establishment was operated by Anthony Thomas "Highway" Simone, an Outfit powerhouse. Those in attendance included Simone, Max Jaben of the Kansas City Outfit, and Anthony Giordano and Jimmy Michaels, both mob figures from St. Louis. After the meeting, Jaben, Michaels, and Giordano were arrested and charged with disorderly conduct. This documented meeting gave law enforcement one more rare look at the Mob's Kansas City and St. Louis connections.

Another victim in the 1960s was turncoat Sam Palma, who was photographed on the courthouse steps with political boss Alex Presta in 1966. He was murdered in a Mafia-style hit, and his body was found at the Mount Olive Cemetery draped over his father's gravestone—a chilling reminder that anyone who might decide to talk against their criminal brother should have second thoughts.

On July 15, 1970 at about 1:00 a.m., as Leon Mercer Jordan walked out of his tavern at the Green Duck located in North Kansas City, he was killed, hit with three blasts from a shotgun. Eyewitnesses at the scene said the shooters were three African Americans. Shortly after the murder of Jordan, a shotgun was found abandoned near the scene and secured by police investigators. It was determined the shotgun had been stolen in a burglary of a hardware store located in Independence, Missouri, in 1965. The weapon was a Remington 12-gauge Wingmaster shotgun. Forensic examination of the weapon could not positively determine this was the murder weapon.

At the time of his murder, Leon Jordan, a Missouri State Representative, was campaigning for a fourth term in the Missouri House of Representatives. Jordan was an ex-Kansas City Police Department lieutenant, the first African American to achieve that position in the history of the department. Jordan had resigned his position from the department in 1952, realizing he had little authority.

In 1951, Leon Jordan had become a member of the National Association for the Advancement of Colored People and developed an interest in politics. His political career began in 1958 when he became a Democratic Party committeeman for the Fourteenth Ward of Kansas City. In 1962 Jordan cofounded Freedom, Inc., an organization advocating political awareness among African Americans in the Kansas City area. They organized a massive voter registration campaign and supported black political candidates.

In 1964, the organization offered eight candidates for office, and seven of the eight secured a win. Jordan was among the seven and was elected to his first term in the Missouri House of Representatives. This would prove to be his first of three terms.

As a result of the murder investigation, three men were charged with murder. One of those charged was affiliated with the Black Mafia, a criminal group in Kansas City. One man was acquitted in a trial, and the charges against the other two suspects were dropped. During the investigation, it was discovered that, in January 1966, a police report was prepared by the Independence Police Department, stating the stolen murder weapon recovered had been sold through a "North End Italian fence." It was suspected the murder weapon could have made its way to the Kansas City mob element. Could Jordan have been wiped out by members or associates of the Kansas City Mob?

Evidence suggests there was a very feasible motive for his death. It was learned later the fence was "Shotgun Joe" Centimano, owner of a local liquor store, who allegedly supplied the murder weapon to the killer he had hired to kill Jordan. The confidential informant who provided this information alleged the "contract" killing was about revenge, and another informant said it was all about politics.

Leon Jordan was not a friend of the Kansas City organized crime faction or their strong political hold on Kansas City and Missouri politics. There were a number of reasons the mob faction, headed by Nick Civella, would have wanted Jordan dead. In the 1970s, the Mob was described by the FBI as "a cold, murderous gang of hoodlums" that didn't like to be crossed. Jordan's long fight for black political power angered the Mob's North End political faction. Jordan's wife, Orchid, told police her husband had refused to change Freedom, Inc.'s endorsement of certain candidates, even after he had been offered money. He had an angry disagreement with the North End politicians shortly before his death about the Freedom, Inc. ballot recommendations.

Jordan, in 1965, had punched fellow Representative Frank Mazzuca on the House floor of the state capitol. Mazzuca supposedly supported mob interests in Jefferson City. Jordan apologized; however, there were rumors that Mazzuca had "friends" on the North Side that were going to kill Jordan, according to one fellow politician.

It was felt by the law enforcement community Jordan's actions over political issues were enough to get him killed. One police informant named Froniabargar, who was a member of the Kansas City Black Mafia, told police this is what occurred. Jordan's killing was "contracted by the North End and carried out by blacks." The payoff man was, he said, an Italian who owned a liquor store on Nineteenth and Vine. Police learned the man's name was Joe Centimano. Froniabargar's story was confirmed by another fellow member of the Black Mafia who wanted to remain anonymous. Another source named Cox said "Shotgun Joe" acquired the shotgun to kill Jordan from a mob associate in March 1970. Centimano then turned the weapon over to the killers.

The FBI suspected the murder was the act of a mob associate who carried out the murder in a freelance hit, to gain favor with the leaders of the mob organization. This motive theory was further supported just a few months later when a second mob hit occurred with eerie similarities.

On November 22, 1970, in the middle of the night, Sol Landie, a high-dollar bettor who co-owned the Square Deal Scrap Metal Company, located at 218 Kansas Avenue in Kansas City, Kansas, was murdered at his residence in Kansas City, Missouri. He was shot in the head as he laid in his bed with his wife, Ann Landie. She had been raped, and the murder and rape were made to appear to be a house invasion rape and robbery. Kansas City homicide detectives Clarence Luther and Gary McGrady, who investigated the crime, noticed a pillow on the bed with a bullet hole in it, a sign there was more than a robbery gone bad. They also noted that expensive jewelry had been left behind.

Four associates were arrested, and one of them, a sixteen-year-old, confessed to the crime, pointing the finger at John Frankoviglia, a member of the Nick Civella crime family, who had hired them to kill Landie. Witnesses at Landie's murder trial testified Frankoviglia had Landie killed because he was to be a witness for the feds in another case. Another witness, seventeen-year-old Gary Johnson, said they were instructed to kill Landie because he was a federal witness and a third associate, twenty-year-old Marquise Williams, testified Landie was killed because of "the indictments."

Evidence at the federal trial documented Landie was caught on wiretaps placing large bets from Kansas City, Kansas, to Kansas City, Missouri, across state lines in violation of federal interstate gambling laws. Landie had been granted immunity and agreed to testify against Nick Civella, Tony Civella, Frank Tousa, and Martin Chess of Las Vegas, who was the Kansas City Mob's betting line source. At the conclusion of the investigation, Frankoviglia and the four assailants were convicted of the murder to wipe out a government witness, one of the very few solved cases against the Mob up to that time.

On April 11, 1973, Nick Spero, a Teamster business agent for Local 41 and member of the Mob, was murdered by the Civella mob faction for failing to carry out a murder contract placed on a Spero associate named Lester Moore, a local car dealership owner, to eliminate Moore from testifying in a Civella mob gambling case. Spero was shot in the head and stuffed in the trunk of a car that was located at the KCI Airport parking lot. Nick's younger brother Carl Spero vowed revenge from his prison cell while serving time for a felony conviction. This would touch off the beginning of a power struggle between the Spero mob faction and the Civella Outfit, lasting for eleven years.

On July 22, 1976 David Bonadonna was murdered gangland-style, a Kansas City mob hit. At the time of the hit, Bonadonna was a lieutenant in the Civella mob, taking orders from William and Joseph Cammisano. His suspected killers, the Cammisanos, assisted by Johnny "Green" Amaro, probably killed him in their garage, shot five times and then left in the trunk of his car. Bonadonna was killed because he had stood by his son Fred Bonadonna, who owned a bar called Poor Freddie's in the River Quay area of Kansas City. The Mob wanted to open bars in the Quay and bring in prostitution. Fred and his dad resisted the Mob's efforts. David Bonadonna paid dearly for his efforts. Fred Bonadonna would seek revenge.

On September 29, 1976, someone placed a pipe bomb at the rear door of the Columbus Park Social Club known as The Trap, located at 1048 East 5th Street, just west of Troost, a mob hangout. It was a warning and possible retaliation for the David Bonadonna hit. This was your author's first involvement in the organized operations in and around the Kansas City metropolitan area. There would be many more cases over the next several years investigated by the ATF Kansas City office agents.

Early in November 1976, Sonny Bowen, a Spero mob associate, found that a blasting cap damaged the back seat of his vehicle. Apparently, it detonated prematurely, injuring the would-be bomber, who left behind blood found on the back seat. Sonny Bowen was also an associate of Fred Bonadonna and became his bodyguard and hit man. On November 17, 1976, a mob associate of Fred Bonadonna named John Brocato was found dead in the trunk of his car parked at the KCI Airport parking lot. He was tortured and strangled on a hit allegedly ordered by Kansas City mob boss Nick Civella. On February 19, 1977, Fred Bonadonna retaliated for his father's murder when he hired his two bodyguards, Sonny Bowen and Gary T. Parker, to kill Johnny "Green" Amaro. The two ambushed Amaro as he pulled into his garage, using shotguns in the murder, which occurred just one block from the home of underworld kingpin Nick Civella.

This hit on their mob associate infuriated Civella. He retaliated on February 22, 1977, when four masked men shotgunned Sonny Bowen to death as he sat in Mr. O'Brian's Lounge located at 3507 Broadway in Kansas City. Informants reported that the killers were Charles Moretina, Pete Tamburello, Anthony Civella, and Carl DeLuna, all high-ranking Outfit members.

On March 28, 1977, shortly after the bars' closing time, a major explosion completely destroyed two side-by-side saloons known as Pat O'Brien's and Judge Roy Bean's located at Fourth Street and Wyandotte in the River Quay area. It was rumored in the mob and law enforcement circles that the building was destroyed by fracturing the gas line in the building after a number of sticks of dynamite were strung up in the building and resulted in a massive air/fuel mixture explosion, supplemented with the detonation of the dynamite. A crime associate of the Cammisanos was the suspected torch.

After the Bowen hit, the Outfit started stalking Gary T. Parker. Parker told federal authorities an attempt on his life occurred on April 1, 1977, when an ambush was set up by mob associate Vincent Picone. Parker had met with Picone at a bar in Kansas City to discuss payment of a debt Picone owed Parker. They agreed to settle the debt later in the day at another bar; when Parker arrived at this meeting, he observed Picone and Willie Cammisano in a car watching for him, and Parker left the area. Parker's life was spared for several months due to Nick Civella's conviction on bookmaking charges. Civella lost his final appeal and began serving a federal sentence on August 1, 1977.

On May 8, 1977 Arthur Eugene Shepherd, Michael Ruffalo, and mob associates set an arson fire at a tire store in St. Marys, Kansas, not too far from Kansas City, Missouri. The arson case was assigned to ATF agent Duane Nichols, who investigated the fire. The defendants were acquitted in a federal jury trial. On the last Sunday morning in July 1977, a bar, Uncle Joe's, located at 223 West Third Street on the River Quay at the River Market in Downtown Kansas City, was destroyed by an explosion. The bar was owned by Kansas City Outfit member Joe Cammisano. The bar had experienced a previous fire on September 28, 1976, but remained open until it was destroyed.

On August 5, 1977 only five days after Nick Civella started serving his sentence, Gary T. Parker was killed with a remote-controlled bomb as he opened the door of his vehicle as he left Louie's Tavern. The tavern, located at 4127 Truman Road in Kansas City, was owned and operated by Tony Mike Bonadonna, Fred Bonadonna's brother and David Bonadonna's son. Then, on November 22, 1977, thirty-eight-year-old Michael Kattou—a former Kansas City firefighter, convicted felon, and associate of the Speros—was murdered in the office of his body shop on Independence Avenue in Kansas City. Investigators concluded Kattou was a victim of an underworld hit as the Mob turned its attention on the Spero Outfit.

On May 2, 1978 Myron "Andy" Mancuso, another associate of the Spero faction, was shot to death gangland-style and found in a vehicle in a parking lot near the Villa Capri restaurant. Information developed to reveal the shooters were William Commisano Jr. and Carl "Cork" Civella. Mancuso had dinner at the Villa Capri that evening, as well as Civella and Cammisano Jr. shortly before his death. Two days later, Michael Massey's body was found in a stolen car on the Kansas City South Side. He was shot in the back of the head. Massey was a federally immunized witness who had testified against Anthony "Tiger" Cardarella, a local mob associate and fence of stolen property. Cardarella was convicted of receiving stolen property primarily consisting of long-playing record albums, and on June 13, 1977, he was sentenced to serve five years at the US Penitentiary in Texarkana, Texas.

On May 16, 1978, Michael Spero, Joseph Spero, and Carl Spero were ambushed at the Virginian Tavern in Kansas City by four Outfit members wearing masks and armed with rifles and shotguns. When the smoke cleared, Michael Spero laid dead, Joe Spero was wounded, and Carl Spero was paralyzed, hit with a bullet in his back.

Harold Nichols, a detective assigned to the Kansas City Police Intelligence Unit, a professional associate and friend of your author, provided a firsthand account of what took place. He and his partner Tommy Walker were checking mob hangouts when they saw Carl Spero outside the front door of the tavern at about 10:00 p.m., talking on the telephone located just inside the door. They drove past onto Admiral Boulevard as the shooting started at the tavern. Detective Nichols said he and his partner were at Admiral and Oak Streets when they heard over their police radio that shots had been fired at the Virginian Tavern. As they returned to the tavern, they saw Carl Spero lying in the street, shot and unable to move. Detective Nichols asked Carl if he knew who had shot him. Carl replied, "Yes." Detectives asked, "Are you going to tell us who?" Carl answered, "No." The detectives proceeded to the tavern and observed Michael Spero on the floor shot in the head and lying dead. Nichols said Joe Spero was shot in the right arm and was taken to the hospital.

Detective Nichols said about two minutes had elapsed from the time they first passed the tavern until they noticed that shots had been fired. Nichols felt the shooters entered the tavern through the rear door and started firing their weapons. They fled through the front door, leaving the scene. Nichols added that the police recovered a 1976 Ford LTD with the motor still running. A shotgun was found near the car, as well as a blue stocking cap lying on the ground. Two pistols were also located in the vicinity of the tavern. Detective Nichols also provided this information to retired FBI Agent and crime researcher William Ousley, who included Nichols' information in his book *Mobsters in our Midst: The Kansas City Crime Family.*

At noon on May 22, 1978, a dynamite bomb was thrown under a vehicle parked at the Red Apple Lounge, located at 117 North Fifth Street in Kansas City, Kansas. The vehicle, which was owned by Jack Anderson, who operated the Red Apple Lounge, was heavily damaged in the explosion. At the time of the bombing, several ATF agents were eating lunch at a restaurant also located on the parking lot and were the first on the scene. A scene examination was conducted, evidence was collected, and an investigation was initiated by ATF and local police.

The investigation developed evidence that the bombing was meant as an intimidation message sent by Kansas City mob boss Carl "Corky" Civella to Jack Anderson. Corky Civella was interested in getting a piece of the Red Apple Lounge. He hired Arthur Shepherd and Michael Ruffalo to do the bombing of the vehicle. The bomb they used was sort of a "John Wayne" bomb (a simple bomb), consisting of sticks of dynamite, a safety fuse, and a nonelectric blasting cap.

Jack Anderson had put the lounge license in the name of Toni LanFranca, a woman who was, at the time, associated with both Corky Civella and Carl Spero. She was also the daughter of a woman who was dating one of the bombers, Arthur Shepherd, an intriguing triangle. This investigation, along with a number of other investigations of criminal acts committed by organized crime figures, were all underway at the time of this incident.

On October 10, 1978, Joseph and Willie "The Rat" Cammisano Sr. pled guilty of conspiracy to extort money and favors from Fred Bonadonna of the River Quay. Willie "The Rat" was sentenced to five years and started serving his sentence in January of 1979. His brother Joe withdrew his guilty plea and was later convicted in a jury trial.

On October 9, 1978, Carl DeLuna was overheard on a telephone conversation with Joseph Agosto, a Civella faction mob associate operating in Las Vegas. DeLuna ordered three long guns with scopes to be used to kill Carl Spero. In January 1979, the police learned the rifles had been delivered to DeLuna in Kansas City. Ironically, also in January 1979, the law enforcement task force team received information from two Spero associates who decided to cooperate with police. They said one of the Speros attempted to kill DeLuna by firing two shots at him with a rifle at DeLuna's Kansas City residence. Both shots missed him.

On January 10, 1979, the body of James R. Harkins, a Local 41 Teamster CPA, was found behind a bar he frequented at 6000 Blue Ridge Boulevard in Kansas City. He had been shot several times in the back, another gangland hit. Harkins had been in the bar earlier in the evening. Federal and Kansas City homicide detectives initiated their investigations with few leads and only a dead body.

On May 5, 1979, two Spero faction members, Joe Spero and Mike Cuezze, placed a remote-controlled dynamite bomb under the vehicle of Civella enforcer Carl DeLuna's vehicle at the parking lot of the Villa Capri restaurant. As DeLuna got into his car early in the morning, the two attempted to detonate the bomb. However, it failed to go off. They retrieved the bomb to try again. The Spero faction was placed under surveillance, and an informant, who was a member of the Spero faction, decided to cooperate with ATF agents and the Kansas City Police detectives.

On May 17, 1979, ATF agents from the Kansas City office seized a remote-controlled bomb consisting of six sticks of dynamite. The bomb was intended to be used by Joe Spero, Conrad Metz, and Mike Cuezze to kill Carl "Tuffy" DeLuna of the Civella faction Outfit. On June 27, 1979, the three were indicted by a federal grand jury, charging them with possession of the explosive bomb. On October 6, 1979, a jury came back with a guilty verdict, convicting Joe Spero and Conrad Metz of illegally possessing a bomb. Cuezze was acquitted.

Late in the month of June 1979, the home of Frank A. Todaro was damaged by a fire and explosion. The fire was intentionally set. Todaro was the owner of the Virginian Tavern (where the killing happened), a bar the Spero brothers and faction members frequented. Joseph Spero Jr., son of Joe Spero, was brought in for questioning after he appeared at a local hospital and was treated for burns on his hand, chest, and face only thirty minutes after the Todaro fire was set. Joe Spero Jr. claimed he burned himself in a lawn mower accident and denied causing the Todaro fire and explosion.

On June 20, 1980 Joseph Spero, the oldest brother, was killed when a bomb exploded in a shed he had rented in south Clay County, where he was hiding explosives. The early theory was that he was making a bomb when it detonated. Spero had recently lost his appeal bid on his bomb possession conviction and was about to start his prison term.

I assisted other ATF agents in the Joe Spero bomb scene examination. We felt during the scene examination that the crime scene told a different story of the cause of Spero's death than the theory that he'd died while making a bomb. Could a booby trap bomb have been placed inside the shed that activated when Spero opened the door, tripping the device and causing it to detonate?

A couple of days after his death, Spero's family members gave the police a handwritten, signed letter he had prepared, instructing them to provide the letter to the police upon his death. In the letter, he wrote about the ambush at the Virginian Tavern on May 16, 1978, naming the shooters as Charles Moretina, Joe Ragusa, and Carl DeLuna, who possessed the shotgun with the other two using pistols. They had committed the shootings at the direction of the Civella crime family.

The answer to Joe Spero's death came ten years later when an FBI source told agents the murder of Joe Spero was carried out by Johnny Joe Calia and Lawrence Tuso, who knew Spero stored a quantity of dynamite in the shed and booby-trapped it, killing Spero most likely when he opened the door to the shed. This explained why we located his body outside the shed. FBI agent Nick Thomeczek testified to this information in an open federal court at a bond hearing for Calia, who was charged in a large multistate drug ring.

On October 10, 1980, mob associates Joseph Ruguso and John Carusso were found guilty of possession of incendiary devices outside a house the two were attempting to burn down in Kansas City. An alert Kansas City police officer arrested the two in possession of the incendiary devices, and ATF agent Chris Sadowski of the Kansas City office perfected the federal case, which was tried in federal court.

On February 5, 1982, a bomb consisting of ten sticks of dynamite was found attached to car dealer Lester Moore's vehicle at his residence. He was an associate of the Carl Spero mob faction and had a contract on his head for several years after he cooperated with the government in a gambling case involving mob boss Nick Civella. This was an obvious failed attempt to kill Lester Moore.

In August 1982, James Duardi, a Kansas City mob insider, attempted to obtain a quantity of dynamite from a source in Oklahoma. He made the pickup with the help of Jack King and Clifford Bishop. King was arrested by ATF agents before he could make the delivery, was convicted, and received a twenty-two-year sentence.

Duardi eventually got his hands on some dynamite in May 1983 and assisted in making a bomb to destroy the Wild Horse Average Saloon, operated by a Duardi associate. The saloon and a bingo parlor were damaged by fire.

In May 1985, after an extensive investigation by ATF agent Dick Curd and the FBI, suspects James Duardi and Thomas Hargrove of Tulsa, Oklahoma, were charged with conspiracy to transport high explosives from Oklahoma to Kansas City and possession of dynamite, all connected to the 1983 delivery of dynamite. In a guilty plea in federal court, Duardi admitted to the offenses charged and was sentenced to eight years in prison.

In the fall of 1983, a large bomb consisting of twenty-three sticks of dynamite was found attached to Carl Spero's vehicle, as it sat in the driveway of his residence in Holt, Missouri, just north of Kansas City. The bomb was found by Spero's young nephew. The Kansas City bomb squad and ATF were called to investigate and disarm the device.

Carl Spero was a marked man, and he knew it. He had already lost three brothers in violent gangland murders committed by the Nick Civella mob faction, and it was just a matter of time for Carl to be the fourth to die.

Carl Spero's crime-filled life came to a violent end on January 19, 1984, when a remote-controlled bomb was detonated under the floor of Spero's small office at his used car lot, located on East Twelfth Street in Kansas City. He was seated in his wheelchair at a desk, talking on the telephone, when he was murdered. He and his wheelchair were blown from the office, landing on the lot. As an ATF supervisor, I was assigned to supervise the crime scene search and collect evidence. ATF agent Dick Curd was assigned as the case agent.

As reported by retired FBI agent Bill Ousley in *Mobsters in Our Midst*, in February 1984, federal Racketeer Influenced and Corrupt Organizations (RICO) Act charges were filed, aimed to prosecute the Kansas City crime family as a criminal entity. The charge cited five "acts of racketeering" committed by the Nick Civella crime family. The charge also included, "from January 1978 to January 9, 1984 Carl and Tony Civella and Carl DeLuna conspired to murder Carl Spero, who was murdered in a bombing on January 9, 1984." All men pled guilty to the charges.

On September 9, 1984 Anthony "Tiger" Cardarella was killed gangland-style, shot and found in the trunk of his car in Kansas City, Missouri. Cardarella had recently returned to Kansas City after serving a five-year sentence for a federal conviction for receiving stolen property that he was fencing and selling. The items were stolen record albums, being sold out of his two stores in Kansas City and Overland Park, Kansas.

With the death of Nick Civella of natural causes and most of his Outfit members in jail facing long sentences on various federal charges, coupled with the death of the four Spero brothers, the city was resting easier as the 1980s moved along. The federal agents and the Kansas City Police Department detectives moved on to investigate other crimes and criminal suspects with a sense of satisfaction at their combined efforts to wipe out the Kansas City mob Outfits of the 1900s.

CHAPTER ELEVEN

THE KANSAS CITY STING
1976-1979

For years, law enforcement managers have searched for scientific methods to aid them in the fight against the increasing rise in crime in United States. During the 1970s, many new and innovative techniques were developed to thwart the efforts of the so-called street or career criminals.

One such investigative technique to surface was the storefront operation. The success of storefront operations has been tremendous. In its simplest form, a storefront operation is a procedure whereby law enforcement personnel establish a storefront that has all the appearance of an illegal activity. Suspected and targeted criminals are lured to the site to sell their illicit and stolen merchandise. Controlled purchases are made at the site under the watchful eyes of video cameras and still photo cameras. The evidence is logged, tagged, processed, and eventually traced to the rightful owners, and the suspects are identified through established procedures.

In November 1976, the Kansas City District Office of the ATF, in cooperation with the Kansas City Missouri Police Department (KCMOPD), initiated plans for a storefront project, later to be code-named "Picaroon," an undercover technique commonly known as a sting operation.

Picaroon is to act as a pirate or brigand, watching or searching for a prize or victims. In this project, law enforcement were the good pirates, and the prize or victims were gangsters, outlaws, and mobsters.

Although Operation Picaroon was preceded by several similar projects conducted in other geographical locations throughout the country, culminating in various measures of success, this project produced extensive results and was categorized as one of the more successful stings. Many techniques and innovations attributed to prior operations were used in Operation Picaroon; however, several unique ideas were developed and incorporated in this project, and ideas, both new and old, were modified and improved upon to fit the need as the operation developed.

The project consisted of six major phases: feasibility/funding phase, planning phase, operation phase, pre-arrest phase, arrest phase, and post-arrest phase.

In November 1976, an initial meeting was held between ATF, Kansas City office and the Chief of Detectives, KCMOPD, to consider the feasibility of a joint storefront operation between the two agencies. Both agencies were enthusiastic about the project and subsequent meetings were held to discuss

Law Enforcement Assistance Act (LEAA) funding and ground rules. In addition, initial contacts were made by the KCMOPD with LEAA in Washington, DC, by telephone and in person. It was agreed the project would take about one year; funding was approved in the amount of $250,000. A tentative budget was prepared, and letters of intent were submitted by ATF and KCMOPD.

The Kansas City Standard Metropolitan Statistical Area (SMSA) included seven counties in two states, having a total number of about 1,300,000 inhabitants. Municipalities range in size from Kansas City, Missouri, having a population of 507,409, to numerous villages with less than 100 inhabitants. In 1975, $15,341,568 worth of property was reported stolen to the KCMOPD alone.

The mayor of Kansas City, Missouri was quoted in the *KC Star* newspaper as stating he considered fencing to be the main source of income for organized crime in the area. Experience and intelligence information indicated that many of these same people trafficked in stolen firearms and occasionally in explosives, which made them subjects of interest to ATF, as well as to the police department, especially since the geographical area was divided by a state line.

ATF enjoyed an excellent working relationship with the police department and had, in the past, conducted successful joint operations against burglars and fences who had violated laws enforced by both agencies.

The operation targeted three types of violators in the KC geographical area:
- The career street criminal who makes his livelihood by burglaries, boosting, larceny, theft, and robberies
- The fences of stolen goods and professional theft rings
- The organized crime element

A site for the storefront was selected as well as an apartment for the out-of-town undercover agents.

The site was ultimately located in a commercial building at 2717 Truman Road, Kansas City, Missouri, in a business and warehousing zone on a major boulevard, near the inner city, with ready access to the interstate highway system servicing Missouri and Kansas.

The building was about 50 feet wide by 100 feet long with one-fourth of it finished office space. Access to the building was accomplished on February 28, 1977, through a rental lease agreement. The rent was $550.00 per month with the first and last month's rent paid in advance.

The front for the mock company was a warehousing and repossessing firm to preclude unwanted business from normal people seeking business services. The name selected for the firm was A. Picaro and Associates. A picaro is a rogue or vagabond.

Once the site was selected, extensive renovation took place to make it functional for the operation phase.

Carmine Caizzo, an older experienced ATF Agent, was selected from the East Coast Baltimore ATF office, to be a lead agent. He was of Italian origin to give the appearance of organized crime. The project required him to be in Kansas City for extensive periods.

ATF Agent "Big" John Keating was selected from the St. Louis office due to his past experience with street criminals and fences. He also worked the counter.

Your author had worked with John Keating in the St. Louis ATF office from 1971 to 1976. We were in the same group concentrating on gangsters operating in Madison and St. Clair counties in Illinois just across the river from St. Louis. Agent Keating had developed a reputation as an undercover agent, and I urged case agent Duane Nichols to secure Keating's assistance. I had talked to Agent Keating, and he expressed a strong interest in the taking on the challenge. He lived with me during the majority of the long project.

A third ATF agent, Bill Peterson, was selected from the Kansas City office. He was new to the area and job but had eleven years of prior police experience. He worked the counter also.

In addition to these three permanent undercover agents, several two-man teams of scouts were brought in by management for two-week periods to act as scouts in an undercover capacity. Their purpose was to visit the targeted taverns, burglars, and fence in the area and publicize the storefront and hand out business cards. Included in these teams was a black team and Mexican team, as well as several white teams.

One of my assignments was to communicate with the agents-in-charge throughout the Midwest to secure these undercover agents and to locate undercover vehicles for use in the project located in other ATF offices.

A suitable apartment was selected for the permanent undercover agents assigned to the project. All after-hours telephone calls to the actual site would switch over to a telephone answering device installed in the apartment that would record the messages if the agents were not at the undercover apartment. If they were present, they would take the calls themselves.

No transactions took place in the undercover apartment, but photographs were taken of some offsite incidents that took place in a lot near the apartment. The apartment was also utilized for numerous meetings and strategy planning sessions.

A number of nights I enjoyed hearing stories of the recent days' encounters with the bad guys and girls of the Kansas City area.

The importance of the planning stage cannot be overemphasized. This was a critical period, and all those involved during this period obviously realized this. Much effort and thought went into this phase, which would later reflect positively on the overall success.

During this period, the agents and police officers talked to law enforcement personnel who were involved in prior sting operations in other parts of the United States and actually visited and observed ongoing projects in St. Louis and New York City.

On April 1, 1977, the storefront site was opened for business in the name of A. Picaro and Associates. It was fully operational to December 22, 1977 and then semi-operational until February 15, 1978, the day of the arrests. Seven Kansas City police officers and eight federal agents were permanently assigned during the phase. In addition, numerous federal out-of-town agents periodically acted as "scouts," infiltrating selected targets, drawing them to the site.

At first, business was slow, but as the weeks passed, business picked up extensively.

From April 1 to May 13, 1977, the storefront operation attracted only thirteen outlaws in seventeen incidents. Evidence included six firearms, as well as numerous other fenced stolen properties.

From May 14 to July 8, 1977, the storefront attracted forty-eight suspects involving seventy-three incidents, mostly repeat customers offering their stolen property.

From July 9 to August 17, 1977, the number of suspects identified was seventy-nine in 177 incidents. Business was picking up for the task force.

From August 18 to October 25, 1977, the number of incidents was 528, involving 201 customers, and from October 26, 1977, to February 15, 1978, the number for the past twelve months totaled 756 incidents committed by a total of 288 criminals.

The total retail value of the property recovered was $1.5 million, including 154 firearms and 145 vehicles(59 of which were stolen from dealerships and 13 stolen from car rental agencies). The vehicles stolen included one Volkswagen, eleven Cadillacs, twenty-six Fords, and thirty-six Chevrolets.

The total items of recovered property included vehicles, truck and tractor trailers, credit cards, bicycles, motorcycles, checks and money orders, food, clothing, typewriters, tape players, car stereos, televisions, CB sets, fans, insulation, rifles, shotguns, handguns, explosives, tires, tools, calculators, adding machines, radios, and ammunition.

The types of state violations charged in Jackson County, Missouri, were 217 felonies and 44 misdemeanors. The misdemeanors included stealing under fifty dollars, receiving stolen property under fifty dollars, and riding in a motor vehicle without consent of the owner.

The 217 felonies included stealing motor vehicle, stealing over fifty dollars, receiving stolen property over fifty dollars, robbery in the first degree, driving motor vehicle without consent of owner, burglary in the second degree and stealing, tampering with motor vehicle, stealing by deceit over fifty dollars, sale of controlled substance, stealing mortgaged property, stealing leased property, forgery using uttering, and arson.

Indictments were also returned in Clay, Platte, Mercer, Calloway, St. Louis, Lafayette, and Greene Counties in Missouri and Johnson, Wyandotte and Greenwood Counties in Kansas.

The federal charges accounted for forty-two suspects being charged with numerous federal firearms and explosives cases of the $1.5 million in property recovered during this period.

Approximately 70 percent of the evidence purchased was successfully traced back to the rightful owner or victim of the theft. This was accomplished through police reports on file, newspaper accounts, serial and identification numbers, and several other unique methods.

On December 22, 1977, the storefront site was closed for the Christmas vacation. It was reopened on January 1, 1978, with a skeleton crew of agents and police officers who concentrated on making controlled buys involving firearms or cases needing additional evidence to prosecute. This continued through February 15, 1978, the day of the arrests.

Also, on December 22, a central command post was established in a large GSA facility located at 601 East Hardesty in Kansas City. Agents, police officers, and clerical personnel were taken from the storefront site and regrouped in this building.

This site was selected because a majority of the recovered property, including most of the vehicles, were stored and secured in the storage area of the building, allowing quick access during identification by victim of the thefts. Existing office space was utilized with a minimal amount of renovation required.

Attorneys from the United States Attorney's Offices for Jackson County, Missouri, and Johnson County, Kansas, were advised of the operation during this period and incorporated in the project to assist in preparation of cases and to act as advisors and reviewers of completed case files.

Witnesses and victims of identified stolen property were brought to the site, where they could properly identify their property and make statement accordingly. A portion of the extensive volume of taped telephone conversations made at the site were transcribed during this phase also. Procedures for the day of the arrests were completed, including selection of manpower, processing and interviewing of defendants, press releases, and cooperation with the news media.

The command post remained operational past the arrest stage and through the initial court process.

On February 15, 1978, at about 5:00 a.m., ATF Agents, KCMO police officers, and Missouri Highway Patrol officers met at police headquarters to be briefed on the various arrest and subsequent processing procedures.

Arrest teams comprising of either two or three men were assigned, and previously prepared packets were distributed. Efforts were made to arrest approximately 150 persons on this initial date. Some defendants were charged with both state and federal violations. Additional indictments and arrest warrants were to be secured at a later date, culminating in additional arrests.

At the end of the day, eighty-one individuals had been apprehended and formally charged. The federal defendants were taken before a magistrate and further processed by pretrial services.

Certain members of the news media had been informed by management of the extensive project earlier in the week and advised of the arrest date, therefore, providing extensive coverage both during and after the arrest date. The decision by management to inform the media early proved very wise in that interviews and some press releases were taken care of early, eliminating interference during the arrests. Picaroon was one of the most extensively covered sting projects in the United States.

Even though the media releases on the project started early in the day, the site stayed in operation all day in an effort to make arrests at the site and attempt several final controlled buys of evidence. Ironically, $168,000 worth of stolen merchandise was brought to the site, making it the largest single recovery date of the entire project.

The arrest phase was completed without incident, which can be attributed to the extensive pre-arrest planning by ATF and police managers.

In an agreement with the *Star* newspaper that the news of the sting would not be made public, the police and ATF gave their permission to allow the three counter undercover agents to give details of the day-to-day encounters they were presented with during the year-long project.

The media showed great interest in the day-to-day workings of the operation and the cops and agents involved.

In *Kansas City Star* articles, published shortly after the arrest phase was completed, detailed these actions through interviews with ATF Agents John "Big John" Keating, Bill Peterson, and Carmine "Tony" Caizzo.

Keating talked about how he temporarily infiltrated the mob. The *KC Star* reporter wrote:

> One of the unachieved goals of Operation Picaroon was to snag some major organized figures in Kansas City.
>
> The Alcohol, Tobacco and Firearms bureau (ATF) managed to infiltrate the Mob socially as part of this effort, but made cases only on a few minor figures with known Mob ties.
>
> John Keating, the ATF agent who posed as 'Big John,' counterman in the joint ATF-police department 'sting,' was the agent who gained short-lived social respectability with the mob.
>
> But, according to Duane Nichols, the ATF agent who coordinated the project, the Mob found out about 'the sting' on Nov. 11, killing Keating's chances of catching any big Mob fish in the ATF net.
>
> Keating was able to form a friendship with a peripheral Mob figure who had access to The Trap at 1015 E. 5th—officially known as the Columbus Park Social Club, located on the first floor of a building owned by Nick Civella, gangland chieftain of Kansas City the last 25 years who went to prison and has since passed away.
>
> Keating drove his new friend to The Trap several times in a white truck with 'A. Picaro & Associates' on its sides, then made it a practice of sitting behind the wheel of the truck in full view of the Trap regulars while his friend went inside.
>
> This way Keating was able to establish something of an identity for himself in their mind. A. Picaro & Associates already had a reputation known inside the Trap.
>
> Eventually Keating started going inside The Trap with his friend, only to find the large room divided by partitions that served to identify the Mob's pecking order. The further from the front door one went, the higher his rank, Keating said.

A view of Missouri State Penitentiary look west, January 2, 1908. Postcard 3881, published by Sam'l H. Smith & Co., Jefferson City (120566).

The Lorraine Motel, now known as the National Civil Rights Museum, where King was assassinated.

Edna Murray

Sonny Liston, 1963

Sonny Liston in prison.

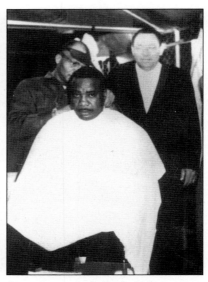

Sonny Liston in the barber's chair at prison.

Estelle and Benny Dickson

Glennon Edward Engleman

James Earl Ray, 1955

William Underhill

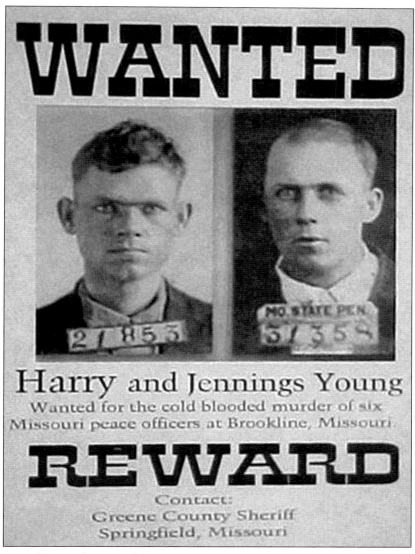

Wanted poster of Harry and Jennings Young, issued by the Greene County Sheriff's Department, 1932.

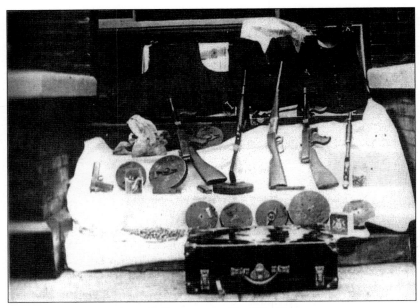

Arsenal of weapons used by Killer Burke.

Aftermath of the St. Valentine's Day Massacre.

Al Capone, 1930

Fred Burke

Thompson Submachine Gun

Kansas City's Union Station filled with travelers, June 1974. (EPA photo courtesy National Archives and Records Administration)

The Union Station Massacre in Kansas City.

Pretty Boy Floyd

Blanche Barrow in Jefferson City Prison. She was the wife of Buck Barrow of the Bonnie and Clyde gang.

George B. Kahler, a Misouri Highway Patrol trooper who was involved in the Bonnie & Clyde shootout in Joplin, MO.

E. Tom Whitecotton, a Misouri Highway Patrol trooper who was involved in the Bonnie & Clyde shootout in Platte City, MO.

Bonnie and Clyde

Bonnie and Clyde vehicle after they were killed in an ambush in Louisiana.

Arsenal found in the car of Clyde Barrow following his death.

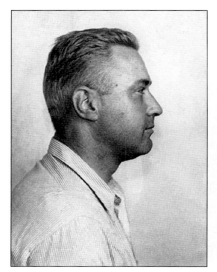

Machine Gun Kelly

The St. Louis Arch on August 10, 2006. (U.S. Air Force photo by Tech. Sgt. Justin D. Pyle)

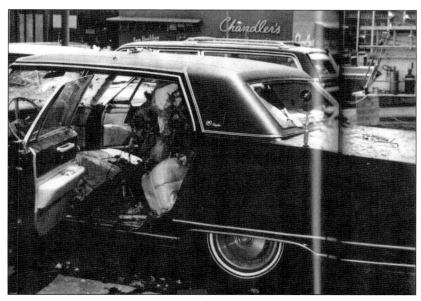

Aftermath of the Phillip Lucier bombing, 1970.

Aftermath of the Jimmy Michael Sr. bombing.

John Paul Spica bombing.

John Paul Spica bombing.

Close-up of the car interior in the John Paul Spica bombing.

The Paul Leisure bombing, 1981.

William T. "Wille" Egan

Charlie Birger Gang at the Shady Rest Hangout, 1926.

The Charlie Birger execution in Benton, Illinois, April 19, 1928.

Bombed vehicle of John Paul Spica.

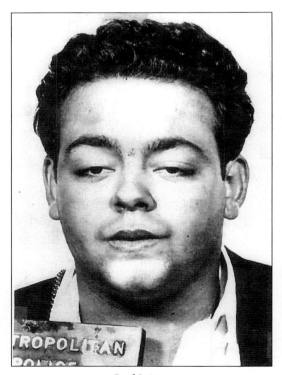

Paul Leisure

178

Thomas Egan

Undercover mugshot of the author, ATF Agent Dave True, 1971.

Bryant's Barbecue, Kansas City, MO

Country Club Plaza, view from 47th Street at Wornall Road, Kansas City, MO. (Public Domain)

Joe Spero bombing, Kansas City Mob, 1980.

Roy Williams, Teamster leader.

The remains of David Bonadonna were left in the trunk of this vehicle.

The body of David Bonadonna was found in the trunk of this abandoned car, a typical gangland-style murder.

An artist's rendering of The Kansas City Sting undercover operation.

ATF agents who worked The Kansas City Sting.

Bowman's house searched by law enforcement officials in Northern Kansas City.

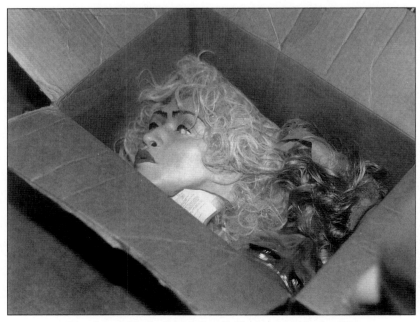

Disguise used in the Trench Coat Robberies, siezed by the ATF.

ATF agents seized these long rifles at Bowman's residence.

An ATF agent displaying a seized handgun from the Bowman residence.

A sack of money from a bank robber seized by ATF agents.

Michael Coy, vehicle bombing victim, Southwest Missouri.

Ben Shriver's burned-out residence in Springfield.

Ben Shriver's burned-out warehouse in Springfield.

Interior damage to the warehouse owned by Ben Shriver after he had it torched.

David Tate, the neo-Nazi who shot and killed Trooper Linager.

ATF agent Duane Nichols with a little girl at the Covenant, the Sword, and the Arm of the Lord campground. AP Photo by Cliff Schlappa

Hand grenades found at the CSA campground.

ATF team photo at the CSA campground; this group snuck in and took fourteen buildings in the plateau area the day before the CSA members surrendered.

Author Dave True in the hole where explosives were detonated at the CSA campground.

Firearms seized at the CSA campground.

Explosives seized at the CSA campground.

Firearms seized at the CSA campground.

ATF agents securing the CSA campground. Author Dave True is pictured center facing the camera.

ATF Agent Dave True discussing a murder contract with Bad JoAnn Cunningham.

Outline of a firefighter killed in the Ryan Fitness arson fire.

Alice Lundgren being led out of National City Police headquarters by an ATF federal agent. San Diego Union photograph

The family of Dennis and Cheryl Avery with their children, Rebecca, Trina and Karen, 1988. Their bodies were found buried under a barn on an Ohio farm after being murdered by the Lundgren cult.

The vehicle of murder victim Christine Elkins, pulled from the Missouri River.

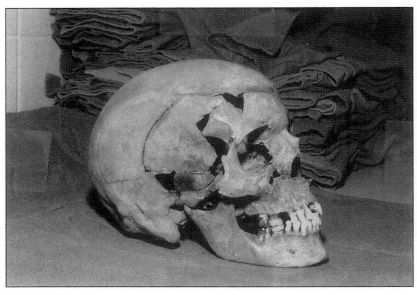

The remains of Christine Elkins.

Keating brought with him certain goods which those inside were supposed to think were 'hot' or stolen property. Popcorn poppers, electric can openers, radios, phonograph records—all for sale at low prices.

But the goods were not 'hot,' Keating said. He had bought them at wholesale or discount house prices, then lowered the price a little more and sold them to Trap regulars.

'I'd go out to Dolgin's, for instance,' he said, 'and pay $20 for a $30 item. Then I'd charge $15 for it at The Trap. It didn't cost us much money.'

At first Keating, the only 'peckerwood' (mob parlance for a person not of Italian descent) in the place, had to content himself with small talk near the front of the building as he watched men play cards—21 and gin rummy.

He overheard no incriminating conversations from anyone. He did notice that numerous private conversations were held, but always away from the tables in a corner of the room.

The Trap would accommodate from 25 to 30 persons at one time.

ATF agents taught Keating how to play both card games and eventually someone invited him to play.

The stakes in the front of the room were low—$1 for each game of 21, $5 to the gin rummy player first to hit 100 points.

In the back area, however, bigger games were under way.

Keating found the only way he could gain a glimpse of the backroom games was by going to the bathroom as often as possible, because the toilet was in the back.

Answering nature's call at The Trap was not always easy. At times, he said, when he arose from a game and announced his forthcoming bathroom trip, someone would say, 'Wait a minute,' and scout the route visually before giving Keating the high sign to proceed.

'Corky (a Mob boss) was clearly the one treated with the most respect there,' Keating said, not just because of the chair but the nature of the interrelationships observed at The Trap as the various regulars roamed here and there, talking with one another.

Suddenly, after Nov. 11, Keating found himself no longer welcome at The Trap. No one would talk or play cards with him.

Nichols believes this is what happened:

A low-ranking Mob associate had been selling stolen property to A. Picaro & Associates. He made four sales, in fact, then a fifth one—a large supply of cake icing.

One of the AFT's and police's jobs near the end of 'the sting' was to trace the property they had recovered to its original owners to determine if it had been stolen.

When they went to the original owner of the cake icing, they were told that he had sold it legitimately to the Mob figure, but for a very low price.

Immediately afterward, word reached the authorities that 'the sting' was known to the Mob.

Nichols concludes that the Mob figure, aware that he probably would be arrested for the four earlier sales, was trying to establish an alibi of sorts for himself when he went to court.

Nichols speculated that if the man could document that his last sale was legal, perhaps he could persuade a jury that he did not know the items sold in the first four transactions had been stolen.

After Keating started receiving the cold shoulder at The Trap, Nichols told him to stop frequenting the place. His role-playing had been so persuasive, the ATF feared that someone might think he was an informant rather than an actual federal agent, and kill him.

In a *Star* news article published on February 11, 1978, the task force junkyard dog Curly was featured. It read:

One of the hazards police and ATF agents faced during Operation Picaroon was from an Airedale named 'Curly.'

Curly was purchased to roam the rear of the building at 2721 Truman Road at night as a watch dog. The law enforcement officers did not want the stolen property they had bought from thieves to be stolen again. But Curly was mean during the day as well as in the night.

'He bit practically everyone who was in on the operation at one time or another,' said Maj. Sidney Harlow of the police department.

Curly's temper was so frequently aroused that the ATF agents and police finally posted a scoreboard on a wall in the garage, keeping a daily record of the number of attempted bites and actual 'hits' Curly made while serving the forces of law and order.

The year long operation encountered a number of obstacles that could have undermined the operation.

In June of 1977 just five months into the project, an inquisitive patrolman, Arnold Rider, assigned to the intercity, learned from an informant the site was a big fencing operation. He surveilled the place for four days and reported his findings to Major Harlow, who was in charge of the police phase of the operation.

Major Harlow told Officer Rider the operation was being run by ATF and the police. Once Rider uncovered the operation, Major Harlow made him a member of the Sting.

In another article published by the *Star*, the agents provided a number of the incidents they encountered during the year-long operation:

All three men carried fake credentials—driver's licenses and Social Security cards—but only Bill ever was asked to show his. Tony claimed that he was from New York and that members of his immediate family operated a string of legitimate trucking businesses in different cities as a convenient front for fencing. Keating said he was from Chicago. Bill told clients he had served time in the federal penitentiary in Atlanta.

The agents' biggest worry, they said, was not their safety but the fact that one serious mistake could ruin the project, for which the Law Enforcement Assistance Administration (LEAA) and the police department spent $180,000.

The longer the three men operated, the more cases they made against the persons who were selling them stolen property. To blow their covers early would mean fewer arrests, less evidence, fewer convictions, fewer jail sentences for those who would plead or be found guilty and, ultimately, a smaller drop in the city's crime rate in the months ahead.

They were well prepared for violence. At least one policeman or agent was hidden nearby at all times with a loaded shotgun while others took videotape and still photographs of each visitor of the room in which most transactions took place.

Special windows had been installed so that if shooting began inside the room no bullets would go through the windows (a playground was across Chestnut to the east) but instead would ricochet inside the room.

Tony told of one instance in which he was certain he was about to be robbed. A man and woman had entered the building. Big John referred the man to Tony, who took him into an adjacent office (which was also covered by video camera) to negotiate a price for his goods.

Once alone with the man, Tony watched as the man reached toward an ankle and pulled a pistol from one of his stockings. Braced for action, Tony was relieved to hear the man offer him the pistol for sale.

Meanwhile, in the front room the woman, for some reason disenchanted with the man as her pimp, was trying to talk Bill into letting her go to work for him as his prostitute.

Chain saws, credit cards, automobiles, trucks, typewriters, adding machines, furniture, jewelry, hub caps, sawed-off shotguns, TV sets, radios came in day after day.

And 90 per cent of the time it was Big John who greeted visitors from behind the counter, smiling sometimes, glowering at other times as he pored over merchandise catalogs to determine the retail value of what he was being offered, then gave the seller the news—he'd pay him 5, 10, 15, 20 or maybe as much as 25 per cent of the listed value, seldom more.

'You're a cold-blooded man,' he recalls being told.

Only for firearms would Big John go higher than 25 per cent. The ATF wanted every one they could get—that took the firearms off the streets.

After they had grown used to their roles, the agents began to pry more into the details of how their visitors had obtained the items they were trying to sell. Where had they stolen them? When had they stolen them?

Surprisingly, most did not hesitate to tell what the agents wanted to hear (and record on videotape).

Often, the agents said, the visitors would boast of other crimes they had committed or knew about. The agents were gaining invaluable information on crime in Kansas City.

They had worked hard in the beginning spreading word around the city that they were available for business. Their notoriety spread slowly but surely by word-of-mouth. Friends would bring in friends who would bring in other friends, and so on.

Big John, Tony, Bill and the officers hiding in the back room would try to establish the identify of each visitor. Sometimes this was difficult. Other times it was no trick at all.

One woman eluded identification until one night one of the agents was watching television and saw the woman on his set. She was part of a documentary about an institution that was trying to rehabilitate women criminals.

'Who is this guy?' Big John would say to a repeat visitor as he brought in a newcomer. 'He looks like a cop. Let me see your I.D.'

Usually the stranger would produce an I.D. card.

One prostitute whom the agents were having trouble identifying finally helped them out by producing four photographs of herself in the nude. She thought they might want to buy the pictures. On the back of one was her name.

Not all of their visitors were especially bright. When Big John offered two thieves $12.50 for a radio, they asked him to knock the price down to $12.40 because then the money would be easier to divide between them, Big John said.

Potential customers were urged to telephone ahead when they had goods to bring in, but not all observed this amenity and some showed up unexpectedly.

One man who called asked whether they wanted a late-model Corvette. They told the man they did. He said he would be right over.

A few minutes later a Corvette came streaking down Truman Road at 60 miles an hour. The caller obviously had stolen it after making sure he could sell it. A police helicopter was hot on its tracks. The agents opened their garage door and he sped inside, losing the chopper and, he thought, the police.

Another car thief one day told the agents a story of extraordinary luck. He had just been on the verge of selling two stolen cars to a fence in St. Louis, he said, when he read in the St. Louis newspapers that the fence was actually a police 'sting' operation.

'Yeah,' grunted Big John, 'ya gotta know who you're dealin' with.' And he bought the cars from the man.

Another visitor brought a touch of humor to the project when he started primping his hair in the mirror while waiting for Big John to name him a price on what the visitor had brought.

'Smile,' said Big John.

'Why?' asked the thief. 'Am I on Candid Camera?'

'Yeah,' said Big John. 'There's a guy behind that mirror takin' a picture of you right now.'

They both laughed, and the man behind the mirror continued taking his pictures.

Their most sophisticated visitor was a salesman who said that he earned $24,000 a year legitimately but that his salary was not high enough. He stole cars as a sideline.

Always dressed immaculately in a suit, tie and vest and carrying an attaché case, he would go to the car he intended to steal, open his attaché case, remove his car theft tools, enter the car, start it and drive away. No one seeing this ever stopped him because of his respectable attire. He claimed to have stolen 100 cars that way.

The undercover agents saved money at times by photographing some of the goods brought to them while the thief was not looking, then refusing to buy the goods. This was often done on personal belongings from house burglaries.

The agents could show the pictures to the victims afterward and presumably locate the thief and the goods later.

One visitor showed up with a $400 U.S. Treasury check he said he had just stolen from the mail. The agents paid him $40 for it and asked him how he had suffered the severe cut he had on his forehead.

He explained that he had been cut by glass while breaking the front window of a liquor store.

'You grab what you can and then run when the man's coming,' he said, explaining one of the subtleties of his vocation.

The 'sting' snagged five members of 'The manhole Cover Gang,' which has been plaguing store owners for more than a year, the agents said. The gang's technique has been to back a truck up to the front window of a store, roll a 75-pound manhole cover through the glass, gather up all they can as the electric alarm goes off and speed off before police arrive. The whole operation would take only a few minutes.

The agents said they understand there are a total of nine men in the gang, leaving four yet to catch.

Among the lessons the agents said they learned were:

Never leave your keys in your car.

Car salesmen should be more careful with cars on their sales lots. (One car showed up at 2717 Truman Road that had been stolen three weeks earlier from a car lot in Phoenix. The owner did not even know the car was missing).

The organized crime element here apparently has high respect for the ATF and the Drug Enforcement Administration (DEA). Big John said that while he was chumming around with mob figures here, they were meticulous in their avoidance of even talking about stolen guns or drugs.

Thieves vary from one city to another. As already noted, Kansas City's thieves seem to have more independence of spirit than those in the East. The agents don't understand why, but another difference they found here was that there is no market in stolen food stamps, although there is in other cities.

It is not necessary to receive approval from the organized crime group in Kansas City before setting up your own, independent fencing operation.

The intense activity in the 'Sting' operation did not go unnoticed by business neighbors near the site.

Shortly after the success of the operation was published, a number of business neighbors told newspaper reporters they knew something was going on at the mysterious business operation.

A news article by *Kansas City Star* reporter Richard Serrano reported in part:

> Businessmen on Truman Road couldn't figure them out. In April they took over an old tire shop, hung their name out front, posted credit card signs on the wall, pulled down the window blinds, locked the front and garage doors—and then virtually disappeared. No one saw them arriving in the morning or going home at night.
>
> The operators of the Royal Craft Boat Company, next door at 2715 Truman Road, figured the men must be operating an illegal fencing operation. They often saw people drive up in fancy cars, go inside and come out stuffing their wallets into their pockets before catching a bus. Other times they would hear a car roaring down the street; just as it reached the shop next door, the garage doors would rise and in would go the car—never to be seen again.
>
> Other area shop owners had similar problems. 'I didn't know what they did,' said Lyle Leas operator of L & M Ornamental Iron, 2701 Truman Road. 'I never saw any traffic over there. I never saw anyone. People wondered what it was. No one knew.'
>
> Bill Sloan, whose father, Lee Sloan, owns the Sloan Automotive Service, 2704 Truman Road, said the Picaro men never associated with neighbors. He saw them just once a month, he said.
>
> 'They never said a word one,' Bill Sloan said. 'They just gave us a check in an envelope and said it was the payment for the rent. They always paid right on time.
>
> 'People would say they never seemed to be open. But I never thought anything was wrong, I mean the cops weren't around or anything.'
>
> The manager of Auggie's Transmission Repair and Parts Co., 2712 Truman Road, acted as though he had a little inside information on the whole operation.
>
> 'I knew something was up,' he said. 'I wasn't born yesterday, you

know. You can't live in Kansas City for 60 years like this and not know something was up.'

A *Kansas City Times* news article published on February 16, 1978, provided some history on storefront operations throughout the United States.

The first storefront operation was set up in Washington, DC in 1976. Over the next several years there were 42 storefront projects in 28 different cities in the United States bringing in $66 million in stolen property. More than 3,100 people have been sought in connection with the fencing operations.

About $2.6 million in 'buy money' supplied by grants from the Law Enforcement Assistance Administration has been used to finance the clandestine operations.

Former FBI Director Clarence Kelley has said the operations are 'a prime example of the effectiveness of federal and local law enforcement working together.'

A report on a study of sting operations last year, which was released in October by the Westinghouse Corporation's National Issues Center, showed that the operations help combat trafficking in stolen goods and do not increase crime or lure normally law-abiding citizens into committing crimes. The report showed that property crime offenses dropped 5 to 26 percent over the 12 months following the operations, compared with crime statistics in the 12 months preceding the operations.

James O. Golden, director of the LEAA enforcement division in Washington and the man considered the father of sting operations, said in an interview Tuesday that 'numerous' other stings are operating in the country.

These news articles were not actually news to me. As the incidents occurred when "Big" John came to my safe house, we would sit in the kitchen and have a beverage of our choice and he, Bill, or Carmine would recount the day's interesting developments at the storefront. This was an exciting time in my career, living the undercover tails vicariously through these courageous law enforcement agents and officers.

Not all the unique techniques used by the task force were reported in the print news media.

On certain occasions, after a successful purchase of evidence, the countermen would pour a glass of whiskey for the suspect, have him pick it up, and join in a toast. When he left, they would have the glass dusted for latent fingerprints and processed to identify the yet unidentified bad guy.

Quite often the sellers of stolen property asked if they could have a job with the apparent criminal enterprise. The countermen would have them fill out an application for possible employment. This was probably the only time in some of their lives they provided identification information, including their real addresses and social security number, making the identification process a little easier.

The post-arrest phase continued and consisted of additional grand jury sessions, processing of tape recordings and videotapes, preparation for trials, and actual participations in trials in defendants. This phase also consisted of numerous preliminary hearings and conferences with defendants and their attorneys to establish dates for guilty pleas and related hearings.

The federal docket, consisting of forty-two defendants, had been disposed of completely. This was in marked contrast with the state docket, which required about four more months to complete. This caused a hardship on the out-of-town agents who have been required to return to Kansas City for extensive periods. The proceedings in Johnson County, Kansas, had proven very difficult because they had no grand jury and, therefore, defendants had to have a preliminary hearing prior to setting a trial date.

A large quantity of electronic equipment had to be acquired to set up adequate systems to allow the judges and jury to listen to taped telephone conversations and to view videotapes that identify the defendants.

On several occasions as many as eight or nine trials were scheduled at the same time and date, creating an impossible situation for the agents involved. This required extensive hours of review of tapes and video recordings by the agents involved.

Federal and state status logs were prepared to establish accountability of all defendants processed, which showed the breakdown for federal dispositions.

Much of the recovered property was disposed of during this period by either returning it to the rightful owner or by auctioning or selling the merchandise.

Sentences ranged from probation to eight years in prison, with about 90 percent of the defendants pleading guilty to their charges.

The federal court system was more prepared to handle and dispose of a large criminal docket. The backlog of cases on the state dockets can, of course, be attributed to the inherent backlog of state cases, other than the sting operation.

Overall, Operation Picaroon was considered an immense success, both operationally and administratively. Although numerous problems developed as the project's daily operations escalated, managers and street personnel repeatedly overcame the problems, allowing total success in the end.

All the agents and police officers stated that, if they had it to do all over again, certain actions would be modified to allow for an even smoother operation. The facts and figures stand for themselves in evaluating the total success of this project by all involved, coupled with their dedication and innovative ideas assured this success.

With the success of the Kansas City sting operation in hand, the agents from the Kansas City ATF office initiated two more projects. In 1979, the agents teamed up with the Overland Park [Kansas] Department, to operate a sting undercover operation out of two homes in Johnson County, Kansas, resulting in the federal indictment of seventeen thieves and the recovery of 213 stolen firearms—including shotguns, rifles, handguns, sawed-off shotguns, and a semiautomatic rifle—and a stolen trailer containing a combine and two cases of dynamite. The operation ran for six months between May and October 1979.

Following this project, a third sting operation, code name operation "Jag," conducted by ATF in cooperation with the Grandview Police Department and the Jackson County Sheriff's Department, from May of 1981 to May 1982, netted sixteen thieves and $500,000 in stolen property, including nine firearms.

During the operation, the undercover agents were also offered a tractor trailer rig loaded with video games valued at $150,000 and a carnival ride valued at $175,000. Rather than make the purchase, the FBI was notified and made the arrests since these items were stolen in another state and transported to Missouri in violation of federal law.

Three very successful operations. I was proud to have played a part in their successes.

CHAPTER TWELVE

THE TRENCH COAT BANK ROBBERS
1970s-1990s

O n September 3, 1982, two outlaws, a tall man and a shorter man, both wearing coveralls and ski masks, using sawed-off shotguns entered the First National Bank in Annapolis, Missouri, just west of Cape Girardeau shortly after it opened. They took control of about twenty people, including employees before they could set off an alarm, and robbed it of $30,000–$40,000, making a clean getaway.

No one was hurt, and no shots were fired. The robbery caused only area media coverage. It was assumed the FBI, who had jurisdiction over the federal bank robbery laws, would quickly solve the crime.

That was not the case, and for the next fifteen years, this pair of outlaws, switching coveralls to trench coats, hats, and sunglasses, were responsible for robbing as many as twenty-eight banks across the nation, stretching from New York to the state of Washington.

As reported in the *Kansas City Star*, "The robbers hopscotched around the northern half of the United States." Here are a few examples of the locations from sixteen states: Schenectady, New York, February 1984; Des Moines, Iowa, November 1987; Green Bay, Wisconsin, March 1989; and Portland, Oregon, February 1994. From one to three holdups happened every year.

The FBI said the previous twenty-seven robberies attributed to the Trench Coat Robbers netted $3.5 million. In addition to their trademark trench coats and detailed preparation, the robbers had one other distinctive trait—they weren't hesitant to become violent. In one holdup, they took a hostage and exchanged gunfire with police. Another time, they kidnapped a banker and his family at his home before robbing his bank. And on another occasion, "they shot a teller."

Their daring robberies have been featured on television's *America's Most Wanted*, *Unsolved Mysteries*, *The Today Show*, and *Court TV*. In 2002 *The New Yorker* magazine published their story in a six-page article, covering the fifteen-year history of the small gang's criminal history. In addition, the print media both locally and nationally has published numerous news articles of the history, the investigation, and results.

Their final robbery occurred on February 10, 1997, at the Seafirst branch banks in Lakewood, Washington. Wearing trench coats, sunglasses and hats, they entered the bank about fifteen minutes after it had closed, confronted three employees with a weapon and tied them up. In the next hour, the two outlaws hauled away $4.5 million in cash, a haul that was the largest bank robbery in the United States history, according to the FBI.

The FBI formed a task force in Seattle code-named "Trench Rob," hoping to identify and capture the two. A $100,000 reward was posted, and the FBI prepared and distributed police sketches of the two suspects, prepared with the help of the employees and customers. The mystery continued.

Then in 1997, following the February bank robbery, two events occurred, one in Kansas City, Missouri, and the other on the highway near Lincoln, Nebraska, that would unlock the mystery of the "Trenchcoat Robbers."

The first event occurred on May 22, 1997, in Kansas City, Missouri. Ironically, it was a lead not developed by the FBI—no, it was a lead followed by ATF agent Paul Marquardt of the Kansas City ATF office, a crack agent who was regarded by the United States Attorney's Office and his professional peers as a thorough investigator and a top-notch federal agent. I had the privilege of working with him from 1976 (when I was transferred to the Kansas City ATF office from the St. Louis ATF office) until May 7, 1997 (when I retired). We worked together on numerous investigations during this period of time. He's an agent whose abilities I admire, and he's a friend whom I still socialize with and share our stories today.

This is his story; this is his case; this is his investigation assisted by the Kansas City Police Department's intelligence division. His investigation developed information and evidence that was provided to the FBI task force in Seattle, Washington, and Kansas City, allowing them to perfect the bank robbery cases still within the statute of limitations and prosecutable in federal court. This is how it all started.

On May 22, 1997, ATF Special Agent Paul Marquardt responded to Federal Van & Storage Company, 4006 Washington Street, in Kansas City, regarding information that two footlockers contained illegal firearms. The footlockers had been in storage and were opened by the company after the storage account had remained delinquent for a period of six months. One footlocker contained three .45 caliber pistols, a bulletproof vest, a scanner with an earpiece, two winter coats, a windbreaker, a blue baseball cap with "Police" printed on it, and a purple Crown Royal bag containing silencer components and other miscellaneous items, including ammunition and magazines. One of the .45 caliber pistols had been stolen in Independence, Missouri in 1970 from a TG&Y store break-in. Forty-eight other firearms were taken during this burglary.

A person identifying himself as Charles Clark had placed the footlocker in storage on October 12, 1985. Mr. Clark used the address 5510 NE Seminole. A subsequent investigation revealed that 5510 NE Seminole did not exist; however, there was a 5510 NW Seminole address in Kansas City. There were no other identifiers of Mr. Clark in the file.

Federal Van & Storage records indicate that the individual known as Charles Clark had picked up the footlocker on December 12, 1990, and returned on December 13, 1990. In addition, the footlocker was picked up by

Mr. Clark on November 2, 1991 and returned on November 25, 1991. On April 3,1992, Mr. Clark placed in storage a second, slightly smaller footlocker. Records indicate that the storage of these lockers was periodically paid for by cash in advance, totaling approximately $2,000 over the previous twelve years.

The second footlocker contained a legal-size briefcase containing books regarding such subjects as *How to Kill, Volumes 1–7, The Anarchist's Cookbook*, and *The Poor Man's James Bond*, as well as books on stage makeup, military manuals for improvised explosive devices, conversion of firearms to fully automatic, disguises and false identification, and how to make improvised silencers.

Also contained in the footlocker were the following books: *U.S Silencer Patents, Volumes 1–2*; *Silencers, Snipers and Assassins*; and *Improvised Modified Firearms, Volumes 1–2*.

In addition, there was a box containing eight videos, with titles such as *Expert Lock Picking: State-of-the-Art Lock Picking Secrets*; *High Speed Entry: Instant Opening Techniques*; *B and E, A to Z—How to Get in Anywhere, Anytime*; *Tactical Use of Explosive*; *Deadly Explosives: How and Why They Work*; *Terrorist Weapons and Explosives*; and *How I Steal Cars*. (Subsequent lab analysis of a latent fingerprint inside the videotape case containing *B and E, A to Z—How to Get in Anywhere, Anytime* was identified as the known left thumbprint of Ray Lewis Bowman.)

All the aforementioned items were taken into custody by ATF, and an investigation was initiated to determine the identity of Charles Clark.

On June 12, 1997, during the afternoon, ATF received a call from the Federal Van and Storage company advising that Charles Clark had come in and paid his storage bill. Agent Duane Nichols responded to the storage shed, learning that the man using the name Charles Clark was driving a dark green Ford Crown Victoria, with Missouri License plate 714BAL. While at the storage shed, he had provided a new address to the manager—PO Box 11070, Kansas City, Missouri— and paid his bill of $135.29 in cash. The bills were taken into custody, and a description of Clark was provided to Agent Nichols. Back at the office, the license plate was checked and found to be in the name of Wayne Wells at 8538 North Troost, Kansas City, Missouri. Could Clark really by Wayne Wells?

On June 20, Agent Marquardt learned from postal inspectors that the post office box address was opened by a person named Ray Bowman of Bowman Security, using a Missouri driver's license number B158-6039-3005-8264 with an address of 3510 NE 67th Street in Kansas City. There were two other names receiving mail there, identified as Delamotte and Well's Mowers. Bowman had been developed as a suspect by Agent Marquardt and from a check on ALERTS network. He also learned that Bowman and a woman named Cheryl Clark had used the address of 5510 NW Seminole; however, neither one of them had ever lived at that address. He also learned that the address and telephone number given for the post office box rental was bogus.

Ray Lewis Bowman was also developed as a suspect in this investigation due to an arrest report dated February 15, 1988, when he was arrested for driving under the influence, and his passenger, Cheryl Clark, was arrested for carrying a concealed weapon. They both listed 5510 NW Seminole as their address in the arrest report. A photo spread containing a photograph of Ray L. Bowman was shown to three employees at Federal Van & Storage on June 23, 1997, and they all positively identified Ray Bowman as the individual who had represented himself as Charles Clark on June 12,1997, when he paid for the storage rental.

The last employee interviewed was Allen Powell. Mr. Powell stated that he was a controller at Federal Van and Storage and was the individual who had accepted the cash payment from the suspect on June 12, 1997. Mr. Powell positively identified the picture of Ray Bowman as being the man and initialed and dated the back of the photograph. Powell asked the man for an updated address the man gave him; it was Post Office Box 11070, Kansas City, Missouri. Mr. Powell further stated that when he asked the subject for an undated phone number, the subject stated, "no phone number," and promptly left the establishment.

On June 27. 1997, SA Marquardt sent the $155.30 in US currency to the lab, along with a certified copy of Ray Bowman's fingerprints. In addition, SA Marquardt sent another package containing one gray plastic gun case, three ten-inch .45 caliber magazines, one Mac-10 flash suppressor, the three .45 caliber pistols, four boxes of Remington .45 caliber ammunition, and one purple Royal Crown bag containing suspected silencer parts to the lab.

On July 9, 1997, SA Marquardt met with KCMOPD Intelligence Unit Sgt. Cy Ritter. Also present at the time of the meeting was Captain Mike Hand. The purpose of the meeting was to discuss information developed regarding Ray L. Bowman and the contents of the footlockers taken into custody from the Federal Van and Storage and the fact that Mr. Bowman was driving a car registered to Wayne Wells, 8538 North Troost, Kansas City, Missouri. Investigation had revealed that Mr. Wells was a twenty-one-year KCMPD veteran who had retired within the last two-and-a-half years on disability. Sgt. Ritter stated that his unit would assist in gathering intelligence on Mr. Bowman, as well as Mr. Wells. Background information was developed by Marquardt and the police intelligence unit detectives.

It was learned that Ray Bowman and his younger brother Dan had started as small-time outlaws, shoplifting or "boosting" for a low-level Kansas City mobster named Tiger Cardarella, who was later murdered in a mob hit. Cordarilla had provided Bowman with a shoplifting list of record albums and other items that were currently in demand. Cordarilla, who owned a record album shop in town, would fence the goods. During these days in the early 1970s, Bowman had hooked up with Billy Kirkpatrick, another Kansas City outlaw, and they began boosting together, wearing oversized trench coats to conceal the stolen items. Marquardt learned the only arrest of the two together was in Springfield in 1974 when they were caught with thirty-eight albums at a Kmart store.

Their actions caught the attention of the Kansas City Police Intelligence Unit and the ATF office, who opened a joint investigation under the name Kirkpatrick.

Bowman attended Paseo High School from 1959 to 1963 before dropping out. His earliest arrest was for a burglary, and he was sentenced to six months. During the next thirty years, Bowman was arrested at least five times for burglary and stealing and once for simple assault and drunk driving. His records show he was involved in a number of violent incidents. In the early 1990s, he settled down when he met a single mother named Jenny Delamotte, who gave birth to two daughters. They were married and living together in a rental house. Delamotte would later become a witness at Bowman's eventual trial.

On July 14, 1997, a laboratory report by Fingerprint Specialist Richard E. Canty was received, and it indicated that the currency had been processed and examined for the presence of identifiable latent prints with negative results.

On July 16, 1997, Det. Danny Reynolds and Det. Gary Wantland interviewed Cheryl L. Clark, a white female born January 7, 1949, at her apartment at 9613 Truman Road, Apt. 3. Clark had been arrested with Bowman on February 15, 1988, and was his girlfriend from about 1980 to 1988. She stated that she hadn't seen Bowman in approximately three years and that, the last time she had seen him, he just appeared at her apartment to talk.

During the time that she lived with him, it was on Seminole Street in Parkville, Missouri, but she could not remember the address. She stated that during her time with Bowman, he never left a paper trail and all the utilities were put in her name. He would leave town frequently and stay away for up to six weeks at a time. He stated she didn't know Bowman to ever have an honest job and believed Bowman was a con man and a booster (thief).

Clark stated that Bowman always wore expensive clothes, and it would not be unusual for him to spend $600 on a night out with her just for dinner and limo service. She stated that Bowman didn't have many friends, and the only friend that came to mind was P. J. McGraw. She stated that Bowman liked to hang out at strip bars and that P. J. McGraw once gave him a .45 caliber handgun for Bowman's birthday. Clark further stated that she had purchased several handguns for Bowman at his request and would always register the handguns. She stated that Bowman always carried a gun on his person for protection and that, on one occasion, he had retrieved a large amount of cash from a post office box located in a bank in Downtown Kansas City, around Ninth and Grand.

Bowman once arrived home with material used to make bulletproof vests and had her sew the material inside his black leather jacket as lining for the jacket. She stated Bowman was physically violent with her and had even pointed a gun at her and threatened to shoot her on one occasion. He had also struck her, leaving a scar under her chin from his ring. The only way that she knew to contact Bowman was through his post office box, which she still remembered as Post Office Box 11070. She advised that Bowman was born and raised in Asheville, North Carolina. She stated that Bowman had a son who was approximately thirty years old and his mother, Gladys Bowman, lived somewhere on Quality Hill in Kansas City, Missouri.

Clark said that she had lost her birth certificate and driver's license when she was living with Bowman. Recently she had requested a copy of her birth certificate and was told that she had already been sent copies on four other occasions, but she had not requested those copies.

The Postal Inspection Office advised Post Office Box 11070, Kansas City, Missouri, 64119 was rented in July 1979 by Ray Bowman and—among others receiving mail there—was Jenny Delamotte. Delamotte's address was determined to be 17006 NW 76th Street, Kansas City, Missouri. Her full name was Grace Virginia Delamotte, and she had three children—Savannah, Samantha, and Taylor.

During the latter part of July 1997, Detective Gary Wantland observed Ray Bowman leaving 17006 NW 76th Street, driving a 1994 Crown Victoria, license number 714-BAL.

On July 17, 1997, Firearms Examiner Doug Craze determined that the parts contained in the purple Royal Crown bag constituted a silencer, and the seizure of the item was initiated. On July 18, 1997, an ATF Lab Report dated July 11, 1997 was received, regarding negative fingerprints examination of firearms that were sent to the lab. Also, on July 18, 1997, SA Marquardt checked with Jackson County Deputy Del Rey Reynolds, who stated that their records indicated that Cheryl Clark had purchased eighteen handguns between 1984 and 1988. On July 22, 1997, Bowman, identifying himself as Charles Clark, stopped by Federal Van and Storage and paid his current storage bill to Beverly Pace, the officer supervisor of Federal Van and Storage. He did not ask to see the footlockers. On July 23, 1997, SA Marquardt talked to Mary Lewis and Allen Powell of Federal Van and Storage regarding their continued concerns that Mr. Bowman would become agitated if he found out that they have opened up the footlockers. SA Marquardt had originally advised them to call 911 when the identify of Charles Clark was unknown.

This scenario occurred on June 12, 1997, when Mr. Bowman appeared at Federal Van and Storage, representing himself as Charles Clark; however, he was long gone before anyone responded to the 911 call. Since that meeting on July 12, 1997, it was jointly decided with employees of Federal Van to accept money from Mr. Bowman for safety purposes so as to not reveal that the footlockers had actually been opened. During this meeting, Mr. Powell and Ms. Lewis suggested that the footlockers be returned to them so that they would have something on hand to show if Mr. Bowman wanted to inspect the footlockers.

SA Marquardt felt that this was not feasible due to the fact that Mr. Bowman would realize that the footlockers had been broken into by employees of Federal Van and Storage. SA Marquardt stated that he would prepare a letter to Mr. Clark from ATF stating that ATF had custody of his property and that he should contact ATF. This would be used as a safety device to give the Federal Van employees a way out if he became irate with them and insisted on inspecting his footlockers. On July 23, 1997, SA Marquardt met with Deputy Reynolds, and he turned over a list of the firearms purchased by Cheryl Clark. Subsequently, this list was entered in a suspect file with ATF Tracing.

On July 29, 1997, SA Marquardt met with Mary Lewis of Federal Van and Storage and gave her a letter addressed to Mr. Clark, explaining that ATF had custody of his property. This letter was to be used *only* in the event Mr. Bowman insisted on seeing his footlockers. It was jointly agreed that, if he merely came in to pay the bill, they would accept the money to avoid a conflict with Mr. Bowman for safety reasons. On July 31, 1997, SA Marquardt and detectives with the Intelligence Unit made copies of the pamphlets that were in the legal briefcase in one of the footlockers. Up until this time, they had been preserved for prints, and on this occasion, they were handled with latex gloves. Copies of the titles of the pamphlets were made and it was discovered one pamphlet from Cobray, Inc. from Smyrna, Georgia, was stamped "Bowman R., P.O. Box 11070, Kansas City, MO 64119," which is the post office box that Mr. Bowman used.

This advertisement was sent on September 20, 1990. There were approximately 100 pamphlets and numerous other books on how to convert weapons, make explosions and disguises, and obtain false identification. On August 4, 1997, the Firearms Technology Branch report written by Doug Craze and dated July 21, 1997 was received, documenting that the parts contained in the purple Royal Crown bag constituted a silencer.

On August 5, 1997, SA Marquardt began making copies of the seven VHS videotapes contained in the second footlocker. AFT completed the copying of the tapes. Marquardt forwarded them to the AFT laboratory to be processed for latent fingerprints. On August 7, 1997, SA Marquardt requested grand jury subpoenas from AUSA Bill Meiners for the unlisted number for Jenny Delamotte at 17006 NW 76th Street, Kansas City, Missouri, and also for toll records going back to September 1996. Intelligence gathered by the police department indicated that Bowman was living with Delamotte at the above address.

On August 12, 1997, a court order was obtained from US Magistrate Robert Larsen for a pen register (used to record phone calls from a given line) for Jenny Delamotte's number. On August 13, 1997, the pen register was installed.

On August 21, 1997, Bowman came to Federal Van and Storage and paid ninety-two dollars to Beverly Pace to prepay until December 1997. On August 21, 1997, an NFA check for Bowman and Clark regarding a registration of silencer was initiated by SA Marquardt. On August 22, 1997, the toll records were received. On August 25, 1997, SA Marquardt dropped off a "police report" with Mary Lewis at Federal Van and Storage, which was, in fact, a fictitious document to make it look like they were the victim of a burglary. This was put in place of the letter to Mr. Bowman in case he came in and insisted on looking at the footlockers. The fictitious police report would be shown to Ray Bowman only if he asked to see the footlockers. On August 26, 1997, a second copy of toll records was received for Southwestern Bell Telephone Company, and the NFA check for Bowman and Clark registration of silencer came back negative.

On October 1, 1997, the ATF Laboratory identified Ray Bowman's left thumbprint on a VHS case for one of the videos found in one of the footlockers. Marquardt started case reports to be presented to the United States attorney's review.

The second event occurred on November 10, 1997, when a person named William A. Kirkpatrick, fifty-seven, a former Kansas City resident, was stopped for speeding on Interstate 80 near Lincoln, Nebraska, by a Nebraska state trooper. The Nebraska state trooper became suspicious of Kirkpatrick while questioning him and called for backup, including a narcotic-sniffing K-9 unit. The dog hit on an item in the car, and the trooper searched the vehicle, including the trunk, where he found four guns and two bags of fake mustaches, a key making machine, and locksmith tools. Also, in the trunk was nearly $2 million in cash.

Kirkpatrick was arrested for possession of firearms and the Omaha ATF office was notified, who joined in on the arrest and investigated firearms charges on Kirkpatrick in federal court. He was held on a $100,000 bond. His wife Penny drove to the courthouse in Lincoln, intending to post his bond. She was arrested and charged with aiding and abetting. A search of Kirkpatrick's house turned up three trench coats.

As reported in crime stories, published in the *Kansas City Star Newspaper,* William Kirkpatrick encounters with law enforcement started early.

He entered Westport High School in 1954 after transferring from McCune Home for Boys, an independent facility for delinquent children involved in Jackson County Juvenile Court cases. Kirkpatrick turned 14 in 1954. In the 1960s, his name appeared often in Kansas City Star crime stories:

He pleaded guilty to taking $30,000 in diamonds and jewelry from an Overland Park store. He was arrested in connection with a $11,940 burglary from a Springfield savings and loan. Charges were dismissed later. He was arrested in connection with the burglary of a Mission optical company. Mission police chasing the burglary suspects fired two warning shots at a car driven by Kirkpatrick. Once, again the charges were dismissed.

Once he was severely injured in a high-speed car crash that killed the car's 27-year-old driver. A jury found him guilty of displaying a deadly weapon in 1968, court records show.

He was arrested in southern Illinois in 1987 on charges of breaking and entering at a car lot, according to court records. Kirkpatrick pleaded not guilty but never showed up for subsequent court dates. A federal warrant was issued, but in 1989 a judge dismissed the original charge.

Not too long after their arrest, Penny decided to cooperate with investigators and convinced Kirkpatrick to plead guilty and cooperate also. He pleaded guilty; however, he refused to name his accomplice Bowman.

In December 1997, Penny pleaded guilty to conspiracy to commit money laundering in Minnesota and was sentenced to three years' probation. Penny told the agents that Kirkpatrick's partner was named "Ray" and was living in Kansas City.

In a related court action, a judge in Nebraska ruled the search of Kirkpatrick's vehicle was illegal, making the evidence inadmissible. However, her evidence could be used against his partner Ray Bowman and later was used in Bowman's trial.

In November and December 1997, ATF Agent Marquardt and an FBI agent from the office in Seattle, Washington initiated preparations of an affidavit for a federal search warrant for the Bowman house, as well as numerous bank safe deposit boxes in the name of Doug Bowman and his mother Gladys. To ensure that the proper information was provided in the affidavit, the United States attorney and the local Kansas City FBI office held a meeting to determine if all the probable cause information was included in the document.

During that meeting, one of the FBI agents said it would be more helpful if they had any strong documentation to directly connect Bowman with the recently arrested Bill Kirkpatrick. ATF Agent Marquardt raised his hand, replying that he had convincing documentation linking the two suspects. The two outlaws had been arrested together at a Walmart store in Springfield, Missouri, in 1974 and charged with shoplifting. He handed the FBI agent a copy of the arrest report. Marquardt then told the FBI agents that the ATF records reflected that Kirkpatrick and Bowman were periodically surveilled together by ATF agents and the Kansas City Police Department detectives from May 1981 through July 1981. On several occasions, Kirkpatrick was seen visiting Bowman's residence. He also told the agents attending the meeting that, in 1988, Detective Harold Nichols of Kansas City Police Department reported in a police report that he had observed Kirkpatrick getting into the Corvette Vehicle belonging to Ray Bowman, which Bowman was driving. Both were known to Detective Nichols.

The FBI now had the connection they needed, and the important information was included in the search warrant. An FBI agent who was attending the meeting offered to review ATF Agent Marquardt's voluminous file of his investigation and asked him "Why did you do all of this?" Marquardt just smiled and said, "It's called investigation, that's what we do." He knew his documentation put the nail in the coffin of bank robbers Bowman and Kirkpatrick.

As the affidavit was being filed and a request for arrest warrants issued, Ray Bowman was seen leaving his house and arrested at the Northland strip mall by Kansas City Detectives with the Intelligence Unit, who were working in connection with Agent Marquardt. Both the suspected bank robbers were now in custody and available to talk. Not surprisingly, Bowman wasn't talking, and Kirkpatrick wasn't naming his partner.

On December 19, 1997, Agent Marquardt filed an affidavit with United States Magistrate Judge Sarah Hayes, charging Bowman with possession of a silencer, using the evidence developed since May. Time was of the essence since Bowman by now knew his partner Kirkpatrick had been arrested in Nebraska and was in custody.

Shortly after his arrest, Bowman's house and a number of the safe deposit boxes in his name were searched pursuant to a federal search warrant being signed by a judge.

ATF Case Agent Marquardt and ATF Agent Randy Roberts were involved in the search. The ATF agents located a locked firearm safe in the basement of the house. A locksmith was called and eventually unlocked the safe, and the agents seized over sixty firearms that were taken into custody. Agent Robert would later testify at Bowman's federal trial in the state of Washington.

Regarding the recovery of the weapons, also seized in the search warrant was more than $1 million in cash, including bills linked to the bank robbery in Tacoma, Washington. Bowman and Kirkpatrick were now both linked to the robbery. The agents also found two notes with the name "Billy" Kirkpatrick, further evidence linking the two bank robbers.

Soon after Bowman was arrested, his younger brother Dan turned over two satchels that Bowman had given him before his arrest, telling Dan the satchels contained money to be provided to Bowman's daughters if something happened to him. He assured Dan it was not drug money. The two satchels contained $480,000. One of the bundles of money contained a stamped band from the Seafirst Bank robbery. This was introduced as evidence against Bowman introduced by Dan during questioning at the trial.

On January 5, 1998, the federal grand jury in the United States District Court for the Western District of Missouri returned a one-count federal indictment charging Ray L. Bowman, a.k.a. Charles Clark, a.k.a. C. Clark, with federal firearms violations, enforced by the ATF. The indictment read:

> Between on or about November 25, 1991 and May 22, 1997, both dates being approximate, in the Western District of Missouri, RAY L. BOWMAN, a/k/a Charles Clark a/k/a C. Clark, defendant herein, did knowingly possess a firearm, a defined by Title 26, United States Code, Section 5845 (a)(7) and Title 18, United States Code, Section 921 (a)(24), namely, a firearm silencer, more particularly described as component parts intended only for use in assembling or fabrication a device for silencing, muffling or diminishing the report of a portable firearm, which was not registered to him in the national firearms registration and Transfer Record, as required by Title 26, United States Code, Section 5841.
>
> All in violation of Title 26, United States Code, Section 5861 (d) and 5871.

On January 9, 1998, during a hearing before US Magistrate Sarah Hayes, Roy L. Bowman pled not guilty to his federal firearm charge. The court date was set for February 9, 1998, and Bowman was ordered held without bond, continuing an order the judge first entered on December 30, 1997. All investigators involved applauded the order.

ATF Agent Paul Marquardt and FBI Agent Butch Roll testified that agents recovered more than $1 million in cash, including marked bills traceable to the February 1997 bank robbery outside Tacoma, Washington.

It was the largest bank robbery recorded in the history of the United States, with the robbers escaping with $4.5 million. On June 3, 1998, Ray Bowman was convicted by a jury in the District Court for the Western District of Missouri of possession of unregistered silencer components in the United States v. Ray L. Bowman, case number 98-00001-01-CR-W-GAF. Bowman was subsequently sentenced to thirty months.

In July 1998, Agent Marquardt traveled to Seattle, Washington, and met with FBI agents assigned to the large bank robbery outside Tacoma, as well as other bank robberies committed by Bowman and Kirkpatrick dating back several years. All were still within the statue of limitation for federal prosecution. Agent Marquardt provided key information on the bank robbers and turned over evidence in the custody of ATF to facilitate the FBI's case. In addition, he provided firearms trace information on several firearms found in the footlocker seized at the storage shed on May 22, 1997, as well as firearms seized in the search of suspect Bowman's house and the safe deposit box in several banks belonging to Bowman.

On August 19, 1998, Kirkpatrick was sentenced to fifteen years and eight months. Also, on August 19, 1998, Ray L. Bowman was indicted in the Western District of Missouri on eleven counts of money laundering, six of which involved the use of safe deposit boxes to secrete currency and valuables either taken from the robberies or proceeds thereof. In Count Twelve, vehicles, items of jewelry, and a money judgment in the amount of $366,919.89 were included in the indictment, forfeitable pursuant to 18 U.S.C 982. On October 12, 1999, Ray L. Bowman pleaded guilty nolo contendere and agreed to the forfeiture of the property listed in the indictment and a money judgment in the amount of $366,919.89. He appealed the sentence entered by the district court on March 10, 2000, by challenging the facts stipulated in the plea agreement. On December 28, 2000, the Eighth Circuit affirmed eleven of the twelve counts.

On November 6, 1998, Bowman was convicted by a jury in District Court for the Western District of Washington of conspiracy to commit bank robbery, armed bank robbery, use and carrying a firearm, and interstate transportation of stolen property in United States v. Ray L. Bowman, Case No. CR98-5121FDB (W.D Wa). Bowman was sentenced to 295 months incarceration and restitution in the amount of $5,228,122.00.

On February 19, 2000, Bank of America was closing its facility at 14 West Tenth Street, Kansas City. Letters were forwarded by the bank, notifying customers regarding the facility closure and removal of safe deposit items prior to that date. Safe deposit box number 4419 had been rented by Ray Lewis since November 1974 under the name of "Ray Lewis/Gladys." The lease on the safe deposit box was paid up until November 2000. No one came forward to claim the contents of the box.

The bank facility drilled open all unclaimed safe deposit boxes. Upon initiating inventory of Box 4419, several firearms were observed in violation of bank policy. The Kansas City Police Department was notified of the firearms in the safe deposit box and noticed unusual items located in the safe deposit box, such as handguns, silencers, gold coins and bars, United States currency, blueprints to the Kansas City Federal Reserve Bank, safes ,and identification cards. Both ATF and FBI were made aware of the finding at the bank.

On January 23, 2001, the court entered a final order of forfeiture and order of restitution. The court granted a money judgment of $366,919.89 and the 1995 Ford Crown Victoria, VIN:2FALP74WXS144343, was ordered forfeited to the United States. All other property listed in the indictment were ordered to be sold by the United States Marshals Service and the proceeds to be sent to the clerk of the court for the Western District of Washington to be applied against the restitution ordered in that case.

An interesting historical footnote, the two outlaws operated undetected for fifteen years, just one year less than another pair of Missouri outlaws, Jesse and Frank James. Bowman was serving his sentence in a federal prison in Leavenworth, Kansas, just outside of Kansas City. However, he did not complete his sentence, dying of natural causes before his release. Kirkpatrick did serve out his sentence and was released, fading into obscurity. So ends the dynamic saga of "The Trench Coat Robbers."

Had it not been for the efforts of ATF Agent Paul Marquardt and the diligent search efforts of the Nebraska Highway Patrol Trooper, assisted by ATF agents investigating firearms charges, the two modern-day yeggs might still be traveling the backroads of America, causing havoc with the banking industry.

CHAPTER THIRTEEN

CRIME, VIOLENCE, AND JUSTICE, SOUTHWEST MISSOURI STYLE 1932-1996

S outhwest Missouri and the hills of the Ozarks have produced its share of gangsters and outlaws throughout the 1900s. I will first highlight a few of the early 1900s.

The Notorious Young Brothers
Jennings Young and Harry Young of Greene County, Missouri, were responsible for the deadliest law enforcement shootout in the history of the United States on January 2, 1932, leaving six lawmen dead.

The Underhill Brothers
Wilber, Ernest, George, and Earl were all born in Southwest Missouri in the early 1900s. All four brothers served time in the Missouri State Penitentiary for numerous crimes, including burglaries, theft, and even murders. Wilber Underhill, the most notorious of the brothers, committed five murders himself before he was shot and captured by law enforcement authorities on December 30, 1933, dying of his wounds in prison on January 6, 1934. He was the first federal fugitive caught by the FBI.

Adam "Eddie" Richetti
He was raised in Bolivar, Missouri, just east of Springfield, a member of the notorious "Pretty Boy Floyd" gang and a close criminal associate of Floyd, pulling off numerous robberies during the 1920s and '30s. Richetti was executed in the Missouri gas chamber on October 1, 1938, after he was convicted of killings committed during the Union Station Massacre in Kansas City.

Jimmie Creighton
A member of the Barker-Karpis Gang, he was a bank robber who was wanted for a heist in Hastings, Nebraska. In 1931, he killed a man in Webb City, Missouri, for simply bumping into him on the street. He was convicted of this murder and sentenced to life in the Missouri State Penitentiary. He, at one time, lived with Fred Barker in Joplin.

Herb "Deafy" Farmer
He owned a chicken farm just south of Joplin and, throughout the 1930s, sheltered outlaws on the run, housing more criminals than he housed chickens.

On January 4, 1935, Herb Farmer was convicted of conspiracy to obstruct justice in the Kansas City Union Station Massacre and was sentenced to serve two years in the federal penitentiary in Leavenworth, Kansas.

Ray "Arkansas Tom" Daugherty

Daughtery was the last survivor of the 1890s Bill Doolin Gang. He robbed a bank in Ashbury, Missouri, was convicted of murder, and was later killed by police in Joplin, Missouri, on August 18, 1924.

"Ma" Arizona Donna Clark Barker

She was born near Ash Grove, Missouri, the mother of Lloyd, Herman, Fred, and Arthur Barker, all Missouri-born between 1893 and 1903, and all members of the villainous Barker-Karpis Gang, declared by J. Edger Hoover as the most notorious gang of the time.

The Bald Knobbers

They were vigilantes operating in the Missouri Ozark hills during the 1880s. There were events occurring in Southwest Missouri that gained national media attention.

Jake Fleagle

The leader of the infamous Fleagle Gang, involved in bank robberies and murder in the Midwest and West, Fleagle was a fugitive, shot and killed in Branson, Missouri, on October 14, 1930, by local and federal officials while he was trying to board a train.

Bonnie and Clyde

They were involved in a deadly shootout in Joplin, Missouri, with law enforcement officials. The criminal histories of these early gangsters and outlaws are each documented in detail in several other chapters in this book. In this chapter we will detail the gangsters and outlaws operating in Southwest Missouri in the 1980s and '90s.

The Ben Shriver Gang

The Ben Shriver Gang was operating in Springfield during the Bar Wars period in the 1980s. They were involved in arson, bombing, fraud, and attempted murder before all members of the gang were caught and sentenced to long prison terms.

The Jimmie Lineger Missouri Trooper Murder

On Highway 65, near Springfield, Trooper Jimmie Lineger was killed by David Tate, a neo-Nazi, during a car stop on April 15, 1985.

The CSA Camp Raids

The ultra-right-wing, radical neo-Nazi paramilitary group known as the Covenant, Sword and the Arm of the Lord (CSA) maintained a compound in northern Arkansas at the Missouri state line with the leader, Jim Ellison, living in Pontiac, Missouri.

The Michael Coy Bombing Murder

Michael Coy was killed when a bomb attached to his vehicle detonated while he and his ex-wife were traveling on a highway just west of Springfield in 1989. She lost her left arm.

The McDaris, Short, and Bridwell Gang

The McDaris, Short, and Bridwell Gang included a large group of burglars, arsonists, robbers, assaulters, and drug sellers operating in and around Springfield and Christian County, Missouri.

The Bad Joann Cunningham Gang

Also of Springfield, they were involved in arson, fraud, and murder attempts in and around the city until captured by a law enforcement task force in 1992. All three members were convicted.

The Bad Jack Moad Gang

Operating in and around Lebanon in the 1990s, all previously were convicted felons committing arson, firearms violations, threats, intimidation, and insurance fraud.

We begin with the Ben Shriver Gang.

THE SPRINGFIELD BAR WARS AND THE BEN SHRIVER GANG

On November 13, 1982, a remote-controlled bomb containing three sticks of dynamite was found lying on the parking lot of the Get-N-Go service station and convenience store located on Battlefield Road in Springfield. The device-receiving portion of the bomb apparently fell off a vehicle while parked in the parking lot.

The Springfield Bomb and Arson Unit was contacted, responded to the scene, and disarmed the device. The detectives suspected the device may have fallen off a vehicle passing through Springfield from St. Louis on the way to a Table Rock fishing resort area, since St. Louis law enforcement was experiencing similar types of incidents regarding mob violence in the past several years.

On November 18, 1982, Dick Mann of the Bomb and Arson Unit contacted the Kansas City ATF office requesting assistance, since ATF had federal jurisdiction of the federal explosive laws.

In my capacity as a federal ATF agent, I received the assignment to investigate the incident and responded to their unit in Springfield. I met with the investigators. We did not know it at the time, but ATF agents would be spending an extensive amount of time in and around Springfield over the next several years, investigating a series of bombing, arsons, and murder attempts involving area mobsters and outlaws.

The information presented to the readers in this chapter is firsthand knowledge developed by the investigators assigned to this case. Any information published in the printed media was information presented to them from those officials who developed the information.

We met with arson investigators Jerry Codey of the Springfield Police Department and Richard Mann of the Springfield Fire Department and inspected the recovered remote-control bomb parts after it was disarmed on the parking lot.

Detective Cody said his unit was investigating a series of suspicious fires that had occurred over the past year or two at country-and-western bars, and it seemed to be related to someone or group "wanting to monopolize the country-western business in town," as one of the bar owner victims reported to the local Springfield newspaper.

Larry Holmes, a Springfield firefighter and owner of the Back Forty Lounge on Glenstone, had experienced three arson fires since May 1, 1982. In one of the incidents, which had occurred on July 25, two witnesses reported they had observed two men running from the rear of the Back Forty Lounge before the fire department arrived.

In another incident early in 1982, a bomb exploded in the parking lot of "Wild Bill's" tavern on Glenstone, and two years earlier, an arson fire had caused minor damage to the tavern.

In late November 1981, a fire damaged the Southfork Bar, also located on Glenstone. Five separate fires were set inside the building, an obvious act of arson that had caused heavy smoke damage and moderate structural damage.

On December 28, 1980, an explosion at the Outlaw Lounge on Sunshine leveled the building. Someone had opened a natural gas valve and lit a candle, which touched off the explosion.

More recently, on October 20, 1982, at about 6:45 a.m., Douglas McQueen was shot in the hand by his employer, Ted Fred Ehlers. This incident occurred at Ehlers's residence, located at 3541 South Carriage in Springfield, during a dispute between the two men and Ehlers's wife. The shooting incident was witnessed by Ehlers's wife, Jo; his son, Randy Ehlers; and his father. An investigation was conducted by the Springfield Police Department, resulting in the subsequent arrest of Ted Ehlers, who was charged with an assault against Douglas C. McQueen.

During the early part of 1982, Douglas McQueen had been introduced to Ted Fred Ehlers, a local Springfield bookmaker. This introduction took place at McQueen's place of employment, the Hitchin Post Lounge, located on Kearney Street in Springfield, a country-and-western bar owned and operated by Benny G. Shriver and Shriver's parents. McQueen was subsequently hired by Ted Ehlers to act as a bodyguard for Ehlers and his family. Ehlers felt he needed a bodyguard after he was victimized in an armed robbery in which he lost approximately $25,000 in bets and wagers. It was common knowledge that Douglas McQueen had previous experience as a bodyguard through his continued boasting.

During the brief period of time that Douglas McQueen was employed by Ted Ehlers as a bodyguard, he openly displayed a firearm that he carried in a shoulder holster. McQueen escorted Ted Ehlers to various Springfield locations, gaining an insight on the locations requested by Ehlers and meeting Ehlers's business and social contacts. During this period of employment, McQueen befriended the wife of Ted Ehlers.

Based on this background information, ATF agreed to work together to determine if and what the connections to the various acts of violence might be. While at their office, the recovered bomb was inspected. The receiving portion of this device consisted of three sticks of Trojan brand 60WR brand dynamite (1-1/4" X 8"), batteries, an Atlas brand electric blasting cap, a Cox Sanwa brand servo and radio receiver with antenna, a pencil for support, an off/on switch, and an arming device. The entire bomb was wrapped in black shiny electrical tape. The date and shift codes had been removed from the sticks of dynamite with a sharp object in an effort to avoid tracing the dynamite.

ATF was provided with a number of photographs of the device component parts. The agents and investigators went to a local hobby shop on East Sunshine and learned from the owner that he had sold the identical remote device and had sold only one or two since he started handling them. However, he did not keep records of the sales.

Information was also developed that a person named Ernie Wells, who was a detention officer for the Springfield Police Department, had a source who told him an employee at the Sheppard Sign Company was selling dynamite on the street. He agreed to keep us informed if he heard information of interest on the street.

On December 14, 1982, the local FBI office provided information that a local criminal character named "Big" Bob Moore may have been the intended target of the bomb device recovered from the Get-N-Go parking lot.

His full name was Robert Leslie Moore, and he was known to be involved in operating a gambling operation in Springfield. Moore also owned a tavern in Springfield, the Locker Room Sports Bar, and operated a prostitution ring from the bar. He employed a woman named Brenda McReynolds, who managed the bar and operated the prostitution ring at Moore's direction.

Investigators started watching the place and would drop into the bar occasionally, making it known who they were. These distractions became an irritation to Moore, who started complaining to his employees about law enforcement watching his actions.

On December 20, 1982, Gary Wallace, the owner of the hobby shop, told us the unit recovered by the Springfield Police had the same frequency as the one he had sold to his customer. He provided a description of the man to whom he had sold one of these devices.

On December 22, Springfield Police Reserve Officer Wells informed us that he heard the Back Forty Lounge was about to be victim again of another bombing over the Christmas holidays. Plans were made to conduct a surveillance on the building. A surveillance was initiated on this date and continued through December 25, 1982.

On December 25, Detective Jerry Codey, ATF Agent Steve Hnatt, and I initiated a surveillance at 10:30 p.m. At just after 11:00 p.m., an explosion blasted a hole in the roof of the building on the Glenstone side. ATF Agent Hnatt said a person had just walked past the building about five minutes prior to the explosion. He did not observe any suspicious actions, and the person walked away out of site. Efforts to locate him were negative.

In the morning, an examination of the scene was conducted, and a number of suspects were developed and investigated, including a man named Jerry Sifford, the brother-in-law of Larry Holmes, who was at one time a partner with Holmes in the Back Forty Lounge until Sifford and Holmes had become involved in a family rift. Information was also received that the task force should look at Ben Shriver, who was currently the manager of the Hitchin Post Lounge located on Kearney Street in Springfield and the previous owner of the Back Forty Lounge. The rumor around town was that Shriver was upset over the fact the Back Forty Lounge was affecting his own bar business.

On December 30, 1982, a confidential source of Detective Jerry Codey's provided information that investigators should look at a person named Douglas McQueen. He said McQueen was an employee at the Shriver-run Hitchin Post Lounge.

The investigators recognized that McQueen was the same person who was shot by the local bookmaker, Ted Ehlers, on November 20. The task force's suspicions of a connection were starting to add up.

During the month of January, the investigators inspected the local explosives company records to see if they had sold dynamite to any of our suspects during 1982. The results proved negative. Investigators received reliable information that the Back Forty Lounge, which had recently reopened, was going to be hit again.

Investigators set up another surveillance on January 19, 1983. A subject was observed stealing hubcaps and damaging vehicles on the customer parking lot and arrested. No other actions were observed.

On February 4, 1983, a house located at 3540 South Carriage and a business located on National in Springfield were heavily damaged by intentionally set arson fires. Both properties were owned by Ben Shriver.

It was reported that Shriver had arrived at his house that was on fire with a friend, an off-duty Springfield police officer named Don Pippin. Shriver told Investigator Mann he was currently staying at another location the past week due to a shooting incident in an attempt on his life the previous Sunday evening. He felt someone was out to get him. Shriver said at the time of the fires he was hosting an event at his Hitchin Post Bar during the evening and Officer Pippin, who was attending the event, could vouch for his whereabouts.

Shriver said he did not know who shot at him or who set the two fires. He refused the offer to take a polygraph. This all seemed highly suspicious to the investigators.

A substantial amount of evidence of arson was collected at the scene, including an incendiary device found at the house consisting of extension cords, timers, wires, alligator clips, a hair dryer, flash bars, electrical plug connectors, glass container, fuse links, cups, foil, and flammable liquid.

On February 26, 1983, our first break in the Shriver Gang investigation occurred when Robert Hood Jr. and a criminal associate named Olen Dale Neal were arrested by Springfield Police detectives after robbing a family in Springfield. They were placed in custody in the Greene County Jail in Springfield.

In March 1983, we interviewed Robert Hood for the first time. He was told we knew about his involvement in serious issues, including his current arrest for robbery, and other serious state and federal crimes (including firearms and explosive violations, arson, and attempted murder). He decided it was in his best interest to cooperate with our task force team.

He verbally admitted his involvement in the burning and bombing of the Back Forty Lounge and named his coconspirators as Ben Shriver, Doug Mc-Queen, and Rudy Haldiman. He also told us who was involved in the attempted murder of local gambler, Ted Fred Ehlers, along with him. In addition, he named who was involved in the arson fires at Ben Shriver's house and Ben Shriver's warehouse in Springfield. He said Ben Shriver had faked an alleged shooting attempt on his life to portray himself as a victim to law enforcement.

The task force team developed information to support his information of a major conspiracy carried out by the gang of conspirators in 1982–83.

On June 9, 1983, at the Greene County Jail, Robert C. Hood, after being advised of his rights against self-incrimination, told Springfield Police Detective Gregory Shafer that he had purchased a quantity of dynamite on August 5, 1982, from Springfield Explosives. He told Detective Shafer where he could recover these explosives. Later that day, Detective Medlin recovered twelve sticks of Trojan Brand dynamite, date shift code 60WR26JAN81W and twelve blasting caps from 2001 North Douglas in Springfield.

In July we met with federal and state prosecutors and requested subpoenas for a federal grand jury. On August 1, 1983, we conducted another interview with Robert Hood at the Springfield Police Department Special Investigation Unit (SIU)

On September 12, 1983, a federal retainer was filed against Robert C. Hood, Jr., on Federal Bench Warrant #80-46 for the Federal Judicial District of Delaware. This involved Hood's illegal manufacturer of drugs investigated by DEA agents in Delaware and Texas. This retainer was filed by the United States marshals for the Western Judicial District of Missouri, Kansas City, placing a hold on Hood, who was incarcerated at the Greene County Jail, Springfield.

Also, on September 12, we met once again with Robert Hood at the Springfield Police Department. He continued to provide significant firsthand knowledge and involvement in federal and state criminal conspiracy violations. We were already focused on the rest of the Shriver Gang.

For the next several months the investigators completed files on the incidents involving fire, explosives, and acts of violence, and leads were followed upon. We focused primarily on the bombing of the Back Forty Lounge, the explosive device recovered from the Get-N-Go parking lot, the arson fires at Shriver's house and warehouse, the reported murder attempt on Ben Shriver, and the shooting of Doug McQueen by Ted Ehlers. Numerous interviews were conducted, and statements were prepared.

We continued to receive information from several sources about our suspect, Robert Hood, related to his involvement in the Back Forty bombing and the Shriver arsons.

On September 14, 1983, Detective Medlin, Shafer, and I conducted an interview with bookmaker Ted Ehlers regarding his association with McQueen, Hood, and Shriver. He provided us with more insight about our suspects and a number of leads to follow.

On December 26, 1983, an arson fire occurred at the Scorpios Massage Parlor located at Highway 61 North, Scott County, just outside the city limits of Sikeston, Missouri. The property was owned by Roger Skaggs, a Springfield resident who had been identified as a suspect in the ongoing investigation of Ben Shriver. The suspected torch in the Shriver investigation was an associate of Skaggs. This fire incident was added to the list of suspicious events.

Realizing the number of open investigations required more manpower, ATF Agent Duane Nichols of our Kansas City office joined in the investigation.

Also joining were detectives Tim Medlin, who was already involved, and Ray Fite of the Springfield Police SIU, as well as two investigators from the Internal Revenue Service of the Treasury Department. They were Bob Hawkins and Steve Hart. They also provided ATF with office space in Springfield. With the added manpower, a task force approach was initiated at the time.

On April 30, 1984, the task force received a big break in the case when Patty Skaggs, wife of Roger Skaggs, offered to provide information on certain bombings and arsons that had occurred dating back to 1978 in and around Springfield and Sikeston, Missouri. She was motivated to come forward after she was injured during an argument with her husband. We also learned a person named Rick Young, a criminal associate of Roger Skaggs, had offered to provide information about illegal activities conducted by Roger Skaggs.

Richard Young was interviewed at his apartment and provided information about two fires that had occurred in Sikeston. He named who he thought was involved and felt Roger Skaggs directed the settings of these two fires.

Young also told us the fire at Roger Skaggs residence in Springfield in 1978 was an arson fire and Roger Skaggs had directed the setting of this fire. The motive behind the setting of this fire was an arson fraud scheme to collect the insurance proceeds. Young provided the names of other people with either involvement or direct knowledge of these criminal acts.

On May 3, 1984, the task force members conducted a lengthy interview with Patricia Skaggs, the wife of Roger Skaggs. At the direction of her attorney, she said that, on July 7, 1978, her husband had conspired with a man named Larry Stahl and other individuals to burn their residence just outside

Springfield, so they could collect the insurance money for financial reasons. A woman named Judy Jordan had helped remove certain items from the residence before the fire and claimed these as lost in the fire. Skaggs removed a bedroom set before the fire and sold it to a person named Melinda Tayler. She mentioned a person named Jon Gillespie, who had direct knowledge of the fire and agreed to cooperate with us and Jon named others who were also involved in removing items and filing the insurance claim.

Patricia also provided her knowledge of two intentionally set fires in Sikeston at two massage parlors that were set at the direction of Roger Skaggs and named the person who set the fires for her husband. These fires she said had occurred in September and December of 1983 and were set by a local criminal named Bobby Gene Rantz.

The task force initiated an all-out effort to develop charges against Roger Skaggs and his criminal associates, conducting interviews, reviewing documents, obtaining federal subpoenas, and meeting with Assistant United States attorneys in the federal courthouse.

Interviews were conducted with Jon Gillespie, an associate of Roger Skaggs, who offered his personal knowledge of Skaggs's involvement. On several occasions, Skaggs had confided in Gillespie, admitting his own involvement and that of others who had helped set the fires. Gillespie was asked to call investigators if he learned anything about others who may have been involved.

We all agreed we could not have too many sources in an investigation this involved, and we developed our share who were in the know.

On June 5, 1984, I interviewed Ina K. McQueen. During this interview, Mrs. McQueen said she was a social acquaintance of Robert Hood Jr. from 1981 through the first part of 1983. She had met Hood through her husband, Douglas McQueen. She had direct knowledge that Hood was wanted by federal authorities during the summer of 1982, and at the time, he made a purchase of explosives in Springfield. She said Hood knew he was wanted by authorities during this period.

On July 17, 1984, a case report was submitted regarding Hood's illegally purchasing dynamite on August 5, 1982. This report included a cover letter detailing Hood's cooperation since March 1983. In return, the United States Attorney's Office in Springfield, along with the Greene County Missouri Prosecutor's Office in Springfield, agreed not to use the information supplied by Hood to incriminate himself in the illegal purchase of the twelve sticks of dynamite and twelve electric blasting caps.

On September 7, 1984, Robert Hood pled guilty to a federal felony drug charge as a result of a federal indictment charged against him in 1980 in the Federal District of Delaware.

On September 13, 1984, Robert C. Hood Jr., signed a fourteen-page confession he provided to us at the Springfield Police Department, admitting he was a central figure in various serious federal and state violations. He had hoped to reduce his criminal exposure by cooperating and telling the truth.

Hood detailed his involvement in numerous felony acts he had committed during 1982 and 1983 in Springfield. He named his coconspirators who also participated in these acts of violence. He had previously provided drawings of a sawed-off shotgun that Doug McQueen had given to him to use in the efforts to kill Ted Ehlers.

According to Hood, McQueen told him he had acquired this sawed-off shotgun from Rudy Haldiman to give to Hood.

McQueen provided a drawing of the description of the dynamite date shift code of JUN26,81 removed from ten sticks of dynamite by McQueen and Hood and a drawing of the bomb Hood had received from McQueen, which was constructed by Rudy Haldiman, consisting of five sticks of dynamite contained in a coffee can and a brown paper sack. This was the bomb he had thrown on the roof of the Back Forty Lounge on December 25, 1982, at the direction of gang leader Ben Shriver. These drawings were filed as evidence documents.

The task force efforts continued to produce results, and on October 30, 1984, Roger Dale Skaggs, acting on the advice of his attorney, provided a detailed signed confession, admitting his involvement in the arson fire of his house in 1978. He also admitted to having his massage parlors in Sikeston and Springfield burned down in 1983. Charges were soon to follow.

On November 28 and December 3, 1984, Glenda Denise Fal provided tape-recorded interviews advising us she was a girlfriend of Rudy Haldiman from December 1982 to the end of February 1983. During this period, Haldiman confided to her his involvement in burning down Ben's house and warehouse and was hired by the person who owned the house and the warehouse. She did not know that Haldiman was talking about Ben Shriver. He told her he was hired to set this fire, so the owner could collect insurance from the fires.

Afterward, Haldiman left the truck he had used to set these fires in Fal's garage. She said Haldiman also left explosive devices, dynamite, electric blasting caps, and a pistol in her garage for a period of time in a bag. Fal said she had become nosy and looked into the bag and realized what she was holding.

Haldiman also told her he was involved in shooting the windows out of a car, using a shotgun in a staged shooting. He said a police report was filed by this man. He said the man was the owner of the Hitchin Post Lounge on Kearney Street in Springfield.

Haldiman told her there was a middleman involved who Rudy called "Cuz." He was involved in all the criminal acts according to Rudy. Denise Fal said a person named Johnny West loaned his car to Haldiman the night he committed the fake shooting.

Fal was shown numerous photographs of men and women and certain items. She said the man called "Cuz" was named "Doug," and she had met Doug on one occasion. Haldiman talked to this man on numerous occasions on the telephone about the money Haldiman was to receive and the rifle he used that had a scope on it.

Fal was shown a list of seven names and asked if she recognized any of the names. She identified the name Ben Shriver, who hired Rudy to set the fires. She also identified a number of items in our possession that Rudy had left in her garage, including electrical tape, a type of fuse, wires, caps with wires on them, batteries, phone wire, insulation, lids off a Folgers coffee can, adding that Haldiman drank Folgers brand coffee. The items also included a battery holder and a plastic trash bag brown in color and a Johnny Walker brand Scotch bottle, adding that Haldiman drank Johnny Walker brand Scotch. Fal also identified a shotgun and black alligator clips.

Haldiman had told her that, on the night of the two fires, he had parked that truck in Shriver's driveway and entered the house with a key and he cut the alarm wires before he entered the house. During this photo spread, she identified Rudy Haldiman as her one-time boyfriend.

On November 30, 1984, an arson fire occurred at the business of Jon Gillespie, one of our key government witnesses against Roger Skaggs. The building and business were totally destroyed.

The task force investigated the fire, along with the Missouri State Fire Marshal's Office and the Springfield Missouri Police Department. Jon Gillespie strongly suspected Roger Skaggs since Gillespie was testifying against Skaggs.

On December 28, 1984, Roger Skaggs was involved in a fight at a bar in Springfield with his wife Patricia, Jon Gillespie, and Rick Young. All three were offering testimony on Roger Skaggs. Injuries were reported to the Springfield Police Department, who documented the incident in police reports.

Realizing the witnesses were being victimized, threatened and injured, the task force presented the incidents to the United States Attorney's Office, encouraging a quick return on grand jury indictments.

On March 21, 1985, Roger Dale Skaggs was charged with willfully and knowingly conspiring with uncharged coconspirators Patricia Skaggs and arsonist Larry Noland Stahl to defraud the insurance company of insurance proceeds after destroying his house by fire.

On this same day, Roger Skaggs pled guilty in federal court to one count arson and one count mail fraud, our second conviction in our investigation.

In a press release to the Springfield media, Springfield Police Chief Troy Majors announced that the pleas entered by Skaggs marked the completion of Phase I of a Special Investigative Task Force effort by members from his department, agents from the ATF's Kansas City office, and members of the Springfield Arson Unit. The task force effort had been initiated in March 1983 to look into a series of arsons, bombing, insurance fraud, mail and wire fraud, gambling, prostitution rings, pornography, and murder attempts that had occurred in and around the Springfield area over the previous several years.

Chief majors said that the task force investigators received continued assistance from several enforcement agencies, including the Springfield Fire Department, the Missouri Highway Patrol, the State Fire Marshal's Office, the IRS, the FBI, and the prosecutors' offices at both the state and federal levels.

Chief Majors said this task force, which had conducted interviews with over 500 witnesses and recovered an extensive amount of evidence, was the longest-running investigation ever conducted by his department. In addition to the Skaggs arsons, the task force focused on organized criminal groups involved in violent criminal acts and arson-for-profit schemes.

Chief Majors said that the task force investigation was continuing and that additional charges citing various felony violations by other individuals would be submitted to the Greene County prosecutor's office and the United States Attorney's Office in Springfield as subsequent phases of the investigation are concluded.

The task force efforts in Phase II were already in full swing, and more federal indictments and state charges were about to be announced.

On August 21, 1985, a federal grand jury in Springfield indicted Rudy M. Haldiman, Robert C. Hood Jr., and Douglas G. McQueen on arson, explosive violations, mail fraud, and conspiracy charges. They were charged with the arson fire of the Back Forty Lounge on Glenstone (a business owned by the gang leader Benny Shriver and located at National Avenue and Central Streets) and Shriver's residence, located in south Springfield.

Named as unindicted coconspirators were Benny G. Shriver and Ina Kathy McQueen of Kansas City. She was Doug McQueen's wife.

In addition to the federal charges, Doug McQueen and Rudy Haldiman were charged in state court by the Greene County prosecutor with conspiracy to murder Ted Fred Ehlers, a business associate of McQueen's after Ehlers shot McQueen on October 20, 1982, during an argument at Ehlers's home in Springfield.

The state's charges included allegations that McQueen and Haldiman had built explosive bombs to use against Ehlers, attaching one of the bombs on Ehlers's vehicle. The remote-controlled bomb fell off Ehlers's car on November 13, 1982. This was the device that was recovered by the Springfield Bomb and Arson Unit and safely disarmed.

The task force and United States Attorney's Office announced to the media the return of these indictments, marking the completion of Phase II of the Federal State Task Force's investigative efforts. They added that the task force was now working on Phase III and hoped to have more indictments by the end of the year.

On September 4, 1985, Robert Hood pled guilty to one count of conspiracy involving the plot from May 1982 to June 1983 to bomb and burn the Back Forty Lounge at 631 South Glenstone Avenue and to commit mail fraud in an attempt to collect insurance money from the fires he had helped set at Ben Shriver's house and place of business on February 4, 1983.

In a separate hearing in federal court, Douglas McQueen pled guilty to counts charging him with Rudy Haldiman in the December 25, 1982 bombing of the Back Forty Lounge, the February burning of the Crescent Music Company Warehouse in Springfield, and mail fraud between December 1982 and June 1983. Both men were held without bond, and sentencing dates were to be set at a later date. Both men had agreed to cooperate with authorities on these and other criminal violations.

On November 20, 1985, Douglas McQueen signed a twenty-three-page confession detailing his involvement, along with coconspirators Rudy Haldiman, Ben Shriver, and Robert Hood.

McQueen admitted setting the fire in July 1982 at the Back Forty Lounge, along with Robert Hood and Rudy Haldiman, at the direction of Ben Shriver. He also admitted bombing the Back Forty Lounge in October 1982, along with coconspirators Rudy Haldiman and Robert Hood, again at the direction of Ben Shriver.

McQueen also cleared up the attempted murder of illegal bookmaker Ted Ehlers after Ehlers had shot him in the hand during an argument when he was Ehlers's bodyguard.

McQueen said Ben Shriver wanted Ted Ehlers dead, so he could take over Ehlers's illegal gambling and bookmaking operation in Springfield.

McQueen had directed Rudy Haldiman to construct a remote bomb and to purchase a rifle with a scope to be used in the murder attempt on Ehlers. McQueen owned a sawed-off shotgun, and Haldiman provided McQueen with a .25 caliber pistol. Ben Shriver also provided a .38 caliber revolver. The plan was to either shoot Ehlers or place the remote-controlled bomb on Ehlers's vehicle. The task force learned Haldiman had purchased the remote-control device at the Wallace Hobby Shop in Springfield, just as we had suspected.

McQueen said Haldiman placed the bomb on Ehlers's vehicle; however, it fell from Ehlers's vehicle at the Get-N-Go fast food shop on Battlefield Road—the one disarmed and recovered by the Springfield Bomb and Arson Unit.

McQueen said Robert Hood was enlisted to help kill Ehlers and had Haldiman make a second bomb that was placed on Ehlers's vehicle.

Ehlers was stalked with the help of Hood and Shriver. Haldiman did his own stalking. Hood made several attempts on Ehlers's life without success. McQueen said the attempts continued through February 1983. He added that these efforts were discontinued when Ehlers was sentenced to eighteen years in prison for shooting McQueen.

McQueen also confessed to assisting in the Christmas night bombing of the Back Forty Lounge. Haldiman made the delay bomb, and Hood threw it on the roof of the lounge, all at the direction of McQueen and Ben Shriver.

Cleaning up this bombing was particularly satisfying to me since I was surveilling the building when the bomb went off, which was rather embarrassing.

McQueen said Shriver asked him to burn down his house and his business, so he could collect the insurance money covering the loss. He said Haldiman had constructed incendiary devices with timers that were used. McQueen, with the help of his wife, purchased the fuel that was used in setting the fire. This made Ina McQueen a coconspirator and eliminated her defense of not testifying since they were married. McQueen added that Ben Shriver had staged a fake attempt on his life to give the appearance that someone was out to get him. This set the stage for the fires. This faked incident occurred shortly before the fires were set, and the police were called by Shriver to investigate the shooting attempt after Shriver reported it.

On the night of the two arson fires, Shriver held a special events night at his nightclub—the Hitchin Post Lounge—and hired a Springfield police officer who performed Elvis impressions, which attracted numerous police officers. This established Shriver's whereabouts while the fires were set.

McQueen provided a truck to Haldiman to hold the incendiary devices and fuel and gave Haldiman keys to access Shriver's house and business, the Crescent Warehouse in Springfield.

Shriver confided in McQueen that he had moved a number of valuable items out of his house and rented storage sheds to secure these items and then claimed them as destroyed in the fire.

He then submitted his proof of loss statement to the insurance company. He had McQueen help him with completing this proof of loss statement to collect the insurance proceeds in the arson fraud scheme.

McQueen said, throughout 1983, Ben Shriver provided his coconspirators with updates on the ongoing investigation being conducted by the task force investigators. McQueen said he moved out of Springfield due to the "heat." He lived in Kansas City; Sedalia; Houston, Texas; and Miami, Oklahoma, for periods of time to avoid being located.

He said Shriver was very concerned, fearing a number of people were providing information to the law enforcement task force officials, closing in on his gang of criminals.

Doug McQueen identified numerous pieces of evidence the task force had recovered from the various arsons and bombing, and he provided the task force with additional physical evidence, including tapes of recorded phone calls, phone bill records, and copies of money orders he had received from Shriver as payment to keep him quiet.

He was escorted to the numerous locations where acts of conspiracy were committed and where device parts were purchased. Photographs were taken of these locations and secured as evidence. It was a very telling confession, and there was more to come!

On December 26, 1985, Rudy M. Haldiman signed an eleven-page confession he had provided to us, detailing his involvement in the numerous crimes he had committed and naming those who were involved in the conspiracy, including Douglas McQueen, Robert Hood, Jr., and Grand leader Ben Shriver. The investigative task force continued to focus on Ben Shriver and prepare our case against him.

On March 20, 1986, Hood signed a second confession, providing additional information on felony acts he had committed in Springfield in 1982 and 1983 and naming his coconspirators involved in these criminal acts.

In these statements, Hood said these acts included arsons, bombings, attempted murders, possession of and manufacture of bombs, illegal possession, sale and use of explosives, and conspiracy, which occurred in Springfield and Green County.

He named those who were involved, including Douglas G. McQueen, Rudy Haldiman, Ben Shriver, and a person nicknamed "Gunrunner," as well as himself.

Hood provided drawings of the bomb that he had received from Doug McQueen, constructed by Rudy Haldiman, that Hood had thrown on the roof of the Back Forty Lounge on December 25, 1982. This would be the second of several interviews conducted with Hood over the next several months in which he confessed to his involvement and others.

Hood provided the task force with several additional drawings he had prepared of the bombs, the dynamite, and a sawed-off shotgun that were used to commit these crimes. Evidence was coming to us, and the task force members were feeling good about the recent developments.

On June 20, 1986, Sergeant Darrel Crick of the Springfield Police Department and I arrested Ben Shriver in Springfield. He was arrested after a simple car stop and charged with a federal warrant, naming him with the bombing of the Back Forty Lounge on December 25, 1982.

Later in the day, Greene County authorities filed a charge of conspiracy to commit second-degree murder on Shriver for his part in the attempted murder of Springfield bookmarker Ted Ehlers.

As a result of the task force intensive investigation, on September 22, 1986, the federal trial of Benny G. Shriver started with the picking of the jury.

After opening arguments by the federal prosecutors and defense attorneys, numerous witnesses were called and testified, each one adding a piece to the complicated puzzle of crimes committed. McQueen, Hood and Haldiman all testified; ex-girlfriends testified; victims of fires testified; insurance agents testified.

On October 1, 1986, Benny G. Shriver was found guilty of all twelve counts of the indictment. The task force announced to the media the conviction of Shriver marked the conclusion of Phase III of the team's multiagency efforts.

We closed the books on the Shriver-Skaggs criminal enterprise, or so we thought.

Shriver was out on bail, pending the court's decision on his appeal, when, on July 11, 1987, a federal affidavit was filed in a bail revocation motion, contending that Ben Shriver had violated his bail conditions by making a false report to law enforcement officers for the purpose of implicating another person in a crime. The *Springfield News-Leader* newspaper detailed the incident reported at the hearing.

Here is their account:

> He told Green County sheriff's deputies he was shot and stabbed early Tuesday morning near Lake Springfield. Shriver said he was shot and stabbed by two masked men, who he said were Springfield police officers [or a federal agent].
>
> The affidavit said Shriver told deputies he recognized the voice of one of the men as that of Springfield Officer Tim Medlin. Springfield

Police Detective Richard Stokes said in the affidavit that he interviewed Medlin and Medlin's wife, who said they were both at home with their month-old baby Monday night and early Tuesday when the incident allegedly occurred.

When he left his home Tuesday morning, Medlin found a brown paper bag in the bed of his pickup truck, the affidavit said. The sack contained a .25 caliber semiautomatic pistol Medlin said he had never seen.

Shriver told officers one of his attackers had fired six shots at him.

An attempt also apparently was made to frame Alcohol, Tobacco and Firearms Special Agent David True, the affidavit said.

Several weeks ago, True received a letter with a Springfield postmark. The letter told True to be at the Top Rail Lounge in Springfield at midnight Monday to receive a telephone call concerning the Shriver investigation.

Medlin told Stokes he conducted a surveillance at the site. He answered the phone when it rang at midnight. The caller hung up, Stokes said in the affidavit.

The letter and call may have been part of an attempt to have True stay overnight in a Springfield motel, where he would not have anyone available to account for his whereabouts, Medlin told Stokes.

At Shriver's bail bond revocation hearing, the federal Judge directed a medical doctor to examine Shriver's wounds and his eyes. The doctor told the judge the injuries were self-inflicted and there was no evidence of liquid burns to his eyes.

After hearing all the evidence in the four-hour hearing, the judge ordered Shriver to remain in jail, pending the conclusion of his appeal process.

He had lost his appeal process, and Benny G. Shriver began serving a sixteen-year prison sentence.

With all the coconspirators in jail serving their imposed sentences, the city of Springfield and its country-and-western bars and taverns were resting easier. The federal and state investigators were now able to close the books on the Springfield Wild Bunch gangster organization.

THE CSA NEO-NAZI CULT ORGANIZATION

On April 15, 1985, the Springfield task force investigation of the Shriver gang was interrupted when a Missouri State Trooper, Jim Lineger, was tragically murdered, machine-gunned to death at close range. The killing occurred during a routine traffic stop of a driver on Highway 65 at Ridgedale, Missouri.

Jimmie Lineger, a smart, dedicated officer, a father of two, died just four days before his son's third birthday. His fellow officers described Lineger as "a gentleman who enforces the law, a good Christian man and a good father."

The driver was identified as David Tate, a neo-Nazi who was anti-government and considered himself a survivalist. Trooper Lineger's partner, Allen Hines, was wounded in the shootout with Tate. It was a senseless murder of a law enforcement hero.

At the time of this murder, numerous ATF Agents were gathering in Springfield and Branson, preparing to serve a search warrant and arrest warrants at a white supremist compound located near Mountain Home, Arkansas, just outside the Missouri-Arkansas state line.

The search warrant would have to wait. A manhunt was underway to capture David Tate, who had fled from the scene.

Roadblocks were set up, and ATF and other federal and state law enforcement officers were assisting the Springfield Troopers office in locating and arresting David Tate.

On April 16, with the manhunt underway, another Neo-Nazi and companion of Tate named Frank Lee Silva was arrested in a campground just north of Gentry, Arkansas.

House-to-house searches were conducted in Hollister, Missouri. The Missouri National Guard assisted with machine gun-equipped helicopters, which joined in with hundreds of lawmen in the search for Tate.

On Saturday, April 20, Tate was arrested in Forsyth, Missouri, near Branson. Law enforcement officials and ATF agents believed Tate was making his way back to the CSA camp in Arkansas, seeking refuge.

After the arrest, the federal and state task force of over 300 law enforcement officers moved in on the search of the Covenant the Sword and the Arm of the Lord (CSA) compound, located near the state line of Missouri and Arkansas in the hills of the Ozarks, an ultra right-wing radical order that practiced and preached anti-black, anti-Semitic, pro-Nazi attitudes and beliefs.

To better understand why the federal government conducted a search warrant at the CSA compound in April 1985, the history of its organization and its leader is provided to the readers.

The Covenant, the Sword, and the Arm of the Lord (CSA) was founded by a Texas minister named James Ellison in 1970 at his residence near Elijah, Missouri, located on the Missouri-Arkansas state line. It was a military-style organization, loosely affiliated with other white supremacist organizations in the United States, consisting of between 90 and 120 men, women, and children. The Ku Klux Clan, the Aryan Nation, and the Order and the Militia of Montana are some examples of their affiliations.

In 1976, Jim Ellison purchased a 220-acre piece of farmland in Marion County, Arkansas, near the Bull Shoals Lake, located on the Missouri-Arkansas borders and about seven miles southwest of Pontiac, Missouri.

In 1978, Ellison developed a guerilla training camp on the farm, which was located in a predominantly white populated area. Ellison's purpose was to take advantage of multijurisdictional responsibilities.

The group's ideology supported hostility against any form of government above the county level, expressing total dislike of Jews and non-whites. Their goal was to achieve religious and racial purification of the United States.

From 1976 to 1982, the CSA members involved themselves in various illegal acts, including the illegal acquisition of weapons, robbery, arson, counterfeiting, murder, and terroristic threats.

The camp compiled stockpiles of supplies, built firing ranges, and afforded a place to stay for several hundred followers and fugitives from justice.

By 1982, law enforcement at the state and federal level estimated the active CSA membership at over 100.

In 1983, CSA member Richard Wayne Snell, with the assistance of members Steven Scott and William Thomas, attempted to dynamite a natural gas pipeline that ran from the Gulf of Mexico to Chicago as an A.T.T.A.C.K. Operation. They hoped this would result in riots, according to Kerry Noble, a fellow CSA member. Fortunately, they were not successful in accomplishing the attack of terror.

Then, in 1984, CSA active member Richard W. Snell shot and killed Louis Bryant, a black Arkansas State Police Trooper, during a traffic stop. At the time of the murder, Snell was also under investigation for the murder of a Jewish pawn shop owner in Texarkana, Arkansas. Snell was charged with capital murder, convicted, sent to prison, and sentenced to death

The federal agents investigating the illegal activities involved with the CSA camp leader Ellison and some of his followers needed to develop current probable cause of illegal possession of weapons at the camp.

In 1985, the opportunity presented itself when Larry Scott, an ATF agent in the Kansas City office, received a call from an individual that wanted to tell law enforcement what he knew about the CSA camp members stockpiling illegal weapons and explosives.

This confidential source told Agent Scott he was a member of the CSA, living in the camp in Arkansas. He had left the camp to get away from the illegal activities going on there, providing Agent Scott with detailed information. He described the types of weapons and explosives that were stockpiled at the camps. Based on this information, a file was opened, and Agent Scott initiated surveillances near the camp.

During these surveillances, the ATF agents documented hearing machine-gun fire and fully automatic weapons fire. During the same period of time, the highway patrol conducted a traffic stop on Highway 71 South (now Highway 49) of Eric Coleman and a second man. The two men were traveling to the CSA camp in possession of a stolen trailer and illegal firearms.

The owner of the trailer saw the thieves driving his trailer and called the highway patrol, who made the stop. The search of their vehicle revealed they were in illegal possession of a Mac-10 fully automatic weapon. The traffic stop and arrests occurred near Harrisonville, Missouri, and the troopers contacted the ATF office in Kansas City for assistance regarding the illegal weapon. ATF Agent Larry Scott was assigned to conduct the investigation.

This information added to the mounting evidence of wrongdoing and illegal possession of weapons by those at the CSA camp. Agent Scott took his information to the Assistant United States Attorney's Office in Springfield and met with Assistant US Attorney David Jones.

The two of them drafted a probable cause affidavit for a search warrant for the camp, which was presented to a state judge in Arkansas, who signed the warrant affidavit to search the camp.

On Sunday, April 21, a special search team of six heavily armed ATF employees was sent into an area of the CSA compound known as the "Plateau". The team members were Explosive Technician Taylor; ATF Special Agents Adamcek, Scott, Ash, and Dennis; and, in my official capacity as an ATF agent, your author, True.

Our assignment was to conduct a sweep of fifteen or more structures located in the area, including cabins and outbuildings, and to take custody of any CSA members.

You can imagine our team's heightened concerns and anticipations, realizing that just six days earlier David Tate, a Neo-Nazi, had just shot and killed Missouri Trooper Lineger, only a few miles from the camp. We all were certain Tate had just left the CSA compound prior to his violent act. We felt the members in the camp were well-armed and were open to reacting in the same manner, especially since the federal government and state law enforcement authorities were raiding their camp.

I assisted Explosive Specialist Taylor in a sweep of the fifteen structures to locate and render safe any and all explosive hazards. During the course of the sweep, we located and identified numerous explosives and firearms. As the explosive items were located, after rendering them safe, we placed them on the kitchen table of each structure for safekeeping.

Once the structures were determined safe, we assisted the other team members in the thorough search of each building; I was assigned as evidence custodian. As we located or were directed to items of evidence, they were photographed in place, secured, and recorded on the ATF evidence log maintained by me. We documented a total of thirty-four-line items of evidence, which were tagged and secured.

Once the search of the Plateau area was completed without a shot being fired, we took the evidence from the compound to the command post and secured the explosives in a safe place and placed the firearms and ammunition at a designated evidence area within the command post.

The evidence we recovered included a Mac 11-A1 automatic weapon with the serial number obliterated. This weapon was found in one of the closets of a cabin in the bedroom lived in by CSA senior member James Wallington.

Agent Scott field tested the firearm, revealing the firearm was a fully automatic weapon with the serial number removed—both serious violations of federal firearms violations.

In the bedroom of a cabin previously occupied by senior CSA member Jefferson Butler, the team located hand grenade casings, electric blasting caps, nonelectric blasting caps, safety fuse, hand grenade spoons, safe pins and firing pins, several sticks of dynamite, tubes of glue, and cans of smoke-

less powders, all in violation of federal explosive laws. It was a very successful day.

On April 22, we were assigned to arrest Wallington and Butler, who were
still on the compound. The two were transported to the Baxter County (Arkansas) Sheriff's Department, where they were fingerprinted, photographed,
and processed. After we turned over the prisoners to the interview teams, we
returned to the CSA compound and once again initiated a sweep of additional
buildings.

During the sweep of the quartermaster supply room adjacent to a large
machine shop, we located a false floor. Three large metal containers were located in the ground under the false floor. We observed the three containers
contained a quantity of electric and nonelectric blasting caps; a blasting machine; military surface flares; C-4 explosives; fuse ignitors; spools of detonating cord; detonating cord connectors; and a large quantity of explosive kinetic
and kinesak.

Upon this discovery, the team notified all other search teams to take cover
in a safe distance while we conducted a sweep of the room for possible booby
trap devices.

Just inside the supply room doorway, we also located three fully armed improvised hand grenades. Once we felt the area was safe, the other search teams
reinitiated their assigned search process. All explosive items were removed to
a safe storage area.

On April 23 and 24, we assisted ATF explosive Technician Taylor with ana-
lyzing all the explosives recovered at the Plateau and main compounds and
assisted in the rendering safe of numerous improvised hand grenades and
other improvised explosive devices.

The procedure consisted of separating the firing mechanism from the main
charge explosives contained in the grenade casings, safing the firing mechanism, and removing the main charge explosives from the hand grenades. A
representative sample of suspected explosives was retained from various de-
structive devices.

The team then took the explosives to the middle of the CSA camp's airfield and destroyed all the explosives by detonation, putting a big hole in the
middle of their airfield that rendered it unsafe to use in the process.

The search of the paramilitary survivalist groups compound, which lasted
four days, resulted in the arrest of its leaders Jim Ellison; Randall Evans, thirty, of Los Angeles; Thomas Day Bentley, fifty-seven, of Hayden Lake, Idaho;
James Wallington, thirty-nine; and Jefferson D. Butler.

A federal indictment that had been handed down in Seattle on April 12
charging Evans and Bentley with participating in the $3.5 million robbery of
an armored car in Ukiah, California, the previous June was also executed on
the two men.

Among the items recovered during the search were over seventy long guns,
thirty handguns, forty boxes of ammunition, thirty machine guns, six silencers, fifty armed hand grenades, an M-72 light anti-tank rocket, and a large

assortment of explosives. One of the weapons was a World War II .303 caliber Lewis machine gun designed primarily as an anti-aircraft weapon.

The explosives were recovered hidden behind false walls, under trap doors, and buried underground. The hand grenades had to be disarmed.

Also discovered was the control box for a command-detonated minefield surrounding the compound that had detonated about three weeks earlier during a storm, a homemade armored vehicle with gun ports, a large quantity of anti-government literature, a target painted to look like a police officer with bullet holes in it, and a picture of Hitler next to a photograph of CSA Leader Jim Ellison. The search team recovered over $55,300 in gold Krugerrands and gold bars and thirty gallons of cyanide.

The CSA members intended to use the potassium cyanide to poison the water supply of several large cities in order to expedite the coming of the second Messiah.

The search and arrests were carried out without a shot being fired. The names of the agencies that participated in the extensive project were prominently displayed at the secured area of the command post. It read:

> The Arkansas State Police; the Missouri State Highway Patrol; the Baxter County Sheriff's Department; the Marion County Sheriff's Department; the Ozark County, Missouri Sheriff's Department; the Missouri State Water Patrol; the Minneapolis, Minnesota Police Department K-9 Unit; the United States Army Corps of Engineers; the United States Army Explosive Ordinance Division; the Missouri State Conservation Services; the Bureau of Alcohol, Tobacco and Firearms (ATF) and the Federal Bureau of Investigation (FBI).

James Ellison and many of his leadership followers were charged in federal court with various violations, including illegal weapons possession and racketeering charges.

By 1986 after many of us had testified in federal court trials in Arkansas. Ellison, Kerry Noble, and four other members—Gary Stone, Timothy Russell, Rudy Loewen, and David Giles—were convicted and sentenced to lengthy prison terms.

Another CSA member, Stephen Scott, pled guilty in an Arkansas federal court to charges he had dynamited a natural gas line near Fulton, Arkansas, in 1983, and ex-CSA member Ken Yates pleaded guilty to conspiring to make and transfer automatic weapon silencers.

As a result of the 1985 raid on the camp, the CSA became nonexistent.

On April 19, 1995, exactly ten years after the CSA camp raid, Richard Wayne Snell, the CSA member who had shot and killed Arkansas State Trooper Louis Bryant and a pawnshop owner, was executed by lethal injection the same day and twelve hours after the deadly Oklahoma City bombing carried out by Timothy McVeigh.

There are plausible links to these two events. Richard Snell had planned a similar attack on the Murrah Federal Building in 1983 after he became upset with the Internal Revenue Service.

Prior to his execution, Snell was documented taunting jailers that something "drastic" would happen on the day of his execution. Could he have known? Surely Tim McVeigh knew Snell was to be executed this day.

Before his own execution, however, McVeigh had claimed he chose this date to coincide with the tragic violent end of the Waco, Texas, siege just two years earlier. He claimed this was his primary motivation for his brutal acts of domestic terrorism resulting in numerous deaths and injuries in Oklahoma City, Oklahoma.

Many of us ATF agents who were part of the successful raid at the CSA Camp ten years earlier also were assigned to the Oklahoma City bombing. Your author was assigned as the ATF's Midwest National Response Team Leader, directing the activities of three teams consisting of over ninety ATF, FBI, Oklahoma City homicide detectives, and Oklahoma Fire Department professionals.

THE MICHAEL COY HOMICIDE BOMBING

On noon, Sunday, October 23, 1989, Michael Coy was killed when a bomb—attached to his vehicle—detonated while traveling on State Road 125 just east of Springfield. His ex-wife Donna Coy, a passenger in the car, survived the tremendous blast but lost part of her left arm. Investigators conducting the scene examination suspected the bomb contained a timer.

Michael Coy was a suspicious man and once had told a neighbor of his in Florida that he was an informant for the FBI and had put a lot of people in jail. He said they might want to get even with him.

Due to the nature of the gruesome murder, ATF got involved and your author, in his capacity as an ATF agent, was assigned the investigation as case agent. We learned he and his ex-wife dealt in real estate and had a number of enemies.

Coy had married his wife in Kansas City in 1963, and they were divorced in 1984 but remained close. The Coys moved to Florida in 1982.

The motives behind the homicide bombing were multiple, and the suspects included bikers, family members, the Mob, several businessmen he had bilked during real estate deals, and his own family members. Michael Coy even took $50,000 from his mother in real estate and never paid her back. We also learned Coy had possible ties to Kansas City's organized crime.

Michael and Donna Coy were musical performers and once had worked at Poor Freddie's, a restaurant located in the River Quay area of Kansas City, owned by Fred Bonadonna. His father, David Bonadonna, was a made mob member and was murdered gangland-style in Kansas City in the late 1970s.

Coy's brother, Patrick Coy, said his brother had a friend named Tiny who rode motorcycles. Federal authorities suspected Michael Coy was associated with "Tiny" Mercer, who was the leader of two motorcycle gangs located in Belton, Missouri. Another relative, who wished to remain anonymous, said Coy knew the Missing Links Motorcycle Gang and sold stolen motorcycles to them.

Mercer had been executed by the state of Missouri earlier in 1989 after being convicted of murder.

Michael Coy's older brother Patrick confirmed that Michael was a good mechanic and welder. The older brother said Michael Coy hung around with known criminals and once told him he had helped with a professional hit.

The relatives said Coy stole coins from a brother and a $60,000 certificate of deposit from a sister and took more than $135,000 in loans from his parents that were never repaid—motives that could not be dismissed. The suspect list just kept growing.

Michael Coy was known as a wheeler-dealer and lived an expensive lifestyle. He created a lot of enemies. He concluded by saying his brother had "hundreds of enemies" and was messing with some real "tough people."

ATF investigated the homicide, along with numerous other investigations ongoing at the same time. Our primary focus was on a disgruntled family member wanting to get even and take revenge. The case remains unsolved.

THE MCDARIS, SHORT, BRIDWELL GANG
CRIMINAL VIOLENCE, CRIME, AND JUSTICE

On May 6, 1988, an explosive device was found in the bed of a pickup truck by a person named Lonnie Asher, who was living at the Homestead Trailer Park in Ozark, Missouri, just south of Springfield. The device was rendered safe by members of the Springfield Police Bomb and Arson Unit and members of the Missouri State Fire Marshal's office.

An investigation was initiated by Deputy Fire Marshal Bill Farr, who contacted ATF for assistance. Your author, in his capacity as an ATF agent, was assigned to assist in the investigation.

For the next five years, a team of investigators from the Christian County Sheriff's Department, the Missouri State Fire Marshal's Office, the Springfield Police Department, and the ATF conducted a joint investigation in Southwest Missouri.

The intense investigation uncovered a gang of criminals involved in making bombs used to cause harm or murder, as well numerous other crimes, including arson, burglaries, theft, fencing, criminal assaults using firearms and acid, and illegal possession of firearms and explosives.

The leaders of the gang included career criminals named Everett McDaris of Fair Grove, Dennis Short of Sparta, and David Bridwell of Battlefield, Missouri. The gang also included girlfriends, a known burglar and convicted murderer, a known meth cooker, and another known burglar recently charged with murdering a burglary victim.

The investigation revealed the gang was on a criminal rampage and felt they were immune from getting caught. In the end, they would be proven to be very wrong.

The first phase of the investigation focused on one of the gang leaders, Dennis Short, who was the ex-mayor of Sparta, Missouri, and who was the person who had constructed the bomb and assisted in placing the bomb on victim Lonnie Asher's pickup truck.

Short was upset over Asher having an extramarital affair with Short's estranged wife. Evidence developed that revealed Short had attempted to detonate the remote-control bomb after it was placed on Asher's truck and was assisted by Everett McDaris, who also helped construct the bomb.

A gang member, Larry Allen, who had served jail time for burglary and murder, helped with the construction of the bomb. Another gang member, David Bridwell, was with Dennis Short when they purchased the remote-control kit at the Hobbydashery Hobby Shop in Springfield. Short signed Bridwell's name to the receipts when making the purchase.

The investigation continued throughout 1988 and 1989.

In July 1989, Dennis Short was convicted by a jury in federal court with possession and construction of the bomb. To the surprise and disappointment of the investigative team and United States Attorney's Office, the judge placed Short on probation.

We appealed the judge's sentencing decision, and the Eighth Circuit overturned the sentencing and ordered the judge to resentence Short properly.

The judge, obviously upset over our right to appeal, sentenced Short to a split six-month sentence and allowed Short to serve time at night in the Greene County jail in Springfield.

I remember a newspaper reporter asking me "off the record" what I thought of the judge's ruling. I told the reporter "I felt he was like an umpire who lost control of the strike zone." The reporter laughed and assured me he would not print this.

During this sentencing of Dennis Short, the judge admonished the government and ATF for attempting to "bootstrap" Short's possession of a bomb conviction to the actual murder attempt on the life of Short's wife's boyfriend, Lonnie Asher, of Ozark. In effect, the judge challenged the government and ATF to find the evidence to prove that Dennis Short was part of an alleged plot to kill the victim, Lonnie Asher, with this bomb, and further that Dennis Short was part of an organized criminal group that was involved in criminal activities during this period of time in 1987, 1988, and 1989.

The task force team of investigators set out to develop the evidence to prove the gang did exist and provide this proof to the judge. At the time of the federal trial, it was highly suspected Short and the gang was involved in:

- The arson of Lonnie Asher's father's outbuilding and barn, located in Cape Fair, Missouri, on November 6, 1987.
- The shooting, attempted murder, and first-degree assault of Charles Dillman, an associate and fellow employee of Short's wife, Susan Short on January 29, 1988.
- The arson of Charles Dillman's mother's barn, located in Ozark, Missouri, on May 5, 1988.
- The attempted murder of Lonnie Asher, using the remote-control bomb that Short was convicted of possessing, on May 6, 1988.
- The first-degree assault on Susan Short, the wife of Dennis Short, by an individual using acid, which was thrown on her face and neck in Springfield, Missouri, on May 10, 1988, a few days after she was interviewed by ATF agents.

During this investigation, which continued after the July 1989 trial of Dennis Short, information and evidence was developed, linking Short to a number of criminal associates including:

David Bridwell—a known drug dealer and fence, living in Battlefield, Missouri, and fellow employee of Dennis Short's at the Sweetheart Paper Company in Springfield.

Annette Melonie—girlfriend of David Bridwell, and fellow Sweetheart paper cup employee of Dennis Short.

Everett McDaris—a known drug dealer and fence, living in Fair Grove, Missouri, and multi-convicted felon.

Connie Lane, a.k.a. Connie McDaris—wife of Everett McDaris, and criminal associate.

Donald Wright—a known burglar, convicted murderer, and nephew of Everett McDaris.

Mike Kinder—known meth cooker and close associate of David Bridwell and Everett McDaris.

Yolanda Helmick—girlfriend of Mike Kinder and known meth cooker, and associate of David Bridwell and Everett McDaris.

Dana Higgins—close associate of David Bridwell and Dennis Short, and fellow employee at Sweetheart Paper Company, located in Springfield.

Larry Arnold—known burglar and fence of stolen property, and criminal associate of Everett McDaris and Dennis Short. Currently in jail charged with burglary and murder.

Beth Crozier—girlfriend of Larry Arnold, and associate of Everett McDaris.

Beginning in February 1990 and continuing throughout the year, the task force team received information from various law enforcement agencies including, but not limited to, the FBI, the Springfield Police Department, the Greene County Sheriff's Department, and the Christian County Sheriff's Department, that documented alleged criminal activity by Dennis Short, David

Bridwell, Everett McDaris, Donald Wright, Larry Arnold, Connie Lane, Dana Higgins, and Mike Kinder, as well as numerous other associates.

Throughout 1990 and 1991, the team correlated the information being forwarded to them by the above listed agencies, initiated a number of interviews, and collected physical evidence and documents, which substantiated the various criminal activities conducted by Dennis Short and his above listed criminal associates.

In April 1991, Detective Tim Medlin of the Springfield Police Department and I initiated contact with meth cooker Mike Kinder of Springfield. Kinder subsequently made undercover contacts with David Bridwell and introduced an undercover Springfield police officer to Bridwell. This undercover investigation has resulted in the purchase of large quantities of narcotics, the transfer of a short-barreled weapon for the purpose of committing a violent crime, and the verification that David Bridwell and his girlfriend, Annette Melonie, as well as Bridwell's sister and a number of criminal associates were involved in a large-scale drug sale operation.

During the investigative interview process conducted throughout 1991 and 1992, we obtained a number of taped admissions and confessions from various criminal associates of Dennis Short, Everett McDaris, David Bridwell, and Dana Higgins.

During this investigation, it was learned that suspect Dennis Short and a number of his associates were allegedly behind a number of additional criminal felony violations, including the first-degree assault of Dennis Short's wife using acid, the burning of barns and other property, the fencing of stolen property, the sale of drugs, and the obstruction of justice during the federal trial by intimidating, threatening and harming certain witnesses, causing them to lie during the actual federal trial.

A break came on February 6, 1990, when Everett J. McDaris was arrested for eleven different criminal charges, including the distribution of controlled substances with three of the charges of selling within 100 feet of a school, which added a lengthy jail sentence.

During an interview with FBI Agent Ben Cagle, McDaris named his methamphetamine dealer and that his girlfriend, Connie Lane, was also buying drugs from this contact. He said Connie was selling drugs to Gus Kizer.

McDaris then said he also bought his drugs from Dave Bridwell and his right-hand man was Dennis Short. McDaris said he sold guns to Bridwell and Short. McDaris added that Short used Bridwell's name when Short purchased parts to construct the bomb he was convicted of possessing.

McDaris said he found out earlier in the day that Dennis Short found out that Steve Ijames was an undercover police officer. Short told Connie Lane they were all going to get busted soon and a black-haired woman named Angie Griffin was informing to police on their illegal fencing activities.

McDaris named Larry and Tommy Rivera as burglars and associates of Dennis Short and said that Bridwell also bought stolen firearms from David Davis and Lonnie Fields. This information was provided to the task force, and it was suggested we conduct a follow-up interview with McDaris and Lane.

On September 20, 1990, Beth Crozier, ex-girlfriend of Larry Arnold, who had broken up with him due to his criminal behavior, was interviewed in Shawnee, Kansas. She said she knew Arnold, a burglar, was in jail, charged with murder. Crozier said Arnold had sold his stolen items to Dennis Short. She said that, during December 1989, she was with Arnold at the Drury Inn in Springfield when Short called find out if Arnold had stolen property for sale.

The items she knew Short had purchased included four-wheelers, firearms, VCRs, barbecue grills, and chainsaws. She said she learned from Larry Arnold and E. J. McDaris that Short was involved in bombing a pickup truck, and McDaris told her he had made the bomb with Dennis Short. On one occasion, Short told her that if anyone messed with him, he had people who could take care of it.

On January 7, 1991, during an interview with Carol Smith, she said she knew Dennis Short and had worked with him at Fort Howard Paper Company in Springfield. She said some of Short's associates at Fort Howard were employees Lester Nimmo, Mike Kirkwood, and David Bridwell. On one occasion, she had watched Bridwell weigh a drug called "crystal" on a scale at the place of business. She had also seen Dennis Short very near Lonnie Asher's house just before the bomb was found on his pickup truck.

On April 15, 1991, Mike Kinder was interviewed at the Springfield Police Department. The interview was tape-recorded. Kinder was in the Greene County Jail on state charges and requested we interview him. He provided knowledge about several individuals and crimes related to their activities, including Dennis Short, David Bridwell, E. J. McDaris, and a person named Dana Higgins including drugs, guns, and stolen property.

Regarding his knowledge about the making of a bomb, Bridwell showed him a blasting cap, and E. J. McDaris told him he had helped make the bomb to blow up a truck. Kinder said Dana Higgins admitted to him he was also involved in making and placing the bomb in the pickup truck. He suggested we talk to Connie Lane, who was E. J. McDaris' girlfriend or wife because she also had knowledge and involvement. Kinder went on to give details of the fencing of stolen property by Bridwell, McDaris, and Short.

On February 5, 1992, Connie Lane was interviewed by us at the Chillicothe Correctional Center. She said she was doing ten years for selling drugs. Lane said she was married to E. J. McDaris and was involved with him in criminal activities. She said she had firsthand knowledge about McDaris and Dennis Short making a bomb. Also involved were David Bridwell and Dana Higgins.

In April 1988, she was present when E. J. McDaris delivered the bomb to David Bridwell at the Western Auto on Chestnut in Springfield. She said her son was with her on this date. Lane described firsthand that E. J. McDaris was the person who had splashed acid on victim Susan Short at her doctor's appointment in Springfield.

Lane said this upset her, so she gave a picture of McDaris to a friend, who showed it to victim Susan Short. She was told Susan Short identified the picture as the man who splashed acid on her face and neck. The persons that had showed this picture of E. J. to Susan were named Sharon and Loren Main or Karen and Chuck Stockdale (she was unsure of their names).

In concluding this taped interview, Lane told a chilling story. She said she had learned some of the witnesses at the federal bomb trial were threatened and intimidated. She said two witnesses named Chuck and Karen Stockdale, who were related to Susan Short, were the planned targets for a bomb on their trailer, but they did not carry this out.

Then they ran Karen off the road, and her little child's leg was broken. When they got up to testify, they changed their story. Lane agreed to testify in our ongoing federal investigation.

As damaging as her information was, there were some problems using it. She was married to E. J. McDaris and was scared of him and his violent ways. She was not involved in the fencing or bomb making activities and could not testify against her husband.

Her testimony against the other coconspirators was limited; however, she did provide some significant leads to follow and interviews to conduct. We were slowly making progress.

On February 14, 1992, we conducted a follow-up interview with Larry Arnold, who was in jail charged with second-degree murder and burglary. He had pled guilty to the burglary and was awaiting the outcome of the murder charge.

In a seventeen-page, tape-recorded interview, Arnold provided additional damaging firsthand information against gang members E. J. McDaris, Dennis Short, Donald Wright, David Bridwell, Dana Higgins, and Les Niemo (or Nimmo). He talked about their involvement in making the bomb, fencing stolen goods, drugs, vandalism, threats, and other crimes.

Allen also verified the information his first taped interview made in September 1990 in the Webster County Jail.

On August 26, 1992, during a tape-recorded interview with Samuel Lee Pyatt, the son of Connie Lane, damaging information was provided against E. J. McDaris, Dennis Short, and David Bridwell regarding the making of the bomb, the fencing of stolen items, and other criminal activities.

Pyatt confirmed he was present with his mother, Connie Lane, the night E. J. McDaris had given the bomb to David Bridwell at the Western Auto store in Springfield. Pyatt said he had received a threatening letter from E. J. McDaris, telling Pyatt if he talked to police he would also end up in jail or he would have someone come and get him and he would never be seen again.

On October 19, 1992, we interviewed Donald M. Wright at the Missouri State Prison in Jefferson City. During this tape-recorded interview, Wright provided damaging information against E. J. McDaris, Dennis Short and the bomb plot against his wife's boyfriend, with whom she was having an affair.

Wright admitted he helped make the bomb and purchased the black powder for the bomb. He also provided the frequency for the detonator. Wright said Dennis Short offered him a contract to burn down two storage buildings on a farm. He turned down the contract but learned the building was, in fact, burned down.

On one occasion, he was with Dennis Short at a restaurant in Springfield when Dennis Short took credit for having his wife splashed with acid in the face. Wright also provided information about Dennis Short being involved in fencing stolen items and dealing in methamphetamine.

During the interview, Wright said he was in prison doing life without parole for murder and his case was under appeal. It was interesting information, but we doubted he could ever be called as a witness in our ongoing investigation.

During this period of time in 1992, an undercover drug operation by Springfield Drug Unit and ATF was in progress, and purchases of drugs were being made from our suspect David Bridwell by Rick Headlee of the Springfield Narcotics Unit.

During the undercover contacts, Bridwell was bragging that he had participated in the acid splashing of Susan Short in May 1988. He also admitted he was with Dennis Short at the Hobby Shop in Springfield with Dennis Short when Short purchased the remote kit used in making the bomb to try to kill Lonnie Asher in May 1988.

Bridwell was going down. It was just a matter of time.

On November 12, 1992, a case report was submitted to the Christian County Prosecutor's Office, citing first-degree assault charges against Dennis Short, Dana Higgins, Everett McDaris, Jr., and David Bridwell. Donald Wright was cited as an unindicted coconspirator.

We hoped to seek prosecution of these state charges in Christian County.

Subsequent to Christian County Prosecutor's receipt of this case report, he traveled to the ATF Lab in Rockville, Maryland, and met with various forensic specialists who have been involved in assisting in this ongoing investigation.

In December 1992, various Springfield police officers and ATF joined in the arrest of David Bridwell of Battlefield, Bridwell's girlfriend, Bridwell's sister, and several other associates who were indicted and charged with a large-scale narcotics distribution conspiracy. ATF assisted in the search of various properties, seizure of vehicles and other property, and the interview of David Bridwell and his girlfriend, Annette Melonie.

In 1993, David Bridwell entered guilty pleas to a number of federal drug and related charges before Federal Judge Russell Clark in Springfield. While Bridwell was awaiting sentencing, efforts were made to gain Bridwell's assistance and testimony in the aforementioned case. All efforts to gain his assistance have been negative.

After entering his guilty plea, David Bridwell was sentenced in federal court to a number of federal drug and related charges before Federal Judge Russell Clark. Although Bridwell had received a lengthy prison sentence, at that time no efforts had been made by him to offer his assistance in the investigation.

The case remained in an open status.

As we entered into the last decade of the 1900s, the various law enforcement agencies and the prosecutors at the city, county, state, and federal levels felt a sense of accomplishment in the pursuit of justice involving the McDaris, Short, and Bridwell Gang.

THE "BAD" JOANN GANG

On February 1, 1991, the BZ Truck Stop, located on Highway 13 just north of Springfield and owned by JoAnn Cunningham, burned down.

The fire was investigated by State Fire Marshal Deputy Bill Farr after the blaze was contained by the Ebenezer Township Volunteer Fire Department and the embers had cooled down. Deputy Farr determined the fire was suspicious, requiring further investigation, and requested law enforcement assistance from ATF at the federal level since the business was involved in interstate commerce and ATF had federal jurisdiction. ATF Agent Randy Roberts of our Kansas City office was assigned the investigation as case agent.

What started out as a simple fire investigation of a small commercial business outside Springfield escalated into a multiagency federal and state law enforcement investigation, involving arson, fraud, money laundering, federal firearms violations, and conspiracy to kill. The investigation also involved treasure maps and a hunt for $1 million.

Agent Roberts learned early in the investigation that Cunningham had some association with criminal fraud schemes in her past. Her husband, Steve Babbidge, was serving time in the federal penitentiary in Leavenworth, Kansas after he had pled guilty on October 23, 1989, to structuring transactions and conspiracy to commit fraud. He was sentenced to forty-one months for the two counts. The fraud scheme was described by the media as one of the largest ever investment fraud cases in Missouri history. It was reported Babbidge had bilked as many as 1,000 senior citizens out of over $6 million in the scheme. IRS agents who investigated the scheme estimated that $1 or more million was hidden by Babbidge before he was arrested.

It was suspected JoAnn Cunningham knew where the money was allegedly hidden and possessed handwritten maps to its location.

Agent Roberts learned, in October 1990, that JoAnn Cunningham had lost her insurance license after the Missouri Division of Insurance looked into several complaints filed in 1988–89 that had accused her of her bilking senior citizens out of their insurance premiums through an insurance company she co-owned with business partner Eric Ikemeier.

The investigators learned the convenience store business was in a poor state of affairs, and Cunningham, during the end of 1990, was complaining about the poor financial condition with certain employees, customers, and business associates.

In January 1991, Cunningham met with her ex-business associate Eric Ike-meier and a part-time employee at the store, Robert Cook, for the purpose of discussing ways she could raise money by defrauding the insurance company.

Robert Cook had recently been released from prison after serving a lengthy sentence for the murder of a young child and was on parole. He was currently a fire captain with the Ebenezer Township Volunteer Fire Department, located near the BZ Truck Stop business. She decided she wanted to burn the convenience store and solicited their help. They agreed and joined into the conspiracy.

The plan was to burn the convenience store on February 1, 1991, at about 9:00 p.m. Cook's role was to start the fire at her direction, and Ikemeier's role was to call 911 at a predesignated time and report the fire, also at her direction.

On February 1, just hours before the fire, in a foolish move, Cunningham called her insurance agent to verify the insurance coverage on the BZ Truck Stop, and she was also overheard by one of her employees complaining about the poor financial condition of the business and the possibility of filing for bankruptcy.

The investigators also learned she had been trying to sell the business for the past year without any success. All these actions were signs of arson fraud to the investigators.

Their criminal conspiracy was now in place, and at approximately 9:00 p.m., Robert Cook and JoAnn Cunningham were the last two people at the BZ Truck Stop. Robert Cook started the fire, at Cunningham's direction, in the northwest part of the building, the office area, on top of a desk utilizing available paper material. Cunningham then proceeded to lock the store, without making an attempt to stop the fire.

In furtherance of the conspiracy, at approximately 9:10 p.m., Ikemeier visually observed smoke coming from the front of the BZ Truck Stop and then traveled to the Crossroads Convenience Store, as prearranged, and made a 911 call to report the fire.

More than fifty firefighters from ten Green County Fire Departments battled the blaze, including the Ebenezer Volunteer Department. Robert Cook, who had returned to the firehouse after starting the fire, responded, and according to Bob Wagner, president of the fire department, recalled that Cook fought the fire with his usual enthusiasm.

One Logan-Rogersville firefighter was slightly injured while fighting the fire. The convenience store was destroyed.

On or about April 8, 1991, JoAnn Cunningham provided to the Farmers Insurance Group, through her attorney Michael Cully, the proof of loss relevant to the fire at the BZ Truck Stop. She was eager to collect her insurance proceeds of about $69,000, which covered the convenience store loss.

On May 2, 1991, Cunningham, along with her unsuspecting attorney, Todd Thornhill, provided a statement under oath to Thomas Hearne, the attorney representing the Farmers Insurance Company, at which time JoAnn

Cunningham denied any knowledge of the fire. She felt confident her scheme to defraud the insurance company was on course just as she had planned.

What she did not know was one of her coconspirators, Robert Cook, got cold feet and, on April 3, 1991, met with Fire Marshal Bill Farr and ATF Agent Randy Roberts, telling them he had information regarding the fire that had occurred on February 1, 1991, at the BZ Truck Stop on Highway 13 and Route 5, just north of Springfield.

Cook said on or about January 31, 1991, he was contacted by JoAnn Cunningham, and she requested him to come to her residence located at 2211 Norton Road, Springfield. Present at her residence at this time was Mr. Cook, JoAnn Cunningham, and a white male named Eric, later identified as Eric Ikemeier. Mr. Cook said that, during this meeting, JoAnn Cunningham and Eric discussed ways to raise money to help the convenience store, as it was doing poorly financially. Mr. Cook said that JoAnn Cunningham and Eric decided to burn the BZ Truck Stop on Friday, February 1, 1991. It was decided that the fire would be started in the office area, where the Styrofoam cups and paper products were kept.

Cook said his purpose for being present was because he was a volunteer fireman for the Ebenezer Fire Department. The Ebenezer Fire Department services the geographical area where the BZ Truck Stop was located. Since Mr. Cook was part of the fire department, Mrs. Cunningham wanted Mr. Cook to delay the fire trucks when the fire call came in.

Cook added that Eric's purpose for being at the meeting was to discuss his part in the fire scheme, that after the fire was started, he was to wait a few minutes and then make a 911 phone call from the Crossroads Convenience Store to the Greene County Sheriff's Department.

On Friday, February 1, 1991, Cook was present at the BZ Truck Stop at approximately 8:30 p.m. This time, Mr. Cook observed JoAnn Cunningham remove from the business papers related to the operation of the business, the daily receipts, and accounts receivable, so they wouldn't be destroyed in the fire.

Since the April 3 meeting, Cook had cooperated in the investigation, and on approximately eight separate occasions, he met with JoAnn Cunningham at her residence in an effort to obtain recorded conversations relevant to this fire for the purpose of defrauding the insurance company. During at least one of these meetings, conversation was recorded between Mr. Cook and JoAnn Cunningham relevant to how the insurance proceeds from the fire would be distributed.

In early June, Case Agent Randy Roberts asked me, your author, to assist in his investigation. JoAnn had provided Robert Cook with a treasure map of gold or money located in the St. Louis area. Agent Roberts thought I (as a St. Louis native) could help find the mysterious location identified on the hand-written map—a treasure supposedly hidden by JoAnn's husband, Babbidge, before he went to prison.

On June 7, 1991, a team of law enforcement agents, along with Investigator Bill Farr and informant Robert Cook, conducted a day-long search of a vacant building located in East St. Louis, Illinois. The search was conducted without JoAnn Cunningham's knowledge.

The results of the search proved negative, and we discontinued our efforts at the end of the day. Agent Roberts and I returned to Kansas City empty-handed.

Bill Farr and Cook returned to Springfield, where Cook was contacted by Cunningham and, in a startling development, solicited his help in finding a hit man to kill two men in Springfield.

One was an ex-fire chief and the second man was the mayor of Springfield. The undercover assignment was given to me since I was about her same age, and she wanted an older criminal hit man to talk to. This conversation set into play a series of events that heightened the level of drama in the arson investigation.

In reviewing the undercover tape made by Cook, it was clear Cunningham intended to have two people killed and was looking for a hit man to do the job. A plan was developed for me to be introduced to JoAnn Cunningham as a hit man from St. Louis.

The first meeting took place on June 11, 1991, at about 9:00 p.m. in the parking lot of a shopping mall located at the intersection of Kearney and Glenstone in Springfield. The conversation began after introductions were made, and JoAnn patted down the hit man, as she was very apprehensive about talking in the vehicle. She said she had two people she wanted killed. One was a man named Monty Sowerby, the ex-chief of the Ebenezer Volunteer Fire Department, and the other she wanted killed was the mayor of Springfield, Thomas Carlson.

She said she did not want them killed at that time, adding she was involved in an investigation and there was too much pressure right now.

She wanted Sowerby wiped out over money she thought he took from her, and she wanted Carlson killed because he had represented her husband, Steve Babbidge, as an attorney, and she was unhappy with how Carlson was handling the legal process.

The meeting ended with the agreement that, if she needed to make any future contacts, it would be arranged through Robert Cook. It did not appear the hit contract was going anywhere. It did not take long to find out we were wrong.

On June 13, 1991, Cunningham contacted Cook and requested he meet with her. At this meeting, she told Cook she now wanted to have someone kill her ex-business partner, Eric Ikemeier. Cook immediately contacted Investigator Bill Farr and Agent Randy Roberts and told them of JoAnn's plan to kill her ex-business partner.

On June 17, 1991, JoAnn Cunningham requested that Cook accompany her to the Republic Gun and Pawn Shop for the purpose of purchasing a shotgun. Cook said JoAnn Cunningham purchased a shotgun and transported this firearm back to her residence, where it was stored.

She told Cook the shotgun was for her protection and could be used to kill Ikemeier, who she claimed had learned about the hidden money and was feuding with her, and she wanted him out of the picture.

On June 18, 1991, a second undercover meeting took place between JoAnn Cunningham, Robert Cook, and the "hit man" from St. Louis at the same parking lot in Springfield. She insisted on talking outside the undercover vehicle and directed us to her house located at 2211 Norton in Springfield, where we talked in her parking area outside the vehicle.

The hidden microphones in the trunk of the vehicle were able to record the conversation and the quality of the voices were clear.

Cunningham started talking about the ex-business partner, Eric Ikemeier, whom she now wanted to have killed. Here are portions of the conversation that was later published in the *Springfield News-Leader*:

> David True: Tell me what you've got and I'll let you know if I can do it.
> JoAnn Cunningham: Okay, one, this is I've got to have this guy taken out, cause evidently he's, he's the one that's launching this war and I thinking once he's done, a done deal, his little morons will be gone, too. Another thing is I have a job that I've hired Robert to do, he's got to go to St. Louis and pick something up for me and bring it back. This moron that's waging war against me has indirectly adrift of this, not knowing anything, but, it didn't come from me, evidently a leak source somewhere else, but I need Robert's back covered. I need him to be protected up and back.
> DT: To St. Louis and back?
> JC: Yeah
> DT: We can take care of, that's easy, that's no problem.
> JC: And then this guy needs to be handled. He's bad. . . .
> DT: What do you want done to him?
> JC: I want him wiped, erased.
> DT: Killed?
> JC: Killed.
> DT: Now, are we talking about something totally different than our meeting last week?
> JC: Yeah.
> DT: Okay, well let's get down to business, tell me what you want.
> *Later in the conversation. . . .*
> DT: I need to see you tomorrow with the barrel.
> JC: Okay.
> DT: The pay phone by the Crazy Horse there. You guys get the barrel.
> JC: Okay.
> DT: When the job's done, you'll know it. You'll read about it in the papers.
> JC: Yeah, that's all I want to do is read about it.
> DT: Then we get back and take care of this little trip to St. Louis.
> JC: And you'll get.
> DT: Get my money.

JC: Get your money right away.

DT: I'll give you the watch, give it to you.

JC: Okay.

DT: And that's it, we won't see each other unless there's some business in the future.

JC: Okay and there might be.

DT: But, Eric is dead.

JC: Good.

DT: It's simple.

JC: Yeah

JC: It's loaded

DT: Yeah, I can tell.

JC: It's ready to go.

DT: I got, it's without reason, you got some problems here . . . right dear?

JC: Uh huh.

DT: Okay, let's toast to it and that's it, I'm history. I'm getting out of here.

JC: Okay.

DT: We don't talk anymore. You have any questions.

JC: No, I don't.

DT: You have any reservations?

JC: Not a one.

DT: You want the guy killed?

JC: Out, history, erased.

DT: Okay, then I'll take the job.

JC: I'll just read about it.

DT: I get $25,000 when he's dead and you know it.

JC: And he delivers my package.

DT: Yeah, that's your package, that's your deal?

JC: Yeah.

DT: You get your watch back. The guns are gone. I'm going to throw them away, they're in the river.

JC: I won't miss them, I won't need them, will I?

DT: Eric Ikemeier is a dead sucker.

JC: Good.

DT: Any questions?

JC: No.

JoAnn agreed the price to kill Ikemeier would be $25,000, paid upon his death. She provided a gold $20,000 watch as collateral. In all, she provided:

- One Mossberg, Model 500 CT, 20-gauge shotgun, Serial #KG258068
- One Titan .25 caliber semiautomatic pistol, Serial #ED48090
- One photograph picture of Eric Ikemeier
- One piece of paper with Ikemeier's home and work addresses
- One 18 karat gold Piaget brand watch as collateral down payment

By providing these items, she committed a very firm, overt act in further-ance of this conspiracy to kill Ikemeier.

The next day, a second meeting with Cunningham took place at the same parking lot on Kearney and Glenstone in Springfield at about 1:00 p.m.

She was supposed to provide a shorter barrel for the shotgun, but she was unable to get the barrel sawed off. During the meeting, she provided her alibi during the evening while the "hit" took place.

She said she would be playing bingo at a location in Springfield and would meet the "hit man" after the job was done. It was agreed the .22 pistol would be used; it would be "less messy."

At 3:00 p.m., JoAnn was contacted by telephone, and she provided the ex-act location of the bingo hall and confirmed she would meet the "hit man" there in the parking lot to confirm the murder had been completed.

She was given multiple opportunities to back out of the conspiracy, and she was firm on wanting the hit on Ikemeier to happen.

Time was of the essence, so the investigative team (consisting of ATF In-vestigator Bill Farr and the Springfield Police Department Detectives, direct-ed by Detective Tim Medlin) contacted Eric Ikemeier at about 6:00 p.m. and informed him of the bad news that someone had been hired to kill him. He was also told the good news that the hit man was actually a federal ATF agent who was acting in an undercover capacity.

Concerned for his health, Ikemeier agreed to cooperate and provided his wallet, driver's license, and various credit cards. He also assisted in a staged murder, "a house invasion hit." A Polaroid photo was taken of him sitting at his desk with his head down and a fake blood running down the back of his neck and shoulder in a simulated deceased pose.

Ikemeier was not told who issued the murder contract and was told to keep quiet and not communicate with anyone the remainder of the afternoon and evening until he heard from us. Two Springfield detectives stayed with him until the meeting with Bad JoAnn was completed.

A surveillance was set up, and at about 9:45 p.m., JoAnn Cunningham was met in the bingo hall parking lot and provided with Ikemeier's wallet and the Polaroid photo of his "dead" body. She took the items and placed them in her purse, satisfied the job had been done.

Cunningham was told Ikemeier was dead, and she responded, "Well, now you have to take Robert, my baby, to St. Louis for the rest of the deal." Just like it was business as usual.

At this point, Cunningham was placed under arrest and handcuffed. The items she had placed in her purse were recovered and held as evidence.

Fire Marshal Bill Farr advised her of her Miranda rights against incrimina-tion, and she was taken to the Springfield Police Department for questioning and processing. During the questioning, Cunningham admitted her involve-ment with the arson of the BZ Truck Stop and was placed in the police jail.

According to a media press release by the United States Attorney's Office:

after Cunningham was arrested, she was described as a 'hard lady on a crime spree' and was determined to have her former business partner, Eric Ikemeier, be killed. It seemed evident in what a federal prosecutor described as a 'Blood curdling' tape recording of Cunningham and True arranging the killing.

The press release continued:

The case 'quickly evolved into a complex multiagency investigation involving insurance fraud, arson for profit, money laundering and eventually attempted murder' Assistant U.S. Attorney David C. Jones said, during the press conference.

The investigation continued, and on June 20, 1991, Eric Ikemeier provided a tape-recorded confession to Special Agent Randy Roberts, confirming the meeting at JoAnn Cunningham's house prior to the fire, between he, JoAnn Cunningham, and Robert Cook, in which it was decided that the BZ would be burned. He also confirmed that his subsequent 911 telephone call reporting the fire was prearranged.

On June 26, 1991, Robert Cook provided a complete handwritten confession to Investigator Bill Farr and Special Agent Randy Roberts, revealing his total involvement in setting the fire at the BZ Truck Stop, at JoAnn Cunningham's direction.

The Springfield media had a field day publishing and reporting every detail of the entire conspiracies, including the playing and publishing the undercover tape recordings made during the course of the investigation.

Subsequent to their confessions, both Eric Ikemeier and Robert Cook pled guilty in state court to second-degree arson. On August 21, 1992, after being jailed for more than one year, JoAnn Cunningham pled guilty in Greene County Circuit Court to conspiracy to commit murder. She admitted to hiring a hit man, a federal undercover agent. She also pleaded guilty to the arson of the BZ Truck Stop.

Cunningham entered into a plea agreement and received a ten-year sentence for her criminal actions. She also pled guilty in federal court to transferring a firearm to commit a violent crime. The sentence of the federal charges was to run concurrent with the state charges.

In a press release on August 28, 1992, after Cunningham had pled guilty, Jean Paul Bradshaw, United States Attorney for the Western District of Missouri, and Rick Cook, Special Agent in Charge of Kansas City's ATF, praised a group of ten law enforcement agencies and offices that had cooperated with the US Attorney's Office in the Cunningham investigation. They were ATF; Missouri State Fire Marshal; Criminal Investigations Division of the Internal Revenue Service; the US Postal Inspection Service; US Marshals Service; Springfield Police Department; Greene County Sheriff's Department; Greene County Prosecutor's Office; Missouri State Highway Patrol; and the Missouri State Division of Probation and Parole.

The Bad JoAnn Gang was no longer was in business and the case was closed.

ATF Case Agent Randy Roberts, Springfield Detective boss Tim Medlin, and Missouri State Fire Marshal Investigator Bill Farr received high praise for their efforts in bringing this case to its successful conclusion—and your author was happy to get back into an undercover role after many years, a role I had enjoyed playing early in my ATF career.

THE "BAD" JACK MOAD GANG

On May 1, 1991, a fire occurred at a residence in Lebanon, Missouri, a city just a short distance east of Springfield, Missouri. The local rural fire department responded and suppressed the fire. On May 2 the fire rekindled, resulting in a total loss to the house and garage.

The owners of the house, Jack and Myrtle Moad, were away on a "vacation" in Las Vegas, Nevada, learned about the fire, and returned to survey the damage and loss of approximately $93,000.

Due to the extensive damage, the cause of the fire was undetermined by an investigator with the GEICO Insurance Company. It was a seemingly tragic loss to the family in terms of the residence, contents, and a late model vehicle located in the garage.

Local police and fire investigators were not involved in investigating the cause. The owners went about filing a loss claim with their insurance company—just another residential fire loss in rural Missouri, or was it?

On June 9, 1991, Missouri State Highway Patrol Trooper Dwell Isringhausen, assigned to the Laclede County enforcement area, made a traffic stop of a car driving with a headlight out. During the stop, the driver, Dennis Long, seemed very nervous for such a minor violation.

Trooper Isringhausen requested consent to search his vehicle, and Long consented to the search. During the search, Trooper Isringhausen recovered a Rohm Model 38-S .38 caliber revolver with serial number FF341803, loaded with five rounds of ammunition with additional ammo under the driver's seat. Long claimed he did not know how the revolver got in his truck or who had put it there.

Trooper Isringhausen ran a record check on Long, which revealed he was a three-time convicted felon for two separate robberies he had committed in St. Louis County in 1976 and a conviction for stealing and assault in Jackson County, Missouri, in 1987.

Long also had a third felony conviction for escaping from the federal penitentiary in Leavenworth, Kansas. Long was definitely a candidate for federal prosecution under the law, and if convicted, the court would impose a sentence of not less than fifteen years to life in federal prison.

On October 8, 1991, the Laclede County Prosecutor's Office and the Missouri Highway Patrol requested that Dennis Long be prosecuted federally regarding his possession of the firearm recovered from his vehicle on June 10, 1991.

ATF Agent Joy Branch contacted the United States Attorney's Office in Springfield and accepted the case for prosecution under "Operation Triggerlock," a federal project targeting multi-convicted felons caught in illegal possession of firearms.

Shortly after S/A Branch initiated the investigation of Dennis Long, she was contacted by Dennis Long's wife, Kathy Long, who advised Branch she had information about other criminal activity conducted by her husband. Kathy Long said that she had direct knowledge of and had participated in setting the fire that had occurred at Jack Moad's residence on May 1, 1991. She said her husband, Dennis Long, and an individual by the name of Ky Haskew had helped set the fire. Kathy Long added that she also had information about a burglary that her husband and Haskew committed during the summer of 1991 that resulted in the theft of firearms. Arrangements were made to conduct an interview with Kathy Long.

On January 15, 1992, S/A Branch told me of the alleged arson at the Jack Moad residence and requested assistance. Upon review of the Dennis Long file, S/A True said that he was familiar with Jack Walter Moad, in that he was a previously convicted felon arising out of an ATF investigation that True had conducted in Illinois during 1973 and 1974.

On January 16, 1992, ATF agents conducted a tape-recorded interview with Kathy Long. During this tape-recorded interview, Kathy Long explained in detail her knowledge and involvement in the setting of a fire at Jack Walter Moad's residence during the first part of May 1991. She also detailed what plans were made in preparation of the setting of this fire, as well as the fact that her husband, Dennis Long, received about $2,000 in payment from Jack Moad for setting his fire. In addition to providing the agents with a tape-recorded interview of these criminal acts, she also agreed to assist ATF in securing conversation from her husband.

On February 2, 1992, at the direction of ATF agents, Kathy Long met with her husband at a prearranged location in Lebanon, Missouri. During the ensuing conversation, her husband, Dennis Long, admitted his involvement in setting the fire at Jack Moad's residence near Lebanon and also admitted receiving money for setting that fire. Long told his wife, Kathy Long, that he would take the rap for the fire because he was not going to tell about somebody who had already paid for the job. He also threatened to kill his wife during this conversation.

This conversation was monitored and tape-recorded. Knowing that a multi-convicted felon had threatened his wife and it was on tape, the investigative team had to take swift action. A federal warrant was secured and on February 4, 1992, and Dennis Long was arrested on a federal complaint, charging him with federal firearms violations. He was transported to Springfield from Lebanon by United States Marshal John Heitman and S/A Branch.

During the trip to Springfield, Dennis J. Long provided a tape-recorded confession to ATF. During the interview, Long confessed to possession of the firearm on June 9, 1991, and that the weapon actually belonged to Jack Moad of Lebanon and was registered to him. In this interview, Long denied he took the weapon from the Moad residence the night he set the house on fire, a lie that would later be cleared up.

Long claimed he acquired the handgun from a person named Ky Haskew, also of Lebanon. He admitted he had helped Haskew attempt to burn the Moad residence, claiming Haskew attempted to set the fire; however, the attempt failed. Long claimed he did not go into the house, only in the garage or the attic.

He claimed they left, and the house burned down the next morning. Long also denied he knew Haskew took the handgun out of the house—another lie.

Long admitted he was approached by Jack Moad to burn his house down for $5,000 payment but that he only received $2,000 for the job after Moad collected some insurance money in July or August of 1991. Long said Moad established an alibi by visiting Las Vegas, Nevada, at the time of the fire.

At this point in the interview, Long said he would not name anybody else who went to the Moad house to set it on fire, that he would take the rap first.

Long admitted he tried to make the fire look like an electrical accident by exposing some house wires located in the attic, "but it didn't work." He did say he poured some liquid from a pint can of charcoal starter on the wires; the can of starter was provided by Jack Moad. Long denied striking any matches while in the attic.

Long was asked about an incident involving the theft of a number of firearms Ky Haskew had stolen from his father and brother. Long said he stayed in the truck while Haskew brought the weapons out of the house and put them in his truck. They then took the firearms to Long's house. Long said he gave the firearms back to Haskew, and Haskew sold them at a pawn shop. Long said Haskew also sold some of the weapons where he worked, and Haskew had paid him sixty-five dollars for helping with the burglary.

Later in the interview, Long said Moad's stepson was also involved in the fire at the Moad residence. The interview was concluded, and Long was taken to the marshal's office for processing regarding the federal firearms charges.

ATF now had a taped confession from a participant in an arson fraud case, additional suspects names to follow upon, and a case expanding in scope and violations of law—more work to be done.

With this lead information, S/A True and S/A Roberts conducted an interview with suspect Ky Haskew at his place of employment, the Independent Stave Company in Lebanon. During this interview, which was tape-recorded, Ky Haskew admitted his involvement in setting the fire at Jack Moad's residence in May 1991, as well as his involvement in the burglary of his father's farm, located in Wright County, Missouri. In addition to providing the agents with a taped confession of his involvement, Haskew provided names of individuals who had purchased the firearms removed from Jack Moad's residence and the firearms stolen from his father's dairy farm in Wright County. Two of the firearms were recovered on this same date. It was a very productive day for the law enforcement team of investigators.

Shortly after Dennis Long was arrested, a telephone message was left on his and his wife Kathy Long's answering machine.

Kathy Long: "Hi. Thanks for calling. I can't come to the phone right now, but if you'll leave your number, I'll call you back as soon as possible."

Unknown Caller: "You'd better tell your old man to keep his mouth shut or he won't be safe in any jail or prison."

End of call.

ATF received the taped message and listened carefully to the voice. It was a male caller who sounded similar to the voice of Jack Moad. We realized Moad was the only person involved in the arson and illegal firearms conspiracies who had previously served time in prison, had previously threatened to have a federal agent killed, and who was looking at jail time if Dennis Long named him as the person who had hired him to burn down the house. The members of the investigative team were not about to rush to any conclusions. The team did realize this was an obvious threat on Dennis Long.

During March, April, and May 1992, the investigative team was very busy gathering incriminating evidence against Jack Moad and his group of conspirators, including documenting that Jack Moad had purchased the .38 caliber firearm, falsifying a form that he was not a prior convicted felon when in fact he was, convicted of federal firearms violations in federal court in 1974. It was an element very easy to prove since Moad had sold the firearms to me, your author, while I was acting in my official capacity as an ATF agent in an undercover operation in Granite City, Illinois. The case had involved fifty-six criminals who were indicted and convicted, including Jack Walter Moad.

The team also secured insurance records from GEICO Insurance Company and bank drafts of insurance checks cashed by Jack Moad in payment for his false claims regarding his residence fire. There were also telephone records of calls between the subjects of the fire investigation documenting phone calls between them during the arson conspiracy.

On March 19, 1992, suspect Dennis Long appeared before the federal grand jury in Springfield and testified truthfully regarding his involvement in the arson conspiracy and firearms possession by Jack Moad.

The multiagency investigation was fast gaining momentum.

On April 4, 1992, ATF requested the assistance of Bill Farr, fire investigator with the Missouri State Fire Marshal's office. Farr was asked to look at the evidence developed regarding the fire of the Jack Moad residence and information on additional fires that had allegedly occurred by Camdenton, Missouri, and possibly in Illinois. Investigator Bill Farr joined the team, expanding the investigative efforts.

On April 8, 1992, Dennis J. Long, through his attorney, entered into a federal plea agreement to accept a federal sentence of fifteen years in prison in return for his cooperation in the arson fire of the Jack and Myrtle Moad residence in 1991. The firearms he was caught with were actually owned by Jack Moad, who was previously a convicted felon when he had illegally purchased the revolver in 1987.

In addition, in return for his cooperation, Long would not be charged with the fire he had set at the direction of Jack Moad in furtherance of an arson fraud scheme, tampering with a witness, or several additional firearms violations he had committed in 1991.

Shortly after the plea agreement was entered in federal court in Springfield, Dennis Long appeared before Federal Judge Russell Clark, who sentenced Long to fifteen years in federal prison, admonishing Long that as long as he continued cooperating truthfully with the law enforcement team, Clark would not increase his sentence.

In November 1992, the investigative team secured handwritten examples from Jack and Myrtle Moad to be compared to handwritten documents in the investigative teams' custody regarding the fraudulent felony by the Moads to the insurance company and the documents regarding the illegal purchase by Moad of a firearm in 1987.

Also developed during November were documents secured from a furniture store in Granite City, Illinois, verifying that Moad's claim of purchasing furniture from their store that he later claimed was destroyed in the arson fire was a false claim in furtherance of the arson fire and fraudulent claims to his insurance companies.

Following this development, the team located neighborhood witnesses to the arson fire who provided additional eyewitness evidence of the arson fire. These were two critical pieces of evidence required to confirm the arson fraud conspiracy.

On December 11, 1992, a federal grand jury returned an eight-count indictment charging Jack Moad, Myrtle Moad, Ky Haskew, and Herbert Lynn, Moad's stepson, with federal conspiracy, federal arson violations, and federal mail fraud violations.

In January 1993, coconspirator Ky Haskew pled guilty in federal court to conspiracy to destroy and damage by fire the residence of Jack Moad and Myrtle Moad for the purpose of committing mail fraud in violation of federal law. Haskew entered into a plea agreement to provide a truthful account of the fire and a burglary, including testifying if needed.

In the early months of 1993, with the indictments secured and the evidence mounting on the association of this gang of outlaws, the focus continued on the gang leader Jack Moad.

On April 1, 1993, Jack Moad pled guilty in federal court to conspiracy to commit arson, mail fraud, and making a false statement to acquire a firearm.

His wife Myrtle and stepson Herbert were spared prosecution in concert with the Moad guilty plea and subsequent plea agreement by Moad.

On this same date, coconspirator Ky Haskew was sentenced in federal court to probation, primarily due to his cooperation with the investigative team and the United States Attorney's Office.

During Moad's presentence investigation shortly after he pled guilty and entered into a federal plea agreement, it was learned that he had divested himself of substantial assets to circumvent the court's authority to set potential fines and restitution. Moad's actions were in violation of federal laws, including obstruction of justice and defrauding the government.

If the United States Attorney's Office had learned this earlier, they would not have entered into the plea agreement with Jack Moad and would have indicted him on additional federal charges resulting in a longer prison term— more evidence of a Missouri career criminal at work.

On June 6, 1993, Jack Walter Moad was sentenced to serve thirty-seven months and began serving his sentence on July 12, 1993.

With the guilty pleas of Dennis Long, Ky Haskew, and Jack Moad, ATF Case Agent Jay Branch was closing the file on the "Bad" Jack Moad Gang, and the other members of the team were all confident the investigation was over, or so we thought.

In 1996, ATF was advised Jack Moad was scheduled to be released from federal prison and initiate his supervised parole process. He was to report to his parole officer, Ken Kabonic, of the Federal Probation and Parole Department in Springfield. Senior Special Agent Kabonic in the release process conducted an initial interview with Jack Moad, the multi-convicted felon with failing health expressing little desire to live, with only one final goad to carry out.

He told Agent Kabonic he intended to seek out the federal agent who had put him in prison, not once but twice, and he intended to "take him out"—and he did not mean to dinner.

Agent Kabonic, realizing he was dealing with a violent ex-con who had previously killed a man and beat the rap, knew Moad meant what he was saying, and contacted ATF to report the threat. Agent Kabonic was aware that Moad had tried to hire a hit man to take out this same federal agent once before in 1974 after his first federal conviction, only to fail in that attempt in St. Louis.

As plans were being made to address this unsettling development and as Moad was about to be released, Senior US Probation Officer Ken Kabonic made a follow-up call to ATF, advising them that Jack Walter Moad had suffered a fatal heart attack and died prior to his release from prison.

Thus, concluded the criminal career of "Bad" Jack Moad, a Missouri outlaw to the end, completing a twenty-nine-year saga between a career criminal and a federal ATF agent.

LUNDGREN CULT MURDER; RYAN FITNESS CENTER FATAL ARSON; RSBI ARSON KICKBACK FRAUD 1990-1996

THE CULT MURDER CASE

The 1990s began in a dramatic fashion for the citizens of Kansas City, when on New Year's Eve, an ATF agent assigned to the Kansas City office, Larry Scott, received a phone call from a man who identified himself as the ex-husband of a woman who was a member of a religious cult group that was responsible for a murder.

He told Scott these were some people he had met recently. The caller related a bizarre story. He claimed these people were members of a religious cult group that was involved in a massive cleansing execution of a family of five from Independence.

The caller said the murders occurred in a barn on a farm located in Kirtland, Ohio, just outside Cleveland. He said the leader of the cult group was named Jeffrey Lundgren, who was also from Independence.

Agent Scott immediately informed his supervisor Rick Van Haelst, who notified the special agent in charge, George Rodriquez, of the grisly tale. He directed Agent Scott to contact the police department in Kirkland, Ohio, to inform their chief there may be five bodies buried in a barn on a farm.

Chief Dennis Yarbrough of Kirkland told Scott his department was aware of the group and sent a team of officers and ATF agents to the barn to conduct a search.

The team's first efforts proved negative, and no bodies were located.

A persistent Agent Scott recontacted the caller, who provided additional details and drew a diagram of where the pit in the barn was dug and where the bodies should be found. It was apparent to Scott the caller was familiar with the barn and could have, in fact, been in the barn himself.

Agent Scott recontacted Chief Yarbrough and sent the diagram to him, persuading him to make a second effort with the help of the diagram.

A team returned to the barn, rather skeptical of the information yet determined to locate the bodies if they were there.

On January 3–4, 1990, the bodies of five individuals were unearthed in the barn, exactly where the caller said they would be.

They were identified as Dennis Avery, forty-nine; his wife Cheryl Avery, forty-two; and their three daughters Trina, thirteen; Rebecca, nine; and Karen, only five years old. They had all been shot—allegedly by Jeffrey Lundgren—with the help of some of his cult members who had also lived at the farm.

The Murders

Lundgren had met with several of his coconspirators on April 10, 1989, telling two of them to dig a pit six feet by seven feet by four feet deep to conceal the bodies after they were killed. The members all made plans to flee the area after the murder ritual was carried out.

On April 17, 1989, Lundgren again met with his cult members, including Greg Winship and Richard Brand. He displayed a gun and asked the men if they were in on the murders. They all gave Lundgren their support. Later on the seventeenth, after the cult members had dinner, coconspirator Ron Luff had brought Ron Avery to the barn from the house. He was bound by Danny Kraft and Richard Brand. While Gregory Winship ran a chainsaw to muzzle the sound of the shots fired, Lungren shot Avery, firing two shots into his body, while Damon Lundgren, Jeff's son, stood lookout. Ron Avery's wife was next killed by Lundgren with three shots to her body before she was placed in the pit next to her husband.

Trena Avery, the thirteen-year-old, had her feet and hands wrapped with duct tape and was placed in the pit with her dead parents. She was shot in the head two times, and Lundgren put two bullets in her back.

Cult member Ron Luff then brought nine-year-old Becky to the barn, telling her he wanted to show her a horse. Once in the barn, she was bound and taped then placed near the pit. Lundgren shot her in the hip, and she fell on her mother's body. As Becky touched her mother, the second shot hit Becky in the back. Winship later recalled Becky was unconscious, still breathing, and making "rasping sounds."

Finally, five-year-old Karen was brought into the barn by Ron Luff, also under the guise of seeing the horses. She also was duct-taped. She was visibly frightened as she was placed in the pit. Lundgren fired one shot into the little child's head and one in her chest, wiping out the entire Avery family.

The murderers spread lime on the victims to speed up the decomposition of the bodies. According to the county coroner, it was possible that Dennis, Cheryl, and Becky were buried alive.

After the killings, the entire cult group fled Kirtland. The victims, originally from Independence, had lived off and on at the Lundgren farm as members of the religious cult.

In a very rapid developing case, ATF agents were provided with extensive information about Lundgren and the group.

The Jackson County, Missouri *Examiner* reported on January 6, 1990:

> Lungren left the Reorganized Church of Jesus Christ of Latter-day Saints in 1988 after his ministry credentials were revoked. He formed his own religious group, said Dale Luffman, president of the northeast Ohio chapter of the Reorganized Church.

Luffman said the group was conspiring to take over the RLDS temple there, and that Lundgren had made threats on his life.

Lundgren was head tour guide at the RLDS visitors' center in Kirtland before leaving the church in October 1988. He was asked to leave the historic center after financial improprieties were discovered, Luffman said.

'He was extremely conniving and manipulative, as you might guess,' Luffman said. 'He began a very subversive kind of teaching, and very cult like behavior began to be expressed. He became a very divisive force.'

Many of the people at the commune 'became quite subject to his leadership, his control and his manipulation,' Luffman said. 'They turned over their paychecks to him.'

'He was silenced for ethical reasons,' Luffman said. 'He would have been expelled from the church on the basis of un-Christian conduct had he not withdrawn his membership. They formed a radical splinter group.'

The splinter group apparently disbanded late in December after members became disgruntled over 'sexual indiscretions,' according to a Kansas City Times report.

ATF spokesman Rodriquez said the group following Lundgren consisted of 29 men, women and children, but some members, including the Avery family, came and went.

One church official described the splinter group as a "fanatical religious group with paramilitary leanings." Through the interviews and confessions, the ATF agents learned the family of five was sacrificed in what was described as a "cleansing execution," meant to fulfill a prophecy as interpreted by the leader of the religious cult, Jeff Lundgren.

Jeffrey Lundgren had considered the Avery family weak and only wanted strong members in his group. According to the former husband of one of the women charged in the vicious murders in Kirtland, Lundgren declared the executions were "meant to fulfill a prophecy."

At one point, Jeffrey Lundgren described the murder of the Avery family as "pruning the vineyard."

On April 18, 1989, the day after the brutal murder, the local police and FBI agents came to the Lundgren farm to talk to him, unaware bodies were buried there.

Information had been received that the cult group had disbanded in December 1989 after everyone moved away, fearing law enforcement could find out about the murders. Most of the members had moved back to Missouri and were living in the Kansas City area. Thirteen former members were charged with the murders or conspiracy.

The prosecutor handling the case, Steven C. LaTourette, of Lake County, Ohio, in a news conference said "these people are not crazy. They are the cruelest, most inhumane people this town has ever seen." The news conference was called after a grand jury in Lake County, Ohio, returned indictments charging Lundgren, his wife, his son, and ten members of his religious cult with the deaths.

Those charged in the indictment as reported by *The Examiner* were:

Lundgren, formerly of Independence; his son, Damon Paul Lundgren, 19; Richard Eugene Brand, 26, of Independence; Daniel David Kraft, no age given, of Navoo, Il; and Ronald Boyd Luff, 29 of Independence, are charged with five counts each of aggravated murder with death penalty specifications.

Each of the other eight is charged with five counts each of conspiracy, complicity to commit murder and kidnapping. Those eight are Alice Elizabeth Lundgren, 38; Deborah Sue Olivarez, 37, of Independence; Dennis Simms Patrick, 35, of Independence; Sharon Jean Bluntschly, 31 of Independence; Gregory Scott Winship, 29 of Euclid, Ohio; Tonya J. Patrick, 33, of Independence; Susie Luff, 31, of Springfield; and Kathryn Johnson 36, of Holden.

The Lundgrens, Johnson, Bluntschly and Kraft are at large. Kraft and Bluntschly had not been previously identified by authorities.

Brand and Winship surrendered in Kansas City Friday. The Luffs, the Patricks and Olivarez also are in custody.

By the time the indictments were returned, ATF in Kansas City had four members who had given a full written confession of the involvement in the murders.

SAC Rodriquez assigned a team of Kansas City agents to drop whatever they were doing and to concentrate on the Lundgren investigation.

Agent Larry Scott remained in charge of the activities as the case agent; Group Supervisor Rick Van Haelst coordinated interviews with those in ATF custody in Kansas City; in my capacity as the ATF Public Information Officer, I prepared press releases for the agent in charge and took numerous calls coming to our office. Other agents were put on standby to conduct follow-ups on leads coming into the office.

By Thursday, January 5, 1990, seven of the members were either arrested by ATF agents or turned themselves into law enforcement.

In a press release, Agent in Charge Rodriquez informed the public of the arrests and that six other members were being sought. He added that some of those arrested had confessed to the ATF agents about their part in the murders. He said there were no federal charges filed and that the defendants would be extradited to Ohio to face state murder charges.

ATF learned from those members providing written confessions that the murders had taken place on April 17, 1989.

On Friday, January 5, 1990, ATF agent Floyd Owens was assigned to conduct an interview with Alice Lundgren's mother, Donna Keehler. He met with her at a house of relatives she was staying at in the Lee's Summit, Missouri area.

She was very concerned for her daughter's safety after she had learned about the murder allegations and the arrest of several of the Lundgren cult members. During Agent Owens's interview, he told her if she heard from her daughter, she was to call him and provide him with the contact information and to inform Agent Owens what she had learned.

At about twelve midnight, Agent Owens received a phone call from Keehler, advising him she had received two phone calls from Jeff Lundgren, who was calling from a location in California. She said she had made arrangements to take custody of her daughter's children.

Lundgren told her that, after the children are turned over to her, they were going to turn themselves into law enforcement. She felt her daughter, her son-in-law Jeffrey, and Damon, were going to flee to Mexico to avoid the indictments.

Keehler provided to Agent Owens a telephone number in California where she was to contact Lundgren. She said her sister Margaret Patterson and her husband Vern Patterson were going to travel to California with her in the morning to take custody of the children.

We traced the phone number that Jeffrey Lundgren wanted her to contact him on at 9:00 p.m. on Saturday, as she traveled to California. The phone number was located in National City at a pay phone near a restaurant next to a motel.

Agent Owens told her he would meet with her in the morning, advising her a team of ATF agents would follow her to California. He then contacted agent Scott and Agent in Charge Rodriguez and advised them of the development.

A plan was put into place to follow her to the location in California, with the hopes of taking Jeffrey, Alice, and Damon in custody and securing the safety of the children first.

SAC Rodriguez contacted the ATF office in San Diego and surveillance was set up at the pay phone in Nation City, just a few miles from the Mexican border. I documented in my ATF official report prepared on January 19, 1990 as follows:

Special Agent Owens and Miller rode together in Owens' government-assigned vehicle, and Agent Scott and I traveled in Agent Scott's vehicle.

On January 6, 1990, at approximately 9:00 PM Kansas City time, Donna Keehler placed a phone call from a pay phone in Oklahoma City, Oklahoma to (619) 477-3856. Her grandson told her everyone was okay and he instructed her to call back on Sunday at noon San Diego time. Damon Lundgren's activities were under constant surveillance by ATF agents from the San Diego Post of Duty during this phone call and subsequent to this phone call throughout the evening of January 6, 1990.

While this phone call was in progress, we remained on a second pay phone next to the phone Donna Keehler was using. As the conversation unfolded, we relayed information to Special Agent in Charge Andy Vita of the San Diego office. We were on a conference call during the course of this conversation. We learned from Special Agent in Charge George Rodriguez that the agents from the San Diego office had followed Damon Lundgren to a motel located near the vicinity of the pay phones.

On January 7, 1990, at approximately noon San Diego time, Donna Keehler placed a second telephone call from the Ranger Station in the Petrified Forest National Park near Holbrook, Arizona. Damon Lundgren answered the phone again and he insisted that everyone was okay. He told Donna to call back at 12:00 midnight San Diego time, when she arrived in the San Diego area. He also told Donna that Jeff and Alice would send the kids to her at a predetermined public location in a cab.

During the course of this second telephone conversation, we again remained on a second phone next to Donna Keehler and once again forwarded the information as the conversation unfolded to Special Agent in Charge George Rodriquez in Kansas City, Missouri, as well as to Special Agent Charles Stimely in the San Diego office. Surveillance was in place at this time on Damon Lundgren as well as the motel room being utilized by an unknown number of the individuals wanted by the Ohio authorities. We were advised that if the opportunity presented itself, agents in place at the motel would effect an arrest of Jeffrey Lundgren if he separated himself from the rest of the individuals inside the motel.

A short while later in the afternoon, we learned from Special Agent George Rodriguez that Jeffrey Lundgren, Alice Lundgren, and Damon Lundgren had been arrested as the mole and that the three children were detained. The children were to be later turned over to Donna Keehler upon our arrival to San Diego, California.

At approximately 11:00 pm on January 7, 1990, the three children were turned over to Donna Keehler at the San Diego office.

Two days later Daniel Kraft, Jr. and Kathryn Johnson were arrested on a highway in California and taken into custody. All of the co-conspirators were now in custody.

In a press release shortly after we had all the cult suspects in custody, Special Agent in Charge George Rodriguez exclaimed, "We caught them pretty quick."

When asked why ATF did not involve the FBI, he said we, meaning ATF, "had the leads," and we were well on our way to catching Jeffrey Lundgren. He added actually enlisting the FBI might have slowed the investigation. "We would have had to stop and take time to go to the beginning telling those guys [the FBI] what we had."

Ohio State prosecutor Steven LaTourette echoed these sentiments, praising the ATF for their proficient and speedy arrest of all the Lundgren cult members. They were very capable in handling the serious situation themselves, he told the press.

Justice Served

As a result of the investigation, the legal process was completed the sentences were handed down.

Alice Lundgren was sentenced to five life sentences (140 years to life) for conspiracy and kidnapping; Damon Lundgren, her son, was sentenced to 120 years to life; Ronald Luff, who was the key planner and facilitator of the murders, was sentenced to 170 years to life; Daniel Kraft was sentenced to 50 years to life; Richard Brand was sentenced to 15 years to life; Sharon Bluntschly, Debbie Olivarez, and Susan Luff were all sentenced to 7 to 25 years. Some of the followers (such as Kathryn Johnson, Tonya Patrick, and Dennis Patrick) were found to have not been involved in the murders and each only received a one-year sentence for obstruction of justice.

As for cult leader Jeffrey Lundgren, he was given the death penalty and sentenced to die by lethal injection.

On July 24, 1991, a special recognition was presented to the ATF investigators in a ceremony in Washington, DC. *Kansas City Star* reporter John Dauner reported the recognition in a new article published in July 1991. It read as follows:

"FEDERAL AGENTS HONORED FOR LUNGREN CASE WORK"

Five federal investigators from Kansas City have been awarded the Treasury Department's highest award for their investigative work on the Jeffrey Lundgren cult murders.

The recipients are Bureau of Alcohol, Tobacco and Firearms agents Larry Scott, David R. True, Floyd Owens, Richard Van Haelst and Tom Miller. Van Haelst and Miller have since been assigned to the bureau's headquarters in Washington.

The awards will be presented Wednesday in Washington by Treasury Secretary Nicholas Brady.

During an 11-day period from Jan. 1 to Jan. 11, 1990, the five agents received and developed information that uncovered the murders of five members of the Avery family, originally from Independence. They were shot to death and buried in a Kirtland, Ohio, barn by Lundgren and 12 followers of his religious cult, the bureau said.

Further investigative work by the agents set off a manhunt from West Virginia to California that led to the arrests.

All 13 have been convicted and Lundgren has been sentenced to death.

The agents were cited for their investigative ability, dedication to duty and ability to organize and work with other federal, state and local law officers 'under extremely dangerous circumstances and severe time constraints.'

On October 24, 2006, Jeffrey Lundgren was executed at the Southern Ohio Correctional Facility in Lucasville, Ohio.

THE RYAN FITNESS CENTER ARSON FRAUD INVESTIGATION

On January 1, 1990, a fire broke out at the Ryan's Fitness Center located in West Burlington, Iowa. The fire, which destroyed the building, resulted in the death of two West Burlington volunteer firefighters. It was determined to be arson.

Two firefighters that perished in the fire were Bill Klein and Joe Wilt. They were the first of numerous firefighters to arrive at the scene. Steve Sands of the Des Moines *Hawkeye* newspaper wrote in a news article an account of their actions:

> Klein and Wilt were the first firefighters inside the fitness center, 1017 Broadway St., when the blaze was reported at 8:33 pm.
>
> Dragging a hose, both were equipped with air packs containing between 20- and 30-minutes' worth of air. Wilt came back out once to ask for more hose, and went back inside.
>
> A second hose team followed the pair inside and found the end of their hose by a pool table, but couldn't locate the men.
>
> Subsequent searches were unsuccessful as the fire raged out of control inside the steel-sided building.
>
> At 9:50 pm, a city backhoe finally tore the building open, allowing firefighters to pour water on the racquetball courts and office area. At 11:40 pm, the Burlington rescue team found the bodies about 30 feet from their hose. Klein, a two-year veteran of the department, was married and had two young children, the youngest less than two months old. Wilt, a three-year veteran, also was married.
>
> Klein and Wilt are the first two West Burlington firefighters to die in the line of duty. Klein's brother, Rick Klein, is a 17-year veteran and was working at the fire scene all night.

Soon after the fire, thousands of donations poured in for the families of the two deceased firefighters. In January 1990, Iowa senator Mark Hagerla of West Burlington, Iowa, introduced a bill stating any arson that results in a death would be a Class A felony, punishable by a mandatory life sentence. It was approved by the state senate in a 46–2 vote.

On February 27, 1990, committee chairman Daniel Jay from Centerville failed to allow it out of his committee, killing its passage for the year.

In July 1990, Iowa Governor Terry Branstad presented the state's highest award for the bravery of the two dead firefighter heroes—an award that has been presented only four times since its inception in 1978.

In October 1991, a final tribute to the two fallen heroes Joe Wilt and Bill Klein was set on the lawn of the West Burlington Fire Station for all to see—a black granite monument that took the artist 400 hours to complete.

Dale Ryan of Kansas City, Missouri, who was the owner of the business that was in trouble financially and recently shut down, was eventually charged with arson by a federal grand jury in Des Moines, Iowa. Due to the business being involved in interstate commerce, ATF was called in to assist in the investigation. ATF Agent Chris VanVleet of the Des Moines office was assigned to the case as case agent.

In my capacity, I was assigned later in the investigation to assist Agent VanVleet in conducting interviews and to assist the United States Attorney's Office in the preparation for the federal trial that was held in Des Moines, Iowa. During the trial, I sat at the prosecution table assisting the prosecutor.

The investigative team, directed by Agent VanVleet, consisted of the West Burlington Police Department, led by Chief George Renker, and the Iowa State Fire Marshal's Office. The team worked together for eighteen months before the federal indictment was returned, charging Dale Ryan with arson.

Investigators learned Ryan was insured for $640,000 at the fitness center. He was reimbursed for $307,000, the fair market value of the business after he filed his claim.

The suspect, Dale Ryan, was born and raised in Kansas City and ran two businesses in Kansas City. He had purchased a Mexican restaurant that failed and closed just six months after he opened it. He also opened and operated a hologram business in the Westport area of Kansas City. He was bankrolled by his father, a millionaire and businessman in Wichita, Kansas.

In Ryan's trial, federal prosecutor Linda Reade argued that his hologram business was also failing when he closed it. Ryan claimed he only closed it, so he could open the Ryan Fitness Center in West Burlington, Iowa. Also, in his trial, the prosecution showed that just prior to the arson, Ryan was depressed over the condition of the business and also depressed over his broken relationship with a go-go dancer from Gulfport, Illinois.

The prosecution also demonstrated that the fitness center was closed just three weeks before the arson fire and Ryan saw arson as the only way to leave Burlington and return to Kansas City. He also removed an expensive hologram from the fitness center before he set the fire.

Evidence showed he called his mother, Alice Donaldson, in Kansas City on January 2 and told her about the fire. He told her he was concerned he may have left a heater on in the business and two firefighters had died. She assured him it was only an accident. Ryan replied, "Not if two firefighters died."

As reported by newspaper reporter Steve Sands of the *Burlington Hawk Eye* Newspaper on September 22, 1991, the arson for insurance profit was not the first scam Ryan was involved in. He was previously in trouble in Kansas, arising out of a scam in which he had sold what Ryan claimed were capsules as effective as illegal steroids, according to the Kansas Attorney General's Office. Their office reported:

He was selling these capsules out of his house in Kansas City to unsuspecting customers in the Kansas City area.

Ryan's print ads claimed daily use of the boron capsules would cause massive gains in muscle size, strength and endurance. The claim could not be supported scientifically.

Ryan sold 100-day supplies of the capsules for $16.50 and $18.95 according to a spokeswoman for the Attorney General's Office in Kansas.

The boron capsule sold for only $4.50 elsewhere.

Ryan paid a $10,000 fine to cover his investigative costs and agreed to refund customers.

Kansas authorities said Ryan entered into a consent agreement in connection with his mail-order business he operated out of his Kansas City, Missouri, home the previous year.

Any illegal thing to make an illegal dollar.

Ryan has a long history with illegal dealings. According to court records, he was convicted of larceny 13 years ago in Kansas City and was fined $100. 10 years ago, Ryan stole jewelry from his father and stepmother; he was charged with burglary and theft, but his judgment was deferred.

On September 2, 1991, the West Burlington arson trial began in federal court in Des Moines, Iowa, with the picking of the jury, followed by opening arguments by the federal prosecutor and Ryan's defense attorney.

Linda Reade, the assistant United States attorney, who prosecuted the case at Ryan's trial, presented a very strong case, citing very convincing case facts and testimony evidence that were also very damaging to Dale Ryan.

Steve Sand, the reporter with the *Burlington Hawk Eye* Newspaper, covered the entire trial. He reported the daily testimony from the prosecution and defense witnesses and the trial proceedings, including portions of the testimony:

Patrick Delashmutt, a former employee, said Ryan told him during a bar conversation in October 1989 that the business was failing.

'I don't know if he was joking or not, but he said he wished it would burn down,' Delashmutt said he was told.

A former center supervisor, Terry Eagen, said Ryan made a similar remark to her. He then told her if the center ever burned down, he might face trouble for making those remarks.

Debra Swan, a former member of the club, testified today that Ryan also told her he wished the center would burn down.

Ryan also made disparaging remarks about his father.

'He said he couldn't wait for his father to get old so he could take him up in a wheelchair and shove him off a cliff,' Swan said.

When asked whether she thought Ryan was serious about the fire remark, Swan said 'he certainly didn't smile' when he said it.

A neighbor of Ryan's, Bonnie Johnston Smith, testified that Ryan came to her apartment the day after the fire and asked her and her son not to tell investigators about the faulty space heater that was at Ryan's apartment.

'He asked me not to mention anything about the space heater,' Smith said.

Smith also said, 'Dale told me that at one time he mentioned to Sherry that if the club would burn down Dale would have a lot of money.'

Investigators found the remains of a space heater at the scene of the fire. Reade is trying to show that a fan blade had been removed from the space heater, causing it to overheat and ignite nearby flammable liquids.

The second week of testimony began Monday with Ryan's former girlfriend, Sherry Zappa, telling about a space heater shorting out as the couple sat in Ryan's apartment weeks before the fire.

Zappa, a go-go dancer at a Gulfport, Ill., bar, had been living with Ryan but left for Minnesota after a fight with him Dec. 20, 1989, she said. She said that he had earlier expressed the wish that the club would catch fire.

'He made a statement that sometimes he wished it would burn,' she said.

West Burlington officers, Larry Garmoe, testified last week that Ryan drove up in a blue Ford Fairmont during the search.

Cans of linseed oil, motor oil and floor cleaner were found in the back seat of the car during an earlier check of the center's parking lot, Garmoe testified.

The license plates Garmoe recorded that night were registered to a white Mercury Zephyr that Ryan received as a Christmas present from his father.

Garmoe said he saw Ryan driving the same car after the fire, but that the back seat was empty.

But defense attorneys claim Ryan was preparing to sell the center and was taking out his personal property.

Authorities also found a key to the center at Ryan's residence. Prosecutors contend Ryan had the only key to the center after he changed the locks before the fire. Firefighters earlier testified the three doors to the center showed no signs of forcible entry the night of the fire.

The defense attorneys representing Ryan in his defense made two critical errors in their trial presentation. The first error was when attorneys claimed the firefighters died as a result of their own negligence by leaving their hose.

Prosecutor Linda Reade, in an emotional response, said the reason they left their hose was because they searched for someone they felt was in the building. This claim did not sit well with the jury, who recognized the firefighters as heroes just doing their job.

The defense attorneys second error was claiming the fire started in an electrical short circuit in the bar areas of the center, caused by a malfunctioning cash register. Prosecutor Linda Reade presented to the jury that cash registers don't cause fires. We had conducted a search of all reported fire causes during the entire year of 1990.

The Property Loss Information Registry (PLIR) located in Boston, Massachusetts, documents all reported fire losses. We queried and found there were no reported fires that were caused by a defective cash register in the United States in the previous two years.

In addition, the defense team was required to turn over to the prosecutors how their electrical expert found this as the cause of the fire. Assistant US Attorney Reade showed the jury a video documenting their expert in his testing of a similar cash register. He used a propane torch to start his register's fire. The jury saw through this defense argument.

On September 25, Dale Ryan was found guilty of setting the fire that had killed two firefighters. The jury declined to sentence Ryan to life in prison with no chance for parole, leaving Federal Judge Harold Victor to decide Ryan's fate.

The federal prosecutor's office recommended a sentence of thirty-plus years for Ryan.

On February 6, 1992, Federal Judge Harold Vieter sentenced Ryan to 328 months in prison or 25 years and 8 months to be served in a federal prison.

In February 1992, just several days after Dale Ryan was sentenced in federal court, an unknown person vandalized the firefighter's monument, spraying it with orange paint. Five days later, Dale Ryan's cousin John Dale Steward, eighteen years old, admitted to spraying the monument and was fined $135 for the act of defacing the monument.

ATF case agent Chris VanVleet was recognized for his diligent efforts in putting a very difficult case together. Case Agent VanVleet and his investigative team were recognized by the United States Attorney's Office and the West Burlington Fire Department for their efforts in the investigation and successful prosecution in federal court.

A few years after the trial, Assistant US Attorney Linda Reade was appointed to the federal bench, becoming a federal judge.

THE RSBI INVESTIGATION

On November 2, 1991, a major fire occurred at a business known as RSBI Aerospace on 40 Highway East in Blue Springs, Missouri; it was a large warehouse containing many aerospace airplane parts. The damage to the parts and structure was set at over $2 million.

Firefighters from nine different departments battled freezing temperatures to extinguish the fire. Several firefighters suffered frostbite, and one firefighter suffered a sprained ankle while fighting the blaze.

The fire scene examination was conducted by the Blue Springs Fire and Police Departments, the Jackson County Fire Protection District, and the ATF.

The scene examination revealed the fire was intentionally set and declared an arson. Your author, in his capacity as an ATF agent, was assigned as case agent and directed the scene examination.

Due to the fact the fire was set at a business involved in and affecting interstate commerce—a federal crime—ATF became the lead agency, and we conducted the follow-up investigation. We learned the business employed approximately thirty employees. We were provided with a computer disc by one of the employees that contained the entire business activities of RSBI from its inception to just a few days prior to the fire.

Very early in this investigation, the team of investigators learned what we were dealing with and who some of the players were. The owner of RSBI was Ross Barber, a property developer and brother of Anthony Barber, the owner and operator of the Barber Tobacco Company in Kansas City, Missouri. Ross Barber was a vice president in the tobacco company and active in its day-to-day activities.

The manager of RSBI was John Campbell Jr., Ross Barber's son-in-law and a recently convicted felon. John Campbell surrendered himself on September 4, 1991, to begin serving a ten-year prison sentence. Campbell was described by the media as a "virtual one-man wrecking crew in the aircraft-parts industry, starting up a series of brokerage operations that ran up huge debts and then abandoning them."

Campbell had been running the RSBI operation under an assumed name "Michael Morgan," the media reported. Campbell's criminal conviction stemmed from his operation of National Marine located in Lee's Summit, Missouri.

A January 1990 trial in Kansas City federal court showed he had defrauded three banks of more than $600,000.

The interview process was initiated immediately. On November 4, 1991, while at the scene during an interview with ATF Agent Peter Lobdell, Ross Barber pointed the finger of suspicion at RSBI employees Mark Wise and Janelle Cid and suggested that the motive for the fire was to cover up employee theft. Barber also admitted he was having severe financial problems at the time of the fire.

The team of investigators were interested in confirming the financial condition of RSBI leading up to the night of the arson fire and the amount of the insurance coverage in the event of a fire loss.

We learned that on or about May 1, 1991, Ross Barber had increased his insurance coverage at the RSBI warehouse from $750,000 to $13.5 million to cover the warehouse inventory. Barber secured a separate insurance policy with Massachusetts Bay Insurance Carrier in the amount of $200,000 to insure the office furniture and office contents.

The financial situation at RSBI was not good at all. On September 9, 1991, John Campbell Jr., a.k.a. Mike Morgan, left the employment of RSBI and initiated serving a federal prison term at Nellis Air Force Base Prison Facility near Las Vegas, Nevada. Campbell left RSBI with several incomplete sales transactions of large sale of airline parts to various companies located throughout the world. This resulted in a false financial condition at RSBI.

On or about September 15, 1991, during a dinner engagement, Ross Barber was told by Guy Tamburello that a certain large shipment of brakes and wheels, which Barber thought were already sold by John Campbell of RSBI, were in fact still in the RSBI warehouse. Barber became very upset and caused an immediate inspection of the warehouse, only to confirm that the brakes and wheels were still in the warehouse, unsold. This was one of the first occurrences that caused Barber to realize that John Campbell Jr. had manipulated the sales and the books at RSBI, reflecting false profits for Barber.

On September 26, 1991, Ross Barber was notified via certified mail that RSBI was being terminated from using the Inventory Locator Service for violations involving the illegal listing of airline parts, which were being simultaneously listed by another company, Sabena Airlines. Barber was placed on notice that RSBI had until October 4, 1991, to furnish written proof of RSBI's exclusive right to offer for sale the inventory they currently listed, which matched that of Sabena Airlines.

These actions on the part of ILS officials placed RSBI in a very precarious financial condition and caused Ross Barber to hire attorneys located in the state of New York and caused Barber to send employee Guy Tamburello to New York to meet with the attorneys and advance a retainer fee for the attorneys' service. Permanent loss of the use of the ILS System would have put RSBI out of business.

On or about October 24, 1991, Ross Barber was advised by George Worley, senior vice president of quality assurance at RSBI, that the entire Accro Tech inventory, which Barber had purchased in 1990, would fall under the category of "unapproved parts," according to current and forthcoming federal regulations because these parts had not been inspected by a Boeing inspector/representative.

As a result of this information, Barber was forced to place this entire inventory in a "quarantined status," making the inventory unsalable.

Shortly after this evaluation, Ross Barber's company, RSBI, was the subject of a lengthy exposé-type published by the *Kansas City Business Journal*, detailing the fact that RSBI had, in fact, been run by ex-con John Campbell, using the assumed name of Mike Morgan. The article detailed how Barber, while denying Campbell was involved in RSBI, had employed Campbell using an alias of Mike Morgan. This news article was distributed throughout the airline industry, hurting the sales at RSBI, adding to the business's already deteriorating financial condition.

Through this interview process of current and ex-RSBI employees, we received information that certain past and current RSBI employees were allegedly involved in illegal payoffs, bribery, and kickbacks of cash and expensive gifts to certain purchasing agents of various aerospace companies and airline companies located throughout the United States. These alleged cash payoffs and gifts of monetary value were being paid to the various purchasing agents of the firms in return for doing business between RSBI and their particular firm or airline company.

The investigation eventually revealed that the persons involved in making these illegal payoffs were John Campbell Jr. (a.k.a. Mike Morgan), who directed the illegal operation, and Kevin Burke, Denise Mize, Guy Tamburello, and Don Gunter, who by agreement, assisted in forwarding the cash kickbacks to the purchasing agents of various airlines and aerospace companies.

On or about January 7, 1992, we met with Ross Barber, the owner of RSBI. This meeting was held at the ATF office located in Overland Park, Kansas, and was conducted at Ross Barber's request. During this meeting, Barber provided a general background on himself, including information on his personal life, as well as information regarding the various businesses he has been associated with.

Also during this meeting, Ross Barber provided us with direct knowledge he had about the fire that occurred at RSBI on November 2, 1991, as well as information and insight about other activities that he knew or learned about that occurred at RSBI. Barber told us that he would draw an income from RSBI each month and that on certain months he would draw as much as $10,000.

Barber emphasized that he would take out enough money from this income to use to pay his income taxes and then give the balance of cash to his son-in-law, John Campbell Jr., who actually ran the business. Barber said that Campbell would use the cash to pay for various expenses that would occur at RSBI. Barber also emphasized that he was not personally involved in the fire at his business nor was he personally involved in any other illegal activities that may have occurred at RSBI.

Barber offered his continued assistance to federal authorities in this case; however, he insisted that he was not part of any of the illegal activities. Barber told us that John Campbell stated to him, "In order to get ahead with aerospace business, you had to pay off people to do business."

Realizing we needed assistance from agents with specialized experience in the airline industry workings, we made a request for assistance from the Department of Transportation, Inspector General's Office in February 1992. Special Agent James Kelleher, with the Department of Transportation, Inspector General's Office, was assigned to this task force investigation. We also received periodic assistance from special agents with the FBI throughout the course of this investigation.

On March 27, 1992, Special Agent Pete Lobdell and I traveled to Las Vegas, Nevada, and conducted an interview with inmate John Campbell Jr., a.k.a. Mike Morgan, who was incarcerated at Nellis Federal Prison Camp. Also, during this visit, we served Lieutenant Lewis with a federal grand jury subpoena for taped telephone conversations between inmate John Campbell Jr. and numerous other individuals located previously in the greater Kansas City metropolitan area. We subsequently received numerous boxes of cassette tapes containing these taped telephone conversations between John Campbell Jr. and others between September 30, 1991 and March 25, 1992.

During this interview, Campbell revealed during the latter part of August 1991 or first part of September 1991, Ross Barber had told him that, if the business at RSBI failed as a result of Campbell going to prison and leaving the business for Ross to run, that he, Barber, could afford a fire at RSBI—that, in fact, he could get away with a fire at RSBI. Barber informed Campbell that his cousin, RSBI employee Guy Tamburello, had successfully filed several insurance claims and collected money on these claims.

The remainder of 1992 involved numerous interviews with past and present employees from RSBI, as well as individuals employed at various airlines throughout the United States who were purchasing aerospace parts and also receiving illegal cash kickbacks in violation of federal wire fraud and mail fraud.

By the end of the year, a federal grand jury was in place, and numerous admissions were secured. Also, several illegal payments of cash kickbacks were secured by ATF. These were paid to an employee named Tom Kabler, employed with Dowty Aviation in Sterling, Virginia, who confessed to his illegal activities with employees at RSBI. An undercover operation was set up with Kabler's cooperation; phone calls were tape-recorded, and cash payments were taken into ATF custody by agents from our office in Baltimore, Maryland.

By the end of 1992, our task force plan was progressing, and indictments weren't far behind. The plan was simple. Secure evidence of federal violations involving kickbacks and, in the process, develop evidence of the arson and possible insurance fraud. Ron Barber had filed an insurance claim of $13.5 million in losses due to the arson fire.

From July 1992 through September 1993, Special Agent Kelleher and I traveled to Virginia; Seattle, Washington; Miami, Florida; Los Angeles, California; and Indiana. Employees at the various airlines and aviation companies provided statements admitting to taking illegal kickbacks in exchange for purchasing aerospace parts from RSBI. All payments were paid in cash and sent to their residence by Federal Express, hoping to avoid federal prosecution.

It didn't work.

On May 4, 1993, Kevin Burke was indicted by a federal grand jury in the Western Judicial District of Missouri and charged with twelve counts of the following:

> Title 18, USC, Section 1343: Fraud by wire, radio or television. Whoever, having divided or intending to devise any scheme or artifice to defraud, or to obtain any money or property by means of false or fraudulent pretenses, representations, or promises transmits, or causes to be transmitted by means of wire, radio, or television, communication in interstate or foreign commerce, any writings, signs, signals, pictures, or sounds for the purpose of executing such scheme or artifice, shall be fined not more than $1000.00 or imprisoned not more than five years, or both.
>
> Title 18, USC, Chapter 63, Section 1346: Devising a scheme or artifice to defraud or deprive another of the intangible right to honest service.

On this same date, Tom Kabler was indicted by the same grand jury and charged with nine counts of Title 18, USC, Sections 1343 and 1346. Kabler was already cooperating, and Kevin Burke agreed to cooperate with our investigation.

In September, John Campbell Jr. and Donald M. Gunter were indicted by a federal grand jury in Kansas City, Missouri, charged with one count of conspiracy to commit wire fraud and three counts each of wire fraud.

On or about November 2, 1993, Ross Barber, in furtherance of the arson insurance fraud scheme, accepted a check from Hanover Insurance Company in the amount of $80,000 as a result of the fire loss he had incurred in the fire of November 2, 1991. Barber subsequently endorsed and deposited the check in a bank located in Kansas City, Missouri, in violation of federal money laundering laws.

As a result of this fraudulent fire claim, Ross Barber also caused Hanover Insurance Company to pay Superior National Bank $55,000 arising out of their losses and a company known as Aaron Rents $15,000 as a result of furniture they had lost in the fire at RSBI on November 2, 1991.

At the request of the United States Attorney's Office, Ross Barber's personal knowledge that he had previously provided to me about Guy Tamburello's involvement in setting the fire at RSBI was documented in a memorandum by Agent True and forwarded to the United States Attorney's Office, Kansas City, Missouri, at the US Attorney's Office request.

This memorandum was subsequently sent to the attorneys representing Ross Barber in his civil suit and the insurance company attorneys representing the insurance company's interest in Barber's $13.5 million claim as a result of the fire at RSBI.

On March 16, 1994, Guy Tamburello was arrested by federal agents and charged with federal wire fraud violations. At the time of his arrest, Tamburello was told he was also a suspect in the arson fire at RSBI and that the fire investigation was also being actively pursued by federal authorities. Realizing he was in serious trouble; Tamburello secured the assistance of an attorney, who contacted ATF, advising us his client wanted to talk.

In 1994, Guy Tamburello and his associate, Paul Anselmo, provided tape-recorded confessions detailing their involvement in the arson-for-profit scheme, stating that they had set the fire at RSBI, using gasoline and cigarette delay devices at the direction of and for Ross Barber. They admitted they had entered into a conspiracy with Ross Barber the day before the fire and set the fire for Barber, so he could collect the insurance proceeds. They also confessed that Ross Barber had established an alibi that he would be at a local restaurant at the time of the fire. Ross Barber directed Tamburello and Anselmo to remove numerous items of value from the RSBI warehouse before setting the fire for the purpose of reselling these items.

On this same date, Tamburello and Anselmo turned over numerous items that they had removed from the RSBI warehouse at the direction of Ross Barber, before setting the fire for Ross Barber on November 2, 1991. Tamburello added, during the early part of 1991, exact date unknown, Ross Barber told Guy Tamburello that the government investigators suspected Tamburello as the person responsible for the arson fire at RSBI.

Also, during the spring of 1994, exact date unknown, Ross Barber met with

Guy Tamburello and admitted to him that he had confided to me certain facts and knowledge he possessed about the fire at RSBI.

On May 20, 1994, Guy Tamburello appeared before a federal judge and pled guilty to one count of wire fraud, arising out of the kickback scheme that he was involved in with Ross Barber and John Campbell Jr. at RSBI, and pled to one count of conspiracy to commit arson at RSBI and admitted in open court that he had set the fire at RSBI, along with an associate, at the direction of and for the owner, Mr. Ross Barber.

In June 1994, as a direct result of Tamburello pleading guilty and admitting setting the fire for Ross Barber, Federal Judge Fernando J. Gaitan, Jr., granted Affiliated FM Insurance Company a motion for a summary judgment against Ross Barber's insurance claim for $13.5 million. In the ruling, Judge Gaitan cited Tamburello's guilty plea to the arson and Barber's admissions to ATF about Tamburello's involvement, in favor of the insurance company.

In March 1995, the United States Court of Appeals for the Eighth Circuit affirmed the summary judgment of Federal Judge Fernando Gaitan, Jr.'s ruling, granting summary judgment in the circuit court in Kansas City on June 22, 1994.

The $13.5 million claim ruling was affirmed and denied payment—a big win for the insurance company holding the policy and a big win for the ATF task force investigators.

On September 26, 1995, Ross Barber was indicted by the federal grand jury and charged with six counts of conspiracy mail fraud and money laundering.

On April 22, 1996, the federal trial of Ross Barber started in Kansas City federal court. His defense attorney claimed the Mafia had infiltrated his company then set his building on fire.

Barber's attorney told the jury that Guy Tamburello's presence at RSBI proved that organized crime had penetrated Barber's business. The attorney noted to the jury that Guy Tamburello was Pete Tamburello's son and said, "It's a classic Italian Mafia case." He told the jury Pete Tamburello was the bodyguard for the late Kansas City mob boss Nick Civella.

He added the notion that Pete Tamburello, as a member of the Kansas City Mafia, had extorted a position for his son at RSBI, as well as a position for Paul Anselmo, a close associate of Guy Tamburello.

The jury bought the defense story, and Ross Barber was acquitted.

Despite of the jury acquittal, the ATF and Department of Transportation investigation was considered a huge success. Five felony convictions, the denial of a huge insurance claim, and the shutdown of a criminal organization, the book on the RSBI investigation was closed and so were the books on the federal and state investigations on the Mafia in the 1900s.

TONY EMERY, NORTHWEST MISSOURI DRUGS-MURDER CASE 1979-2000

T ony Emery was received at the Missouri State Prison in 1979 after he was found guilty of possession of burglary tools in a jury trial in Atchison County. Emery was sentenced to a term of two years' confinement. Tony Emery's criminal career continued for years after his release from prison on August 5, 1981.

When Emery returned to Maryville after serving his sentence at "The Big House," his vicious, mean reputation reared its ugly head on several occasions. When Ron Coy, one of his criminal associates, was about to go on trial for shooting someone, the prosecutor's house was blasted with a shotgun, sending out a threatening message to all. A mistrial was declared, and then the charges were dropped when the witnesses were afraid to testify.

On another occasion, when a road crew foreman for the county tried to have Emery fired for not working, the foreman's house was set on fire. Emery's violent exploits continued when a competing company decided to bring their own sanitation business and equipment into the Maryville area. The company lost one of their trucks in a mysterious explosion. Everyone suspected Emery had blown up the truck with dynamite, but no charges were filed.

When the local newspaper released a negative news article about Emery's trash hauling business, someone used a bulldozer to drive through the wall of the newspaper offices. Emery was suspected of numerous crimes, including burglaries, auto thefts and assaults, yet no one would step forward and testify against him. Everyone feared Tony Emery.

Origin of Emery Network

As 1987 arrived, Tony Emery set out to become a trafficker of methamphetamine. He sought out advice from drug dealer Jean Reed. Emery applied his acumen for the drug business through his experience operating and managing his family-owned business of Emery Sanitation Company, located in Maryville, Missouri. He quickly realized the potential for making large profits in his illegal endeavors.

Emery bragged to his criminal associates that he aspired to monopolize the methamphetamine trade in Maryville and eventually all the Northwest Missouri and Southwest Iowa areas.

Unlike many drug dealers, he did not use the drug. He did capitalize on his violent reputation, and despite the fact he was a convicted felon, he routinely used and carried firearms to protect his enterprise and eventually force other competing meth dealers out of business.

Emery included his mother Betty Emery, his brother Terry Emery, his sister Virginia Billings, his cousin Herb Emery, his brother-in-law Richard Allen, and others in growing his profitable, illegal operation. Initially, employees of Emery Sanitation were routinely utilized to distribute his meth. Soon the distribution network grew beyond Emery Sanitation personnel.

Emery built his drug trafficking organization, expanding upon the already established structure of Emery Sanitation, a family business entity that affected interstate commerce—an important element required for federal agent intervention.

His distribution network remained his central focus and, like a good businessman, Emery was always seeking new and better sources of meth to supply the ever-increasing demand for the drug.

Much like any large-scale narcotics network, his coconspirators in the distribution network did not all know each other, but they did share the common purpose of supplying meth that Emery distributed throughout the entire Northwest Missouri area and elsewhere. These sources included fellow gangsters from San Diego, California, and Fort Collins, Colorado.

Emery initially relied on financing from a criminal named Kirby Oglesby from Independence, a city known as the original meth-producing capital of Missouri and beyond. The large sums of money allowed Emery to purchase multiple pounds of meth. Emery used carriers to travel to meet West Coast contacts with these large amounts of money, make the purchases, and return with the meth for distribution through Emery's network.

Tony Emery's trafficking grew from dealing grams and eighth ounces to supplying multiple ounces to smaller distributors throughout Northwest Missouri. These drug distributors numbered no fewer than twenty-one and involved both men and women. Tony Emery was truly the meth drug kingpin in Northwest Missouri, and he was not about to lose that status. Cross him and you were in fear of harm; inform on him to police and you became a candidate for murder.

Firearms Acquisition Episode

Starting in May 1988, Emery, a convicted felon, acquired firearms, using other coconspirators to purchase guns on his behalf. He also made some illegal purchases himself in violation of federal ATF laws. This process continued throughout 1989, reaching as many as eleven firearms in his possession. This large-scale criminal operation did not go unnoticed by local law enforcement agencies, as well as the Missouri Highway Patrol's State Narcotics Unit. As intelligence information came to these departments, they each, in turn, initiated their own investigations and began sharing information with federal and local agencies. The local agencies also had a long-standing reputation with federal law enforcement agencies, including the ATF offices located throughout Missouri. After local police realized they were dealing with criminals possessing and using firearms and conducting illegal drug activities throughout the United States, the call to ATF agents in the Kansas City office came easy.

The highway patrol, as well as Sergeant Randy Strong of the Maryville Police, made contact with ATF Agent Mark James through Dave Linn in the Kansas City office. James was once a Missouri Highway Patrol trooper who worked on narcotics cases. Agent James, who had a strong reputation for being a maverick agent, played a lot of hunches and was quite successful during his law enforcement career.

Agent James's partner on this assignment was Mike Schmitz, a new ATF agent and a former All-American football player at a small college. Involvement of Agent Schmitz would have to wait until he completed new agent ATF training at the National Academy in the state of Georgia.

By May 1988, Emery and his organization was possessing and distributing as much as three to six pounds of methamphetamine throughout Northwest Missouri. In the fall of 1988, Emery directed coconspirators Kirby Leslie and Ron Coy to use his firearms to fire into the dwelling of Terry Sloniker, a drug trafficking competitor, as a warning not to compete for Emery's territory.

Between the fall of 1988 and the winter of 1989, Emery's organization possessed and distributed at least twenty-six pounds of meth, according to law enforcement documentation, not counting an unknown amount of undocumented meth. Throughout this time, the members of the gang, as well as leader Emery, routinely carried weapons in furtherance of the drug operation. Emery usually carried a Desert Eagle .44 magnum semiautomatic pistol.

An Error in Judgment Committed by Tony Emery

In February 1989, Christine Elkins, who had been receiving drugs from Emery for years, joined in the Emery drug distribution conspiracy. Elkins provided transportation for Roger Jackson (a fellow distributor whom she was living with) to Tony Emery's residence on an average of two to three times a week. Jackson would obtain meth from Emery on these trips for resale to customers. These drug amounts ranged from a quarter ounce to an ounce each trip. Emery charged $1,800 per ounce. Jackson, in turn, supplied customers, including Chris Walker of Iowa, Kirby Leslie, Mike Logsdon, Richard Allen, Ed Archer, and Terry Oglesby.

On October 16, 1989, Emery supplied Jackson with a quantity of meth. Jackson got high on some of the drug and physically assaulted Christine Elkins. On October 19, 1989, Jackson, high on drugs, again assaulted Elkins. This time she threatened Jackson that she was going to the police and would tell the police of his drug trafficking if he assaulted her again. Jackson told Emery of her threat, and the two men told her they would kill her if she ever talked to the police. She assured them she wouldn't tell and would stay true to the organization.

During mid-November 1989, Tony Emery met with Christine Elkins, a drug addict herself, to discuss supplying two pounds of meth per week to her at a price of $1,800 per ounce. Elkins had established contacts with buyers of meth. One of the buyers was actually a confidential informant, working with the Nodaway County Sheriff's Department in an undercover capacity.

On November 27, 1989, Virginia Billings, who was Tony Emery's sister and part of the distribution network, brokered a quarter ounce of meth from Tony Emery to Christine Elkins. Elkins, in turn, sold the drug to the confidential informant of the county sheriff's department.

On December 8, 1989, Tony Emery supplied Elkins with one-eighth ounce of meth, which she sold to a cooperating informant of the Missouri Highway Patrol Drug Unit. On December 13–14, 1989, Elkins met with Jim Wissman, who was operating in an undercover capacity and discussed with her an upcoming meth deal supplied by Tony Emery.

On December 15, Tony Emery supplied Elkins with one-half ounce of meth as a sample for a one-pound deal she was unwittingly negotiating with the confidential informant of the highway patrol. Elkins gave Tony $900 provided to her by Highway Patrol Trooper Alvin Riney. Trooper Riney had recorded the serial numbers of the bills. During this transaction, Elkins was under surveillance and was seen with Emery at his residence.

After the transaction was completed, Elkins was arrested by members of the Highway Patrol Drug Unit for delivery of the controlled substance. Realizing she was in big trouble, Elkins identified Tony Emery as her source and agreed to assist the troopers to perfect charges against Emery that night.

Elkins placed a call to Emery to further discuss details of completing the one-pound meth transaction. The phone call was recorded by police. Emery said he would meet with her at her residence. Upon Emery's arrival, he became suspicious of her strained behavior. He went outside and observed the presence of surveillance vehicles. Emery then fled the area, successfully eluding the police.

On December 16, 1989, officers from the Maryville Department of Public Safety and troopers with the Missouri State Highway Patrol executed a search warrant at the residence of Tony Emery, 1408 East Halsey in Maryville. Emery was found to be in illegal possession of eleven firearms that had previously traveled in interstate commerce. Convicted felon Emery was in violation of federal firearms laws.

This event was communicated to ATF Agent James, who was already involved in the investigation. Possessing and using firearms during drug sales was a serious mistake by Emery. Items found at the scene included an assault rifle positioned on his coffee table for easy access, a cutting tray for making meth, cutting agents for diluting drugs, the home and work numbers of Herb "Tug" Emery, the home and telephone number of Bobby Miller, and the $900 of marked bills Trooper Riney had given to Christine Elkins to use with Emery earlier that night.

Tony Emery was arrested later on December 16 and charged with distribution of controlled substances. If proven the firearms were used as protection during his drug distribution operation, he would be looking at serious federal time. After his arrest, Tony Emery made up his mind that Christine Elkins was the key witness against him. He was an ex-con looking at serious prison time if convicted. Emery hoped to convince her to not cooperate with police by paying for her attorney fees and providing her with meth to satisfy her drug habit. If this didn't work, she would have to be silenced.

On December 20, Elkins gave a tape-recorded statement to Trooper Riney regarding her drug trafficking endeavors with Tony Emery. During the week after Elkins's arrest, Tony Emery, out on bond, summoned Elkins to his residence, where he and Augie Sherman conducted a thorough debriefing of her. The two were very concerned about the events leading up to her arrest and how much she had told the law enforcement officers regarding Emery's involvement in the drug trafficking. Emery promised to pay all her attorney fees, gave her $2,000 in cash, and left an unlimited supply of meth at Roger Jackson's residence for her consumption.

Tony Emery was very leery of Christine's commitment to not give him up to law enforcement authorities. Elkins realized she was facing serious charges herself and was concerned about her two children if she had to serve any lengthy prison time. Emery felt she needed to be silenced to avoid testifying against him; she had to be murdered.

Between January 15 and April 18, 1990, Elkins paid attorney John Torrence $4,950 in cash and $1,000 by money order for a legal retainer fee. On February 15, 1990, Christine Elkins began writing a letter to her mother Patricia Camblin, outlining the details of her drug trafficking activities with Tony Emery and his organization. This letter was finished on March 28 and mailed to her mother—a routine of letter writing to her mother she had carried on for years. On June 29, 1990, Elkins's attorney required an additional $2,000 retainer to file depositions and conduct the related investigation regarding her pending drug charges.

The Plot to Kill Christine Elkins Begins

During the period between December 1989 when Emery was arrested in Maryville and August 1990, Tony Emery communicated with his uncle Earl Emery, who was serving a life prison sentence for murder in the Iowa State Prison. Tony told a drug associate named Kenny Poppa that his uncle had an inmate contact in prison who was about to be released and who would do a murder contract for Emery. Long-distance telephone records documented twenty-six calls made to Tony Emery's home phone number from the Iowa State Penitentiary in Madison, Iowa. This part of the conspiracy to kill Elkins did not materialize, and Emery took a different approach, deciding to kill her himself. These were the actions of a violent, dangerous man willing to take violent, dangerous steps to save himself from extended prison time.

Tony's uncle in prison wasn't the only person he talked to about killing Elkins. He told fellow criminal associate Randy Crail that Christine Elkins had set him up and that she would be "taken care of." He also told Terry Swalley on numerous occasions that he was going to kill Christine Elkins because she might testify against him in his pending trial for drug trafficking.

Sometime prior to August 4, 1990, Tony Emery told James Witt he was worried about a female witness who was going to testify against Emery in a drug trial. Emery said that he had paid her attorney fees but was afraid she was still going to testify. Emery said he had been granted his last continuance and that he was going to have to kill her to ensure her not testifying.

During the summer, prior to August 4, 1990, Tony Emery told Kenny Poppa that he was either going to kill Christine Elkins or pay her money to go away.

Over the years each one of these criminal associates, all involved in Emery's meth trafficking network, would get in trouble themselves and provide statements to law enforcement officials of their knowledge of the Tony Emery murder plot.

During the month of July, Christine Elkins's telephone service was disconnected for nonpayment, and for a two-week period, she moved in with Roger Jackson and used his telephone to make and receive phone calls.

During mid-July 1990, Tony Emery asked his cousin Herb to purchase some "cut" used to dilute the meth, thereby creating a bigger profit when sold. Herb talked to Bobby Miller, who acquired the "cut" from a head shop that sold a product for $99 a pound. Herb and Miller purchased three pounds, with money supplied by Tony. Tony also instructed Herb to bring back a gram of pure methamphetamine that Tony had intended to use to kill a female witness that was going to testify against him in a drug trial. Tony told Herb that a drug associate in Maryville, Ron Coy, would give it to her to cause a lethal overdose. Herb acquired the pure meth from James Witt and drove the items to Maryville to give to Tony and Ron Coy.

Tony directed Herb and Ron Coy to take the pure meth to Christine Elkins's house and give it to her. Elkins was not at home; they returned to Tony's, telling him they could not find her. Much like Tony's efforts to hire a hit man to kill Elkins, this effort met with negative results. After this failed attempt, Herb Emery reported to Tony that Ron Coy became extremely nervous, and the two of them agreed they would not use Coy in the next attempt to kill Elkins.

On July 23, 1990, Christine Elkins met with ATF Agent Mark James for the purpose of assisting law enforcement regarding the federal firearms violations in furtherance of the narcotics trafficking committed by Tony Emery and his criminal associates. If proven guilty, the prison terms for those convicted would be enhanced by a considerable number of years in federal prison. During this meeting, Elkins told Agent James she was not receiving any money from Emery for her mounting attorney bills, and he was baiting her with promises of a big payoff for her to leave the area.

A few days later on July 26, under the direction of Agent James, Christine Elkins attempted to engage Tony Emery in incriminating conversation while she was equipped with a recording device. Unfortunately, during the meeting, Emery noticed the undercover vehicle of Trooper Al Riney pass the area. Emery became suspicious of Elkins. He took her to an abandoned residence he owned at 1502 Edwards Street in Maryville and forcibly attempted to search her to determine if she was wearing a wire. His efforts were unsuccessful.

Shortly after this meeting with Emery, Elkins met with Trooper Riney and ATF Agent James and told them what had occurred. Elkins was visibly terrified and so upset she tried to strike Trooper Riney. Elkins said Emery had told her once again he would kill her if she tried to "set him up."

On July 31, 1990, in furtherance of his plan to kill her, Tony Emery met with Elkins and asked her if she was ready to leave the Maryville area for good. Emery told her he was gathering a quantity of meth and $3,000 to $4,000 to give her in order for her to disappear. Also, on July 31, Tony Emery placed three phone calls to Roger Jackson's residence, and about this same date, Emery was seen talking to Elkins at the Bearcat Lounge. Elkins told a coworker she was terrified because of threats she had received.

On one occasion before August 4, 1990, Mia Clizer was with Tony Emery in Tony's vehicle when Christine Elkins drove up to talk to him. They talked about the upcoming trial, and Clizer watched Tony give Elkins a gram of meth. After Elkins drove away, Tony told Clizer that Elkins was blackmailing him for meth and money for her attorney fees, in exchange for her not testifying against him. Emery said he was tired of this and was going to do something about it. Clizer, having been beaten by Emery on several occasions, felt Emery meant he was going to kill Elkins.

The Murder of Christine Elkins

On or about August 2, 1990, Tony Emery made a phone call to his cousin Herb Emery, who was out of jail and lived in Colorado, and told him he was having a big problem with Christine Elkins, and he asked Herb to come to Maryville and help him with the problem. Tony said she was coming by his house wanting money and dope in exchange to not testify against him. Tony wanted her killed.

When the weekend came, Herb went to Bobby Miller's house in Colorado to purchase a gram of meth for the trip. Herb invited Miller to go with him to Maryville and help with the driving. He did not tell Miller about the plot to kill Elkins. He had Miller get a blackjack and bring it with him. Herb took a .45 caliber handgun that he put in the trunk of his car.

During this trip, Bobby Miller used his telephone calling card six times and Herb Emery used his calling card one time as they traveled through the state of Nebraska on the way to Maryville. They two men arrived at Tony Emery's house at about 4:30 a.m. on August 3, 1990, and parked Herb's car in the garage so it wouldn't be seen.

Miller slept while Tony and Herb talked about killing Elkins. They discussed the idea of asking Miller to join in on the murder plot. When Miller woke, Tony talked to him, and Miller agreed to assist in the murder plan. Miller even came up with suggestions on how to dispose of Elkins's body.

One idea was to put her body in a barrel and take it to Colorado to dispose of it in a mine shaft. Another idea was to dump her body in the Missouri River with holes in the barrel. Tony said he could have a person named Dana Clizer direct them to a boat dock on the river. Herb volunteered to hit her in the head and kill her with Miller's blackjack.

Tony provided $800 for Herb and Miller to rent a truck and purchase a quantity of concrete to use in the disposal of their victim. The two men drove to St. Joseph, Missouri, and rented a vehicle then went to a hardware store and purchased about thirteen sixty-pound bags of Sakrete concrete.

Sometime during the late afternoon of August 4, 1990, an unsuspecting Christine Elkins telephoned Tony Emery and the two, per Emery's plan, discussed Emery giving her drugs later that night. Tony told Elkins to meet him at an empty residence at 1502 Edwards Street (which is within yards of the city park), using the guise that he was going to give her several thousand dollars and a quantity of methamphetamine in exchange for her leaving the area. Tony Emery's plan was taking shape.

Sometime just after dark on August 4, 1990, Tony and Herb Emery stole a barrel from property neighboring Tony Emery's property to the east and loaded it onto the Hertz-Penske rental truck for use in the disposal of Christine Elkins's body.

Now with everything in place, Tony and Herb Emery entered the abandoned residence at 1502 Edwards Street, awaiting the arrival of Elkins. Bobby Miller was waiting outside the house in the rental truck, hidden near the rear door of the house.

Around 9:50 p.m., before going to meet Emery, Elkins went to the residence of Jerry Moser in Maryville and made a local phone call. Moser overheard Elkins say something about meeting near the park. Elkins asked Moser to babysit her son, Steven. Elkins told Moser that she was going to get some money from someone and that, if she was not back in ten minutes, he would find her in the morgue. Moser never saw Elkins again.

At approximately 10:00 p.m., Bobby Miller observed a woman matching the description of Christine Elkins arrive at 1502 Edwards Street. Miller watched as the woman entered the darkened residence through an open back door and was heard screaming, "Stop! Stop! Stop hitting me! Why are you doing this to me? Stop!" The screaming lasted approximately one minute.

Once Elkins entered the residence, she was attacked by Tony and Herb Emery, who first struck her with a blackjack in an attempt to render her unconscious. They then continued to beat her until they finally knocked her down a flight of stairs, where she laid semiconscious. The two men noticed her moving and realized she was still alive.

Following the attack, Herb Emery exited the murder scene and told Bobby Miller that there had been a change of plans. Herb Emery instructed Miller to go to Tony Emery's residence and wait for them there. Miller left the scene in the rental truck, turning the wrong direction. Within a few blocks, he encountered a Maryville Police Department patrol car and panicked. Becoming disoriented, he drove north out of Maryville to Burlington Junction, Missouri.

At 11:16 p.m., Bobby Miller placed a call to the residence of James Witt in Fort Collins, Colorado. Miller was attempting to get the phone number of Tony Emery; however, Witt was not at home. Miller returned to Maryville. At 11:43 p.m., Miller called James Witt again by telephone and was successful in contacting him. Miller was extremely agitated and told Witt that the Emerys had committed the murder they had been talking about. Miller said he got scared and fled from the scene. Miller asked Witt for Tony Emery's telephone number, so he could call Emery and tell him he was going back to Colorado.

As Miller made his way back to Colorado, he made two calls to Tony Emery's home. He was unsuccessful and left a message on his answering machine. He just wanted to get away, wondering why he had ever got involved. Herb Emery also left Maryville without finishing the job and headed back to Colorado.

The Cover-Up and Admissions

On August 5, 1990, Tony Emery contacted James Witt, telling him he had killed the female informant. Following the Harley Davidson Motorcycle rally in Sturgis, South Dakota, on or about the week of August 6, 1990, Herb Emery and Bobby Miller confessed to James Witt their involvement with Tony Emery in the murder of Christine Elkins.

Around the same time, James Witt, Herb Emery, and Dean Smith were at the residence of Bobby Miller in Greeley, Colorado. Smith walked in on a conversation between Witt and Emery, who were talking and laughing about Emery having killed a woman who was going to be a witness against his cousin. In the presence of Herb Emery, Witt then elaborated to Smith how Emery had struck this woman over the head numerous times with a "monkey wrench." Emery enthusiastically admitted to Smith that James Witt's allegations were true. Later conversation between Witt, Emery, and Smith revealed that Emery had driven to the state of Missouri to commit this homicide and that the victim was going to be a witness in a drug trial against Emery's cousin. Smith knew Emery's cousin to head a drug trafficking enterprise in the state of Missouri for which he had supplied methamphetamine.

Shortly after August 4, 1990, a complete remodeling of the interior of the 1502 East Edwards Street residence was initiated by Tony Emery. All the floor tiles from the basement floor were removed, and a sealant was placed on the existing concrete floor. Additionally, all the interior walls were freshly painted. Much of the interior work was performed by Roger Jackson, who was paid cash by Tony Emery.

In August 1990, a warrant for the arrest of Christine Elkins for failure to appear for trial was issued and entered into the National Crime Information Center. Additionally, Christine Elkins's vehicle description, including VIN and license plates, was also entered.

In August 1990, Christine Elkins's normal routine of writing or telephoning her mother on a frequent basis abruptly ended with no explanation, which had never happened throughout her entire adult life.

In late August 1990, Lacretia Allen had occasion to view the inside of Christine Elkins's residence (a rental property owned by Allen's father). The residence was left in a condition indicative that the occupant intended to return. Laundry was still hanging on the clothesline. Coffee was in the coffee pot. No clothes appeared to be missing.

The most revealing aspect of her sudden disappearance was that she had left two children she loved behind with no explanation.

On September 8, 1990, an inmate in the Iowa State Penitentiary in Fort Madison, Iowa, named Larry Michael Smith, wrote a letter to his mother stating that he had talked to Tony (Emery) on September 7, 1990. Smith wrote that Tony had told Smith that a state's witness against Tony named Chris had disappeared. As a result, Tony's trial date had been postponed. Smith further wrote that Tony said the police were upset about not having much of a case against him.

Not too long after the murder of Christine Elkins, Tony Emery told Terry Swalley in reference to Christine Elkins that "he had taken care of the problem." Also, after the murder of Elkins, while supplying James Ketcham with methamphetamine, Tony Emery warned Ketcham not to talk to anyone about their drug dealings by telling him that "a girl in town [was] doing some talking. She was warned, now she's come up missing."

On December 18, 1990, James Witt has a consensually monitored/recorded meeting with Herb Emery, who reiterated events concerning the murder of Christine Elkins. (Emery had previously told Witt that they had knocked her down a flight of stairs by beating her over the head.) Emery stated that they had first hit her with a "blackjack" and then a lead pipe or metal case flashlight. He said there was a lot of blood but that they got rid of her and her car. Emery described the rock quarry that they had used to dispose of Elkins and her vehicle. Witt asked Emery if he had recently gone back to the quarry to make sure Elkins's body wasn't floating. Emery stated he had not but was sure it wouldn't because of the depth of the water that the vehicle was submerged in. Emery reaffirmed that Bobby Miller was to have transported Elkins's body to Colorado in a rental truck for disposal but that he "freaked" when the assault on Elkin began. Witt asked Emery if they were concerned about Miller talking. Emery said no because "Miller had been warned". Emery further indicated that he was mad at Miller because he had been given an ounce of methamphetamine for his assistance in the murder.

On December 28, 1990, while conducting a transaction for five pounds of methamphetamine, Herb and Tony Emery made incriminating admissions alluding to the murder of Christine Elkins that were audio- and video-recorded. James Witt, in an undercover capacity for law enforcement, talked about his need for a government witness against him to be killed. Tony Emery offered to kill this witness and stated, "That's the way the fucking bitch did me." Tony talked about on one occasion "shaking down" the woman he was referring to. Emery further stated, "We'll take care of your dirty laundry. . . . We can do something. . . . He's not worth twenty years. . . ." Later in the conversation with Witt after having been alone with Tony, Herb Emery stated, "Tony said he'll take care of that fucking guy."

In December 1990, this drug transaction was actually a sting operation conducted by federal investigators, the DPS of Maryville, the Missouri Highway Patrol, ATF, and DEA regarding the trafficking of meth by the Tony Emery drug organization. They also hoped to get admission about the murder of Elkins.

Proving the Murder

Shortly after this transaction was executed, the task force arrested Tony Emery, Herb Emery, and Ron Coy, who were all-in on this illegal drug transaction. In a press release to the media authorities, the task force authorities announced other arrests were possible, and the investigation would continue. With the three drug ring leaders in custody, the authorities hoped their arrests would break up the growing distribution and drug trafficking enterprise and hopefully solve a murder.

On December 29, 1990, a .45 caliber pistol was recovered from Bobby Miller, who admitted to having received it from Herb Emery. Miller also admitted to having rented the Hertz-Penske rental truck in St. Joseph, Missouri and to having been in Maryville on the weekend of August 4, 1990.

In early 1991, following the arrests of Tony Emery, Herb Emery, and Ron Coy on December 28, 1990, all were imprisoned at the same facility with Dean Smith. Smith overheard a conversation between the three in which Herb Emery stated something to the effect of "they'll never find her body." Ron Coy immediately chastised Herb to not talk about it anymore. Later, while sharing a cell with Herb Emery, Herb told Smith that he meant they would "never find her body" because "she" wasn't dead. Emery elaborated that the female witness was just hiding out. The method by which Herb Emery brought the topic up led Smith to suspect that Emery was trying to make exculpatory statements to make up for the admissions he had made earlier.

During the summer of 1991, Tony Emery's sister, Karen Allen, told Teresa Poppa that Tony had "done away" with Christine Elkins and that "the bitch got what she deserved for snitching her brother off." On April 16, 1993, Larry Michael Smith told ATF Special Agent Michael Schmidt and Maryville Department of Public Safety Sergeant Randy Strong that he had served time with Tony Emery's uncle, Earl Emery, in the Iowa State Penitentiary. Smith said that he had corresponded with Tony Emery by telephone and by mail during his incarceration. Tony Emery told Smith that a witness against Emery named Christy was talking to the police.

On August 1, 1995 Robert "Bobby" Miller, the drug dealer from Greeley, Colorado, provided a confession regarding the part he played in the alleged murder of Christine Elkins. The investigators taking his statement were Randy Strong from the Maryville Department of Public Safety and ATF Agents Mark James and Mike Schmidt. They were eager to hear what he had to say. Miller didn't disappoint them. Miller provided a detailed account of his criminal relationship with Herb Emery.

On August 2, 1995, officers of the Greeley Police Department found and photographed a rusted white barrel at the former residence of Bobby Miller in Greeley Colorado.

Over a period of time, Herb Emery had told Miller about the criminal activities conducted by his cousin Tony Emery, which included drug trafficking and insurance fraud, involving a truck he had blown up in an insurance fraud scam. In the summer of 1990, he had helped Herb Emery acquire twenty-five pounds of a drug-cutting product in Denver, and the two had transported the product to Missouri.

Miller provided his account of how the murder went down, including hearing the victim yelling "Stop! Stop! Stop, Stop hitting me. Why are you doing this to me?" He said the screaming only lasted about one minute, then it was quiet. He detailed their plans to kill her and the continuing cover-up. As payment, he said he had received an ounce of meth and a .45 caliber semi-automatic pistol.

ATF Agent Mark James prepared and filed his report. Both Agent James and Schmitz realized the importance of this information as they continued to build their case against Tony and Herb Emery.

On November 20, 1996, after six years of investigation by ATF, the Missouri State Highway Patrol Drug Unit, and the Maryville Department of Public Safety, a federal grand jury in Kansas City, the Western Judicial District of Missouri, indicted a suspect charged with the murder of Christine Elkins. The man indicted for the 1990 murder was Herbert J. "Tug" Emery, forty-two, of Kelsey, Colorado. The indictment charged "Tug" Emery with one count of murder in relation to major drug trafficking and one count of murder with intent to prevent communication of information to a federal law enforcement officer. Both counts were related to the alleged murder of Elkins, who had served as an informant for state and federal law enforcement in the Tony Emery drug-related investigation.

In a press conference held in the Maryville City Hall, United States Attorney Steve Hill told the public, "Elkins' body has not yet been found, despite extensive investigation but in light of the evidence developed by our joint investigation, the grand jury today formally alleges that there is probable cause to believe that Herbert J. Emery was directly involved in her murder on August 4, 1990."

The indictment alleged Emery "intentionally killed or counseled, commanded, induced, procured and caused the intentional killing of Elkins," while he was engaged in a conspiracy to traffic in one kilogram or more of methamphetamine. Count two of the indictment alleged Emery "did knowingly and intentionally kill and cause [Elkins] to be killed" to prevent her from communicating information to a federal law enforcement officer concerning methamphetamine trafficking.

US Attorney Hill concluded with a stern message to the other coconspirators involved in Christine Elkins's murder: "The indictment today is what we hope to be the first public step toward bringing a resolution to this matter."

On June 17, 1997, Herbert J. "Tug" Emery pled guilty in federal court to the murder of Christine Elkins, in the presence of his attorney and a public defender's office investigator. In a press release subsequent to Emery's guilty plea United States Attorney Steve Hill said:

The search continued for Elkins' body and that additional people could be charged. Investigators at the federal, state and local levels of law enforcement have worked hard in cooperation for almost seven years to bring this matter to a conclusion, and we have no intention of turning away from a task undone.

After entering his guilty plea, Herb Emery provided a lengthy ten-page confession to ATF Agent Michael Schmidt and Investigator Randy Strong of the Maryville DPS. He also provided substantial information about Tony Emery's illegal criminal acts, including Tony's involvement in the murder of Christine Elkins.

Emery also implicated Ron Coy and Robert "Bobby" Miller as directly involved in the murder of Christine Elkins and offered his speculation that a person named Dana Clizer directed Tony and Coy to a boat ramp on the Missouri River where the victim's vehicle and body were submerged in the river. Coy had told Herb Emery that Dana was there when the car was sunk. He felt Tony had given a vehicle to Clizer in return for showing him where to dump the car in the Missouri River.

Tug also told the investigators that Tony's mother, Betty Emery, had knowledge that Tony and Coy did the murder of Christine Elkins. A very convincing and thorough confession was provided by Herb "Tug" Emery, as well as his commitment to testify, in return for serving no more than twenty years in federal prison in a formal plea agreement with the United States Attorney's Office.

On July 27–28, 1997, a small army of law enforcement officers led by Agent Schmitz and Deputy Strong, supported by professionals from the Missouri Water Patrol, US Coast Guard, Army Corps of Engineers, Missouri Department of Conservation, Missouri National Guard, the Naval Investigative Service, and Necrosearch International magnetic survey experts descended on the shores of the Missouri River adjacent to the Nodaway Island boat ramp.

The search team focused on this location after receiving information from coconspirators Tug Emery and Robert Miller, and cooperating witness Dana Clizer, who identified this spot as the place where the victim Christine Elkins's body and her vehicle could be found. It was a long shot, given the strong currents of the river could carry a vehicle down the river all the way to St. Louis. However, it was a long shot that all agreed must be taken to bring these leads to a successful conclusion—finding the missing murder victim, Christine Elkins.

The first step in the search process was conducting a magnetic survey of this area of the river, conducted by Necrosearch International. The survey detected numerous major objects in the waters, and they hoped one of them was the vehicle they hoped to locate. The hits on the objects were numbered, markers were placed in the water, and they examined them under water in numerical order.

After two days of searching the riverbed at Nodaway Island area in Andrew County, Missouri, at 12:51 p.m., a diver surfaced with a license plate in his hand that he held up for those on the shore to read. The plate read Missouri plate number B6E652—it belonged to the vehicle of Christine Elkins. The diver exclaimed he had just removed the plate from a 1980 Oldsmobile Cutlass, the same model Elkins owned. Soon the tedious task of removing the vehicle began.

Once the trunk of the vehicle was secured to avoid accidentally opening, the vehicle was pulled out of the river to the shore. The group of investigators and drivers watched anxiously. The trunk was opened, revealing the remains of a body and female clothing. In unison they all cheered loudly.

On July 29, the body was examined in Kansas City at the Jackson County Medical Center, resulting in a positive identification of murder victim Christine Elkins. A close examination of the skull revealed a large hole fracture the size of a soup can, caused by a heavy metal object. The Jackson County medical examiner ruled this was the cause of death. Her death was ruled a homicide. The long years of tedious efforts from so many were now paying off. They now had a body. Sergeant Randy Strong, who was involved in the long investigation since its inception, said aloud, "Tony Emery is going to pay for this."

Final Justice

On Tuesday, September 31, 1997, a federal grand jury in Kansas City handed down a one-count federal indictment, charging Tony E. Emery with murder in the beating death of Christine Elkins. The indictment alleged that Emery "maliciously, and with premeditation, killed Ms. Elkins, the mother of two sons, by beating her to death."

At the time of this indictment, Tony Emery was in custody at the federal medical center in Springfield for his 1991 federal drug conviction and wasn't going to be able to elude the task force anymore.

Agent Schmidt and Randy Strong paid a visit to Tony Emery in Springfield to tell him they weren't there to talk to him. Agent Schmidt got in Emery's face and simply said, "You're next to be tried for the murder of Christine Elkins. You better get an attorney."

With the recovery of Christine's vehicle and body found in the Missouri River on July 28 and the guilty plea and confession of Herb Emery, the case was now focused on Tony Emery.

The statements of Herb Emery, Robert Miller, James Witt, and Dana Clizer had led the task force of agents and officers to the location of Elkins's vehicle; law enforcement officials, who for seven years had combined resources and searched a 200 square-mile area around Maryville for her body, were feeling pretty confident this case was coming to a successful resolution. The drug lord of Northwest Missouri was going down, and his drug distribution empire would be successfully dismantled.

The Trial

On July 7, 1998, just short of one year after the victim Christine Elkins's body remains were recovered from the Missouri River, the federal murder trial of Tony Emery began with opening arguments. The government's evidence at the trial consisted of numerous telephone records documenting the contacts between the coconspirators and the victim Christine Elkins; the firearms belonging to Tony Emery that were recovered by law enforcement; the testimony of witnesses at the trial documenting their involvement with the criminal acts of Tony Emery; and the physical evidence, especially the recovered vehicle pulled from the Missouri River that had contained the body of Christine Elkins.

This physical evidence, combined with the testimony of "Tug" Emery, Bobby Miller, and James Witt was so precisely presented it was easy for the jury to reach a proper conclusion—a guilty verdict in only two hours of deliberation. Emery was sentenced to life in federal prison with no eligibility for parole.

On July 30, 1999, the United States Court of Appeals for the Eighth Circuit affirmed the judgment of the trial court and denied Tony Emery's appeal, affirming his sentence of life in prison with no chance of ever being paroled.

This senseless murder of a woman hooked on drugs, involved in a major meth distribution ring in Northwest Missouri, and killed for trying to assist law enforcement gained national media attention. The *Kansas City Star* newspaper ran a ten-part serial article by reporter Matthew Schofield between November 4 and 23, 1999, entitled "Justice—The Christine Elkins Story."

Crime writer Steve Jackson published a book, *No Stone Unturned: The True Story of the World's Premier Forensic Investigators*, that devoted one chapter to the Christine Elkins case, which highlighted the work of Randy Strong, Mike Schmitz, and Mark James.

As of December 31, 2020, the final day of a very interesting year, Tony Emery is still serving out his prison sentence for the murder of Christine Elkins.

BIBLIOGRAPHY

Books:

Anslinger, Harry and Will Oursler. *The Murderers: The Shocking Story of the Narcotic Gangs.* New York, NY: Farrar, Straus and Cudahy, 1961.

ATF Book Committee: US Department of Justice Bureau of Alcohol Tobacco Firearms and Explosives. *Protecting the Public Serving Our Nation.* Morley, MO: Acclaim Press, 2017.

Auble, John. *A History of St. Louis Gangsters.* St. Louis, MO: The National Criminal Research Society, 2000.

Bakos, Susan Crain. *Appointment for Murder.* New York, NY: Pinnacle Books, Winsor Publishing Corp., 1989.

Barrett, Paul W. and Mary H. Barrett. *Young Brothers Massacre.* Columbia, MO: University of Missouri Press, 1991.

Betz, N. T. *The Fleagle Gang: Betrayed by a Fingerprint.* Bloomington, IN: Author House, 2005.

Brill, Steven. *The Teamsters.* New York, NY: Simon and Schuster, 1978.

Brown, Cecil. *Stagolee Shot Billy.* Cambridge, MA: Harvard University Press, 2003.

Bruns, Roger A. *The Bandit King: From Jesse James to Pretty Boy Floyd.* New York, NY: Crown Publishers, Inc., 1995.

Burrough, Bryan. *Public Enemies: America's Greatest Crime Wave and the Birth of the F.B.I., 1933–34.* New York, NY: The Penguin Press, 2004.

Cantalupo, Joseph and Thomas C. Renner. *Body Mike: An Unsparing Expose by the Mafia Insider Who Turned on the Mob.* New York, NY: Villard Books, 1990.

Cooper, Courtney Ryley. *Ten Thousand Public Enemies.* Boston, MA: Little Brown and Company, 1935.

Denton, Sally and Roger Morris. *The Money and the Power: The Making of Las Vegas and Its Hold on America, 1947–2000.* New York, NY: Vintage Books, a Division of Random House, Inc., 2002.

Edge, L.L. *Run the Cat Roads: A True Story of Bank Robbers in the 30's.* New York, NY: Red Dembner Enterprise Corp., 1981.

Farrell, Ronald A. and Carole Case. *The Black Book and the Mob: The Untold Story of the Control of Nevada's Casinos.* Madison, WI: University of Wisconsin Press, 1995.

Fischer, Steve. *When the Mob Ran Vegas: Stories of Money, Mayhem and Murder.* New York, NY: MJF Books Fire Communications, 2005.

Gentry, Curt. *J. Edgar Hoover: The Man and the Secrets.* New York, NY: W.W. Norton and Company, 1991.

Hayde, Frank R. *The Mafia and the Machine: The Story of the Kansas City Mob.* Fort Lee, NJ: Barricade Books, Inc., 2007.

Helmer, William J. and Arthur J. Bilek. *The St. Valentine's Day Massacre: The Untold Story of the Gangland Bloodbath That Brought Down Al Capone.* Nashville, TN: Cumberland House, 2004.

Helmer, William J. and Rick Mattix. *The Complete Public Enemy Almanac: New Facts and Features on the People, Places, and Events of the Gangster and Outlaw Era, 1920-1940.* Nashville, TN: Cumberland House, 2007.

Jackson, Steve. *No Stone Unturned: The True Story of the World's Premier Forensic Investigators.* New York, NY: Pinnacle Books, Kensington Publishing Corp., 2002.

Lhotka, Bill. *St. Louis Crime Chronicles: The First 200 Years, 1764-1964.* St. Louis, MO: Reedy Press, 2009.

Life magazine. *Mobsters and Gangsters: Organized Crime in America From Al Capone to Tony Soprano.* Life Books.

Martin, Ronald. *Murder at Pope's Cafeteria.* Lulu Publishing Services, 2018.

Missouri Sheriff's Association. *Preserving the Past, Protecting the Future: A History of Missouri Sheriffs.* Jefferson City, MO: Missouri Sheriff's Association, 2014.

Milner, E. R. *The Lives and Times of Bonnie & Clyde.* Carbondale, IL: Southern Illinois University Press, 1996.

Moore, James. *Very Special Agents: The Inside Story of America's Most Controversial Law Enforcement Agency—The Bureau of Alcohol, Tobacco & Firearms.* New York, NY: Simon and Schuster, Inc. Pocketbooks Division, 1997.

Nelson, Derek. *Moonshiners, Bootleggers and Rumrunners.* Osceola, WI: Motorbooks International Publishers and Wholesalers, 1995.

Ness, Eliot and Oscar Fraley. *The Untouchables. The Real Story: The Gripping Expose of Chicago's Vicious Mob Empire by the Man Who Smashed It Apart.* New York, NY: Pocketbooks, 1957.

Newton, Michael. *Gangsters Outside the Law (True Crimes).* Sywell Northampton, United Kingdom: Igloo Books, 2010.

O'Malley, Terence Michael. *Black Hand/Strawman: The History of Organized Crime in Kansas City.* Copyright by O'Malley, 2011.

O'Neil, Tim. *Mobs, Mayhem & Murder: Tales from the St. Louis Police Beat.* St. Louis Post-Dispatch Book, 2008.

Ouseley, William. *Open City: True Story of the KC Crime Family, 1900-1950.* Copyright by Bill Ouseley, 2008.

---. *Mobsters in our Midst: The Kansas City Crime Family.* Kansas City, MO: Kansas City Star Books, 2011.

Pensoneau, Taylor. *Brothers Notorious: The Sheltons: Southern Illinois' Legendary Gangsters.* New Berlin, IL: Downstate Publications, 2002.

Perry, Douglas. *Eliot Ness: The Rise and Fall of an American Hero.* New York, NY: Viking Press, Penguin Group, 2004.

Pileggi, Nicholas. *Casino: Love and Honor in Las Vegas.* New York, NY: Simon and Schuster, 1995.

Roemer, William, Jr. *War of the Godfathers: The Bloody Confrontation Between the Chicago and New York Families for Control of Las Vegas.* New York, NY: Donald L. Fine, Inc., 1990.

---. *The Enforcer: Spilotro: The Chicago Mob's Man Over Las Vegas.* New York, NY: Donald L. Fine, Inc., 1994.

Schreiber, Mark S. *Shanks to Shaker: Reflections of the Missouri State Penitentiary.* Copyright by Mark S. Schreiber and Jefferson City Convention and Visitors Bureau, Jefferson City, MO, 2011.

Schoenberg, Robert L. *Mr. Capone: The Real—and Complete—Story of Al Capone.* New York, NY: William Morrow, 1992.

Smith, Brad. *Lawman to Outlaw: Verne Miller and the Kansas City Massacre.* Bedford, IN: Jona Books, 2002.

Southwell, David. *The History of Organized Crime: The True Story and Secrets of Global Gangland.* London, England: Carlton Books, Limited, 2012.

Steele, Phillip W. and Marie Barrow Scoma. *The Family Story of Bonnie and Clyde.* Gretna, LA: Pelican Publishing Company, 2000.

Unger, Robert. *The Union Station Massacre: The Original Sin of J. Edgar Hoover's FBI.* Kansas City, MO: Andrews McMeel Publishing, 1997.

Waugh, Daniel. *Egan's Rats: The Untold Story of the Prohibition-Era Gang That Ruled St. Louis.* Nashville, TN: Cumberland House, 2007.

---. *The Gangs of St. Louis: Men of Respect.* Charleston, SC: The History Press, 2012.

Newspapers:
Arkansas (AR) Gazette
Arkansas (AR) Baxter Bulletin
Arkansas (AR) Democrat
Burlington (IA) Hawkeye
Blue Springs (MO) Examiner
Columbus (OH) Dispatch
Denver (CO) Post
Houston (TX) Chronicle
Houston (TX) Chronicle News Services
Joplin (MO) Globe
Kansas City (MO) Star
Kansas City (MO) Times
Las Vegas (NV) Sun
Los Angeles (CA) Times
Maryville (MO) Daily Forum
New York (NY) Daily Tribune

New York (NY) Times
Nodaway (MO) County News Leader
Omaha (NE) Herald
San Diego (CA) Union
Southwest Times (AR) Record
Springfield (MO) News-Leader & Press
Springfield (MO) Daily News
St. Joseph (MO) News-Press
St. Louis (MO) Post-Dispatch
St. Louis (MO) Globe-Democrat
St. Petersburg (FL) Times
Tampa (FL) Tribune
Twin Lakes (AR) Citizen
USA Today
PAPERS AND PUBLICATIONS:
All Theft Acts (ATF)
Americanmafia.com
Biography.com document files
Block Parole, Inc. (OH)
Boston University Libraries
College of the Ozarks (MO) Ralph Foster Museum documents
Court TV Crime Library
Encyclopedia of Arkansas
FBI official files
Fortune magazine
Gangsterreport.com
House Assassination Committee Report, 1978
Kansas City Missouri Crime Commission files
Kansas City Missouri Police Department files
Labor Department memo
Legendsofamerrica.com library digest
Life magazine. 1967, 1970
Livejournal.com
Mattie Howard journal
McKinley High School Goldbug
Missouri Department of Correction files
Missouri Historical Society Documents. St. Louis (MO) criminal court
    documents
Missouri State Archive files, Jefferson City, Missouri
Missouri State Highway Patrol files, Jefferson City, Missouri
National Integrated Ballistic Information Network, ATF
The New Yorker magazine
Newsweek
Playboy magazine
South Dakota State Historical Society documents

Springfield Missouri Public Library files
St. Louis (MO) Metropolitan Police Department files
St. Louis (MO) Metropolitan Police Department Fraternal Order of Police,
    the Gendarme Publication
St. Louis Missouri Public Library documents
Stlouistoday.com archives
St. Louis University archives
Webster's dictionary
Westinghouse Corporation's National Issues Center
Wikipedia
Young Brothers Massacre booklet

TERMS, NICKNAMES, AND PHRASES
QUOTES, DESCRIPTIONS, AND PLACES
1900-1999

This chapter of the book originated as an afterthought, but in reality, it has been one of the most enjoyable and interesting areas of my research.

As I read through books I have obtained over the years, I noticed several authors included a section on terms, nicknames, quotes, and descriptions of people and places. So, I set out to see how many I could find related to Missouri gangsters and have included them here.

I was surprised to learn how many different terms were available for me to provide explanations and answers for the reader—so much that what I initially envisioned as a section turned out to be an entire chapter.

PLACES ASSOCIATED WITH MISSOURI

The Annex—A special section in the federal penitentiary at Leavenworth, Kansas, just outside of Kansas City where the most dangerous and degenerate prisoners were held.

Bad Lands—An area in St. Louis at the turn of the twentieth century located at Nineteenth and Chestnut, so named by locals due to its high crime rate and large numbers of saloons, brothels, and rickety tenements.

The Big Muddy—A term used to describe the Missouri River winding its way through Missouri from Kansas City to St. Louis and beyond.

The Bloody First—Kansas City's first ward, where Boss Pendergast ruled his political machine.

The Bloody Third—The Third Police District in St. Louis, where many of the gangs of St. Louis fought with the police and each other in the early 1900s.

Cow Town—The East Coast's simple-minded image of Kansas City, Missouri. Cow towns were generally viewed as small, isolated, or unsophisticated areas.

The Crime Corridor—An area of the United States spreading north from Texas to Minnesota, including the states of Oklahoma, Illinois, Kansas, Iowa, and Missouri, which is squarely in the center of the corridor.

Dago Hill—A second Italian neighborhood was located on a large hill in the southwest area of St. Louis bound by Hampton Avenue on the west, Kings Highway on the east, Manchester Avenue on the north, and Arsenal Street on the south, identified by its residents simply as the "Hill." Non-Italians referred to the area as "Dago Hill."

The Goldfish Bowl—A notorious soundproof room used for vigorous police interrogations at police headquarters located at Twelfth and Clark in St. Louis.

Kerry Patch—A neighborhood located near Downtown St. Louis where the Edwards Jones Dome is now located, so named due to the large number of Irish immigrants who migrated there or gave birth to future Irish American hoodlums and gang members in the early 1900s.

Little Egypt—A term describing the Southern Illinois area near St. Louis, Missouri.

Little Italy (of Kansas City)—A proud Italian neighborhood in Kansas City in the early 1900s walled in by the produce market square on the west, the Missouri River to the north, a housing project on the east, and old town to the south, was home to 12,000 crowded Italians, 85 percent of whom were of Sicilian extraction, in the early twentieth century.

Little Italy (of St. Louis)—A Downtown Italian colony adjacent to the Kerry Patch neighborhood surrounded by Washington Avenue on the south, Cass Avenue in the north, the Mississippi River on the east, and Fourteenth Street on the west.

The Max Welton Club and Racetrack—Located at the southwest corner of St. Charles Rock Road and Pennsylvania Avenue in St. Louis County, where the Egan's Rats hung out and practiced drive-by shooting skills in the early 1900s.

Paris of the Plains—A writer's impression of Kansas City in the 1930s, describing the city as the jazz capital of the world.

The River Quay (pronounced key)—"An arts and entertainment district developed in the 1970s at the original Kansas City town site of nineteenth century buildings just west of the produce market filled with shops, residential lofts, and nightclubs."

Running the Cat Roads—Term used by bank robbers in the 1930s describing preferred escape routes throughout the Midwest, including old farm roads, trails, and side streets that were difficult to navigate after dark unless you were a cat! It was a process perfected by bank robber Harvey Bailey.

Scatters—A term describing pool halls and taverns throughout Missouri.

The Sharpshooters Club—The Cuckoo Gang's hangout, located on Mt. Olive Street at Lemay Ferry Road in Lemay, Missouri, in the early 1900s.

The Trap—A building located in the heart of Little Italy at 1048 E. Fifth Street that resembled a storefront owned by Kansas City mob boss Nick Civella and housed the Northview Social Club, informally called The Trap.

Twelfth and Vine Streets—"The historic Blues and Jazz district of Kansas City, dominated by surrounding clubs filled with world class musical entertainers that placed Kansas City as the Jazz capital of the world in the 1930s." A place where "Outfit" business (see definition below under Mafia terms) was handled and high-stakes card games and dice games were routinely held from the 1950s to the 1970s. The phone at The Trap was used by Outfit figures in an interstate gambling enterprise, drawing the interest of federal agents and Kansas City detectives assigned to the Intelligence Division.

On September 29, 1976, a pipe bomb was thrown at The Trap, blowing the back door off its hinges. ATF investigated the crime scene and was this author's first involvement in Kansas City organized crime and warring factions, a series of murders, bombings, arsons, and other crimes carried out well into the 1980s, which will be detailed in another chapter in the book.

Uncle Tom's Cabin—A reference to the state capitol in Jefferson, when associating the capitol to Kansas City Machine Boss Tom Pendergast and the political power he possessed throughout Missouri.

The Valley—A raunchy entertainment district in East St. Louis, Illinois, frequented by St. Louisans that self-destructed during the early 1910s.

West Bottoms—An area in Downtown Kansas City in the late nineteenth century that boasted a dynamic mix of heavy industry, agriculture, and rollicking nightlife.

Wettest Block in the World—An area in Kansas City in the early 1900s on Ninth Street named because twenty-three of the twenty-four buildings housed saloons.

TERMS DESCRIBING PEOPLE OR GROUPS

American Boys— phrase Chicago boss Al Capone used when referring to his secret crew consisting primarily of non-Italian gangsters from the battlefields of St. Louis, Missouri.

Boomer—A transient who worked as a handyman on the Midwest oil fields.

Booster—Slang for a shoplifter.

Briefcase Cops—A term local police used when referring to FBI agents, who they didn't consider as real cops.

Flapper—A young woman, especially one of the 1920s, who showed disdain for conventional dress and behavior (Webster's II New Riverside University Dictionary definition). Missouri had its share.

Gangster Moll—A gangster's girlfriend (dictionary definition). Missouri molls included female partners, relatives, and paramours.

Gangsters—People who operate in gangs (Webster's II New Riverside University Dictionary definition). The gangs of Missouri in the early 1900s primarily originated in the St. Louis areas of the state.

G-Men—A criminal's term when referring to federal government agents over the years.

The Green Ones—A Mafia family in St. Louis so named because much of its Sicilian muscle was fresh off the boats. "They got their start in Little Italy," which was roughly west of today's Edward Jones Dome in Downtown St. Louis. They operated their moonshine stills across the river near Ponton Beach in Madison County, Illinois.

Hostesses—Female hostages placed in getaway cars, coined by bank robber Harvey Bailey.

Johnny—A street slang for a man.

Mac—A popular substitute in the early 1900s for the name of someone who was male.

Mobsters—A member of a criminal group (Webster's II New Riverside University Dictionary definition). For the purpose of this book, the term is used to identify the members of the Mafia and organized criminal gangs primarily operating in the Kansas City and St. Louis areas—including Kansas City, Kansas, and the Southern Illinois area adjacent to St. Louis—who had association with Missouri gangsters and conducted criminal activity in Missouri.

Nixie Fighters—A slang term used to describe one who fights the police. Also, the nickname of a gang in St. Louis.

Outlaws—A habitual or confirmed criminal (Webster's II New Riverside University Dictionary definition). The term gained popularity in the Midwest during the Wild West era of Missourians Jesse James, Cole Younger, and the Dalton gang. During Prohibition and the Great Depression, the term was used to identify the bank and train robbers.

Paramour—A favorite FBI expression during the early 1900s when describing female associates of gangsters.

Puddler—A worker in an iron factory.

Stand-up Guy—According to mob parlance "is a manly acting fella who sticks by his word, doesn't forget where he came from or who his friends are, pays his debts, and doesn't squeal."

Yeggmen/Yeggs—A term used by the press and criminals to identify American bank robbers and safecrackers.

The Wops—A term used by gang member Pete Gusenberg of the "Bugs" Moran gang when he referred to Al Capone and his mostly Italian Mob. Gusenberg was one of the St. Valentine's Day Massacre victims machine-gunned by ex-St. Louis Egan's Rats and Capone's "American Boys" from Missouri.

TERMS ASSOCIATED WITH THE MAFIA

Associates—A broad label applied to a wide range of people. An Italian soldier who hasn't been made or a non-Italian who can't be made, a flunky politician, friendly labor leader, or a crooked cop.

The Black Hand—As detailed by Dan Waugh in *Men of Respect* and Bill Ousley in *Open City,* "An illegal process carried out by the Mafia in the Little Italians of Kansas City and St. Louis in the early 1900s against Italian business owners exporting money from them in return for protection or suffer violent consequences including death for failing to pay. They meant business including forty unsolved murders in Kansas City between 1909 and 1919 alone of business owners and family members who refused to pay protection money." (Ousley)

Borgata—A Sicilian term for a crime grouping.

Capo—The boss of a crime family.

Capo Regime—Italian for Mafia captains who commanded frontline soldiers.

Consigliere—Mafia counselor who keeps his ear to the ground with the soldiers and gives advice to the boss.

The Hit—A more modern-day term to describe a "contract killing." The mob boss authorized these acts of violence according to Outfit rules.

La Mano Nero—An Italian word meaning the Black Hand designation for crimes of extortion in Little Italy communities, first coined in America by newspapers reporting murder and extortion, hoping to avoid the word Mafia, which was considered American in origin.

L'ucchiatura—A Sicilian term for "the evil eye" and a menacing hand sign of death. In June 1911 Antonio Sansone, a youthful St. Louis Sicilian, testified during his murder trial that his victim, Joseph Cammarata, a known member of the Mafia whom he had stabbed to death during an argument, had demonstrated this toward him. During his defense, he demonstrated the sign by placing his thumb and forefinger of the right hand together in a ring and extended the other three fingers toward an intended victim.

The Lug—A tax paid to Kansas City mob boss Charlie Carrollo each month by hundreds of illegal establishments, allowing them corrupt police protection. Sixty percent of the tax was divided between himself and the top syndicate men, then the remaining forty percent went to Boss Pendergast at 1908 Main Street. The massive war chest was presented by the Mob in other rackets and the machine used it to grease palms and purchase holiday turkeys to be handed out.

Made Men—Men who are inducted members of the Mafia.

Mafia—According to Daniel Waugh in *Gangs of St. Louis*, "the word 'mafia'" which came into use in the mid-nineteenth century, was a corruption of the Sicilian adjective mofusu, an ambiguous term that roughly described someone as an arrogant bully, but one that was fearless, proud and enterprising. . . . New members were sworn in with a blood oath and a pledge to never speak of their activities. The organization came before everything, even family. Once a man joined, he never left the organization while still alive. . . . Ironically, these men rarely referred to themselves as the mafia. Most used the term Cosa Nostra ("our thing") and/or L'onorata Societa ("the honored society") when speaking of the organization.

The Mafia Don—Best described by Bill Ousley in *Open City*:
The old-world Mafia Don, belying his true nature, was normally modest in his demeanor, speaking and listening with an air of humility. His true power cloaked, he held himself out as but an ordinary man, yet one who spoke for everyone. He dressed with care, but modestly, was generous, a family man who never considered divorce, cherished respect and honor, and was a patriot, outwardly supportive of the government he inwardly despised. Behind the cloak he was proud, suspicious, sly, conspiratorial and deceptive as only those who have long been conquered but never defeated could be.
To maintain his position the Don had to be seen as a prudent, level headed, cunning leader. Outside the clan he took on the role of authority/father figure, a friend to all, protector, mediator and advisor. He regulated social conflicts, maintained a semblance of order, generally over-seeing matters normally within the purview of the establishment. As a preserver of social

order, he was recognized locally, and by the State itself, as guardian of the people. He granted favors willingly, understanding the more people witnessing his ability to help and get things done the greater his prestige. The Don saw himself as that person every society needs, able to put things right when they were out of kilter.

Mafioso—Applied to the individual rather than an organization.

Mustache Petes—A term used by younger mobsters in Kansas City when describing Sicilian-born fathers of organized crime and Black Hand operators, lacking in English language skills, clannish, and wedded to old-world thinking and protocols.

Omerta—A Sicilian term describing a cultish code of silence that defined very clearly how a "man of respect" must behave. To break it was punishable by death; to be a man meant remaining silent.

Outfit—The Americanized term describing the Mafia in St. Louis and Kansas City in later years.

Peckerwoods—Mafia family term for White Anglo-Saxon Persons (WASPs) who carried out criminal activities for the Mafia. Arthur Eugene Sheppard was a peckerwood hired to carry out bombings for the Kansas City Mob.

Sandwiches—A term used to describe how skim money from Las Vegas casinos was brought back to Kansas City in $40,000 cash bundles secured with rubber bands and hidden in the carrier's jacket with specially made pockets to avoid detection. Upon arrival, the money was divided up among mob bosses. Carl "The Singer" Caruso was the usual carrier of the sandwiches, a process that was carried out for several years in the late 1970s to February 1980, when the scam was broken up by federal authorities, Kansas City detectives, and the Federal Organized Crime Task Force.

Spot Killings—An early 1900s term describing gangland killings.

The Sugarhouse Syndicate—Formed by Joe Filardo, a Kansas City mobster, circa 1928, with other prominent members of the North End criminal element, to corner the black market in the ingredients used to make illicit alcohol.

TERMS ASSOCIATED WITH PROHIBITION AND THE ILLEGAL DISTILLERY OF ALCOHOL

A Blind Pig—A speakeasy.

Bootlegger (noun), Bootlegging (verb)—The dictionary definition came from a smuggler's practice of carrying liquor in the legs of his boots; to produce, sell or transport alcoholic liquor for sale illegally.

Canning — The process of putting beer in cans much like canning food in carriers. This process got one of the original St. Louis bottom gang members Edward "Red" McAuliffe killed on September 1, 1908, when he was making too much noise canning and drinking beer in the alley behind a women-only rooming house at 2114 Lucas, causing the woman of the house, Leva Sales, to come out of the house and tell the Mob to stop drinking and making noise. McAuliffe slapped her. She pulled a pistol and shot him in the head, killing him on the spot.

Growler—A common term used in the late 1890s and early 1900s to describe a container of beer. The dictionary definition is a container (as a can or pitcher) for brew bought by the measure, a term familiar in the St. Louis taverns.

Hootch Hounds—A term commonly used in the Prohibition era to describe the federal Prohibition agents from the US Treasury Department, who enforced the federal laws against bootleggers.

Lid Club—An after-hours drinking establishment.

Moonshine—Illegally distilled whisky; to distill (liquor) illegally; to operate an illegal still (a dictionary definition). Its history dates back to the merger of England and Scotland under the "Act of Takers," which proved to be almost fatal to whisky production in northern Europe. A vast majority of the Scottish distillers started distilling secretly at night, thus creating the nickname "moonshine."

Near Beer—A legal product during Prohibition, having an alcoholic content of no more than half of one percent. A product that brewers converted to; also called "Piss Beer" by Chicagoans.

The Noble Experiment—The enactment of the Volstead Act in 1920, a dry law that started the national Prohibition era in the United States and created bootlegging.

Speakeasy—A place for the illegal sale of alcoholic drinks during Prohibition.

TERMS ASSOCIATED WITH GAMES PEOPLE PLAYED

Bank Night—A popular Depression-era promotion for motion picture houses.

Blind Robin—A golf game played by gangsters in which one would lie on the ground with a golf ball balanced on his chin while one of his partners teed off.

Blue Monday—Another Kansas City ritual in the 1930s "was a day long party each week for prostitutes on their day off, hustlers, and musicians who would clean up and hit the club by 7:00 A.M." as described by Frank Hayde.

Policy Games—Illegal lottery games prevalent in the black neighborhoods in the urban Missouri areas.

Quoits—A game similar to horseshoes in the early 1900s, using a flattened ring or iron on a circle or rope thrown at an upright pin.

Throwing Away The Key—A Kansas City ritual observed by jazz club owners in the "open city" era of the 1930s, best described by the famous William "Count" Basie: "in those days when they opened a club they took the key to the door and handed it with a five dollar bill to a cab driver and told him to ride as far that'll take you and then throw the key away." The doors of the club never closed.

Walkathons—A curious popular phenomenon for a few years in the 1930s in which couples walked continued circles around a dance hall for as long as possible—for days on end—in hopes of winning a big cash prize.

TERMS ASSOCIATED WITH MACHINE BOSS POLITICS

Boodlers—Slang term for middlemen who carried messages and/or money for the political machine bosses.

Indians—Gangs of thugs working for the political machines who worked the election polls, presumably because they were on the warpath every election day in St. Louis, in the late 1800s and early 1900s.

Pineapple Primary—A term used to describe Chicago's 1928 election primary in which Al Capone used his St. Louis "American Boys" to toss bombs or "pineapples" at speakers, officers, and homes of rival reform candidates and then supporters. The term pineapple was adopted from the military hand grenade shaped like a pineapple and regularly stolen from army and national guard armories.

Sluggers—Members of the Egan's Rats and Cuckoo Gangs who were hired by St. Louis businessmen or corporations to use their muscle to break up a strike in the 1900s.

Slugging—A term used to describe the act of union busting, usually perpetrated by Egan's Rats members in St. Louis in the early 1900s.

TERMS ASSOCIATED WITH MIDWEST BANK ROBBERS

Casing—The observation of bank guards, alarms, and tellers pioneered by bank robber Herman K. Lamm in 1917.

"Cleaning the Street"—A hoodlum term referring to the job of keeping armed citizens and law enforcement officers away from a bank robbery in progress

Gits—Detailed getaway maps, also pioneered by bank robber Herman Lamm.

Jug—A term used by bank robbers to describe a bank.

Jug Maker—An expert in bank robbery.

Midnight Julep—A slang term used to describe the explosive nitroglycerine used by criminals to open safes.

Tote Bag—A term used to describe what a bank robber would use to pile the cash and bonds in when robbing a bank, usually a pillowcase.

TERMS ASSOCIATED WITH KIDNAPPERS

Fingered—A term used to describe the kidnappers' initial process. The victim is "watched, catalogued, and seized." The kidnappers also determine how much ransom to ask for and ensure that the victim has the ability to pay the ransom demand.

TERMS ASSOCIATED WITH CLOTHING

Kroger Caps—A flat round hat with a small bill, which often was worn by St. Louis Kroger supermarket employees, made famous when five robbers from Chicago, Illinois, attempted to rob the Southwest Bank on South Kings Highway in St. Louis on April 24, 1953, all wearing these Kroger caps. Two were killed, two others were wounded, and the driver escaped. A movie was made about the bank robbery attempts starring actor Steve McQueen in one of his first movies.

The Sixth Street Roll—Referring to a type of hat that became a trademark of the hoodlums of St. Louis. Black hats pushed in at the sides and a glorious roll down the center of the crown manufactured and sold by Levine Hat Company in St. Louis for twenty dollars.

TERMS ASSOCIATED WITH POLICE, FIREARMS, AND NEWSPAPER REPORTERS

AKA—An Acronym for "also known as," used by law enforcement to document aliases used by gangsters.

Blab—In the criminal parlance, to squeal on others. The Webster's II New Riverside University Dictionary definition to talk foolishly, to reveal (secret matters), especially through indiscreet or outspoken talk.

Comparison Microscope—Used "to bring two objects, I.E. bullets, into the same line of vision. The bullets are slowly turned one after another, to match them for the inevitable fingerprinting."

DOA—An acronym for "dead on arrival" used by law enforcement and medical personnel describing a victim's condition upon arrival to the city hospital emergency room.

Frequency Tables—A compilation of the letters of the alphabet that are used most often. In law enforcement forensics, the table used by experts when decoding secret messages between a criminal and his partner to make the process easier.

Going Over the Wall—A term used by police and gangsters to describe a prisoner or prisoners escaping from a prison, literally escaping by physically going over the wall.

Handshake Murder—Perpetrated by New York mobster Frankie Yale when he took out Dean O'Banion in his Chicago flower shop. Yale would later be murdered by Capone's St. Louis American Boys, including Fred Killer Burke and his crew in New York on July 1, 1928.

Helixometer—A ballistics device that could measure left- and right-hand twists of a gun barrel rifling and could reveal both a gun make and model. The St. Valentine's Day Massacre committed by Al Capone's "American Boys" from St. Louis was the first time the start of a new forensic science era in criminology, including the use of the helixometer. Used during demonstrations by noted forensic ballistics expert Calvin Goddard, who included large photographs and projected slides showing how each gun left impressions on bullets and bullet casings.

Juice—A slang term used by police to describe the crime of loan sharking and putting the squeeze on loan victims.

Laid Off—A term used to describe the practice of wagers laid off, re-betted to another bookmaking operation.

Latent—A term associated with "a fingerprint that is difficult to see but can be made visible for examination." (Webster's II New Riverside University Dictionary definition)

Modus Operandi—A Latin phrase meaning a method of operating. (Webster's II New Riverside University Dictionary definition)

Paddy Wagon—Slang for police van for suspects; the term paddy is offensive slang for an Irishman (Webster's II New Riverside University Dictionary definitions)

Racket—By the 1920s, the term had become a euphemism for extortion and eventually referred loosely to any criminal or easy money enterprise. This term was used extensively by the print media.

Snatch Racket—The kidnapping of gamblers and gangsters and associates for large ransoms, often driving the victim across state lines. A crime pioneered by ex-St. Louis Egan's Rat Fred "Killer" Burke in concert with the Purple Gang of Detroit.

Thousand Yard Stare—A term used to describe a defeated man sentenced to many years in prison.

Topliners—A term the thugs in St. Louis called newspaper headlines in the late 1800s and early 1900s.

Ultraviolet Ray—Used by law enforcement crime laboratory experts to expose, as examples, hidden bloodstain splotches on victims, water marks on paper documents in question, powder marks fired at close range and many other uses.

X Marks the Spot—A practice that originated with the press when the body was already removed from the scene and the reporter arrived at the scene to file his report.

TERMS ASSOCIATED WITH WEAPONRY

Chopper—Street term used by bank robbers to describe a Thompson submachine.

GAT—A slang term used to describe a pistol. Also short for Gatlin gun.

Gun Car—The St. Louis Cuckoo Gang's bulletproof maroon Hudson Sudan.

Lupara—An Italian word for a sawed-off shotgun, the weapon of choice for early gangs in America.

Shank—A prison term for a knife.

COLORFUL GANGSTER NICKNAMES

As with the terms and quotes from the gangster era of the 1900s, many of the colorful characters that came and went throughout the United States were dubbed a catchy nickname by newspaper reporters, law enforcement officials, fellow criminals, associates, or relatives. In some instances, how they acquired their nickname is a story as interesting as the name itself.

Criminals who were born, reared, or operated in Missouri were not to be outdone in acquiring their own unique monikers.

In law enforcement, the nickname was important because, although the criminal may have numerous aliases, his nickname in most cases would remain the same. It was so important that the FBI, with the help of local and state law enforcement, set up files to tabulate the nicknames of practically every known crook in America. There are too many to mention, so this section will confine itself to personalities whose nickname origins have been documented by authors and researchers dating back to the early 1900s.

In keeping with the popular Top 40 hits that identify the most notable songs being played in the 1900s, this is the author's list of his Top 40 picks.

Joseph John "Doves" Aiuppa—"A minor Capone Lieutenant in the 1930s and a henchman of ex-St. Louis Egan's Rats member Claude Maddox. He had a reputation as an excellent bank robber. He acquired the nickname 'Doves' in the 1960s of the unlikely crime of illegally shooting some 500 mourning doves in Kansas and transporting them back to Chicago," according to authors William Helmer and Rick Mattix.

Arrie "Ma" Barker—"Ma" Barker was born in Ash Grove, Missouri, and so nicknamed for raising four sons who all became notorious criminals in the 1920s and 1930s. FBI Director J. Edgar Hoover characterized her as "a monument to the evils of parental indulgence." She was killed along with her son Fred Barker in a gun battle with the FBI on January 16, 1935.

Anthony "Tough Tony" Capezio—Involved with Missouri Fred "Killer" Burke in the St. Valentine's Day Massacre, so named after surviving a gasoline explosion and fire while he was attempting to dismantle one of the getaway cars with an acetylene torch on February 21, 1929, following the massacre.

Bob "Gimpy" Carey—An Egan's Rats member and friend of Fred "Killer" Burke, also involved in the St. Valentine's Day Massacre. He picked up the nickname after being injured while in service during World War I (to avoid criminal indictment). The nickname would show up later in police files. Carey was an alcoholic who reportedly committed suicide after killing his wife in New York on July 29, 1932; however, "Bugs" Moran claimed he killed Carey in retaliation for the St. Valentine's Day Massacre.

John "Ironman" Carrol—A famous St. Louis Police officer in the early 1900s, so named for the many hours he spent in the police gym and his build.

Carl "The Singer" Caruso—A mobster with ties to the Kansas City Mob who ran junkets to Las Vegas from Kansas City. He was the usual carrier of $40,000 cash of skimmed money from Las Vegas casinos to Kansas City mobster boss Nick Civella in the mid-1970s. He was nicknamed after the famous opera singer Caruso.

Dominick "The Sugarman" Cataldo—A St. Louis Santino gang member who supplied so much sugar used by the moonshiners to make whiskey in the 1920s that he was called "The Sugarman." He was killed gangland-style on January 19, 1928, in the Dogtown area of St. Louis by Russo gang members.

Joseph "Green Onions" Cipolla—One of the very few Italian members of the Egan's Rats gang, acquired the name as a vegetable peddler. Cipolla was murdered by fellow Rats on December 5, 1921, at their St. Louis clubhouse in St. Louis over a robbery gone bad.

Anthony "Tony Ripe" Civella—The son of Kansas City mobster Carl Civella, he was so named "because when he spoke, it sounded like he had one of his father's ripe tomatoes rolling around in his mouth," as documented by Frank Hayde in *The Mafia and the Machine*. "Tony Ripe" was boss of the family in mid-1980s until his death in 2006.

Carl "Cork" Civella—A Kansas City mob boss, along with his brother Nick in the 1950s–1980s, so named for his explosive temper. When angered, he would pop like a cork.

Nick "Zio" Civella—A Sicilian word for uncle used to convey affection and respect. He was a ruthless Kansas City mob boss from the 1950s to the 1980s.

William "Dint" Colbeck—A longtime Egan's Rats member and gang leader in the 1920s, was a master criminal and a master plumber with big hands that often got in the way, causing him to dent the metal pipes. The nickname went from "Dent" to "Dint" and to "Dinty," which stuck until his death by a machine-gun blast as he was returning to St. Louis from East St. Louis, Illinois, on February 17, 1943.

Willie "The Rat" Cammisano—A capo of the Nick Civella Mob Syndicate in Kansas City, operating in the 1940s and 1950s, and later, he was a tough character with over 100 arrests. Frank Hayde writes, "his nickname is dubious since he never ratted on anyone and wouldn't have tolerated its use to his face. The nickname was probably penned by *Kansas City Star* reporters who wanted to irk the swaggering gangster."

William "Tough Bill" Condon—A fellow co-leader of the St. Louis Walnut Street gang in 1900, so nicknamed for his penchant for fisticuffs, noted for killing fellow gang member "Bullet" Dwyer with a gun after a fisticuffs match with Dwyer in 1900 in a Downtown St. Louis tavern.

James "Wingy" Cox—A St. Louis Cuckoo Gang member and a former member of the Barry Street gang, so named when the lower half of his left arm had to be amputated after a 1924 gang shootout. He was arrested 248 times in six years in the 1930s.

William "Lucky Bill" Crowe—A Cuckoo Gang member in the 1920s who acquired the nickname due to his luck in beating convictions, shot to death in his flat in St. Louis on April 12, 1923, by Egan's Rats. "Lucky" at beating convictions; not so lucky beating the bullet.

Carl "Tuffy" DeLuna—A member of the Nick Civella Kansas City Mob Outfit in the 1950s, 1960s, and 1970s, he "was the family's most feared enforcer. He was a master of the 'Mafia Stare' and had the reputation as the toughest guy in the city," according to Frank Hayde.

John "Pudgy" Dunn—A young Egan's Rat in 1910 acquired the name due to the 240 pounds he carried on his five-foot-eleven frame. He was convicted in 1924 of manslaughter of a criminal partner and sentenced to ten years in prison.

Joseph "Scarface" DiGiovanni—A Kansas City mob leader in the early 1900s, so nicknamed after he burned himself, receiving a facial disfigurement in an arson attempt shortly before World War I.

Edward "Bullet" Dwyer—The leader of the Walnut Street gang in St. Louis in 1900, earning the nickname as the result of his frequent involvement with gunplay, resulting in a body covered with over two dozen bullet and knife scars.

He took his two last bullets on May 4, 1900, in a tavern fight in St. Louis with a fellow gang member, sending him to the morgue with one too many bullets.

Charles "Pillow" Fresina—Boss of the St. Louis "Pillow" gang in the 1920s, so nicknamed by the St. Louis Police due to a habit of using a pillow as a cushion when he sat at a hearing involving the murder of a rival gang member on June 11, 1928.

Charles "Mad Dog" Gargotta—A muscle man for Kansas City mobster Johnny Lazia in the 1930s; "Mad Dog" was a homely-looking gangster also described by federal crime fighters as "rat-faced." He was murdered with Kansas City mobster Charles Binaggio in 1950 in Kansas City.

Fred "Shotgun" George Goetz—An ex-Egan's Rats gang member in the 1920s, picked up the nickname from his choice of weapon, usually a 12-gauge sawed-off shotgun that he hid in his golf bag with his clubs, referring to the weapon as his "twelve iron." A criminal associate of Fred "Killer" Burke involved in 1929 St. Valentine's Day Massacre, he ironically was killed in Cicero on March 20, 1934, when a shotgun blast blew off most of his head.

Benny "Melon Head" Giammanco—A member of the St. Louis Russo gang and a veteran bootlegger in the 1920s, so nicknamed because of his "large, uniquely shaped cranium." He was murdered gangland-style on August 24, 1927, by a rival gang.

Alan "The Genius" Glick—The real estate developer from San Diego, California, so named for his ability to purchase casinos and other properties in Las Vegas in the early 1970s. He made the mistake of borrowing money from the Teamsters Union Central Pension Funds, not realizing he would soon be owned by Kansas City mob boss Nick Civella, who had a hidden interest in his casinos.

Edward "Jelly Roll" Hogan, Jr.—A St. Louis-born leader of the Hogan gang in the early 1900s, gained the unwanted nickname due to his pudgy build, standing only medium height.

Ivory "Seldom Seen" Johnson—A black gangster and a major player in the Eighteenth and Vine Streets jazz center in Kansas City in the wide open 1930s. He earned the nickname because, whenever the authorities were looking for him, he was seldom seen.

Alvin "Old Creepy" Karpis—Co-leader of the Barker-Karpis gang that operated in the Midwest, including Missouri, in the 1930s, so named for having facial features similar to the actor Boris Karloff and a "frosty" demeanor. He spent thirty-three years in prisons and died in Spain of an accidental overdose of sleeping pills on August 26, 1979.

David "Crying Dave" Klegman—"Crying Dave" was so named because of his habit of shedding tears during vigorous police interrogations. He survived a murder attempt in Downtown St. Louis on September 25, 1931.

Thomas "Snake" Kinney—An original Egan's Rats gang member in St. Louis, was given the nickname as a youth in the late 1800s when it was reported to police that he had "sneaked newspapers" from fellow paperboys. The police officer with an Irish accent reported it as "snake" and the nickname stuck with him for life.

James "Jimmy Needles" LaCapra—An associate of Kansas City mob boss Johnny Lazia in the 1930s, his nickname described his addiction to heroin. He provided information on the Union Station Massacre in Kansas City to the FBI and was found murdered in Kingston, New York, in the early fall of 1935 for his efforts.

James Anthony "Horseshoe Jimmy" Michaels—A gunman with the St. Louis Cuckoo Gang during the Prohibition era, he was so named due to his knack for escaping trouble. He served thirteen years in prison, convicted of armed robbery. Michaels was murdered in St. Louis in 1980 as the victim of a car bombing by rival gang members Paul and Anthony Leisure. This author assisted in the investigation as an ATF agent investigator. Michaels' history had not proven so "lucky" after all.

Edna "The Kissing Bandit" Murray—Earned the nickname after she kissed a victim when she and her husband robbed him in Kansas City in 1929. She was also nicknamed "Rabbit" after escaping from prison three times, including the Missouri State Prison for Women in Jefferson City.

Raymond "Crane Neck" Nugent—An Egan's Rat in the 1920s, so nicknamed because he had no neck. He also carried the nickname "Gander" by some criminal associates. During the summer of 1931, he disappeared and was never heard from again.

Thomas "Fingers" Regan—A well-known St. Louis pickpocket and sneak thief who acquired his names for his criminal work. Shot by Egan's Rats in a tavern shootout on December 25, 1911, dying shortly thereafter.

Maishe "Deerhunter" Rockman—"A colorful old-time Jewish gangster who was involved in the Kansas City Strawman Casino skimming investigation as the money carrier for the Cleveland's Syndicate. His code name was 'Deerhunter' because Rockman loved to hunt game," as documented by Frank Hayde.

William "Skippy" Rohan—A legendary St. Louis Egan's Rats gang member who earned the name through his numerous prison escapes during his criminal career in Missouri in the early 1900s.

Elmer "Astor" Runge—A young Egan's Rats member who was always well dressed so his mother gave him the nickname "Astor." He was murdered on December 5, 1923, by a fellow Egan's Rat.

Wilber "The Tri-State Terror" Underhill—A Joplin-raised psychopathic killer outlaw, so nicknamed for his criminal rampage throughout several Midwestern states in the 1920s. Underhill undisputedly earned the most nicknames of any criminal of his time. Early in his career in 1923, he was nicknamed the "Lover's Lane Bandit" after robbing a number of parked couples in various necking areas in Joplin. In November 1933, after his infamous prison break from the prison in Lansing, Kansas, on Memorial Day of that year, Underhill was being called the "Southwest Executioner" by newspapers following his murderous trail to boost the sale of newspapers. He also carried the nickname "Mad Dog" and was known for his homicidal ways. He died on January 6, 1934, after being mortally wounded by FBI agents, the first fugitive killed by the FBI.

Henry "Dutch Snitch" Zang—An early 1900s bartender and pickpocket so named after he testified against a gang member in St. Louis in a murder case on March 2, 1914. During the lunch break of this trial, Zang got into an argument with the gang member on trial and shot and killed him, claiming self-defense. Zang was never charged.

FAMOUS GANGSTER QUOTES

Gangsters, outlaws, mobsters, crime reporters, and law enforcement personalities across the United States and throughout the twentieth century have provided interesting quotes to associates, the media, and investigators, some which have been recorded and printed appearing in research and quotation books.

There is little argument among research authors that Chicago's "Big Fellow" Al Capone was the most frequently quoted gangster of the public enemy era in the early- to mid-1930s.

Criminal personalities who were born, raised, or have roamed throughout Missouri have provided their share of quotes that have either been attributed to them or invented by writers who contend "that if they didn't say it, they probably should have."

I have selected about fifty presented in chronological order by date to provide the reader with a clearer understanding of the mindset of the person at the time of the quote.

EARLY 1900s

Harvey Bailey—The king of bank robbers, who operated with the notorious Missouri-born Barker-Karpis Gang and spent prison time in Alcatraz, provided this quote to L. L. Edge, circa 1980, describing his opinion of J. Edger Hoover: "That damn Hoover was a bigger crook than anybody at Alcatraz." This was an opinion shared by many fellow outlaws operating in the 1920s and 1930s.

Harvey Bailey—After J. Edgar Hoover had claimed to the nation that "Ma" Barker, mother of four Missouri-born outlaws, was the mastermind of their gang after the FBI shot and killed her and one of her sons in January 1935, Bailey was quoted by a L. L. Edge as saying: "The old lady couldn't plan breakfast."

Arthur "Doc" Barker, Member of the Notorious Barker-Karpis Gang—"I'm all shot to hell," his last words uttered after he was shot by guards at the Alcatraz Prison on January 13, 1939, as he was attempting to escape.

George F. Barnes Jr., a.k.a. "Machine Gun Kelly"—Bank robber and kidnapper who participated in the kidnapping of Oklahoma City oilman Charles Urschel on July 22, 1933, resulting in a $200,000 ransom paid to Kelly near the LaSalle Hotel in Kansas City, on July 30, 1933. His most famous quote on September 26, 1933, when arrested in a Memphis rooming house:

"Don't shoot, G-men! Don't shoot," may have been a fabrication by the FBI. FBI Agent William J. Roemer, when interviewed, said Kelly's wife, Kathryn, did say, "Honey, I guess it's all up for us. The G-men won't ever give us a break." Kelly later denied ever making the statement.

Blanche Barrow of the Bonnie and Clyde Gang, and Wife and Accomplice of Missouri-born Marvin "Buck" Barrow—While in prison in Jefferson City, Missouri, in 1933, Blanche wrote, "Across the fields of yesterday she sometimes comes to me a little girl just back from play. The girl I used to be and yet she smiles so wistfully once she has crept within, I wonder if she hopes to see the woman I might have been."

Clyde Barrow of the Bonnie and Clyde Gang—was quoted as saying shortly before being killed in a police ambush on May 23, 1934, "No man but the undertaker will ever get me. If officers ever cripple me to where I see they will take me alive, I'll take my own life."

Charley Birger—Leader of the Birger Gang of Southern Illinois, who grew up in St. Louis, said on April 19, 1928, to a *St. Louis Post-Dispatch* reporter, "I've shot men in my time, but I never shot one that didn't deserve it." This was just two hours before he was hanged for the murder of Joe Adams, the mayor of West City, Illinois. Birger was also quoted as saying, "I kill only bad people."

Leo Vincent Brothers—A St. Louis Egan's Rats member and fugitive from St. Louis, where he had been involved in racketeering, arson, robbery, and murder, on loan to the Chicago Mob who, on June 9, 1930, murdered Jake Lingle, a *Chicago Tribune* reporter, in a Chicago subway before many witnesses. At his 1931 trial for the Lingle murder, in which the state sought the death penalty, the jury recommended fourteen years in prison, to be released in eight years for good behavior. Brothers said, "I can do that standing on my head."

Al Capone—The Chicago mobster, when describing his special crew of shooters of non-Italian descent, all from St. Louis, said, "These are my American boys." The boys were hired by Capone either in the fall of 1927 or spring of 1928 to carry out crimes of violence, including murders.

William T. Egan—Leader of the infamous St. Louis Egan's Rats gang, who, on October 31, 1921, was shot by two gunmen and rushed to City Hospital, where Police Chief Marlin O'Brien asked him, "Do you know who shot you?" Egan replied, "Yes." "Then tell us," the chief said. Egan replied, "No, I ain't saying anything," exercising the criminal code of silence. He died a few minutes later.

Charles Arthur "Pretty Boy" Floyd—"They'll get me. Sooner or later I'll go down full of lead. That's how it will end." This was a very accurate statement, made shortly before he was gunned down on October 22, 1934, by local police officers and FBI on an Ohio farm. This from a ruthless killer whose first felony conviction occurred in St. Louis and who was one of the shooters in the Kansas City Union Station Massacre.

Fortune **magazine Writer**—In a 1934 article wrote, "The one island of law and order is St. Louis, whose police are notably well equipped and whose

Police Chief, Colonel Joseph A. Gerk, is outstandingly able and honest." The article described the writer's opinion of the police operations in St. Louis in the 1930s.

Frank Gusenberg—A Chicago mobster aligned with the "Bugs" Moran Gang and a rival of Al Capone, he was one of the St. Valentine's Day Massacre victims of February 14, 1929, shot numerous times by St. Louis shooter Fred "Killer" Burke and crew. Before he died, he was asked by a police officer, "Who shot you?" Gusenberg answered, "Nobody shot me," shortly before he died of numerous bullet wounds.

Captain Frank Hamer—Famous Texas Ranger who came out of retirement in 1934, hired to track down outlaws Bonnie and Clyde. After accomplishing his assignment, killing Bonnie Parker and Clyde Barrow as they drove past his roadside ambush, was quoted as saying, "I hate to bust a cap on a woman, especially when she's sitting down," in reference to Bonnie Parker.

Raymond Hamilton—Notorious bank robber, convicted murderer, escape artist, and partner of Clyde Barrow of the Bonnie and Clyde Gang. When captured some time between 1932 and 1934, he said, "I'm Raymond Hamilton, and I don't intend to give you any trouble. I'm just fresh out of ammunition, money, and women. Let's go to jail."

William Helmer—Co-author of *The St. Valentine's Day Massacre* and *The Complete Public Enemy Almanac*, stated: "A gunman was welcome anywhere if he arrived from the battle fields of St. Louis." This a quote was also printed on the cover of the book *Egan's Rats* by Daniel Waugh, a St. Louis crime researcher. This quote accurately describes the respect for St. Louis gangsters during the 1920s.

Edward J. "Jelly Roll" Hogan—Leader of the St. Louis Hogan gang, whose house was riddled with bullets from a rival gang on May 19, 1922, was asked by police who did it. He said, "I'll identify them with a shotgun."

J. Edgar Hoover—Director of the FBI during the Roaring Twenties era through the early 1970s, referred to the Midwest, which included Missouri, as "The Cradle of Crime."

J. Edgar Hoover—With the help of his publicist, Courtney Cooper, an ex-*Kansas City Star* reporter, wrote in the late 1930s, "The eyes of 'Arizona' Clark Barker [Ma Barker] by the way always fascinated me. They were queerly direct, penetrating hot with some strangely smoldering flame, yet withal as hypnotically cold as the muzzle of a gun." It is of interest to note there is no evidence Hoover ever interacted with "Ma" Barker in person.

The Mother of George Magness, a minor outlaw in the early 1930s—while visiting her son, who was locked up for robbing a bank in Kansas, she told the local sheriff, "Hell, sheriff, bank robbin' ain't hardly no crime at all." This was the opinion of so many Depression-era poor people living in the Midwest, including Missourians.

Oliver Alden Moore—President of the East St. Louis Central Trades Council and business manager of the Boilermakers Local Union, who, on August 10, 1932, told *St. Louis Post-Dispatch* reporter Carl Baldwin, "Sure, I've been threatened" [by the Shelton Gang]. "Well, let them try it. They can't intimidate East St. Louis Labor." Forty-five minutes later, Moore was gunned down outside his Union office, hit over twenty-five times in a drive-by machine-gun shooting. So much for threats and intimidation taken lightly.

"Bugs" Moran—Chicago mobster, rival of Al Capone, the intended target of the St. Valentine's Day Massacre of February 14, 1929, was interviewed by a reporter four days after the massacre. He was quoted as saying, "Only Capone kills like that," not knowing at the time the massacre was carried out by Capone's "American Boys" from St. Louis. When Al Capone learned of Moran's quote, he replied, "They don't call that guy 'Bugs' for nothing."

Edward Morrow—A journalist for the *Omaha Harald*, wrote of Kansas City in the 1930s, "If you want to see some sin, forget about Paris and go to Kansas City." Morrow based his observations on his tour of the red-light district that stretched for many blocks along Thirteenth and Fourteenth Streets and his "business lunch" at the Chesterfield Club, a fine dining establishment where the waitresses wore nothing but cellophane aprons that revealed their pubic hairs shaved into hearts, diamonds, spades, or clubs.

Francis Nally—A St. Louis police captain and noted tough cop who ran the Carr Street District in the mid-1920s with his fists. A native of Ireland, he arrested mobster John Giannola after Giannola boasted Nally would never arrest him. As Nally was dragging Giannola, sporting a swollen eye and a split lip, into the district station, Nally declared, "John was resisting arrest."

A New York News Writer visiting Kansas City in the 1930s reported, "All one had to do to locate a gambling game was to . . . . ask a Patrolman on the Kansas City streets. He'll guide you. It's perfectly open. You just walk in."

Bonnie Parker of the notorious Bonnie and Clyde Gang—In a letter to a newspaper in the early 1930s, giving her description of fast vehicles, wrote, "Say boy, can't robbers get away fast these days? I'm glad this country is different from what it was when Jesse James lived here."

Bonnie Parker—In April 1933, she was quoted as saying, "Tell the people I don't smoke cigars. It's the bunk." This shortly after a photograph of her posing with a cigar in her mouth and holding a revolver she had taken from a police officer in Springfield, Missouri, was published after a shoot-out with police in Joplin, Missouri, on April 13, 1933, where the photograph was discovered.

Joseph Raimo—A Kansas City police officer assigned to the Italian area who, after receiving a death threat in a letter, said, "If they're going to get me, they'll get me anyway," was killed shortly thereafter from a shotgun blast as he was walking home on his day off, March 27, 1911.

Wilbur Underhill Jr.—A holdup man, bank robber, and twice-convicted murderer born in Newtonia, Missouri. He was the first fugitive killed by the FBI, on December 30, 1933, after a shootout in Kansas, in which he was hit several times and captured, he held a press interview and stated, "Actually I only got hit five times but them shots made eleven holes in me." He added, "I counted each one as they hit me. When I set sail, they sure poured it on me." Underhill survived his wounds for nine days before he died in prison on January 6, 1934, making a dying declaration to the FBI, "Tell the boys I'm coming home."

1950s

John Doherty, famous St. Louis Police Department detective chief—According to reporter John Auble, Doherty took St. Louis ex-con Sonny Liston (before he was a heavyweight prize fighter) to the outskirts of town in the mid-1950s, stuck a gun to his head, and told Liston to leave town. Doherty reportedly said, "If you don't, they'll find you in an alley." As a footnote, this author worked for Chief Doherty in the homicide division in 1970 and part of 1971, and this story was common knowledge amongst fellow detectives.

Anthony "Tony" Lopiparo—In 1954, before going to prison for income tax invasion on illegal cigarette income, he was asked in court when did he last look at his company (Twin City) books. He replied, "I don't remember. I don't know how to read or write."

Anthony Lopiparo—Described by the *St. Louis Post-Dispatch* as "A Notorious St. Louis Mobster," while being questioned by Senator Este Kefauver in February of 1951, he asked, "What's the matter? Haven't I got a constitution?" Kefauver replied in jest, "You seem to have a good constitution," referring to Lopiparo's large size.

Joseph Valachi—The first Mafia member to ever reveal the secrets of Cosa Nostra at the Kefauver Committee Hearings in 1950s. The first hearing was held in Kansas City. Valachi was taken aback when he was accused of smearing the good name of Italians. He answered, "I'm not talking about Italians. I'm talking about criminals."

1960s

Harold Gibbons, St. Louis Teamster Local Union Boss—On March 7, 1967, describing the imprisonment of Jimmy Hoffa, the Teamsters International Union President said they "shipped him off to the shithouse."

Tony Giordano, St. Louis mob boss—A rookie *Post-Dispatch* reporter named John McGuire in March 1967, who, in his first month on the job, was sent to the fourth floor of the St. Louis Police Headquarters to ask for Captain John Doherty to see if they had booked mob boss Tony Giordano. It was lunchtime, and no one was around. The reporter spotted a man in a blue suit in a side room. Thinking it must be a detective, he asked, "Excuse me, officer, I'm from the *Post-Dispatch*. Have they booked a Tony Giordano?" The man replied, "They ain't booked me yet, kid." Giordano smiled.

Robert Kennedy, United States Attorney General in the 1960s—While discussing the Mob's political influence, he said, "The racketeer is at his most dangerous, not with a machine gun in his hand but with public officials in his pockets." This reference included his knowledge and concerns of the mobsters operating in Missouri.

Paul Leisure, St. Louis mobster and classmate of the author—In early September 1962, while being driven by his cousin Rich to SEMO State College in Cape Girardeau, high school mate Paul Leisure told me, "I intend to get a college degree and make my mother proud." Paul Leisure lasted about one or two weeks at college. Homesick, he returned to St. Louis, and within two years, he was the driver and bodyguard of St. Louis mob boss Ton Giordana, and our driver, Rich Leisure, had been gunned down and murdered in a tavern hit.

Paul Leisure would move on and achieve his degree in crime, a degree that brought his mother only pain and anguish.

Herb "Seek and Find" Riley, a St. Louis City Homicide Detective in the 1960s and 1970s—When asked by reporter and author John Auble how he obtained so many confessions, Riley reached into his desk drawer and pulled out a Bible. He said, "All I do is place the guy's hand on the Bible, look into his eyes and ask, 'Isn't there something you want to tell me?'" I had the fortunate opportunity to work with Detective Riley while assigned to the Homicide Unit.

1970s

Tommy Callanan, brother of Laurence L. Callanan, leader of Pipefitters Local Union 562—On June 15, 1973, after losing his legs when a bomb ripped apart a vehicle he was operating in Spanish Lake just outside St. Louis, he told a rescuer named Theodore Heitzler, "They promised they wouldn't do this to me." So much for kept promises in the battlefields of St. Louis. The rescuer, "Tad" Heitzler, testified to this quote at a federal grand jury shortly after the attempt on Callanan's life. He went on to become an ATF agent in the St. Louis office whom I had the privilege of working with for many years.

Unnamed Federal Agent—As one federal investigator put it when describing Kansas City Teamster labor leader Roy Williams in 1976, "That Roy's been tied in with the Mob for years."

Harold Gibbons, St. Louis Teamster Local Union Boss—In an interview in early 1977 describing how corrupt the Teamsters Union was said, " . . . that the labor management has maintained its integrity to the extent that it has always amazed me . . . somebody is always trying to make a deal with you . . . that more guys haven't succumbed is beyond my comprehension."

Labor Department Memo—A great quote from a 1971 Labor Department memo: "It was also learned that Roy Williams is under the complete domination of [Kansas City Mob Boss Nick] Civella. Williams will not act contrary to the wishes of Civella, apparently because of both self-interest and fear."

Morris Shenker, mob attorney in St. Louis—In April 1977, reporter Jim Drinkhall asked Shenker, who was also owner of the Dunes Hotel and Casino in Law Vegas, why he always comped New York mob boss Tony "Pro" Provenzano at his casino. Shenker replied, "Tony's a good player, why shouldn't I comp him? I've known him for twenty years . . . he's out here for the Board meeting," referring to the Teamsters International Executive Board meeting held in Las Vegas at the time.

This is one of the most insightful quotes documenting the intimate connections between the Mob, mob attorneys, the Nevada casino industry, and the labor union.

Edward J. Steska, leader of Laborers Local Union 562 in St. Louis—On February 24, 1972, Steska was at his union office, talking on the phone with a business agent when he uttered, "Uh-oh!" which proved to be his last words as he was shot five times with a .45 caliber revolver found next to his body.

A Teamster Vice President—While talking about Roy Williams, he said, "Roy's not a free citizen—he has to do what these guys tell him," referring to the Mob.

Roy Williams, a Kansas City truck driver who eventually rose as top man of the Teamsters, the most powerful union in the country in the 1960s—Years later while testifying in court, he said, "That's when I became his boy." This occurred after Williams was kidnapped, blindfolded, and told by Nick Civella thugs, "If he didn't cooperate and provide Union pension money for loans, they were going to kill his children, his wife, and him," telling him he would be the last to go.

1980s

Anthony Leisure, a St. Louis mobster, convicted murderer, Laborers Union Local 110 business agent, brother of mob boss Paul Leisure, and high school mate of the author of this book—On August 14, 1981, shortly after his brother Paul was severely injured in a car bombing murder attempt, I, in my capacity as an ATF agent, talked with Anthony Leisure at the Firmin Desloge Hospital in St. Louis. Anthony said, "I don't know who was responsible for my brother's bombing, but if I could get my hands on them, I would choke them to death."

I suggested to Anthony that he allow law enforcement to handle the investigation of his brother's bombing. He replied, "No thanks, I'll take care of this myself." Within the next twelve months, Anthony Leisure was responsible for a shotgun murder attempt on September 11, 1981; a car bombing homicide on October 16, 1981; and a murder hit) on one of his own criminal associates to silence him in July 1982. For his efforts, Anthony Leisure was sentenced to life in prison. So much for "I'll take care of this myself."

2000s

Willie Radkay, Holdup Man—Born in the "Strawberry Hill" area of Kansas City, Kansas, just outside Kansas City, Missouri. When asked by his niece, Patty Terry, in 2005 how he survived being shot six times in 1934 and twelve times in a Kansas City, Missouri jewelry store robbery in 1935 in a shootout with police, Radkay replied, "tough skin, soft bullets, and they didn't hit anything important."

ABOUT THE AUTHOR

David True began his career as a public servant from 1966 to 1968 as an Explosives Ordnance Disposal Specialist (EOD) in the United States Army. From 1968 to 1971, he was a St. Louis Metropolitan police officer and detective, assigned to the Bomb and Arson Unit in the homicide division. He joined the ATF in 1971, assigned to the St. Louis and Kansas City, Missouri offices, performing duties in various capacities as an agent and supervisor. He retired from ATF in 1997 after twenty-six years of service and accepted a position as a corporate security manager and investigator with Yellow/Roadway Corporation (YRC) until retiring in 2013.

He has a Bachelor of Science degree in Administration of Justice. He has lectured extensively throughout the United States during his professional career on crime and criminals. He is the recipient of numerous honors and recognitions and is an active member of numerous professional law enforcement and fire service associations.

INDEX

318

319